J. F. Herring & Sons

To Hélène
with love

THE LIFE AND WORKS OF

J. F. Herring senr

AND HIS FAMILY

J. F. Herring & Sons

by

OLIVER BECKETT

'Whatever I do, I do to the best of my ability'

– J. F. HERRING Senr

J. A. ALLEN & CO LTD

London and New York

Published in 1981 by
J. A. Allen & Company Limited
1 Lower Grosvenor Place
London SW1W 0EL

British Library Cataloguing in Publication Data
Beckett, Oliver R
J. F. Herring and Sons.
1. Herring family 2. Painters – England – Biography
I. Title
159.2 ND496

ISBN 0-85131-335-3

Designed by Eric Stubberfield
Photoset in Great Britain by
Rowland Phototypesetting Limited, Bury St Edmunds, Suffolk
Printed by St Edmundsbury Press, Bury St Edmunds, Suffolk
and bound by Robert Hartnoll Limited, Bodmin

Foreword

by SIR NOEL MURLESS

J. F. Herring senr is undoubtedly best known for his paintings of the prominent race-horses of his day, particularly his long series of winners of the St Leger and the Derby. I am very fond of my painting of the great race-mare, Alice Hawthorn, by him.

However, his farm-yard pictures so painstakingly done, take one right back into the middle of 19th century England, and indeed, many of these scenes would have been quite familiar at the end of the 1914–18 War.

I am glad that at last the task of writing the first history of the Herring family has been tackled by Oliver Beckett, and this readable account will, I feel sure, have great appeal to all lovers of our English country-side.

I was associated with the author, as the original editor of 'Stud & Stable' (now 'Pacemaker'), and I know he has a great love and knowledge of horses and painting, and has written many interesting articles on the subject. Now, after extensive research, most of the facts of Herring's long career have been established.

This beautifully produced book will, I feel, be of great advantage to all owners of sporting paintings, to galleries and the general public. I wish it every success.

Woodditton Stud
Newmarket

Contents

Illustrations

COLOURED PLATES

Acknowledgements

When I started writing a life of John Frederick Herring and his family, I had no idea of the formidable undertaking it would be; perhaps that is why there has, so far, been no such work! And yet it seemed eminently worth-while to attempt to trace the extraordinary career of this peer of sporting artists. How did a young chap with no artistic background, few friends and a scanty education become such a respected and successful painter?

The records to which I have turned are somewhat meagre, and very often contradictory. Inevitably I have leant heavily on Mr J. B. Muir's Memoir, published in July 1893. Indeed, without that prime source anyone who researched Herring would be at a loss. Mrs A. M. W. Stirling's chapter, 'A Painter of Reality', in her amusing book, *A Painter of Dreams*, is of course another volume to which one would refer. She was the daughter of Mrs A. M. W. Pickering, who was a niece of Mr Charles Spencer Stanhope, an early patron of Herring's, and from her pages one gleans some homely touches that have an air of authenticity. But Mrs Stirling has a lively imagination, and one feels that some gaps in the story have been coloured with some graphic prose that pays scant regard to chronology. Apart from these two authors, Herring is of course mentioned by Sir Walter Gilbey, Capt. Seltzer, Basil Taylor, Stella Walker and – at some length – in Walter Shaw Sparrow's important books, although he mentions his work mainly in relation to Landseer.

These sources, the *Dictionary of National Biography*, Graves and Bénezit etc. are open to anyone, discrepancies and all, which indeed in the course of time are mostly copied and repeated from one exhibition catalogue to another.

I have had however the great good fortune to be invited to study the documents, correspondence and family history made available to me by Lady Violet Macfadyen. These have enabled me to put the record straight in a number of respects, and I here acknowledge Lady Violet's kind help with the deepest gratitude. Mr John Warner, too, a direct descendant of Herring's youngest daughter, Jennie, has also been of great assistance. I owe a debt too, to the Doncaster archivist, Mr Leslie Smith, for his invaluable research into the genealogy of the Herring family, and also to the Librarian at County Hall, GLC Reference Library and the Librarian of Kent *County Archives*, *Maidstone*.

I need hardly add that while records and photographs are useful, seeing the pictures is essential, and it is here that the many wonderful exhibitions arranged over the years by the London galleries have provided evidence for one's own eyes of the importance and enduring attraction of the British school of sporting art in general, and of Mr Herring in particular. For, sadly, Herring is not well represented in the National collections, and there must be hundreds in private hands.

Through the generosity of Mr Paul Mellon, who is lending many pictures to the new gallery of British Sporting Art at the Tate, two excellent examples of his work will be on public view; then, perhaps it will be generally recognised that without Herring there would have been a serious loss, not only of an unparalleled record of the best thoroughbreds of the age, but also of numerous charming works of art expressive of rural life in the 19th century.

My grateful thanks are due to HM The Queen and HM Queen Elizabeth, the Queen Mother, and to the following museums, art galleries and private owners who have been so helpful in locating or providing photographs, or information about the Herring family's pictures:

The British Museum
Doncaster Museum and Art Gallery
The Jockey Club
The National Gallery of Ireland
The Royal Academy Library
The Tate Gallery
The Witt Collection
Wm. Woodward Collection, Baltimore Museum of Art, USA
The Victoria and Albert Museum
York Museum

Arthur Ackermann & Son, Ltd
Christie's, Ltd
Fores, Ltd
Pawsey and Payne, Ltd
Richard Green
J. Sabin, Ltd
Spinks, Ltd
Sotheby and Co.
Tryon Gallery

His Grace, The Duke of Beaufort
J. D'Arcy Clark Esq
The Marquess of Exeter

Eric Fawcett Esq
His Grace, The Duke of Grafton
Sir Richard Graham, Bt
Lord Grimthorpe
The Earl of Halifax
Mr and Mrs R. L. Hollins, USA
Lady Violet Macfadyen
Sir Mark Milbank, Bt
Lord Rotherwick
The Earl of Scarbrough
Sir Tatton Sykes, Bt
His Grace, The Duke of Westminster

Please note that in some cases the owners of some of the pictures reproduced are not known; in that event, the photographs are credited to the gallery which provided them, with apologies to these owners.

A Man of his Time

John Frederick Herring was born into a world that was ready to receive him, and to reward his particular talent; not that his name figures largely in the annals of the Fine Arts, nor did he attain financial independence and fame without a struggle. For it was a competitive world, the world of sporting art, and there were numerous other painters with flair and ability practising the art at the time he made his debut. Stubbs died in 1806 and Sawrey Gilpin in 1807, but when Herring got into his stride, the Alkens and Ferneleys were still going strong, and other competitors[1] set a hot pace.

This efflorescence of major and minor figures came about through various causes which will be touched on elsewhere, the principal one being a tremendous upsurge of interest in the breeding and improvement of cattle, sheep, heavy horses and bloodstock, by the people best able to pay for representations of these prodigies of the animal world. No less of an august personage than Sir Joshua Reynolds had complained long before that Mr Stubbs got 100 gns for a picture of a race-horse, whereas he only got 150 gns for a full length portrait.

The emergence of this butterfly from the chrysalis of the early 18th century had been aided by John Wootton who had a classical training, and the Dutch painters, Peter Tillemans, Jan Van Wyjk and Andrew Van Diepenbeck. With the lustre added by Stubbs, Gilpin and Marshall, a specifically British school took wing.

Moreover, the establishment of the Royal Academy in 1769 gave the arts in Britain a certain standing and a new dignity independent of foreign, particularly French, influences. The French Academy, while numbering such men as Baron Gros and Theodore Géricault among them, had been completely dominated by the neo-Classical style of J. L. David, until freed by Eugène Delacroix. The historical situation of France, in the 19th century,

[1] Ben Marshall, d. 1835; John Ferneley senr and junr, d. 1860 and 1862; Philip Reinagle, d. 1833; James Ward RA, d. 1859; George Arnull, d. *c.* 1840; Thos Woodward, d. 1852; William and W. J. Shayer, d. 1879 and 1885; H. B. Chalon, d. 1849; James Pollard, d. 1867; Charles Towne, d. 1840; C. Cooper Henderson, d. 1877; George Garrard, d. 1826; Edmund Bristow ARA, d. 1876 and the brothers Barraud, William, d. 1850, and his brother Henry d. 1874.

with a revolution of some sort every few years, gave little scope for the enjoyment of sporting pastimes, or for pictures of them, apart from rather bloody encounters with wounded stags in the style of Rubens and Snyders. The nearest approach to what we would call a sporting picture was perhaps Courbet's late work of deer in a forest.[1]

The Royal Academy however, under the learned but idiosyncratic leadership of its first great President, Sir Joshua Reynolds, cold-shouldered mere sporting or horse painters,[2] in favour of the more grandiose ideals of History painting and portraiture, given even greater impetus with the genius of Sir Thomas Lawrence. So these exponents of a humbler order were very much out on their own, pursuing a scent that the RAs disdained to follow. And as with all splinter groups, its members – if such they can be called, varied in skill and ability, the more primitive unlettered efforts of the Sartorius tribe and John Cordrey, running alongside the more sophisticated air of the Coopers and Ferneleys, culminating in men like Richard Barrett Davies and Sir Francis Grant, both of whom became RAs and the latter, PRA.

Herring, who exhibited at the RA, came somewhere between the two types; his skill qualifying him for entry to the magic circle, while his subject matter did not.

It is indeed something of a mystery how he gained his ascendancy over his confreres, some of whom had a proper training, when he himself – as far as is known – had little or none. At first sight it hardly seems as though the Doncaster of 1815, the scene of his earliest endeavours, was exactly an Athens of the North. The nearest centre of any importance was Liverpool, but Wm. Huggins, its main protagonist, was really too young to have influenced Herring, although the tradition of painting thin over a white ground does show itself in his work. Much nearer home, was Charles Schwanfelder who lived and practised for many years in Leeds. I like to think he may have had a hand in Herring's education, but there is no written evidence to support the theory. He must have seen James Ward's pictures at some time too, for one or two of his canvases in the years 1820–1830 show undeniable signs of his influence.

One can only assume that a talent bordering on genius, allied to a quite extraordinary perseverance and acute observation got him where it did. To these qualities must be added the purely adventitious support of one or two early patrons, whose encouragement and support gave Herring a head start to his career in Yorkshire.

So, from about 1815 to 1850, Herring was called upon to paint the best race-horses, starting with the St Leger winners, which achievement constitutes a unique record of British bloodstock. Of course, other artists painted the same Derby and other winners, and it is often instructive to compare different versions of the same animal – not always to Herring's advantage.

Nevertheless, over 500 of his paintings were engraved and became a popular – and lucrative – sideline, hanging in many a country house, trainer's lodge, inn and tack-room in the country. The owners, trainers and jockeys he introduced into his better compositions are not without merit as portraits of the leading men of their age too,

[1] Rosa Bonheur, although undeniably a great animal painter, did not concern herself with sport.

[2] Stubbs became an ARA, but not an RA.

although the heads are sometimes too small, the opposite of Marshall's portraits where the heads are usually too large. He soon mastered this failing.

It is easy to see that Herring's work was valued by his patrons, as much for its veracity and polish as for the excellently rendered glimpses of heath and copse, or sunlit cloud, at which he was such a master. There is a certain sameness about many of the profiles of his equine 'sitters', but in fact, he had an acute eye for the proportions and general make-up of a horse, and was able to analyse with the knowledge of a true horseman, the depth of girth of one, the sloping shoulder of another, and the bold eye, well-sprung ribs and sloping pasterns of a third.

True, he may have flattered (and did) the swan neck of one horse and 'improved' the hocks of another, but breeders and owners are hard taskmasters when it comes to the colour and conformation of their favourites, and under such conditions he did manage to vary occasionally the stereotyped side-view, not always successfully, as the picture of Matilda owned by the Jockey Club will testify.

Perhaps trainers were more co-operative with painters than they are now. For at least up to the 1840s, he usually painted the thoroughbreds indoors and fitted in the landscape afterwards, which may account for the rather artificial gloss imparted to their satiny coats. But it must be remembered that it was not usual to allow the racers to be roughed-off once the season was over, so the problem of the change of coat between two- and three-year-olds, did not then arise.

It must be remembered, too, that under his contract for prints for the St Leger winners (and later, for Derby winners), he had to produce portraits very soon after the event; this accounts for the many straight renderings for this purpose, of the horses shown in a loose-box or stall (usually about 9 × 11 ins) which he then worked up into grander compositions of about 25 × 36 ins, to include jockey, trainer and perhaps the owner. So too, the lovely skies he painted, always seem to me to be those of a sunlit, autumn day of high-flying clouds.

In a number of instances he painted later versions of his original pictures, dated up to as much as ten years after the event the picture commemorated. These must have been done from sketches he kept by him (as we know he did) or from the prints that had been taken from them. He seems to have sometimes allowed his eldest son, John F. junr, to do copies of these early pictures too, judging by the inferior style in manner, brush-work and anatomy of some of these small works, still going the rounds.

None of the painters of his day had mastered the true action in the gallop; they had progressed from the Sartorius and Seymour convention, where the hind legs are anchored to the ground in what is called the 'rocking-horse' position, successfully represented the walk, trot, even the extended trot at speed, the canter and the jumping action, and it was Herring who popularised the gallop portrayed with all four legs extended, 'ventre-à-terre'. But until Edward Muybridge published his photographs which proved that there was always one foot touching the ground, except in the 'collected' position, no-one attempted anything different, except for one rather clumsy effort by James Ward.

This convention had its virtues for it imposed a certain rhythm on the picture which was designed to convey a moment in time and not necessarily the speed at which the horses were travelling. The famous picture by Manet of a race at Longchamps gives that impression but at the expense of a very blurred rendering of the anatomy which is not really satisfactory either. The problem still remains as the action which is literally taken from photographs often appears lifeless. The sketches of John Skeaping perhaps have come nearest to solving the equation of anatomical accuracy combined with correct alignment of the limbs at speed. Munnings side-stepped the difficulty by preferring to paint the start rather than the race.

A camera was listed in the studio effects auctioned after Herring's death, but how or if he actually used it we do not know.

But apart from his studies of life on the Turf, Herring of course, turned out many pleasing hunting pictures, coaching-scenes, horse fairs, stables and inn-yards, and farmyard and agricultural pieces, featuring horses, cattle, dogs, ducks and fowl, pigs, ponies and donkeys. He also did one or two paintings of shooting, and some of stalking in the Highlands, but not I think any of fishing.

His hunting pictures have been criticised for being too tidy, and lacking the excitement of a fast scurry across the Shires done so well by the Ferneleys and Wolstenholmes. But he knew what he was at, although he had none of the humour of an Alken or Leach for the disasters of the chase, and his informal pictures of actual hunts are delightfully natural. The other pictures, painted for the express purpose of being engraved as 'sets', although well composed, do perhaps lack the flavour of mud, sweat and swearing inseparable from the cut and thrust of riding across country.

On the other hand, the dress and deportment of the riders is a picture of its day, and from this distance in time, we have a sight of the countryside of England as it became with the enclosure of common land by quick-set hedges, and before railways and telegraph lines, pylons and jerry-built houses spoilt the view. His equestrian portraits of Daniel Haigh, MFH, master of the Old Surrey, and two of 'Mad Jack' Mytton, are masterpieces in the genre.

He may have thought it wiser to stick to his own specialities when there were other artists such as the Howitts, who concentrated on shooting, and James Pollard and Charles Cooper Henderson on coaching. His great-great-niece, Mrs Dulcie Vaughan, owned a most attractive picture of a scene in an inn-yard, at the Swan Inn at Grantham, which shows he could make something of the subject when he chose. Here an immense waggon, with 'London' inscribed on its hood, is picking up passengers and parcels, and six horses are harnessed up, surrounded with onlookers and ostlers. This again is an historical record, as the Swan Inn has long since been demolished.

Two similar works were sold in 1978 at Mr H. J. Joel's sale at Childwickbury for £25,000 and £17,000 – two of his highest prices. This proves that the seven years he spent as a coachman were not wasted, and disproves Shaw Sparrow's assertion that he avoided painting such scenes in distaste at the hardships he had suffered on the road. Some of the most characteristic examples show post-horses awaiting a change at the way-side inn, usually with the coach approaching in the distance.

In his 'middle period' of the 1830s he attempted grouping horses at the start of a race, and his greatest of the kind is perhaps the start of the famous 'Dirty Derby' of 1844, but by 1848 he declared he would not paint another winner unless he could make a 'subject of it'.

As time passed his subject matter widened, and although it is true to say that his style remained meticulously fine throughout his career, it is noteworthy that his brush-work gained a new expressive suavity in middle and old age, when he came under the influence of Sir Edwin Landseer, whom he greatly admired, and with whom he collaborated more than once.

His pictures of horses being shod, or his scenes of Scottish life, stalking and so on, show an altogether admirable appreciation of form, and also of the effects of atmosphere enveloping his subjects and the distant hills and lochs, which is missing from most of his horse pictures, where a desire to show every feature in minute detail detracts from the overall effect.

He and Landseer were truly Victorian in their approach, and if anything, it was Landseer who was the more sentimental of the two. Herring was apt to bestow sentimental titles on some of his pictures, which are quite capable of impressing without them, whereas Landseer could not resist stressing the limpid gaze of a faithful shepherd's hound, given his technical facility which was phenomenal. It is said that Landseer only agreed to paint Voltigeur because of his attachment to a cat, not because he was an outstanding animal or that it echoed the devotion of the Godolphin Arabian to another cat.

Herring's vision of girls and boys with their pets and ponies, bears the stamp of genuine affection – his daughters Emma and Jennie often posed for him, and it has to be admitted that his painting of fur and feather was masterly, though James Ward did not agree. His somewhat biased opinion of Herring was expressed in scathing terms in one of his letters to his son George. 'If I had painted nothing but Horses,' said he, 'why, the Jockeys and Jockey Gents would prefer the works of Herring, and a specimen is now sent to me as one of his crack efforts. This was of three horses' heads, villainously drawn, feeding on a scanty meal of wiry hay and one of them nibbling at vine leaves.' Herring also had a strange passion – shared with his son Charles – for lop-eared rabbits munching lettuce-leaves in circular frames, but at least he never over-sentimentalised the canine creation. In fact, he brought all his expertise to bear on depicting greyhounds, and in two instances at least the results are magnificent.

No account of his work would be complete without a mention of his faithful horse, Imaum, a beautiful white Arab; this was the animal that figured in countless canvases, where Herring has 'taken up the challenge of his colour and mastered it'. In particular, he is shown acting the part of a horse in the last stages of exhaustion and distress, bearing the bound Mazeppa on his back, in the picture painted for Alderman William Copeland, and including a herd of wild horses, that the Art Journal of the day called his 'most poetical and moving creation'. How he came to acquire this valuable, docile and intelligent animal is told in a later chapter.

So what sort of a man was this John Frederick Herring, who started out in life with none of the advantages of heredity, money or useful connections in society, and ended up painting Orville for George IV, becoming Animal Painter to HRH The Duchess of Kent, and a great favourite of Queen Victoria and Prince Albert, and the painter selected by the Duc D'Orleans to immortalise his race-horses?

We have very few letters from which to gauge his character, and those that have come to light are from middle life, when he was already enjoying some success: nothing remains unfortunately, of a memoir of his early days that he wrote for Charles Spencer Stanhope. As with all artists, these letters mention what work he was doing, and what prices he was getting, and mixed up with this is chat about the family and his health and circumstances generally. Transcripts of the letters from which we have freely drawn are printed in the Appendices. There are no opinions expressed about scandals in the racing world, or about other artists; he only mentions that he has married again as an afterthought. He was pretty self-centred.

There are, however, four pictures – three of them self-portraits – which reveal more of the man.

The earliest is a most delightful piece of 1828, of himself and his brother Benjamin (Plate 17). Here we see a pair of Regency gents, posed in front of a neo-Classical temple, wearing – in the height of fashion – top hats, frock coats and sponge bag trousers. Herring's pink and roundish countenance, and agreeable suggestion of *embonpoint*, contrasting with the cadaverous features of his talented younger brother, who was a sick man and died only two years after the picture was painted, at the age of 24.

The next portrait, done some twenty years later by A. Corbould, as one of a pair, the other being of his second wife, Sarah, is a convincing character study, although quite a small scale picture (Plate 39).

Here, his somewhat owlish appearance contrasts with a shrewd, searching expression in those heavy-lidded eyes; this would be a hard man to best in a bargain. The thin, almost pursed lips indicate a certain iron self-control and determination. There is no humour in that face, and there was little in the man's make-up.

As a family man, he was surely a stern parent – if, as often happens, at the same time over-indulgent to a favourite child. The good clothes, stock and watch-chain, the delicate hand, you would think were those of a well-to-do middle-class business man, a banker or solicitor. He clearly means to convey by his whole demeanour the image of respectability, probity and industriousness – the Victorian ideal, and that surely of his Dutch ancestors. These qualities he demonstrated in his life.

The impetuous youth who leaves home on an impulse and sets off for a more or less random and faraway destination has long since matured; the tough coach driver has been forgotten, and in his place we have a sound Council member of the Society of British Artists.

And yet, this studio portrait does not tell us the whole truth. There is a self-portrait in the fine canvas he painted of a horse fair on Southborough Common in 1857 (Plate 20) which gives us the open-air man.

Then in his early sixties, he here appears as the epitome of the bluff, prosperous countryman, from the top of his buff-coloured, jauntily rakish top hat, down to his well-polished booted feet, planted firmly apart.

No matter that to our eyes his bushy side-whiskers, the hint of corpulence under the broad cloth waistcoat, and his white linen surmounted by a black silk spotted stock suggest, perhaps a genial mixture of W. C. Fields and Sir Alfred Munnings, this was a man who met all classes on equal terms, whether in the studio or Newmarket Heath, Burlington House or the cow-byre, and made his own way with a determination and sincerity that raised him above his followers and imitators like Henry Hall.

He included himself, and I think his son Charles, also in a painting published as an engraving by Fores, of the start of a Steeplechase. Here the hair is white, the covert-coat easy and casual, and the great painter is studying the card, which was in itself an innovation. No sign of a sketch-book, but proof of his powerful visual memory.

The last revealing evidence of his character and life-style comes from the imperishable photograph of him in his studio at Meopham, mentioned in the last chapter.

His three sons, of course, painted too, and the confusion between them has resulted in many an arbitrary attribution, which will be dealt with on another page. But it is worth noting here how many of the sporting artists had brothers, fathers or sons who did similar work. And, rather like in the Renaissance work-shops, one member of the family helped another in the actual composition, and no strict boundaries were observed between them. And if, after all, this savours of 'trade' rather than 'Art', in a world that offered patronage on a lavish scale to the favoured few, who would be averse to cashing in on the goodwill of a family business?[1]

His frequent collaboration with other artists such as Thos Faed, A. F. Rolfe, E. Boutibonne, James Pollard, Edwin Landseer, and Henry Bright is more difficult to grasp in these days of extreme individualism, particularly as it seems unimportant by whom these pictures were actually signed. One can only assume that it was brought about either because of pressure of work, or, as in the case of his assistance to William Powell Frith in 'Derby Day', his acknowledged mastery of horse painting.

Herring is said to have 'used' his younger, most talented son, Charles, to finish pictures he himself had started, or by appending his own signature to paintings done by Charles, and here we enter the murky penumbra of attribution which is dealt with in another chapter. What is certain is that Charles was a most affectionate son who worked amicably with his ageing parent, as is evident from the letter in Appendix A6.

He is also said to have been jealous of the ability of his eldest son, John Frederick junr and to have finished off and signed some of the latter's pictures himself. I personally think that this did happen, but if so, it was to the benefit of J.F. Junr's reputation who was never thought as highly of as his father. He had ample time to prove himself as he outlived his father by forty years, dying in the present century in 1907. And he did some good work too, but buyers should beware of the amateurish efforts signed – J. Fred Herring, in a crabbed script.

[1] Thus several generations of the Sartorius family operated, the Alkens too. George Morland's father was no mean portraitist, the brothers James and William Ward both excelled at mezzotint engraving, there were two Barraud brothers, sharing admirable quality in their work, Dean Wolstenholme senr and junr were specialists in delightful small-scale hunting pictures, the Ferneleys, father and son, were experts in the Meltonian 'swells', even Stubbs had a son, and so on.

As an example of the respect in which the family was held, I may quote the experience of Fred Roe, RI, the late Victorian painter of historical subjects. His son, Mr Gordon Roe, FRS, tells me that his father was recommended to approach J.F. Junr, when he was starting out as an artist, to see if he could not take up horse painting as a career that offered a hopeful future.

According to Mr Roe, his father Fred, had a pleasant interview at J.F. Junr's home at Great Wilbraham, nr Cambridge, but he was dissuaded from this course as J.F. Junr felt Fred's heart 'was not in it'. But he did invite Roe to visit him in his studio at any time he wished.

J.F. Junr of course, made farm-yard scenes his speciality, but the incident does serve to show that Herring senr's reputation lived on, long after his demise. That there was some rift between father and son seems to be borne out by the fact that in J.F. senr's very detailed will (Appendix B), there is no mention at all of J.F. Junr.

Whether we put Herring above or below Ben Marshall, whether we prefer the brilliant actuality of his thoroughbreds stripped for action to all the musical metaphors adduced in favour of some of Stubbs's compositions, or whether the hunting man will always admire the Ferneley's Quorn more than Herring's East Suffolk hunt pictures, is a matter of taste; what is sure is that the owner who sold a Herring for £68 in 1947 that came up for sale thirty years later at £24,000, has lived to regret it.

J. F. HERRING Senr

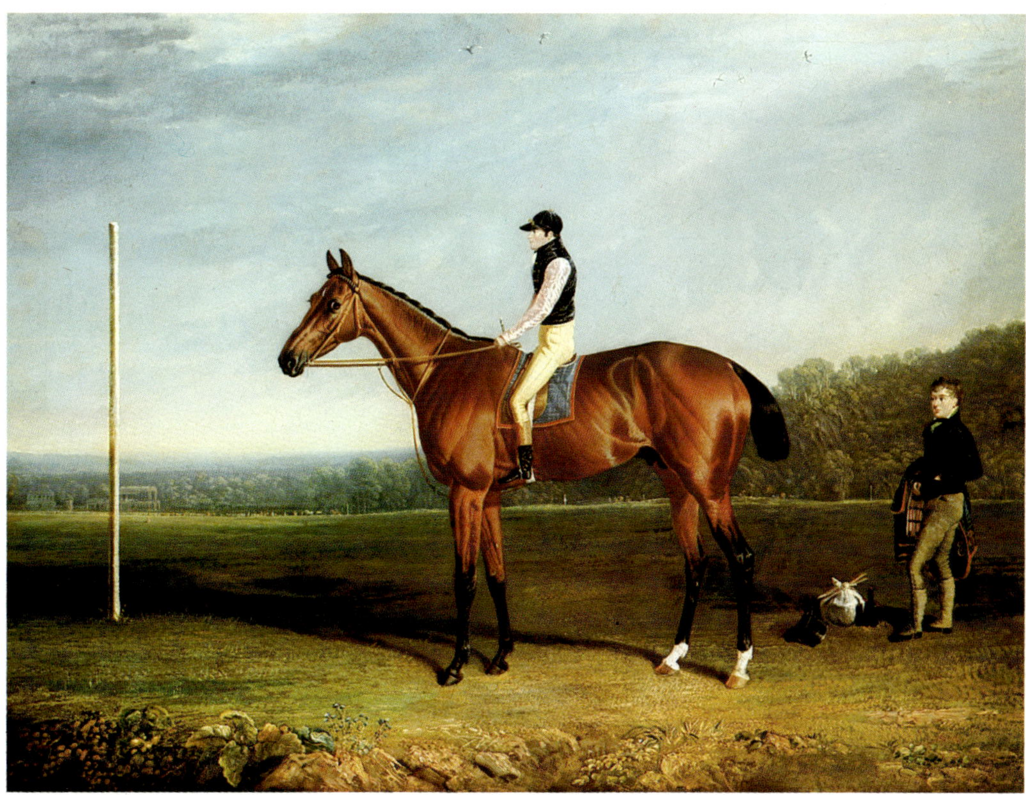

1

Theodore with John Jackson up, and with his lad, at Doncaster. Signed, inscribed and dated 1822.

Courtesy:
Arthur Ackermann & Son Ltd

List No 12

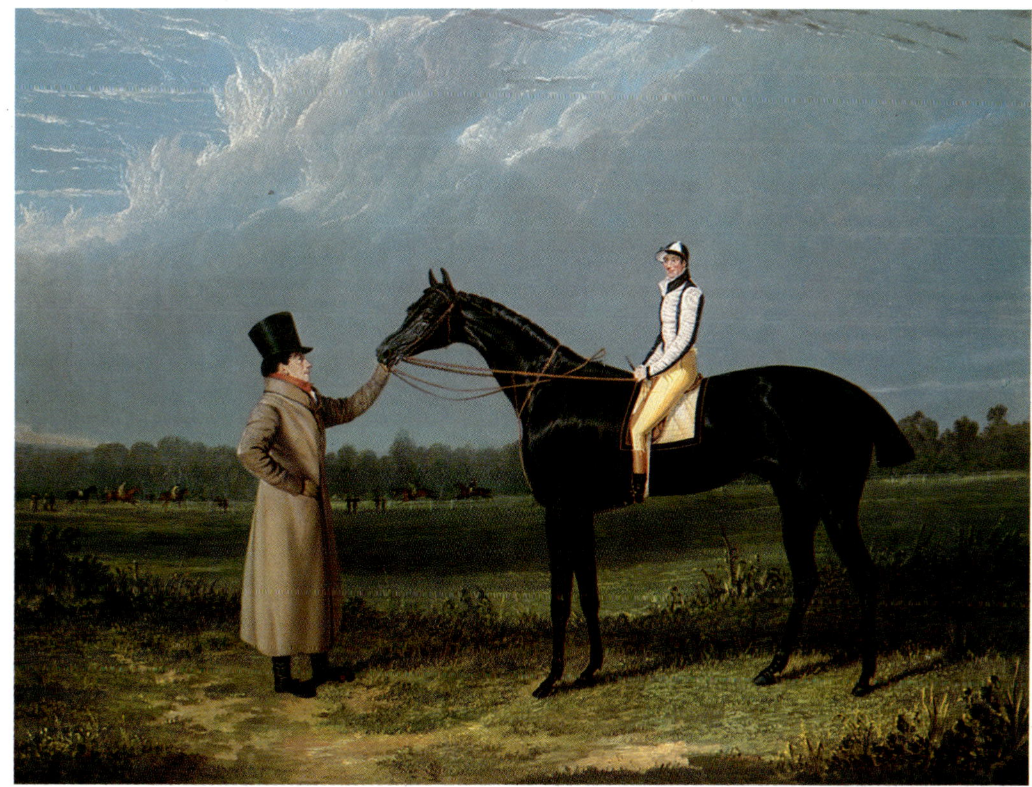

2

Jerry with Ben Smith up, at Doncaster. Signed and dated 1824. 21½ × 29½ ins.

Courtesy:
Arthur Ackermann & Son Ltd

List No 18

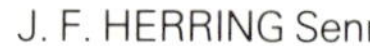
J. F. HERRING Senr

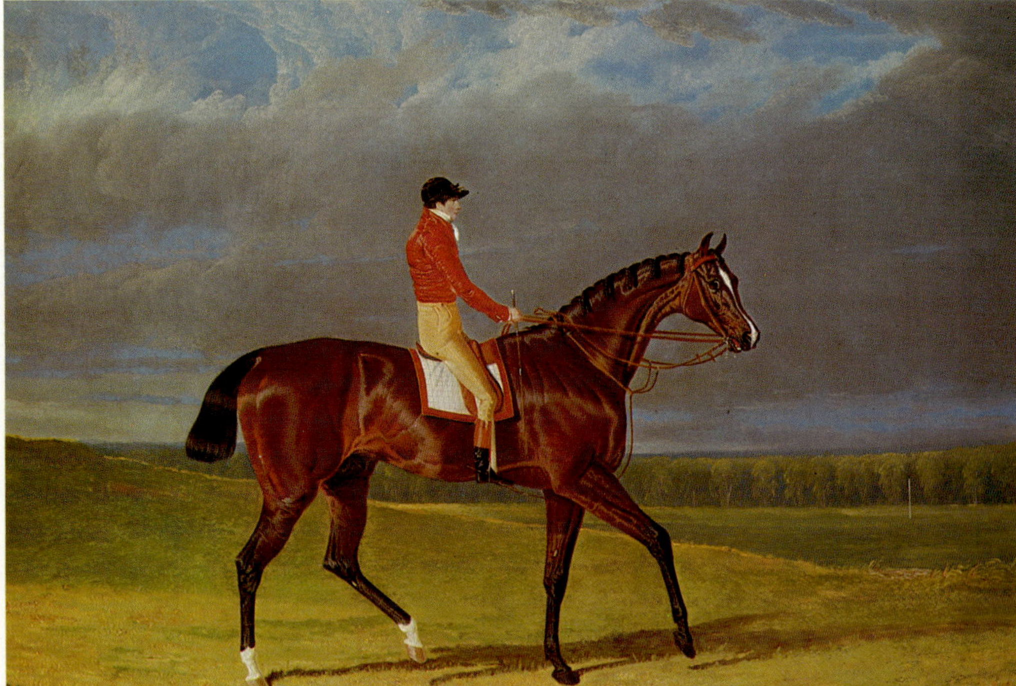

3

Figaro with J. Lye up. Signed and dated 1825. 22 × 30 ins.

Courtesy:
Arthur Ackermann & Son Ltd

List No 20

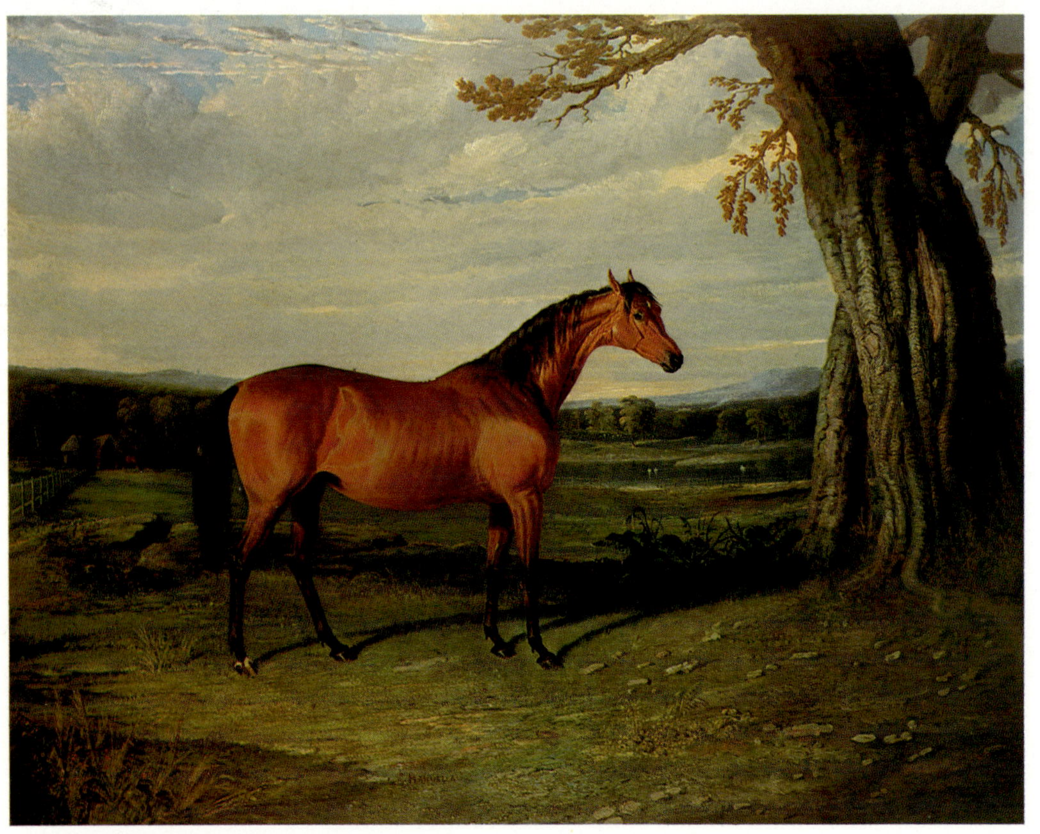

4

Manuella at Mr Richard Watts' stud. Signed, inscribed and dated 1825. 40 × 50 ins.

Courtesy:
Arthur Ackermann & Son Ltd

List No 21

5

Vanish with Sam Darling up
Signed and dated 1830.
22 × 30 ins.

Courtesy:
Arthur Ackermann & Son Ltd

List No 49

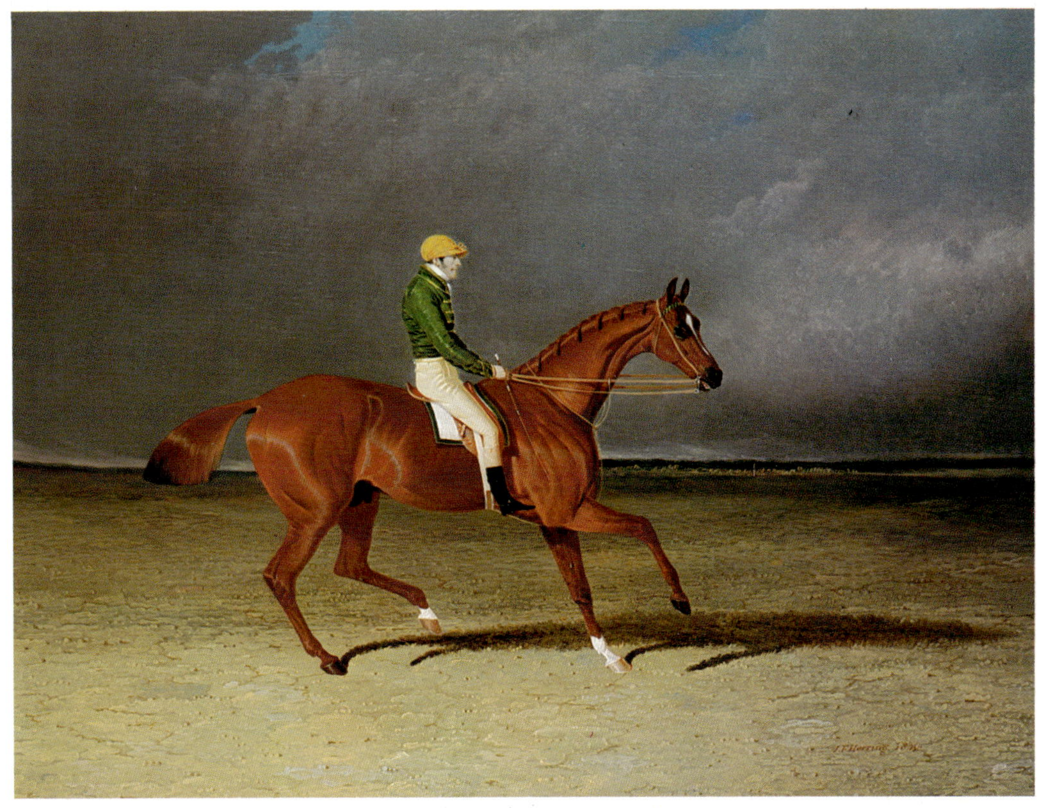

6

Rockingham with jockey Sam Darling. Signed and dated 1833. 10½ × 12½ ins.

Courtesy: Christie's

List No 58

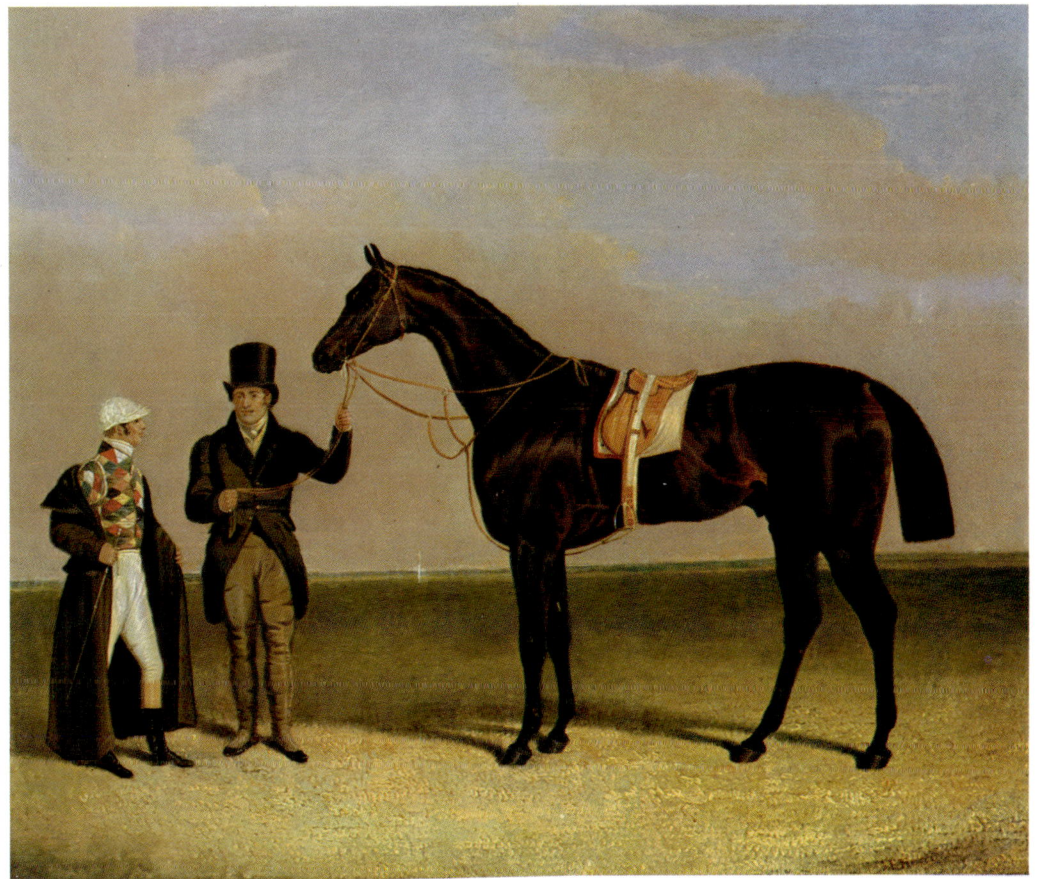

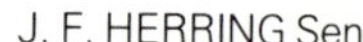

J. F. HERRING Senr

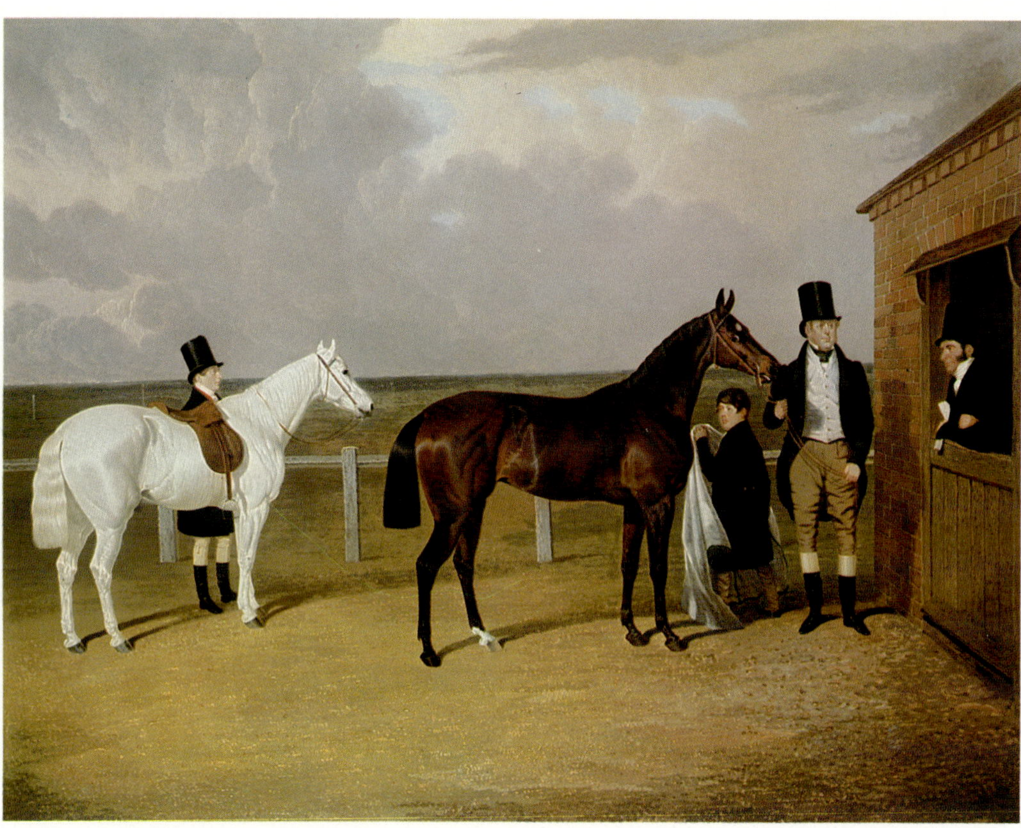

7

Vespa with owner holding bridle, trainer and groom.
Signed and dated 1833.
28 × 36 ins.

Courtesy:
Richard Green Gallery

List No 60

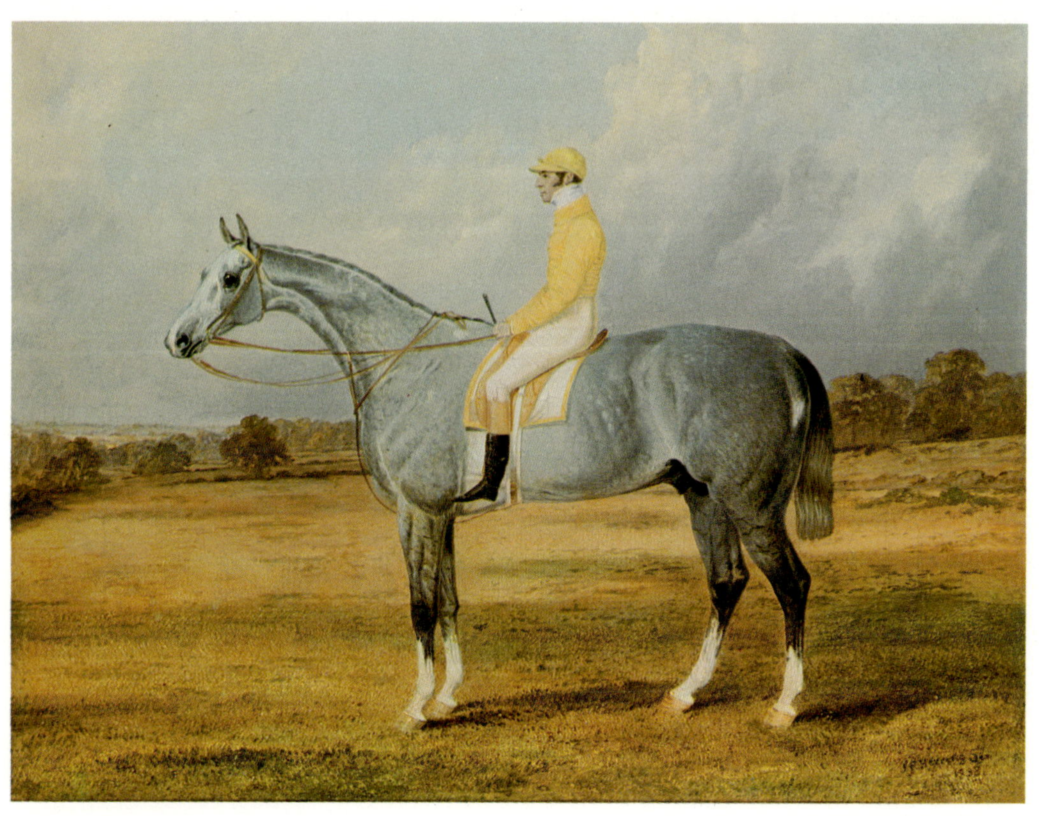

8

Grey Momus with J. Day up.
Signed and dated 1838.
14 × 18 ins.

Courtesy:
Arthur Ackermann & Son Ltd

List No 100

1

Youthful Toil – and Talent

1795–1814

It was no accident when John Frederick Herring[1] took the coach to Doncaster and left the stench of the urban wen behind him.

For some years he had trudged from Blackfriars Road, across Blackfriars Bridge – then just completed – probably cut through Seacoal Lane, past the Old Bailey Criminal Court and then on to work in his father's fringe-making and upholstery shop in Newgate Street; Smithfield Market lay to the North, St Paul's Cathedral to the South, and Newgate Prison to the East.

Now in his nineteenth year, that September day in 1814 was to mark the fledgling's taking wing into a wider world and a new career which was to bring him fame and fortune.

With the family business and home now established at 88 Newgate Street, he would see the Royal Leeds Union coach pass his father's premises every day, with the word 'Doncaster' painted on its door. What dreams that seemingly prosaic destination may have conjured up in the mind of an imaginative youngster can only be conjectured.

His parents had lived at Richmond, in North Yorkshire, before he was born, so he doubtless had some idea where the town was, and he surely realised the importance in the racing calendar of the Great St Leger due to be run in a few days' time – his pals on the coaches must have put him in the picture. Be that as it may, Fate took a hand, and he resolved there and then to leave home, board the coach and travel thither.

There are two theories about this sudden decision. One story goes that he had painted a picture of a horse that a chance visitor to the shop liked so much that he bought it for two guineas – in the absence of Herring's father. When that worthy learned what had happened apparently he was not best pleased, and harsh words were exchanged. Whether this was the picture for the 'White Horse' inn in Fetter Lane, of which Herring is known to be the painter cannot now be confirmed. Anyway, it is assumed that there was some sort of family row about the young Herring's lack of application to business.

[1] Please note that the Herring we now know as 'J. F. Herring, senr', will be referred to simply as 'Herring'; to avoid confusion, other members of the family will be referred to by their Christian names.

The other theory is that young Herring had contracted a marriage with Anne Harris that was frowned on by his parents, with the result that the atmosphere became unbearable to him. As both parties were under age, however, they would have had to have parental consent, as elopement to Gretna Green was then the only alternative, and there is no record of such an adventure.

Unfortunately, there is no record of the marriage either, and the registrars of the two churches in Camberwell where the family were then living have been searched from end to end. Census returns give only the date and place of birth.

It would be unusual for a family to patronise a church in a different parish to that in which they were living, in view of the fact that the Banns would have to be read for three Sundays prior to the proposed nuptials. There is no record of a marriage between them in the church archives in Doncaster where seven of his eight children were baptised, so, what happened?

To work back from the birth of their first child, John Frederick junr, which occurred on 21 June 1815, Herring and his wife, Anne Harris, must at least have known each other since the previous September. So the question arises, did they get married at some church we know not of, or did they not get married at all?

With such a lack of documentary evidence, one can only look for the solution in the characters of the people concerned. It is known that Herring was a regular attender at Doncaster Parish church, where his voice and his musicianship was well appreciated; would he have faced it out, 'living in sin' in those days? It seems highly unlikely. Neither does it seem convincing to assume that a girl who was free, would have followed him to the North, so precipitately, knowing he had no job and few prospects at that juncture.

So perhaps one must concede that they married somewhere before he left for Doncaster, and she joined him when he had found lodgings. Exactly where and when they married will perhaps come to light one day for some researcher who has better luck than the author.

His father, Benjamin Herring, who was a notably home-loving and domestic sort of character, must have been shocked – if not surprised – by this flight to independence of his eldest son. For, although he had employed the lad for some years in his business, he had not apprenticed him, and the time spent by John Frederick in hanging about the local smithies, and sketching horses in the numerous coaching stables, he considered wasted.

Indeed, it must have been hard for someone of John Frederick's temperament not to have been fascinated by the bustle and ordered confusion of the great coaching establishments which were then thriving in London. The glamour of the sparkling equipages, the trotting bays and the cheery toots of the guard's horn as another coach started on its daily journey must have enthralled him.

He was said at this time never to be seen without a whip or a pencil in hand, and what schooling he had is not known for sure, but his bent towards the arts was already in evidence. His first coaching picture of the Hampton Court coach-and-four, was painted at the time, and for sixty years was in the family's possession.

One of the largest coaching-inns of its day, 'The Golden Cross' (mentioned in *Nicholas*

Nickleby) situated where Nelson's column now stands, was, in fact, only a few minutes away from the parental establishment, and one can easily imagine the lad often playing truant to stand and stare or even run alongside holding the bridle of the leader as he turned out of the yard into Pall Mall.

At some time or another he must also have persuaded some driver friend of his to allow him up on the box to take the reins, as his skill as a driver was so soon to be put to the test.

* * *

As the authorities differ in their accounts of his family background, it may not be out of place to sketch it in from information which has been provided by his descendants. His father, Benjamin – a name that recurs frequently in each generation of the family – had had a chequered career, prior to his arrival in the capital. He was British, not American, contrary to popular belief, for he had been born in New York when it was still under the British flag, before America was declared independent. His father, Jan Frederick, was the son of another Benjamin, who had married a Dutch heiress in the island of Curaçao.

This dot in the Caribbean Sea was a prosperous trading centre, producing sugar, coffee and cotton, with 'numerous warehouses always full of the commodities of Europe and the East'.

When the French and Dutch inhabitants fell out, the island surrendered to a single British frigate. It was restored to the Dutch by the Treaty of Amiens in 1802, only to be re-taken by the British in 1867.

This is only mentioned because of the efforts made by Jan Frederick (John Frederick's grandfather), and later his son, Benjamin (John Frederick's father), to claim valuable properties in Surinam that were rightly theirs, inherited from their Dutch forebears. (There was also a daughter, Catherine, who is said only to have escaped the guillotine in the French Terror, by marrying a Frenchman.) Matters were complicated by the fact that Surinam was ceded by the English to the Dutch in exchange for the province of New York (once New Amsterdam) in 1774, and was later re-taken by the English. Jan Frederick, in fact, is alleged to have died of chagrin in 1779, when he failed to prove his title.

His (Jan Frederick's) widow, Lucretia (neé Van Duerson) we are told, 'did not remain in widowhood long', but married a Mr Francis, an Englishman then residing in New York. Four sons and a daughter were born of this match, but the family emigrated to England when Benjamin (John Frederick's father) was about seven years old. They took up residence in Richmond in Yorkshire, and young Ben was apprenticed to an upholsterer in Newcastle-upon-Tyne.

Poor Ben was very harshly treated by his stepfather, whom he believed to be his own father. He bore his name, and was taught to venerate him, having been too young to remember anything of his real father. However, a Colonel Etherington, who had been a close friend of his father's, informed Ben when he was 'almost risen into manhood', that his name was not Francis, but Herring, and he ought to lay claim to a property called Jagers Woude to which he was lawful heir. He also had the papers in his possession, and advised him how to go about the business.

Lengthy correspondence with the various authorities failed to substantiate his inheritance, however, and after expending £4,000 in the attempt, he eventually gave up. Where he found such a large sum to even get thus far, or whether his parents or the good Colonel backed him, is not known. He should also have come into possession of a whole island, Aruba, some five miles from Curaçao, from his uncle William Herring, but this too, we believe, he was more or less swindled out of as well.

So, not being a pertinacious sort of man, and unwilling to venture further than France or Holland in the search for the phantom property, he gave up that claim too, and settled down to the business he had been brought up in. Other members of the family are said to have visited the island, later in the 19th century, but with John Frederick deserting the family home, we hear no more of it. It seems certain that Benjamin was not a wealthy man, and his son cannot have had much money on him to embark on life.

All we know is that John Frederick left four sisters behind, and four brothers, all born at regular two yearly intervals, only one of whom, Benjamin, showed any tendency towards art, and in fact painted quite well. But he died young in 1830.

Before his father, Benjamin, fades out of the picture, we might mention that, on the death of his first wife, (J.F.'s mother) Sarah Jemima (née Howard of Wimborne, Dorset) in 1831, he married again and had a daughter Emily Eliza (born 1832). He himself ended up as Governor of Winchester Gaol. How this remarkable metamorphosis from a small tradesman to a position of some importance was achieved we do not know. Such appointments were usually bought in those days or else in the gift of someone in the government.

Of the other members of this prolific family of John Frederick, his brother Charles (born 1800) married Emma Gale and had eight children, and his eldest son, also Charles, fathered nine children, the descendants of one of whom, the third child, Leonard, has descendants still living.

John Frederick himself, who married twice (his second wife, Sarah Gale probably being a sister to Charles's wife, Emma), had eight children, the three boys, John Frederick junr (born 1815), Charles (born 1828) and Benjamin (born 1830), following in their father's footsteps – as we shall see.

2

The Coachman-Painter

1814–1821

We left our hero boarding the coach for Doncaster, and there is a story that the driver was a friend of his, who had allowed him to take the reins before; but what of the journey he then undertook?

One can imagine his excitement and delight as his chosen conveyance rattled over the cobbles through the Metropolis, along what is now Waterloo Place and up Regent's Street; the delays occasioned by meeting immense hay-wains on their way to the city dairies or herds of cattle being driven to Smithfield Market for slaughter, would only whet his appetite for the adventure.

So, leaving the new-built houses in Portland Place behind, they would take to the open road. For Regent's Park was still a large farm, Swiss Cottage – a cottage, Islington a suburb, and Jack Straw's inn on Hampstead Heath would be the first toll-gate they encountered on their way to Barnet, and the first change of horses.

The whole journey[1] would have taken the best part of two days, passing through Hertfordshire and Stamford on the way, and probably halting at Grantham for the night. The experience was perhaps glamorous enough to confirm him in his ambition to drive such a vehicle himself one day – just as small boys used to dream of being engine-drivers.

Anyway, the attractive legend – which deserves to be true – persists that he arrived in Doncaster on the day the Great St Leger of 1814 was to be run. It is possible that he planned the whole thing so as to arrive in time to see it. With the whole town on the Moor for the last 'Classic' of the year, what more natural than that he should find his way, for the first time in his life, with the rest of the population – not then very numerous – on to the course. And there he saw the Duke of Hamilton's[2] colt, William, cheered home the winner.

[1] A similar odyssey is recorded by Dickens in *Nicholas Nickleby* (Chapter V) where the coach to Yorkshire departs from the Saracen's Head, Snow Hill, via The Peacock, Islington to Eton Slocomb, Stamford, and The George at Grantham and Newark.

[2] Alexander, Duke of Hamilton – portrayed by Garrard *c.* 1786.

As a contributor to the *Sporting Magazine* was later to write of him in the jargon of the day: 'The right chord was touched at once: the silken coats of the horses and satin jackets of the jockeys gave a pleasure in contemplating them he had never before experienced, and back he went, "turf struck", to try his hand at a representation of the scene which had made so vivid an impression on him. But natural genius alone was unequal to the task, and so for awhile succumbed to the difficulties of the subject, from the want of her twin sister, art, to teach the young idea how to carry out her intentions.'

The same author then recounts how the young townling in his wanderings, alone and unknown, round the streets of Doncaster, was brought to a halt outside a coachmaker's painting shop. There, through the open doors, he espied someone with brush in hand, attempting to give the 'pride of the boot' to a new coach, 'The Commander-in-Chief', his aim being an equestrian portrait of the Duke of Wellington, taken from one of Alken's sketches. Too shy to obtrude on his first visit, Herring returned the next day, got into conversation with the painter and offered to try his hand. His offer was gladly accepted and Herring drew in the outline so well that his new acquaintance asked him to colour it also. While engaged on this task, the employer came in and was so struck with his ability that, after a short interview, he took him on to paint the insignia of a new coach he was building, The Royal Forester. This required him to delineate a white lion on one door and a reindeer on the other. Herring completed this work with equal credit, although he can hardly have attempted a reindeer before, and Herring needed no second invitation when the proprietor, Mr Wood, insisted on him getting up for a ride alongside himself, to prove the springs and christen the drag . . .

Having thus made the acquaintance of Mr Wood, Herring, on hearing in the coach office that one of the men on the Wakefield run was about to give up driving, thereupon asked Mr Wood if he might take up the vacant seat. The latter, not unnaturally, was inclined to scoff at the idea of a painter driving a four-in-hand, and told him that as the owners were mainly responsible for the doings of their men, he could not accept the offer. But when Herring assured him that he was quite competent, otherwise he would not have asked the favour, he agreed to give him a trial on one of his coaches, and would accept the verdict of the up and down coachmen of the day fixed.

Their report turned out to be so favourable, that Mr Wood agreed to employ him as a driver, and the very next Monday saw Herring, attired in the regulation frock-coat, top-boots and low-crowned hat of those times, take his place for the first time as a professional, 'on the box', of the important Wakefield and Lincoln 'Nelson' coach. From then on he became known as the 'artist-coachman'.

Mr Wood's caution is understandable when it is realised that the stage-coach businesses were highly competitive ventures. They had been set up in rivalry to the post service by private entrepreneurs, and set new standards of speed and reliability over the much improved turn-pike roads that were being built by Telford and Macadam. They had the advantage of travelling by day, but still charged their passengers less than the Post.

In their wake they brought about a national network of first-class inns, designed to provide passengers with rest and refreshment, and the coaches with fresh teams of horses.

One particular coach would travel about one hundred miles before handing over to a new one. The 'Nelson' for instance, was the name given to the run, and many coaches with the same name serviced the route. But horses would have to be changed about every dozen miles. The ostlers who were good at their job could unharness a tired team and tack up a fresh one in a matter of three minutes, to the astonishment of foreign travellers.

Thousands of horses were involved in the organisation, good, bad and indifferent; it took a skilled man to drive a laden coach, trotting along at about ten miles an hour, with perhaps a kicker teamed with an old fellow with one eye, through fog, snow and – worst of all – floods. He had to judge his pace on the flat, negotiate steep downward hills without tying a wheel, which might upset the load, by coaxing his 'wheelers' to do the braking, and then let 'em loose over a hump-back bridge at the bottom in order to scale the gradient on the other side.

Up to our period, the stage-coach drivers had been mostly unmitigated ruffians, coarse of speech and bullying in manner – especially where tips were concerned. But the new breed of proprietors, like Mr Wood, demanded a higher standard, as they depended on the goodwill of the public to use their coaches. So the drivers became a much better-mannered lot, neatly turned out in their top-hats and buckskin breeches, the élite of the road, or 'swell dragsmen' as they were called.

Herring continued nearly two years on this route, and must have been making a decent living. Although in later life, he seemed to consider his life as a coach driver had damaged his health, and delayed his start in the profession which made his name, he must have earned a real respect and admiration in his new role. The inhabitants of every hamlet through which the coaches went used to turn out to watch them go by, and cheer them on their way. It could well be that Herring's 'Nelson' coach, might have been the first to bring the good tidings of the victory of Wellington at Waterloo, and the final overthrow of 'Boney', to many an outlying village, where the jubilation would know no bounds.

The hard-won experience from such a hazardous and demanding occupation did give him, too, a unique understanding of the conformation of the horse, and a meticulous regard for the detail of bridle and harness which he turned to good account in his coaching pictures. But it also aggravated his tendency to bronchial troubles.

In his spare time he was still painting horses on inn signs, and decorating coach panels, as was his contemporary Charles Towne but nothing remains of those 'prentice' efforts, and it was not until he transferred to the Doncaster to Halifax coach, which went via Barnsley and Huddersfield, that his progress in that career took a new turn.

There were many gentlemen and aristocratic travellers too, who loved to sit on the box with the driver, and would in fact pay extra for the honour. At one time, 'outside' passengers were accorded scant consideration by those in charge of the coach, or by the inn-keepers they encountered on the way, but now, it was 'quite the thing'. And it was Herring's good luck that one day, in the normal course of duty, he got into conversation with a traveller on his box, who turned out to be a distinguished Yorkshire landowner, Mr Charles Spencer-Stanhope, of Cannon Hall, near Barnsley.

The latter evidently realised that this was no ordinary charioteer by his style of driving, and moreover, not much of a Yorkshireman – to judge by his accent, and the conversation took a turn to indicate that Herring had other interests apart from the 'ribbons'.

Mrs. A. M. W. Pickering, who was Mr Spencer-Stanhope's niece, recalled in her memoirs, that her Uncle Charles, who was exactly the same age as Herring, used to tell the following story:

> One day he was on the box seat of the Doncaster coach, sitting by the coachman; they passed a field of cattle and my Uncle remarked to the coachman, "Well, those cows belong to the lean kine!" "Oh, Sir," said the coachman, "but they are so picturesque!" "Picturesque" said my uncle, "that is an odd word for you to use. What do you know about the picturesque?" "Well, something, Sir," answered the coachman, "I'm very fond of it, and I wish when you come to Doncaster that you would come and see me, and I would show you some of my drawings."

Anyway, on arrival at their destination at the Doncaster Arms, afterwards known as The Brown Cow,[1] Mr Stanhope adjourned to Herring's lodgings which were almost opposite the inn in question. He was struck with the cleverness of his drawings, and his remark, on seeing a few of Herring's pictures lying about, proved much to the point. 'What a pity,' he exclaimed, 'you should be driving a coach.'

The result of this chance meeting was a letter from Mr Stanhope, followed by a commission to paint a chestnut hunter belonging to his brother, named as Mr Collingwood, which was sent over to Doncaster for the purpose. As the commentator puts it: 'The portrait was finished to the owner's complete satisfaction, and Mr Herring so secured two of his first and best friends; Mr (afterwards the Reverend) Charles Spencer-Stanhope and Mr Collingwood', with the former he kept up a correspondence for the rest of his life.

Here Mrs Pickering refutes the imputation that Herring became too conceited in later life to acknowledge the encouragement he had received from Mr Spencer-Stanhope, in the following words:

> When he (Herring) was at the height of his fame, my uncle Charles went one day to call upon him. He was delighted to see him, referred to their drive on the Doncaster coach and said: "You were the first friend – the first person who said one word of encouragement to me," and made him a present of some proof prints of his pictures of horses.

Before we leave this account of Herring's early years, there is a puzzling story about an inn sign that he painted for an old pub – The Long and Short Arm – at Lemsford, near Hatfield in Herts, on what was once the Great North Road.

The sign he painted, depicted a horse-drawn wagon and two men, with the wagoner extending an arm at full length for a tankard of beer which the landlord was withholding with his arm held back. To make the meaning clear, the inscription 'Pay before you sip' was written on it. This sign was replaced by an altogether different version showing wooden arms of different lengths supposed to convey a warning to coach-drivers that the road ahead was flooded, or clear.

The original version by Herring was probably stolen or acquired by some collector who knew the value of his signs after he became famous.

(With acknowledgements to 'Hertfordshire Countryside')

[1]*"Brown Cow" anecdote*: This inn had been so named by the publican for whom Herring had painted the sign. Offers to buy it had been turned off by the good wife of the ale-house who firmly declined any money for it, saying in her broad Yorkshire accent that it was worth more to her than anyone else.

9

Launcelot and Maroon.
Signed and dated 1840
27¼ × 40¼ ins.

Courtesy: Sotheby's

List No 119

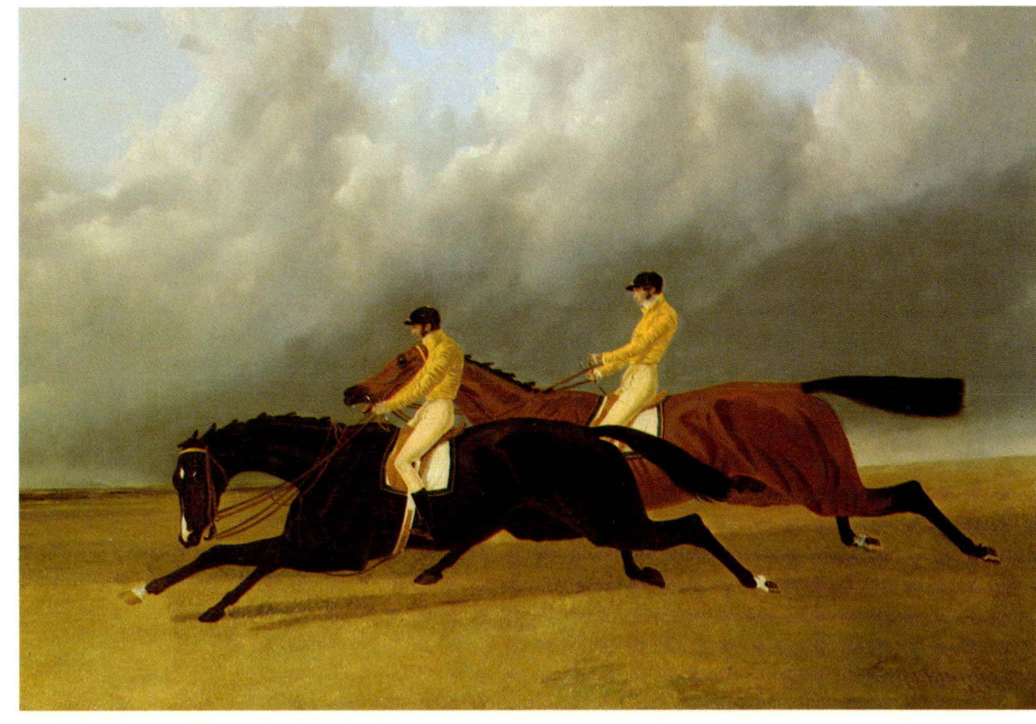

10

Charles XII in a stable. Signed and dated 1843. 28 × 36 ins.

Courtesy:
Arthur Ackermann & Son Ltd

List No 150

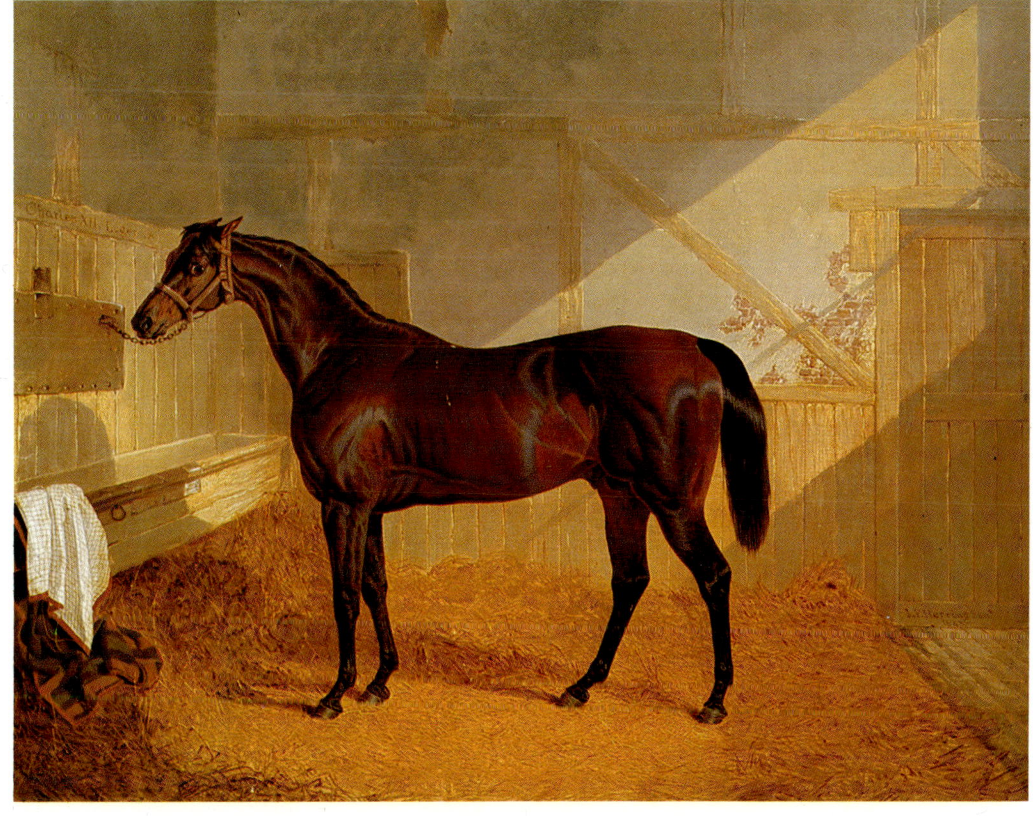

J. F. HERRING Senr

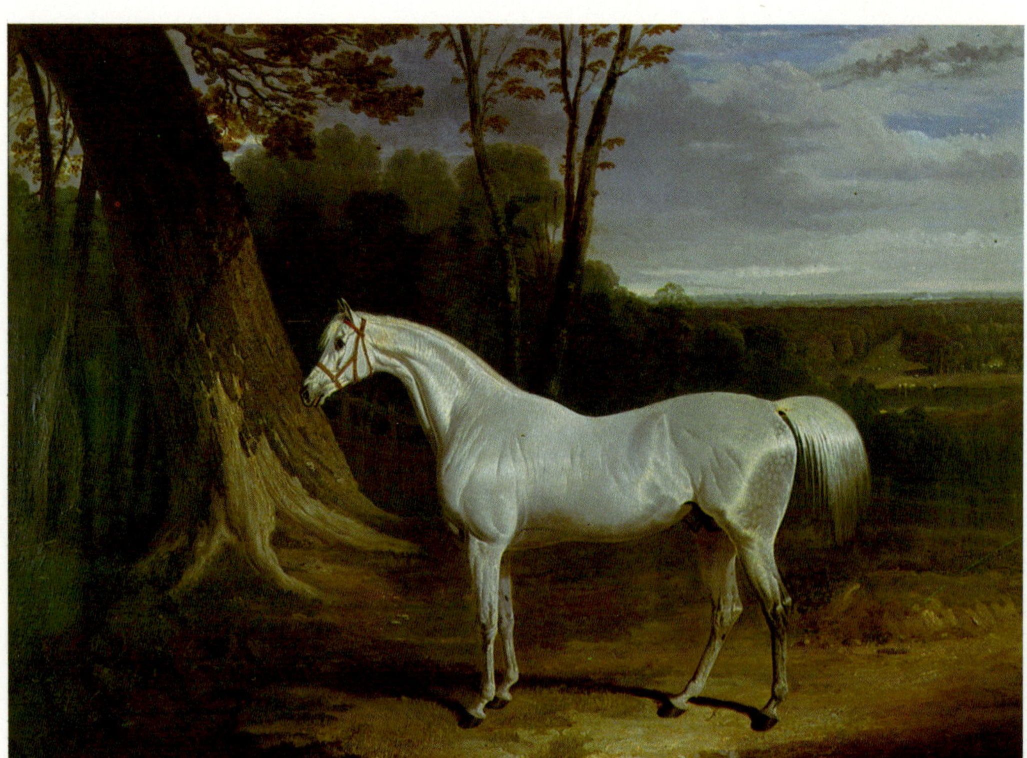

11

Grey Arab Stallion Windsor Castle in distance. Signed and dated 1826. 21½ × 29½ ins.

Courtesy: J. D. D'Arcy Clark

List No 25

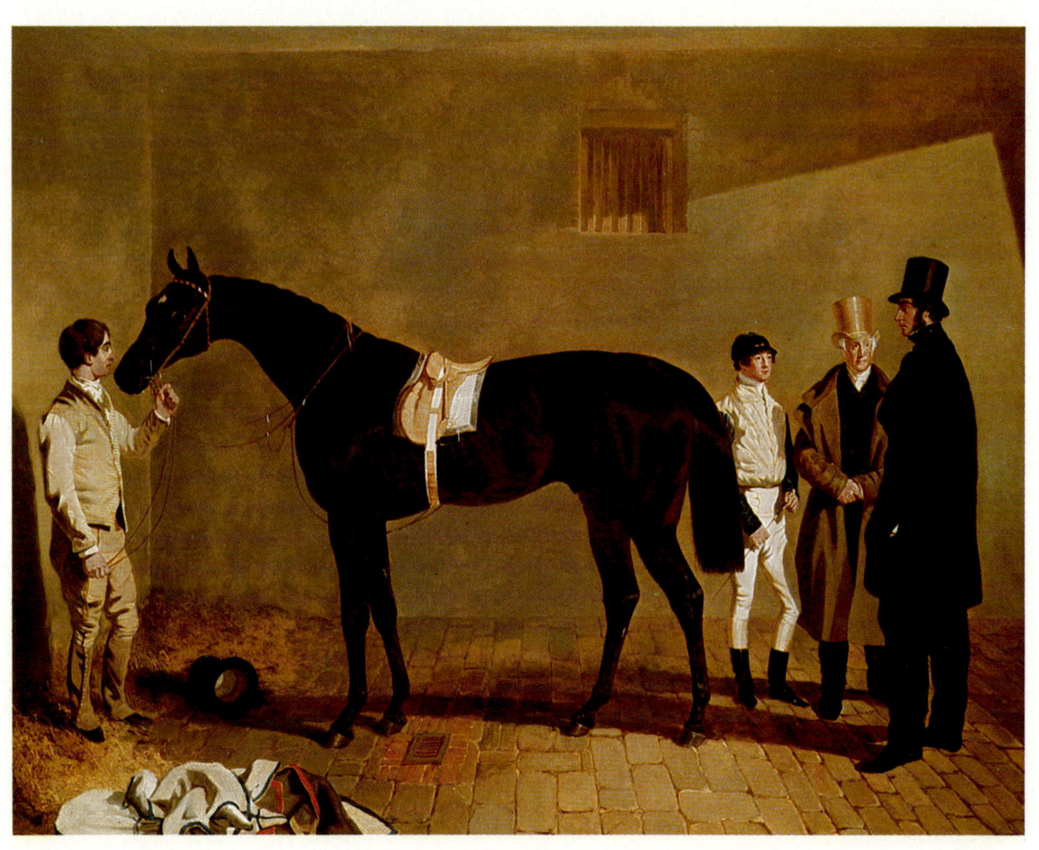

12

Mr Irwin and his brown colt **Faugh-a-Ballagh.** Signed, inscribed and dated 1844.

Courtesy:
Richard Green Gallery

List No 152

J. F. HERRING Senr

13

Allan McDonough on **Brunette** Tom Oliver on **Discount** and Jem Mason on **Lottery**. *c.* 1847. 28 × 36 ins.

Courtesy:
Arthur Ackermann & Son Ltd

List No 190

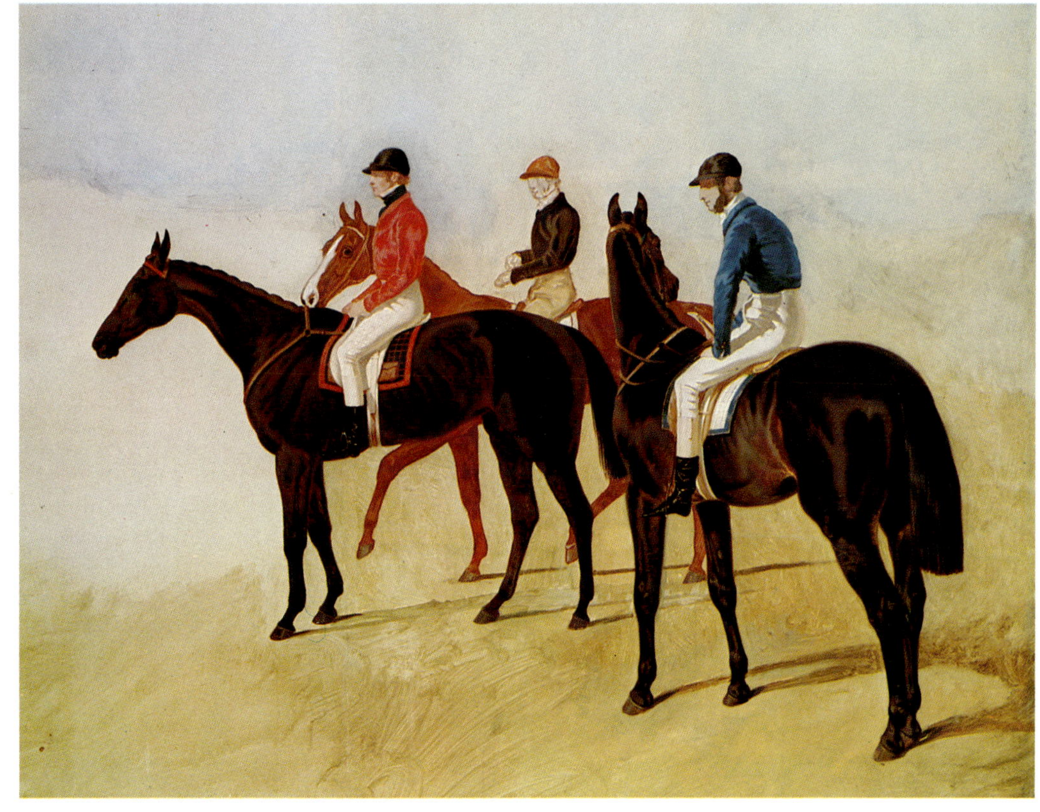

14

Steeplechase Cracks. Signed J. F. Herring senr, not dated. 24 × 44 ins.

Courtesy:
HM Queen Elizabeth the Queen Mother

List No 181

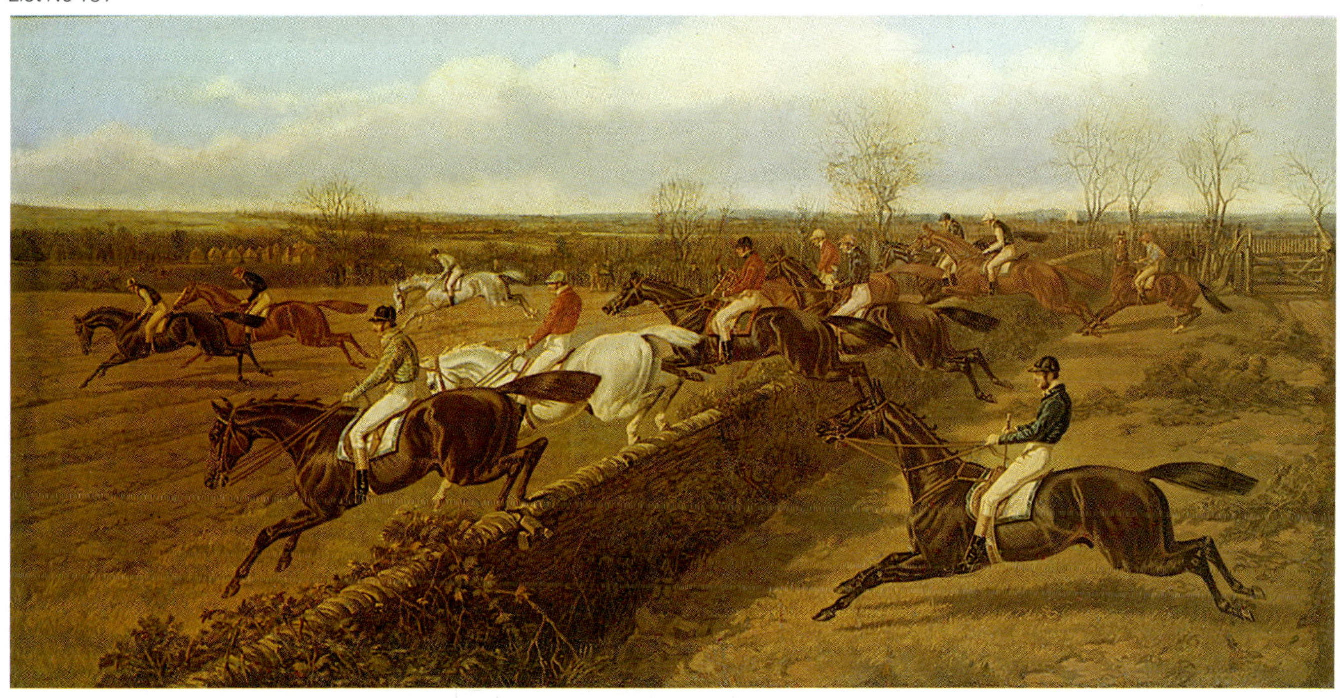

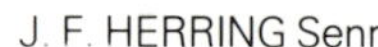

J. F. HERRING Senr

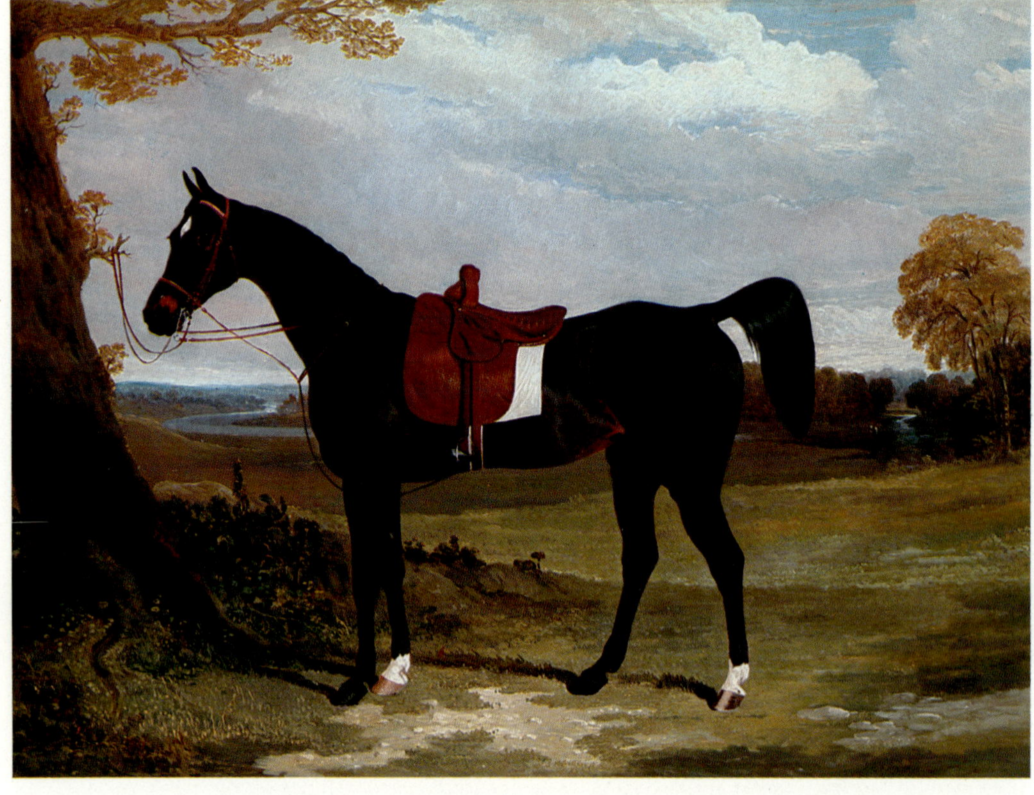

15

Dark bay hunter, side-saddled, and bridled. Inscribed and dated 1833.
$17\frac{1}{4} \times 23\frac{1}{2}$ ins.

Courtesy:
Richard Green Gallery

List No 66

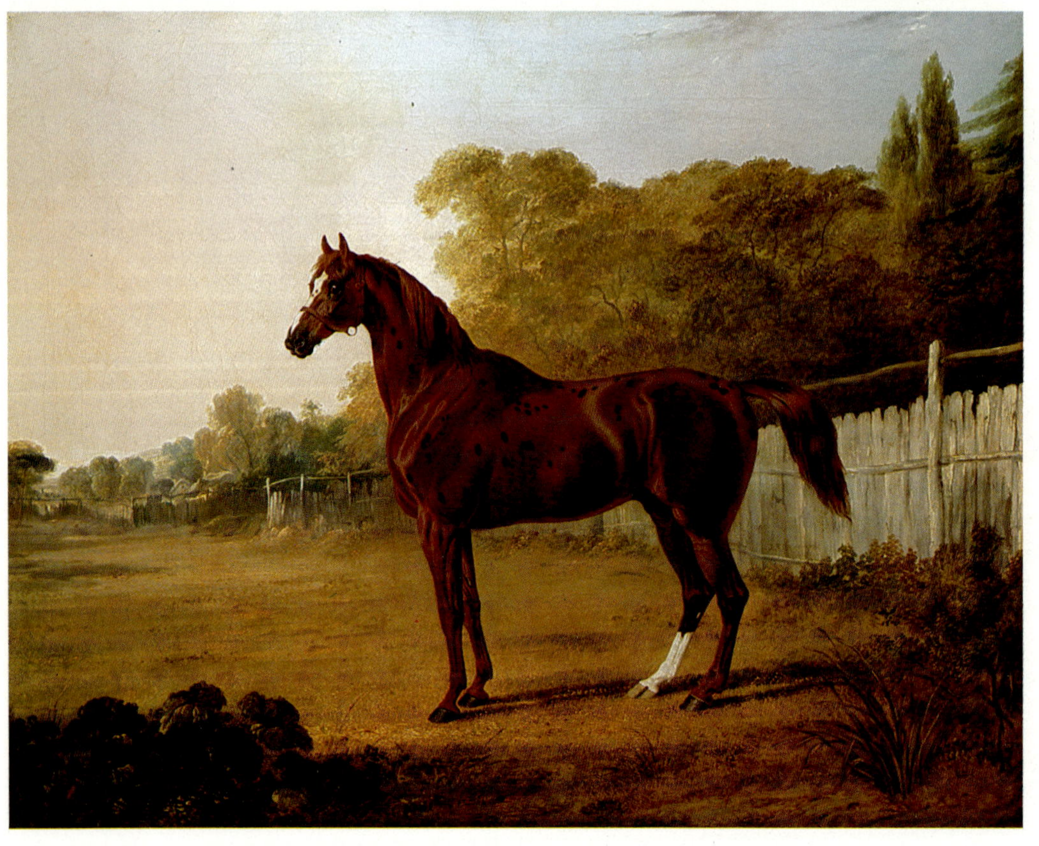

16

Pantaloon in a paddock. Signed and dated 1846.
28×36 ins.

Courtesy:
Richard Green Gallery

List No 175

3

Good Friends in Yorkshire

1821–1830

In such a 'horse mad' district as Doncaster, it is no wonder that the reputation of this 'artist-coachman' should soon spread across the county of broad acres, and bring renewed offers of employment as a painter. The training centres of Middleham and Malton were neither of them too far for owners to think of commissioning him, and with many good examples of his talent already in circulation, his appreciative partrons pressed him to give up driving, and 'abandon the box for the easel'. (Races were also run at Malton.)

Amongst them, none was more insistent in this advice than Mr Frank Hawkesworth, of Hickleton Hall who had admired a painting of a hound he had seen in a window in Doncaster. It was he who made an offer to Herring that must have been hard for a young hopeful of twenty-one to refuse. This amounted to a guarantee of enough work for one year to establish himself, by which time, he argued, he could well manage on his own.

Resist it he did, however, exhibiting a caution beyond his years, which was not uncharacteristic of the matter-of-fact nature of his Dutch ancestors. He felt he needed still more practice in the art, before giving up the substance of a steady income, for the shadow of an uncertain future. (Although the great age of Dutch painting was on the wane, one should not ignore this national strand in the make-up of a personality whose immediate forebears showed no sign of artistic genius.)

His next assignment as a coachman came through a well-known local personage, Mr George Clark(e) of Barnby Moor. He had seen, and been impressed by, a sign-board Herring had painted for an Inn, called 'The Coach and Horses'. He also realised that Herring was something of a wonder on the road as well, and as he himself was involved in the business, he invited Herring to join his firm. Herring thus achieved the pinnacle of a driver's ambition, and found himself in charge of the 'High Flyer' coach, on the York to London route, which ended at the White Horse, Fetter Lane. The name was an apt prophecy of Herring's future, being christened after Mr Tattersall's renowned sire, the unbeaten High Flyer.

He remained on this route for a matter of eighteen months, before acceding to the importunities of his friends. The fact that he was continually plagued with bronchitis and asthma from constant exposure to the biting winds and uncertain weather of the Great North Road, also played a part in his decision to 'go it alone' with his painting. These bronchial troubles afflicted him, off and on, for the rest of his life, and were contributory to his eventual demise.

He was not disappointed by Mr Hawkesworth, who confirmed his previous generous offer, and this determined him to retire from the road. It was actually a gradual withdrawal from the sphere in which he had attained distinction, because Mr Clarke, who had become as much his friend as his employer, paid him a retainer to take up the reins on his coaches from time to time, in order to report how the teams were working. This secret arrangement testifies both to the high opinion Mr Clarke had of his protégé, and to Herring's discretion and skill.

The first commission Mr Hawkesworth instigated was for Herring to paint some pictures for Mr Christopher Wilson of Ledstone Hall, of his stallion Smolensko, and of a black cob and a retriever. From Ledstone Hall he proceeded to Stapleton Park, where he painted eight hunters for the Hon. Edward Petre. This marked the beginning of a long association with that dashing sprig of the Nobility, who had the incredible good fortune to win four St Legers in 1822, 1827–28 and 29, all of which were to be immortalised in paint and engravings in due time by Herring. He also painted other race-winners for Petre such as Matilda, the winner of the Oaks. (Now owned by the Jockey Club.)

His next appointment was to paint no fewer than four hunters, and seventeen foxhounds belonging to Sir Richard Bellingham Graham, of Norton Conyers, Ripon. Here again, his services were later called upon by that satisfied client to paint his winner of the 1816 St Leger, Duchess. That picture is in the US, in the Baltimore Museum, in the late William Woodward, Senr's collection. The present Sir Richard Graham only owns one Herring, of a piebald hunter in a stable, and a copy of Duchess. This was only the fore-runner of his unequalled series of portrayals of St Leger winners for the next thirty years, ending with Van Tromp in 1847. He caught up with the winner of 1815, Sir William Maxwell's Filho da Puta, which actually marked the commencement of that roll of honour.

The year 1818 saw his first entry accepted for the Royal Academy exhibition, which was a 'Portrait of a Dog'. Over the years he only had 22 works hung by the RA, only one of which was a race-horse, Rockingham, probably because that august body thought little of mere 'horse painters', and most of Herring's work at this time was commissioned anyway. In that year also the *Sporting Magazine* published the first of many of his engravings that were to appear in its pages.

For although, in later life he broadened his range of subjects, it was, after all his painting of thoroughbreds that made his name, and, to quote finally from the scribe of the *Sporting Magazine* writing some years later: 'As a pourtrayer (sic) of the thoroughbred horse in high condition he is, and has long been, unrivalled; that beautifully healthy and natural gloss he gives to the skin – the real effect of being well-bred and reared, that union of strength and elegance – the perfect symmetry of the animal which he paints so life-like, so

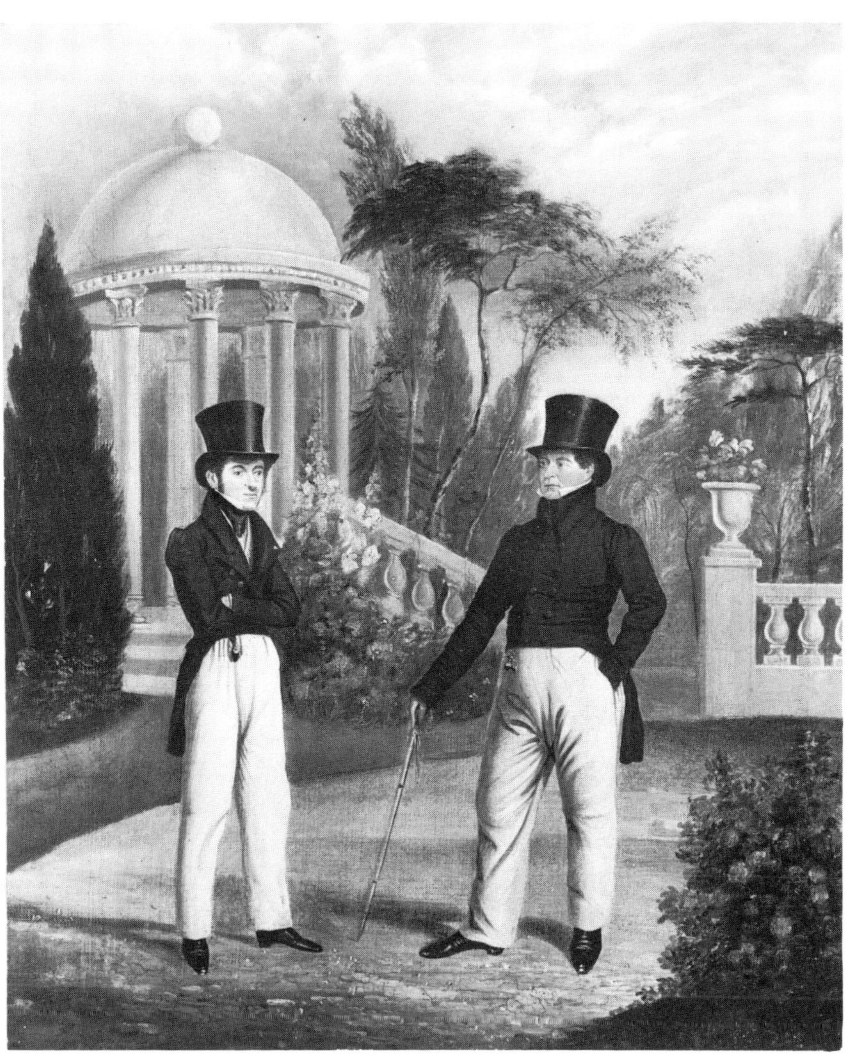

17

J. F. Herring, senr and his brother **Benjamin** by J. F. Herring senr. 20 × 24 ins.

Courtesy:
Arthur Ackermann & Son Ltd

List No 46

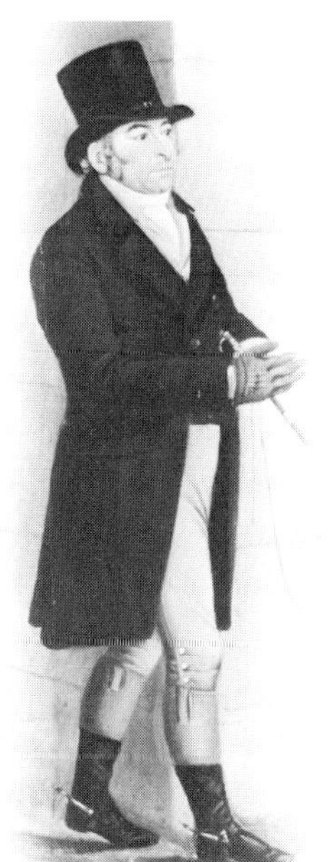

18

Mr George Clark who employed J. F. Herring as a coach-driver *c.* 1820. (Detail from a picture by Clifton Thompson of Nottingham.)

Courtesy: J. D. D'Arcy Clark

effectively, and yet so unexaggerated. And then, if as is said, one true mark of genius be its attention to trifles, prove him by the accompaniments with which his racing subjects are usually finished off: not a buckle or a strap, not a wrinkle out of place or omitted, from the hanging of a throat-lash to the set of a cirsingle. Surely he was born for the place, and the star that led him away on the Leger day was not the slave of idle chance, but the good servant of a happy destiny'.

Even allowing for a pardonable hyperbole in that dithyrambic passage, what is without doubt is that for the next twelve years, he developed and diversified his art by prodigies of industry, turning his hand to hunting and rural scenes, steeplechases and flat races, and an endless stream of individual winners. The pressure brought about by his evident desire for extreme accuracy never led him to skimp his work, which always shows that careful delineation of a particular horse's good points, that he could equally well describe in words in exact detail.[1] He was accused of using a prefabricated sketch of finishes etc. which he then completed by putting in the appropriate jockey's colours and horses' coats, but if he did, it never occurred to him that he was 'pot-boiling', he just did it the way he saw it, and 'The Turf' welcomed him with open arms.

It should not be assumed, as it is often, or at any rate used to be by some critics, that his patrons were besotted with horse-flesh and knew nothing about art, when they included eminent connoisseurs who had plenty of good pictures in their collections.

By 1822, *The Annals of Sporting*, in a lengthy and flattering review of Herring's progress, mentioned that he had 'executed in the finest style of excellence, portraits of animals for the Hon. E. Petre, the Duke of Portland, Lord F. Bentinck, the Earl of Surrey, the Marquis of Townsend, the Duke of Newcastle, the Duke of Leinster, Lord Middleton, Sir George Sitwell and many others', and went on to remark: 'We were struck with the exquisite accuracy of the likenesses, and charmed at the colouring, the shades and the character thrown into each animal and its rider . . . and we may safely predict from these specimens that he will at no distant period rank with the most celebrated animal painters the country has ever patronised'.

They published an engraving of Jack Spigot from his painting to enable their readers better to form a judgment as to the 'extraordinary powers' he possessed. In a later issue however, they make the point that the engraver in reversing the position of the horse has done him something less than justice, as the mane was turned, and owing to the necessarily small scale of the reproduction, much of the attractive background detail was lost.

They also reported that 'the same rising genius' had recently finished a painting of the Earl of Scarborough's elegant little horse, Black Prince. They maintained that the Earl was so pleased with the result, that without making invidious distinctions, he resolved to hang the picture – being of the same large dimensions – alongside Ben Marshall's celebrated picture of Catton in his dining-room at Sandbeck – and it is still there. Herring was also commended for introducing into the composition, Lord Scarborough's training-groom, S. King, and 'with much effect, the horse-cloths lie on the ground, as if just slipped off previous to running . . . all the points of the horse appear well and accurately delin-

[1] c.f. comments quoted in Engravings.

eated with a good share of anatomical study, the course of the veins, which was curious to him, having been traced with minuteness. The Black Prince has since then evolved a castrato in order to be made a hack by its noble owner.'

In the following July, the same journal recounts how Herring tackled a new subject for him, that of military painting. The Huddersfield Yeomanry Corps commissioned him to do a large painting of their commandant, Captain Atkinson on a charger, attended by a trumpeter, with a charging troop in the distance. This he accomplished successfully with all the problems of showing a crowd of galloping horses and was then called upon by Mr George Hartley of Middleton Lodge to carry out a similar task. This was to show the Richmond Foresters and the North York regiment in uniform, drawn up before a landscape showing Richmond Castle in the background, taken from the old race-course.

During these years Herring had also been engaged on a scheme arranged with the *Doncaster Gazette*, to sketch each winner of the Great St Leger, starting with the winner of 1815, Filho da Puta, of which he had made a drawing that he carefully preserved.[1] It was this venture that the *Sporting Magazine* announced in its issue of March 1825, saying that the Duke of York had honoured the publishers, Messrs Sheardown & Co, with his name as subscriber. The *Annals of Sporting* of May that year explained further that the prints were to be continued annually, coloured from paintings by Herring and accompanied by a description of the horse and particulars of the race. 'We cannot for a moment doubt,' said they, 'but that it [*the series*] will meet with general approbation and support, and fully bear out the promise of the design.'

Launched under such exalted patronage, the series was a complete success, and included up to that date, Filho da Puta, Duchess, Ebor, Reveller, Antonio, St Patrick, Jack Spigot, Theodore, Barefoot, Jerry and Memnon. These eleven winners were published as a set in paper covers by Sheardown's. The copperplates were afterwards purchased by Messrs Fuller of Rathbone Place, London W1, who also issued a series with their name and address from the same plates, and for them Herring continued to work yearly until 1839. It was about that date that Messrs Baily of Royal Exchange, Cornhill, engaged him to begin a new series on a larger scale and this arrangement lasted until the year 1847, thus completing thirty-three years in succession. For the Derby, he made a regular series of twenty years, commencing with Mameluke in 1827.

The prices of the Great St Leger prints as originally issued by Fuller's were: 7s. 6d. plain and 15s. coloured, each. The price usually paid for each portrait Herring painted, from which the engravings were drawn for the Fuller series, was £25. His first picture for Fullers alone was of the 1826 winner, the Earl of Scarborough's Tarrare.

Seeing that the best commissions came from the racing fraternity, he decided to make a move to 'Headquarters' at Newmarket in 1830, the year that Priam, one of the greatest

[1] 'The Druid' recounts an amusing story about Sir William Maxwell's horse, Filho da Puta, 'whose name,' he says, 'was rather a puzzler to the hardware youths, who had a vague notion that it was 'Fill the Pewter', and it led to a little difficulty between two of them who had seen the race from the carriage-wheel. "Noo, Jack, what wil't have for a croon?" said one; and "Hang it, man, I'll have Filler" was the reply. "Wilt 'er?" said his mate, "dang it, then, I'll have Pewter;" and anon, when the winner's name was shouted, there came such an angry skirmish of "I'se won, Filler's won", "Dang it, thou'se a leer, Pewter's won," etc., succeeded by a battle royal, that the police had to interfere and explain'.

racers of the century, won the Derby, trained by the then leading trainer at Newmarket, Bill Chifney. But before leaving the scene of his first successes, a word or two about his private life may not be out of place.

He formed many friendships in his years of residence in the town of his adoption, and he was not too busy with all his professional activities to deny himself the pleasure of indulging his musical talents, which were of a high order for an amateur. It shows this hard-working and ambitious family man in another, rather attractive light.

He had a generous bass voice which was considered a 'great acquisition' both at church and in the concert hall, and his clarinet playing recommended him to the Doncaster Amateur Band, in which he performed for many years under the kindly baton of a Dr Haigh, Professor of Music at Cambridge. He even had one or two compositions published, though unfortunately, these seem to have disappeared. But music was certainly an important element in his life, and there is evidence that he encouraged his children in their appreciation and performance of music, too.

He now had a family of six children to support; his first child, John Frederick, had been born on 21 June 1815, his daughters, Sarah on 15 June 1820, Ann on 15 June 1822, and Emma on 3 March 1826, his younger boy, Charles on 8 May 1828, and his youngest, Benjamin, on 12 February 1830.

Another son, also christened Benjamin, was born on 7 March 1818, but he died in infancy on 14 September 1821 which must have caused the parents some distress – although not an uncommon occurrence in those days. The other members of the family, born at regular two-yearly intervals were thriving.

He could look back on his first ten years as a professional painter with pardonable satisfaction: he had emerged from obscurity to become the most popular equine painter in the North, had worked steadily and well on commissions from leading owners and trainers, and had commenced his long series of portraits of the St Leger winners.

So, at the age of just thirty-five, he took another step towards attaining his ambition of becoming the best known racehorse painter in the country, and removed to a house near Newmarket.

4

To Newmarket with the Family

1830–1833

It was an odd sort of place that he found to live in, in that flat bit of country near Six-Mile-Bottom. A rambling sort of mansion in brick and flint with a slate roof, it still stands at the end of a curving driveway, and – presumably because of the low-lying ground and the possibility of flooding – has the appearance of being propped up on its lower floor, as the front door is approached by a causeway from one side, and a flight of steps from another. The tall windows, in an attractive 'Strawberry Hill Gothick' style, overlook many miles of countryside.

It must have been a rather lonely spot, hard by the straggling hamlet of Fulbourne, but it was only half an hour in a trap from 'Headquarters'.

Herring must have had high hopes of more work now he was at the centre of things, but although his output proceeded as regularly as usual, he soon found that the Newmarket of 1830 was not the hub of activity it had been in the previous decades, and he only stayed there three years.

Some of the outstanding trainers of the past era had come to the end of their active lives. Bill Chifney seemed to lose his nerve, or his touch after Priam's Derby victory; he was notoriously hard on his horses in training, and many good youngsters had broken down being over galloped on hard ground. Robert Robson retired at about the same time, and, what was more conclusive, a number of leading owners' strings left the district to be trained elsewhere, such as on the Downs of Berkshire and Wiltshire (close to the popular Stockbridge course). The genius of Malton-based John Scott satisfied the Yorkshire owners, the Earl of Derby trained at Lancaster, Lord George Bentinck's huge string was stabled at Goodwood with John Kent, while the Earl of Chesterfield, for some unaccountable reason, opted for Ashby-de-le-Zouche, in Lincolnshire.

With such an exodus, many great yards closed down and became derelict, only to be revived in the 50's, after the Year of Revolutions in Europe, with the arrival of a number of Scottish trainers, like the Waughs, Matt Dawsoan and the Jarvis's, who picked up valuable premises for a song.

Moreover, the varying fortunes of the town had not only followed the vicissitudes of success and failure on the race-course, but also to a great extent the degree of Royal patronage.

It is well known that King Charles II – often accompanied by Nell Gwynne – was a constant habitué, and James II also favoured the venue. But George IV, who died in June of 1830, although he had been a staunch supporter, had 'a little local difficulty' back in the 1790's, and had been practically warned off. William IV, who succeeded him, was not much interested in racing, or indeed, painting, as two anecdotes aptly illustrate.

On one occasion, when his trainer asked him which of his three horses he wished to run at Goodwood, the old Sailor King replied, 'Let all the fleet go, one of them must win'. It is said they came in first, second and third.

On another occasion he was shown a picture that George IV had liked, and he commented, 'Aye, it seems pretty, I dare say it is, my brother was very fond of this sort of nick-nackery. Demned expensive taste though'. Thus displaying his fear of extravagance after George's much-criticised lavish expenditure on works of art for Carlton House. In fact, Sir Oliver Millar, the Keeper of the Queen's Pictures, says there is no basis for the oft-repeated assertion that King William ever commissioned Herring.

For Herring probably thought he would step into the shoes of his old friend, Ben Marshall, who had finally quitted Newmarket in 1825, having lived in the district for some thirteen years. Aubrey Noakes, in his interesting book on Marshall, says that even when he, Ben, decided to leave London to go there, his friend and sometime pupil, Abraham Cooper, exclaimed 'Why Newmarket? Surely that is a barren spot for the Fine Arts.' And Marshall replied: 'The second finest animal in creation is a fine horse, and, at Newmarket I can study him in the greatest grandeur, beauty and variety'. He made a further comment that may have aptly applied to Herring too. 'A painter should never be satisfied. He should desire always to improve; when he ceases to improve, he should die.'

So, as Marshall had followed George Stubbs, Sawrey Gilpin, Boultbee and the Sartorius's, Herring was to take up the torch, and become – as one commentator put it – almost as official in his capacity of historian of racing, as Mr Clarke was a celebrated Judge, and Mr Weatherby, Keeper of the Match Book.

Marshall and Herring had met early in the career of the younger artist and formed a friendship that lasted until Marshall's death in 1835.

It is on record that Ben gave him a sound piece of advice from his long experience, that Herring, for his part, perhaps heeded too well. 'One of the worst things a painter can do', he said, 'is to send forth to the public too many early productions. Destroy them or paint them over; otherwise they will be, as it were, continually rising up in judgment against you'. This, and the following remark may account for the scarcity of his early work and of his drawings, which are often an inspiring gauge of an artist's ability. This was demonstrated by a recent exhibition of an earlier master's brilliant sketches, namely, James Seymour.[1] These are, for the most part, much more vivid and alive than his studies in oils.

[1] At the William Drummond Gallery, Covent Garden, 1978.

19

The two favourite hunters of John Scott. Signed and dated 1838. 27½ × 35 ins.

Courtesy:
Richard Green Gallery

List No 105

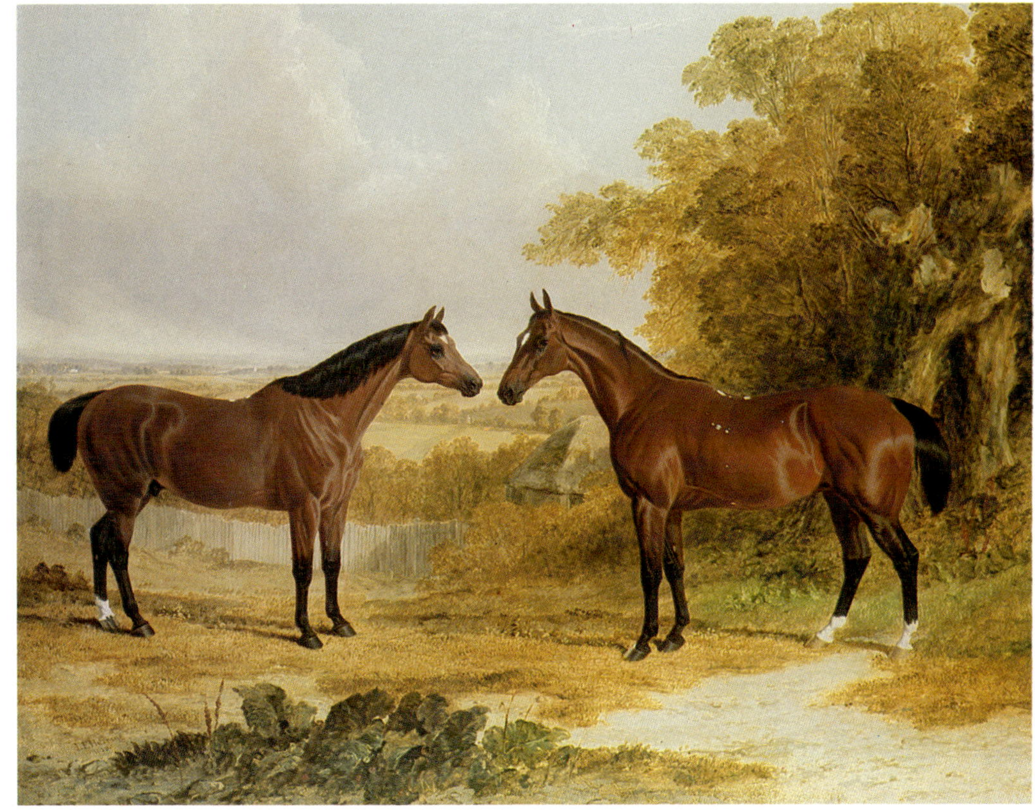

20

Horse Fair, Southborough Common. Signed and dated 1857/8. 39 × 69½ ins.

Courtesy:
Richard Green Gallery

List No 282

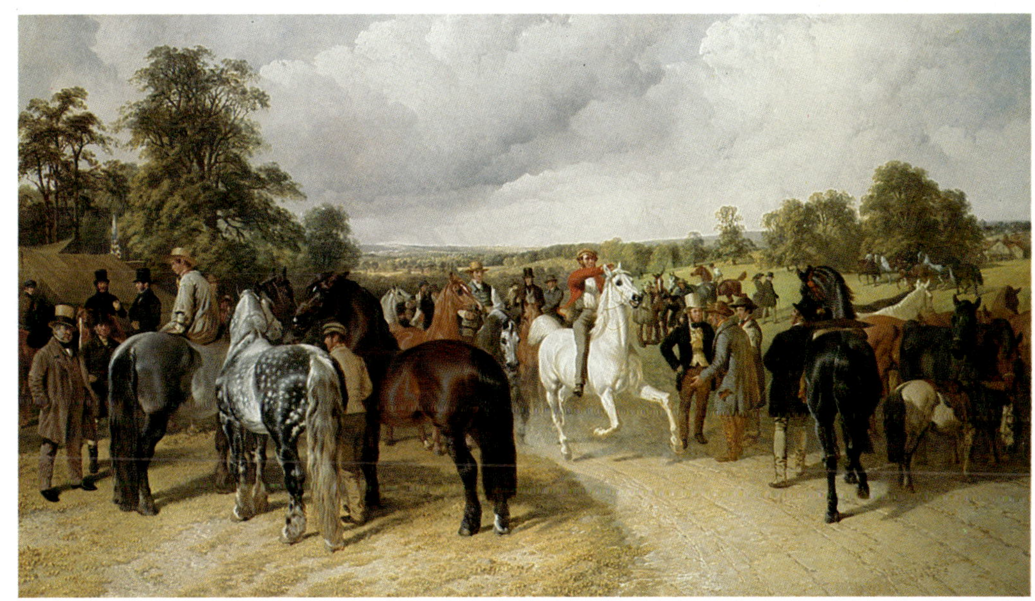

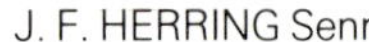
J. F. HERRING Senr

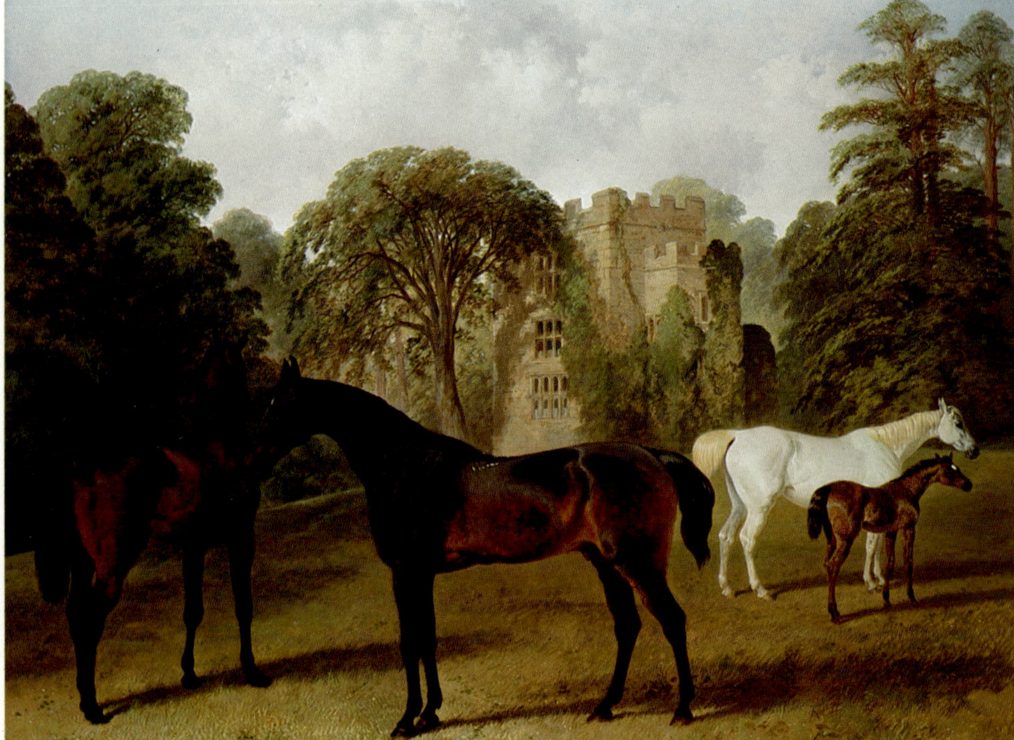

21

Hunters at grass, Haddon Hall. Signed and dated 1851. $40\frac{1}{2} \times 51$ ins.

Courtesy:
Richard Green Gallery

List No 237

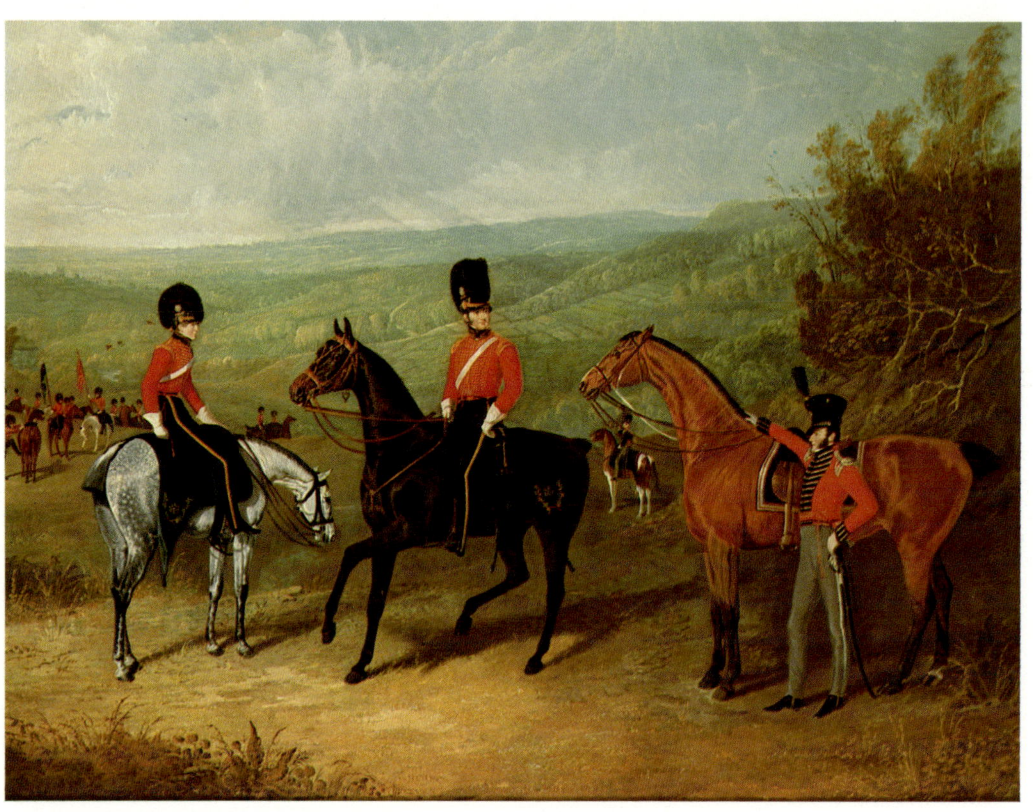

22

Richmond Yeomanry on **Manoeuvres.** Signed and dated 1820. $41 \times 53\frac{3}{4}$ ins.

Courtesy: Sotheby's

List No 5

23

The Meet near Harrold, Beds.
Signed and dated 1837. One of a pair with plate 24.
22 × 27 ins.

Courtesy:
Richard Green Gallery

List No 98

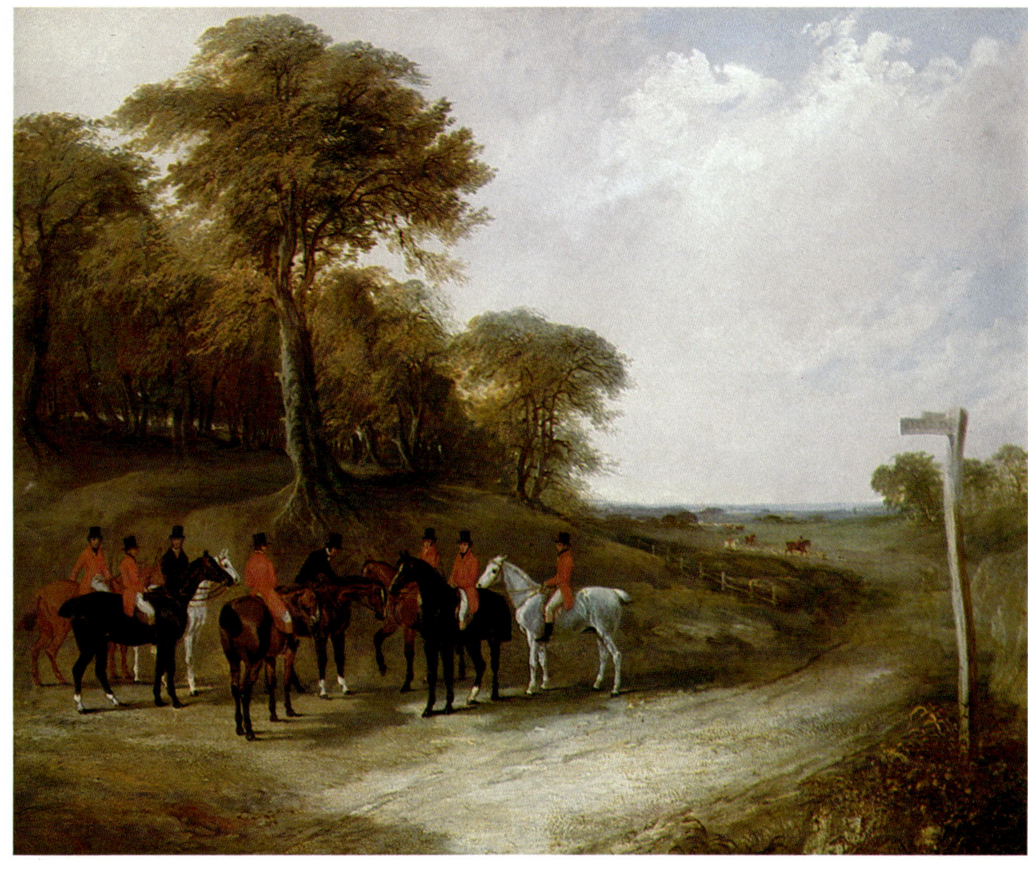

24

The Hunt in Full Cry.
Signed and dated 1837. One of a pair with plate 23.
22 × 27 ins.

Courtesy:
Richard Green Gallery

List No 99

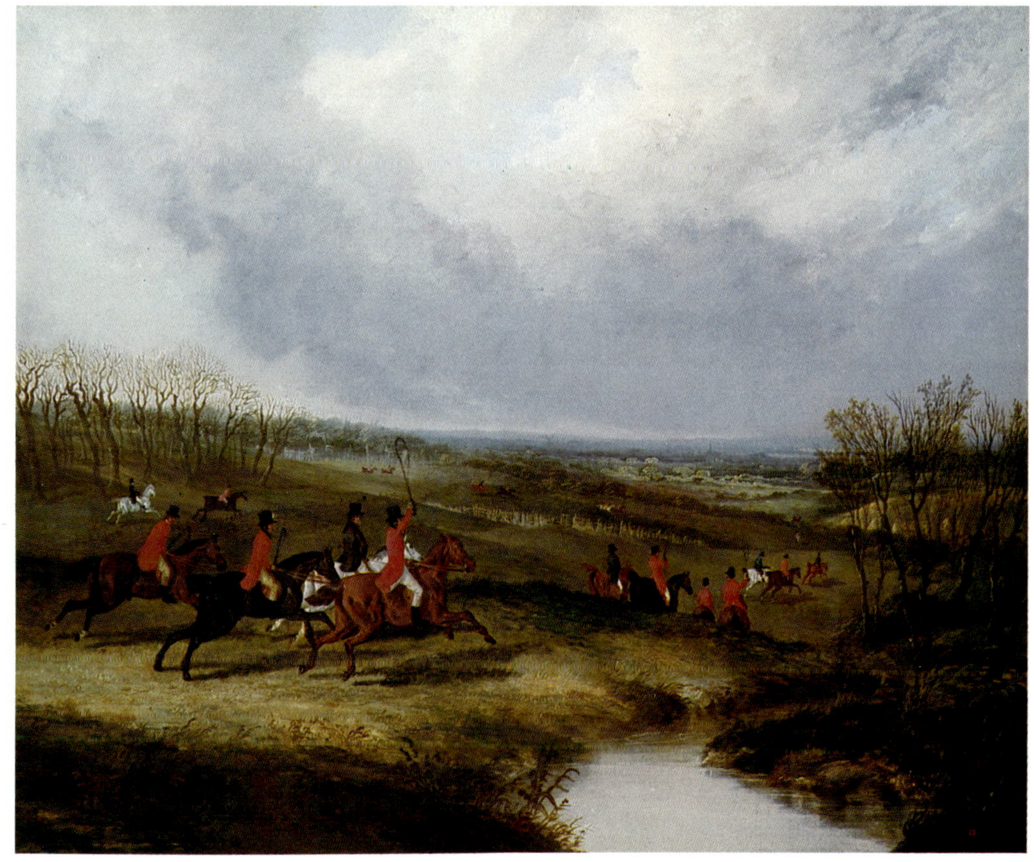

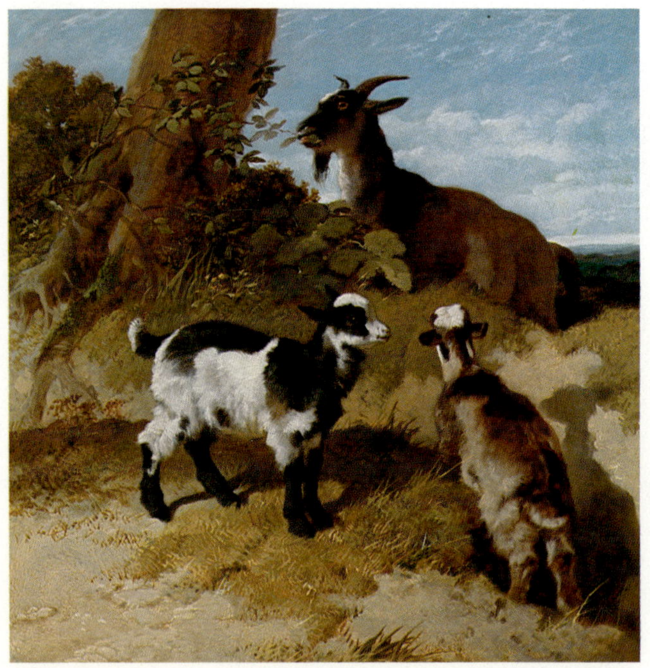

25

Goats in a Landscape. Signed and dated 1852. 16¼ × 16¼ ins.

Courtesy: Richard Green Gallery

List No 241

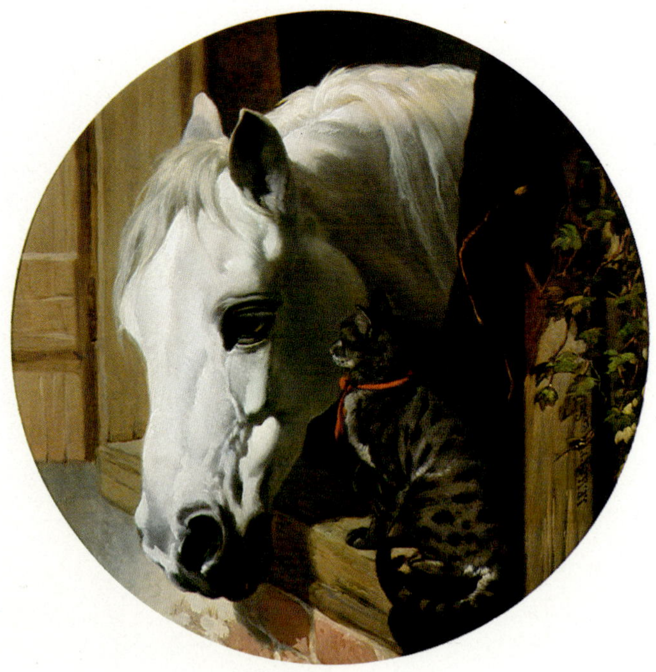

26

Friends. Signed *c.*1848. 13 in diameter panel.

Courtesy: Richard Green Gallery

List No 196

27

Fox Hunting – Full Cry. Signed and dated 1834. 14 × 32 ins.

Courtesy: Richard Green Gallery

List No 73

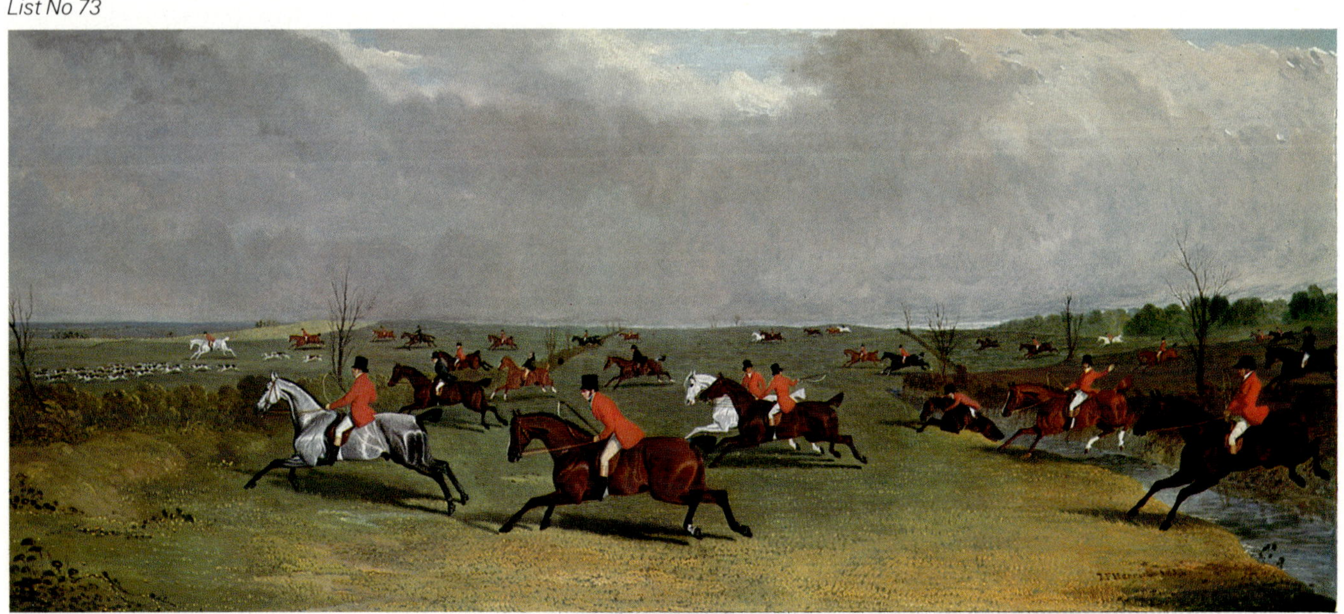

Marshall was once asked if he ever saw Herring sketch; 'No,' was the answer, 'but I once saw him put a pencil to paper, and a horse's head ran out of the end of it.' A tribute to Herring's facility which he apparently hid, or at least disguised from the world at large.

Herring painted several horses that were also painted by Marshall, such as Mameluke, where the latter's ability to flesh out the substance of the anatomy, makes more of a real horse than does Herring's careful – almost maidenly brushwork, at least at that stage in his development. Herring usually managed his skies and herbage more naturally – and effectively – than Marshall, however, whose turf often looks more like a sandy shore covered with pebbles.

Marshall had made the most of a prosperous era in the town, when seven Derby winners had been sent to Epsom from local stables, but that period was followed by a lull.

Such a situation is hard to imagine looking back from today's standpoint, when Newmarket is acknowledged the world over as one of the finest racing and breeding areas, where yearlings fetch millions of dollars at the Sales at Park Paddocks, and the National Stud houses sires mating with the cream of the Stud Book.

Back in the 18th century, when the three great stallions were imported, the Darley Arabian, the Godolphin Arabian and the Byerley Turk, racing was much more localised in the North and the South, owing to the difficulties of transport. But once the Stud Book was established, it was not long before the Jockey Club began to assert its authority over courses everywhere.

Starting in about 1767, when a select group of what has been called, 'Young Bucks and Old Rakes' used to meet in a coffee-house in the High Street, few could have foreseen the prestige it would attain. But through their collective efforts and those of several outstandingly able administrators among them, some order was brought into the chaotic conditions of a gambling sport. Their judicious acquisition, over the years, of farms and Crown Lands in the vicinity, saved too, the incomparable Heath from the depredations of the speculative builders.

By the 1820's the conglomeration of tents, and roped and staked enclosures had given way to a stand, but the majority of patrons still attended the meetings on horse-back. Ladies, in their landaus and broughams drawn up alongside the finishing straight used to send their 'runners' to make their bets, and dispense lobster patties, rich viands and 'cheribums' of champagne to their friends – to use Rosa Lewis's term . . .

The betting-ring, as we see in pictures by Rowlandson, was a hectic shemozzle of anxious backers and urgent layers, all betting on credit too. Entry to the Heath was still free, as it is today, and continues to be at Ascot, Goodwood and Epsom. But here and at other tracks, the policy of railed-in enclosures was gradually adopted to enable the management to charge for admission and thus boost the prizes and cover the overheads.

So, although perhaps some of the glamour was missing when Herring arrived, there were still some well-managed studs, good trainers and the races. Wars, and the alarums and excursions of war, leaving these important events un-touched apparently. So Herring still found much to do. His series of St Leger winners continued with paintings of Chorister (1831), Margrave (1832) and Rockingham (1833), and his Derby series with Spaniel

(1831), St Giles (1832) and Dangerous (1833), and his first Oaks winner, Vespa (1833). His famous Goodwood picture of the Gold Cup of 1833 most probably emanated from his studio in Camberwell.

Unusually, for him, he celebrated a day's shooting with an attractive picture with a Six-Mile-Bottom background. He also must have had a day out with the Suffolk Hunt which brought forth a classic view of a run across an East Anglian landscape (actually dated 1834).[1]

The student of our agricultural heritage will notice that the hunt is crossing three huge fields, rising to the horizon and separated and drained by hedges and ditches. At intervals, along the hedge-rows, still young, are even younger elm saplings. These will have matured, withered and died of elm disease in our life-time. And, no doubt, Coke of Holkham would have preferred to see the broad balks sown with clover or turnips, but, how vividly is encapsulated in this one picture, the trend that had made the country rich and the countrymen poor, of enclosing the common land. Hounds have obviously sprung the fox from the spinney, straggling along the rise, to take his chance in the open, but these ten to twenty-acre fields offered scant cover unless the varmint could find refuge in an earth, some way away.

In this respect, Herring is an accurate observer, but in another, the strictures by Walter Shaw-Sparrow on the lack of realism in his hunting pictures have an element of truth.

For the field to be so strung out argues that hounds have been running for some time, yet no speck of mud besmirches the spotless white breeches and pink coats of the horsemen, no hint of sweat lathers the withers of the cock-tailed hunters whose coats exhibit a gloss that could only come from a final wisp down in the stable. True, one unfortunate is obviously being run away with – but in the distance – and another, having failed to clear a monstrous obstacle is seen climbing out of the water, but these are the only signs of distress. As anyone knows, who has ridden across country, the hazards of the adventure are a good deal more taxing than a gentle canter in Rotten Row, or than Mr Herring allows.

He does not emphasise the cold, wet, miserable aspect of a rainy day in December; his skies are blue, the sward, a verdant green. Lionel Edwards used to depict the overcast skies and muddied gateways of winter with far more realism. And yet he brings to his sets of hunting prints a much more accomplished air than Pollard, Howitt or the Alkens. Here he has the ability of arranging a variety of incident, and, what one can only call a composition in depth that leaves the journeyman of the art far behind. These were, after all, the most hackneyed subjects in the world, but Herring manages to make something dramatically worth-while of them.[2]

Two sets in particular exhibit this 'mouvementé quality;[3] one of which was engraved by J. Harris in coloured aquatint, and published by Henry Graves and Co in 1852, and

[1] Exhib. Arthur Ackerman October 1978
[2] There were four sets 1846, 1852, 1854 and 1874.
[3] Exhibited by Frank T. Sabin, October 1976

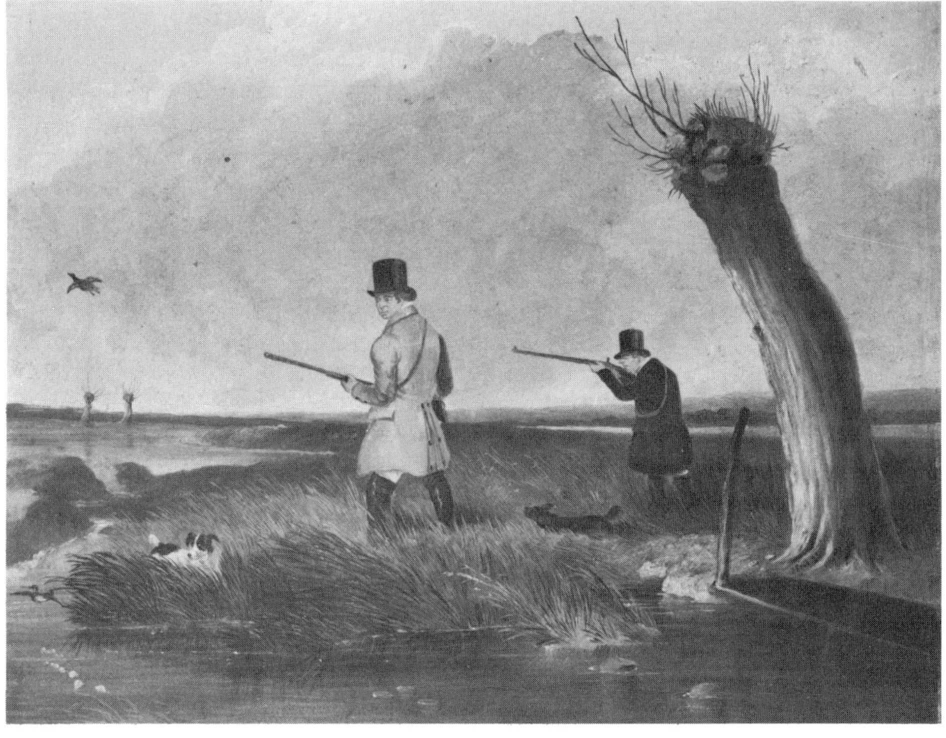

28

Shooting Duck at Six-Mile-Bottom
by J. F. Herring junr.

Courtesy: Sothebys

List No 303

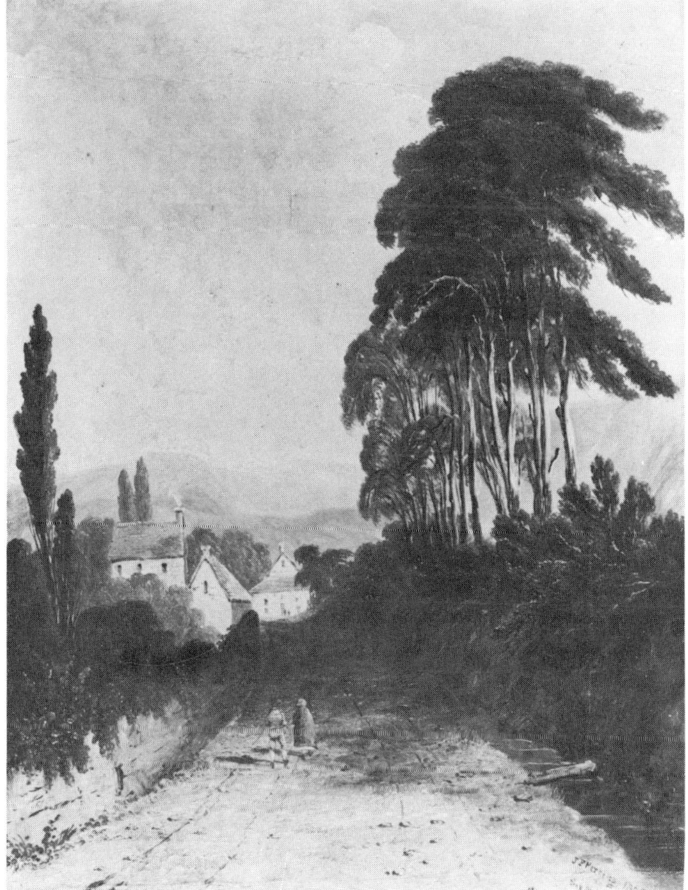

29

A View of Six-Mile-Bottom
by J. F. Herring junr.

Courtesy: The Witt Collection

List No 304

another, again engraved by J. Harris, but published by Messrs Fores, Piccadilly. Each, though titled slightly differently, show 'The Meet', 'The Find', 'Full Cry' and 'The Death'. These were most probably designed from earlier sketches combined with memories of similar events, as Herring was certainly past hunting when these prints were published, and how well he has caught the little incidents that enliven the day's sport!

The lounging chat of the 'Swells' at the Meet, as a groom leads away the hack on which one of them has ridden to the venue, while another tightens his girths; the expectant air of the horses as they hear the pack give tongue, while the master holds up his hand to stay the eager onrush of the field; the drama of a fall during the run, with a good fellow trying to catch a loose horse in the distance; and lastly, with what dash the surviving thrusters take the wall separating them from hounds breaking up their quarry. Apart from the action implicit in the above scenes, Herring – well served by his engravers – always painted his bare trees, fences and skies with a deft touch, and suggested a sense of space within the narrow confines of the convention. His humanity shows in the fact that – except in one instance – the kill is always in the distance, he does not revel in the inevitable bloodshed as some Continental masters, like Snyders seem to do.

He was perhaps a bit old-fashioned in not including any lady riders in these earlier pictures, no 'Lucy Glitters' takes the eye – or the stirrup cup – at the Meet. On the other hand, these riders were shown to be bold jumpers. Not so many years before, when hounds were slower, jumping at the gallop was unheard of. Mr Jorrocks, of course, and his like, never jumped if they could find a gate, 'a fall's a 'orrible thing,' he said, and the posture of the horse and rider taking off as shown by Stubbs or George Morland, indicates that at that time they preferred to get their mounts to jump off their hocks, almost at a standstill.

But hounds were now being bred faster and with a good music as well, so a touch of blood was needed if the horses were to keep up. However enraged the Master of an old private pack might be by the competitive riding that ensued, he could not do much about it if he wanted to encourage subscribers. Herring's preference for the smart and aristocratic means that we have to go the pages of Surtees to observe the hired screws and broken down hacks immortalised by the satirical pencil of John Leach.

This divagation into social history is only one avenue of reflection prompted by the glimpses of the habits and pastimes of an age that has vanished, which is part, and by no means a negligible part, of the pleasure to be had from this school of British painting, of which Herring is such an important exemplar.

The year 1832 had seen another addition to his family, in the shape of a daughter, Jane,[1] and the next year he decided to make another move – this time to London, the 'Great Wen' as Cobbett called it, but still the capital of the country and the centre of the art world.

[1] Jane, born 17 September 1832, married Mr Warner, a solicitor of Tonbridge 23 July 1857 and her descendants are still living.

5

London and Royal Patronage

1833–1853

With his return to London, Herring entered on what is, perhaps, the best and most interesting phase of his career; it brought a broadening of his technique, a wider range of subject-matter, and important new clients, particularly amongst the Royals.

The family took up their abode at 31 Park Street, in Camberwell, where they were to remain for the next seven years. Why he elected to live in this far from salubrious, low-lying district of London, which did his bronches no good at all, we do not know. It may be that he had patched up his quarrel with his father, and therefore wished to be in more or less the same neighbourhood as the rest of the family.

There is another curious lacuna in the evidence for the oft-repeated statement, that he took lessons at this time from Abraham Cooper, RA. In his effusive style, Shaw-Sparrow says that this was the result of his 'fine, modest manliness, patient, kindly, warm and eager – culminating in that humble determination to improve himself'; Basil Taylor[1] repeats this claim also, but no corroboration is forthcoming from the various contemporary memoirs which have been studied. (J. M. Muir says so and the DNB but it is not mentioned in his obituary in the *Sporting Magazine* – who would surely have known about it.)

It may be true, but it seems unlikely that Herring, having achieved the success he had, and being the determinedly independent character he was – not notably 'patient' or 'kindly' etc. etc. – would seek tuition from a man only eight years his senior. That Cooper did give lessons we know from the fact that he taught William Barraud at one time, and Harry Hall, Herring's 'successor' with the Derby winners.

Cooper, as another self-taught artist, had not had the benefit of teaching at the Academy Schools as other contemporary painters had, but had done very well for himself as a painter of cattle and horses – especially Arabs – with the help of some tuition from old Ben Marshall. He had also made something of a name as an illustrator of battle scenes. He had worked as a lad in the mimic battles staged by Astley's Circus, too, but what could he

[1] *Animal Painting in England*

teach Herring? – I surmise, very little. They were, in all probability, acquaintances, and, as possibly one of the first Academicians Herring had met, he would seem an important man to know; but apart from nourishing Herring's latent ambition to be accepted by the RA, he could hardly have taught him anything about the art of race-horse portraiture Herring did not know already.

Be that as it may, signs of some professional jealousy between the two appears in a publication of 1836, where it is implied, somewhat slanderously, that Herring unfairly procured an advantage over his rivals in being the first to be allowed to sketch Sir Gilbert Heathcote's Derby winner, Amato. A touch of spleen gives a spice to the anecdote which concludes with the following words: 'Cooper and Hancock, imcomparably his [*Herring's*] superiors, were obliged to wait the second day after the race for three hours till the trainer had finished his potations in one of the tents!' The mere existence of such a piece of gossip indicates that some envy was provoked in the breasts of his compeers by his acknowledged pre-eminence in creating his famous series of portraits of winners of the big races, afterwards to be engraved.

Their feelings can hardly have been assuaged by the announcement in *Bell's Life* in September of the same year, that the Company would be publishing a series of portraits by Herring of Celebrated Thoroughbred Stallions in Folio Imperial at 5s. plain, and 10s. coloured. The first two, Whistler and Blacklock, were published together, and with the remainder, numbering 19 in all will be found in the list on p. 156 of this book.

With competition as keen as this, it may perhaps be asked whether Herring was so superior to his contemporaries as it seems – or was it merely a superior business ability that won him these contracts?

In this connection it will be of interest to our readers to quote from some comments made by 'Nimrod' (C. W. Apperley), the most respected equestrian correspondent of the day, to the Editor of the *New Sporting Magazine*, in 1833. Now Apperley was more at home in the hunting field than on the race-course, but no one can deny his expert testimony as regards the points of a horse.

He was asked whether he had seen Little Weeper, who had beaten Glaucus (also painted by Herring) for the Criterion from the 'Turn of the Lands', and he replied: 'I saw her twice – once on canvas in Mr Herring's painting-room at Six-Mile-Bottom, and afterwards in the stable. I had a great desire to see her, because I never met with so thick and so low a two-year-old as she appeared on canvas; but I found the representation a faithful one.' As regards Beiram, Apperley said he particularly asked permission to see him, to satisfy himself he was such a racing-looking nag as appeared in the drawing in the magazine. And, although a painter could scarcely fail to catch a likeness of him from his very peculiar features, he thought Herring's likeness was striking, and 'he is very happy in preserving the blood-like form of the race-horse'.

Herring's intimate association with so many outstanding thoroughbreds over a long period, and the fact that he often had painted the sire or the dam – or both – of his present 'sitter', gave him an unequalled knowledge of the bloodlines of those days. So when he says that Ardrossan, the sire of Jack Spigot, was 'the coarsest thoroughbred he had ever known', as his neck was really heavier than Stubbs's sketch of the Godolphin Arabian; and that Welbeck, the sire of the neat little Bedlamite, ranked nearly as high in his list of the 'ugly club' – we feel convinced of the rightness of his judgment.

Equally, by inspecting his pictures of such beauties as Mr Lambton's Don Juan by Orville (who wrought such wonders among the Cleveland mares), Magistrate, Filho da Puta, Duchess (who always ran in high company and was his 'prima donna' among the smaller mares) and Crucifix and Queen of Trumps, which were his favourites among the larger mares, it can be seen that his ability to depict the true shape and form of a race-horse was won in a hard school and by long experience.

It may be worth giving just one of his graphic descriptions of a horse, many of which appeared regularly in *Bell's Life* alongside the engravings of his work to which they refer. Stubbs may have uncovered the truth of a horse's anatomy, layer by muscled layer, for the veterinarians of future generations, but painters who can analyse their subjects with the acuity of observation evident in Herring's prose, are rare birds indeed.

Here is his commentary on Mündig, the winner of the Derby of 1835, whose dam, Emma, he had painted, in a letter to the Editor of *Bell's Life*:

PROPERTIES OF 'MUNDIG'

To the Editor.

Sir, In compliance with the wish expressed by your Manchester correspondent, by whose remarks on my former portraits of the winners of the Derby and St Leger I cannot but feel pleased, I shall endeavour to the best of my ability to give you my opinion on the properties of Mundig, the winner of the late Derby, the portrait of which I herewith forward, in the persuasion that neither you nor the thinking part of your readers could have anticipated that justice could be done to the subject in a shorter time. [The notice appeared in the issue of 14 June with the woodcut, so could hardly have been drawn and processed any quicker. – Author].

Mundig, it will be remembered, is by Catton, and generally speaking the Cattons have not the most pleasant head. The head of Mundig is certainly large but lean, but though I have heard him called 'sour-headed', when saddling, I cannot see it myself.

His neck is strong, but not loaded; perhaps this may be owing to Mr Scott's good management. His breast and shoulders are the strongest for a three-year-old I ever recollect, at the same time not heavy, but beautifully formed. His withers not particularly high, his arms are very large, with legs that seem to defy any sort of ground to affect them. He is very deep in the girthing-place, with capital fore-ribs, but if anything low in the back, though in a very trifling degree, with good loins and back ribs; his hips are large and his quarters very long, with immense thighs, hocks; and made in the best form for climbing a hill, being higher behind than before. His colour is a good chestnut with one white hind-leg.

May I take the liberty to add that my portrait of Mundig will be published without delay by Messrs Fuller, Rathbone Place, and that I hope in this, as in all my former efforts as an animal painter, while I afford satisfaction to my friends, I shall not detract from the reputation which it has been my good fortune to secure.

In this instance particularly have I received the most liberal assistance from Mr John Scott (the trainer) allowing me every facility in the getting up my portrait, and also by Mr William Scott (the jockey), who has very kindly sat to me. Of the success of my labours the public will (as soon as the print is out) be able to form their own opinion.

I am, etc.
J. F. Herring

[1] The picture in question of Mundig was called 'superb' by Mr Muir in his memoir.

It's all there, recognition of the family's characteristics, indications of the temperament of the horse, the sort of going likely to suit him, his height and colour, the care of the trainer in building up his physique – and a tribute to the co-operation he received from trainer and jockey. And not merely, as Mr Jorrocks was wont to comment, a praising of his bad points better to allow the good points to speak for themselves! Henry Alken could have done no better . . . and Munnings not so well.

It was about this time, 1835, that according to a memoir published by the Stoke-on-Trent potters, W. T. Copeland, Herring got into serious financial difficulties, owing bills totalling some £500.

It is hinted that this may have been caused by his over-reaching himself while studying under Cooper, but this hardly seems likely as he was selling pictures and collecting royalties from his engraved prints. It is more likely that it was caused by the increasing expense of bring up a growing family in London, and perhaps the cost of having had a large studio built at his house.

Whatever the cause, it was a happy chance when he was introduced to William Taylor Copeland, who had been in partnership with Spode, the famous maker of porcelain. Copeland generously took up the bills and invited Herring down to his Essex estate, at Leyton, where he provided him with a house, and commissioned many pictures which are still in the family's possession, 'Mazeppa' for one.

Herring made good his indebtedness by painting his benefactor's race-horses and many pictures of hunting and rural life in the neighbourhood.

Mr Copeland, who became Lord Mayor of London, and was for many years Member of Parliament for Stoke-on-Trent, had been in partnership with Josiah Spode, who founded the porcelain factory in 1770.

Copeland bought out the Spode interest, however, and it was under his aegis that the scientific formula for fine bone china was evolved, and the technique of underglaze blue printing was developed and perfected to take hand-painted designs. On this ware, that is so brilliantly white, durable and translucent, with hand-laid borders in various colours, particularly dark red and apple green, a whole series of hunting scenes painted by Herring were adapted and transferred, to make a highly attractive possession.

Each plate, dish cup or saucer bears a graphic portrayal of one phase or another of the sport. (These sets are rare.)

Sets were also made in monochrome in the gadroon-edged style, with the design hand-painted under the glaze in black on a fine cream earthenware body.

The comment has often been repeated that Herring was no hunting man, but surely the accuracy and vivacity of his hunting pictures – and the prints which were made from them and are still so popular, belie this criticism. It should be borne in mind too, that there are two types of Herring hunting pictures: one is the view of an actual hunt meet, or view of a run, and the other is a composite of events in the chase, but of no particular hunt, specially drawn for engraving.

The scenes of particular hunts are, of course, much more informal, more naturally grouped and thus, really more attractive.

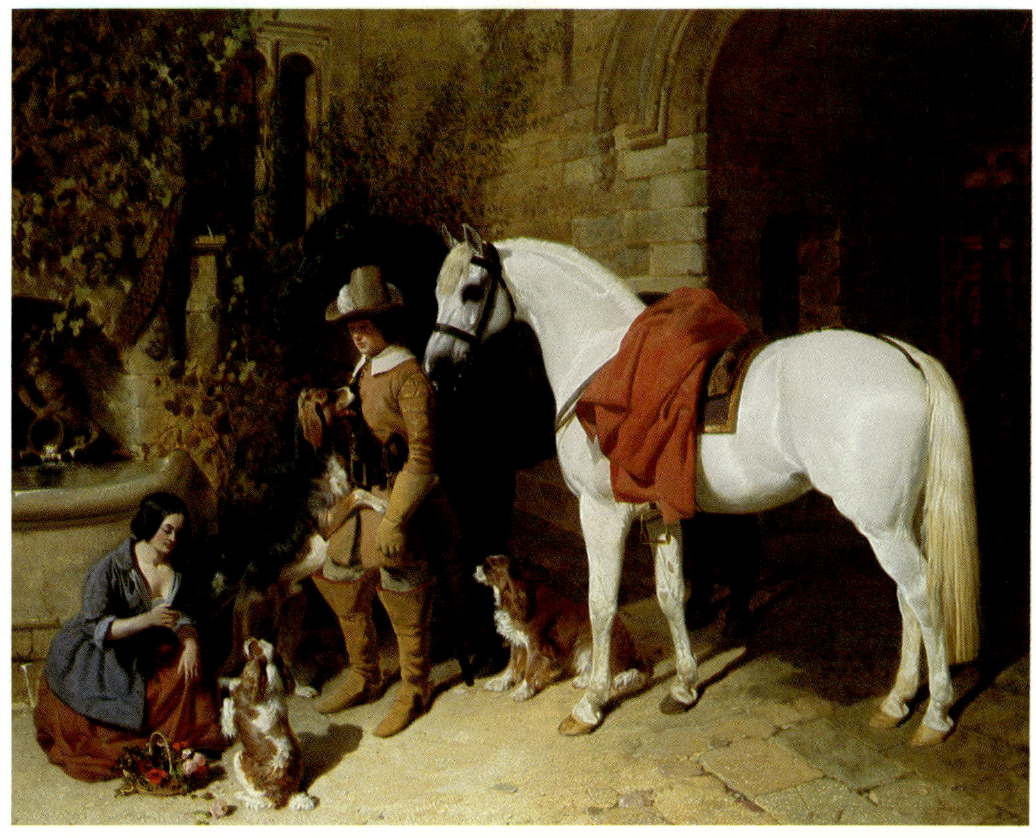

30

The Baron's Charger. *c.*1850.
36 × 45 ins.

Courtesy:
Richard Green Gallery

List No 222

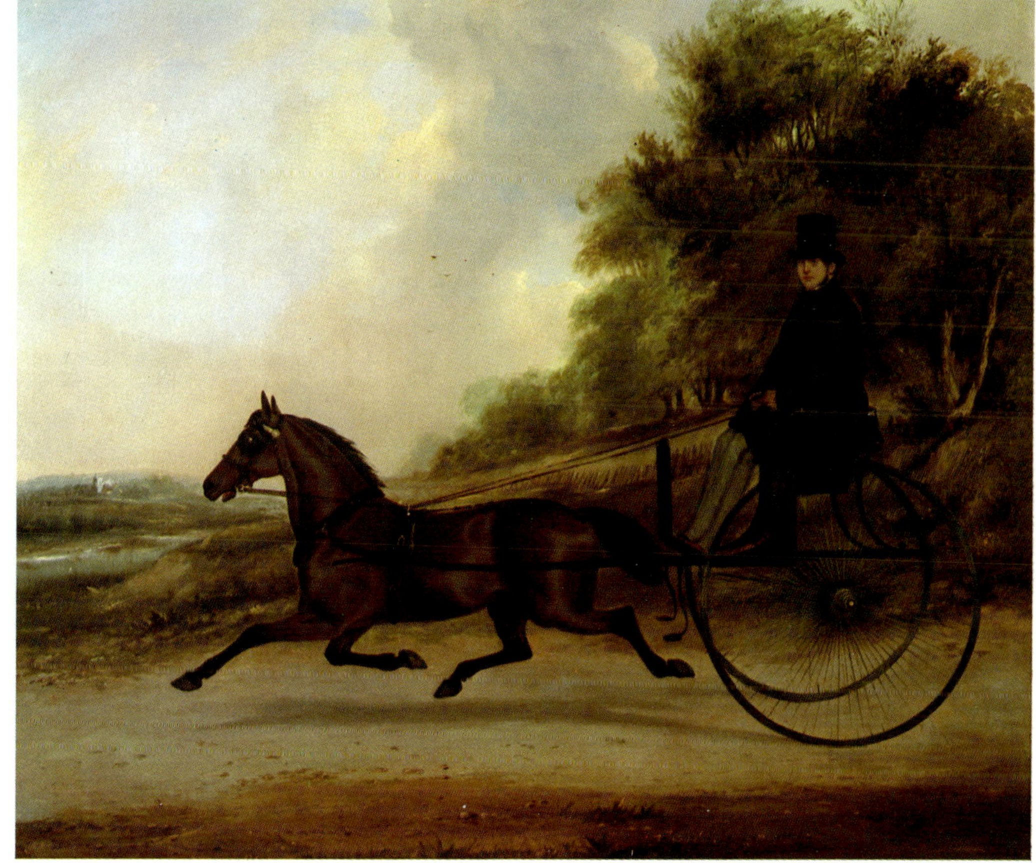

31

Sir Joseph Hawley in a gig,
c. late 1850's. 24¾ × 29½ ins.
Owner of four Derby winners.

Courtesy: The Jockey Club

List No 229

J. F. HERRING Senr

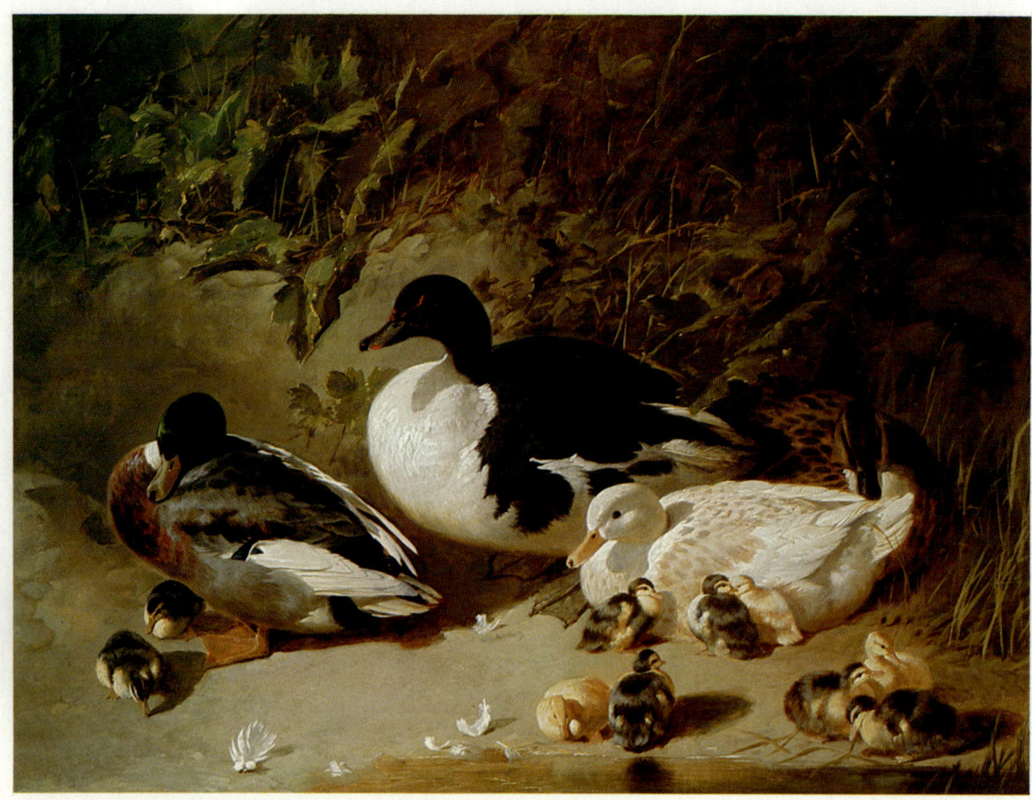

32

A Happy Family. Signed and dated 1844. 19½ × 26¼ ins.

Courtesy:
Richard Green Gallery

List No 163

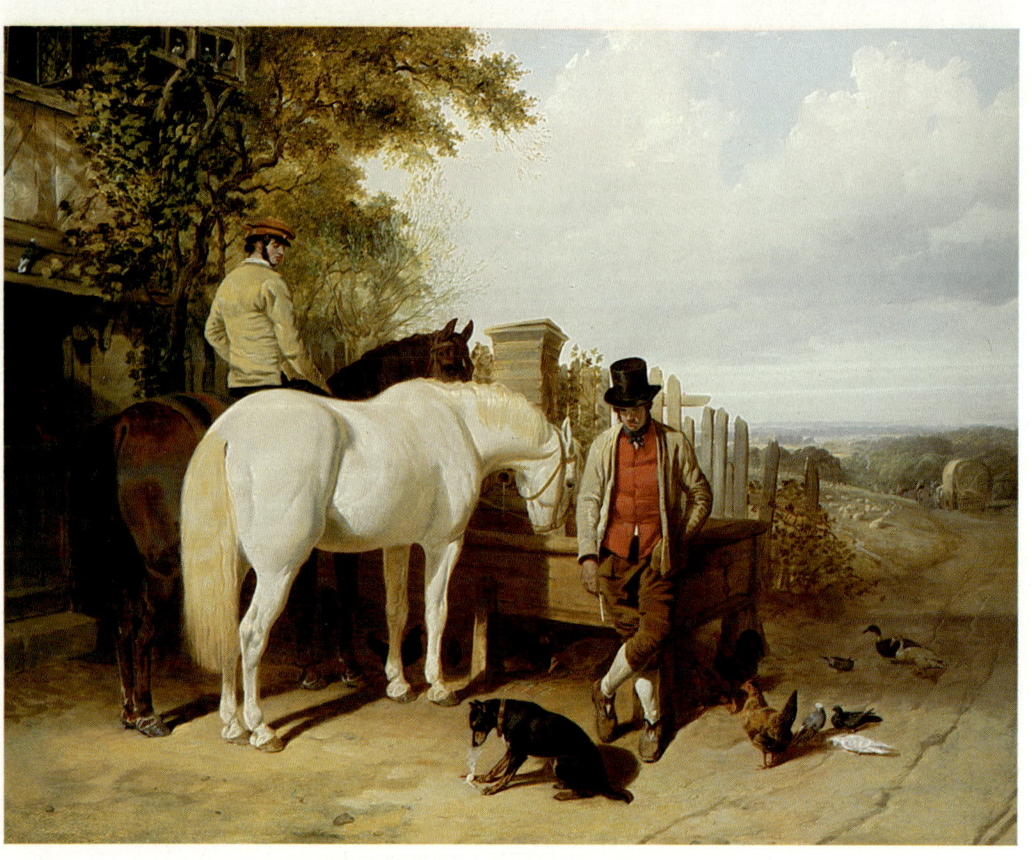

33

The Broken Pipe. Signed and dated 1844. 28 × 36 ins.

Courtesy:
Richard Green Gallery

List No 159

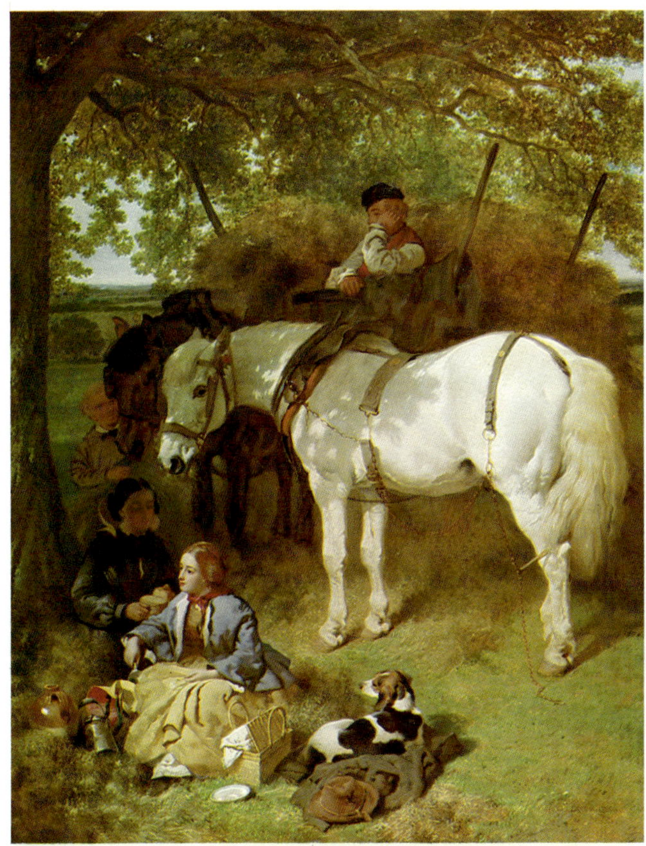

34

The Noon Day Rest. Signed and dated 1855. 49½ × 39½ ins.

Courtesy:
Richard Green Gallery

List No 272

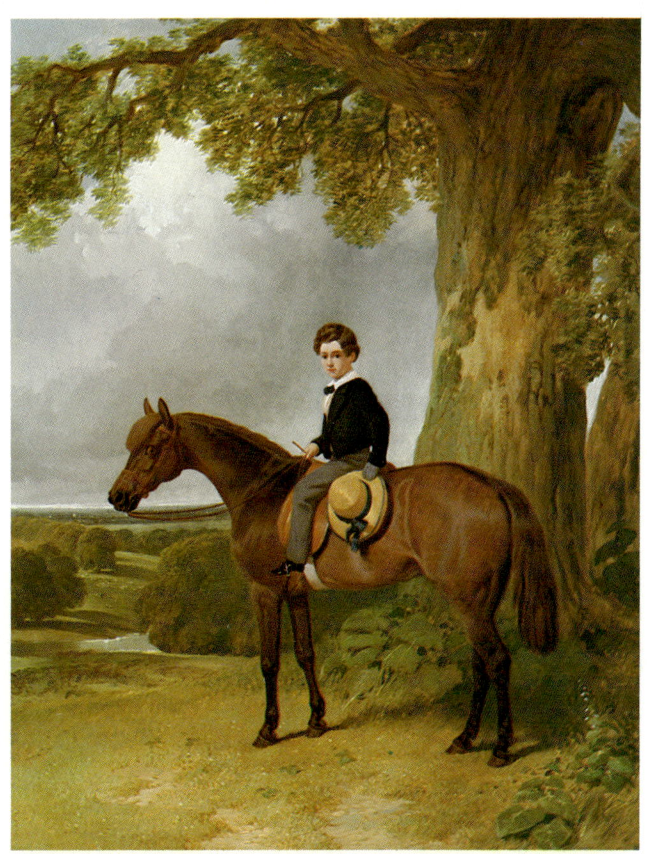

35

Henry Willis, aged 10 astride his Pony. Signed and dated 1851. 36 × 28 ins.

Courtesy: Richard Green Gallery

List No 232

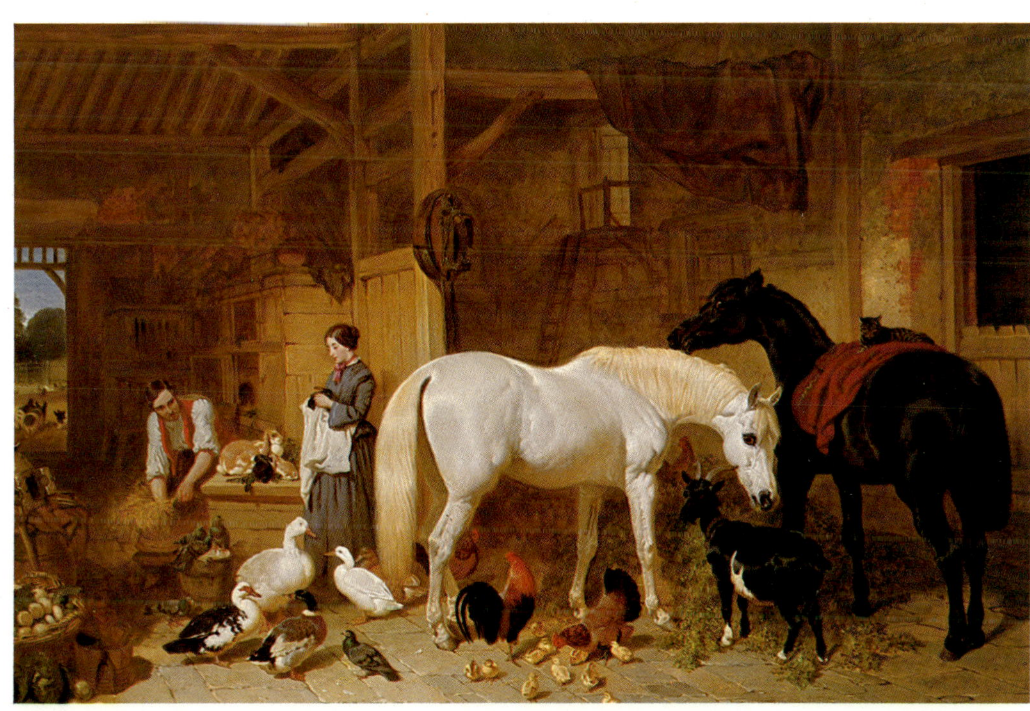

36

Horses, figures and livestock at Meopham. Signed and dated 1852.

Courtesy:
Richard Green Gallery

List No 240

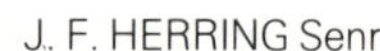
J. F. HERRING Senr

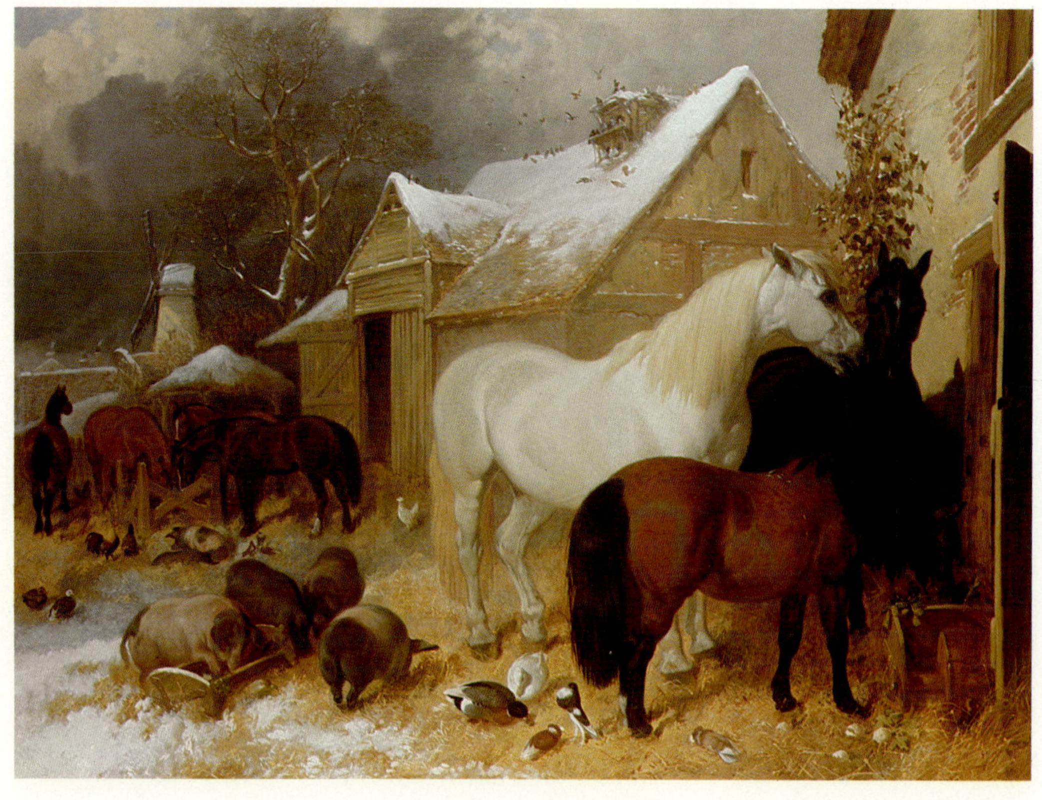

37

Stableyard in Winter. Signed and dated 1847. 28 × 36 ins.

Courtesy:
Richard Green Gallery

List No 189

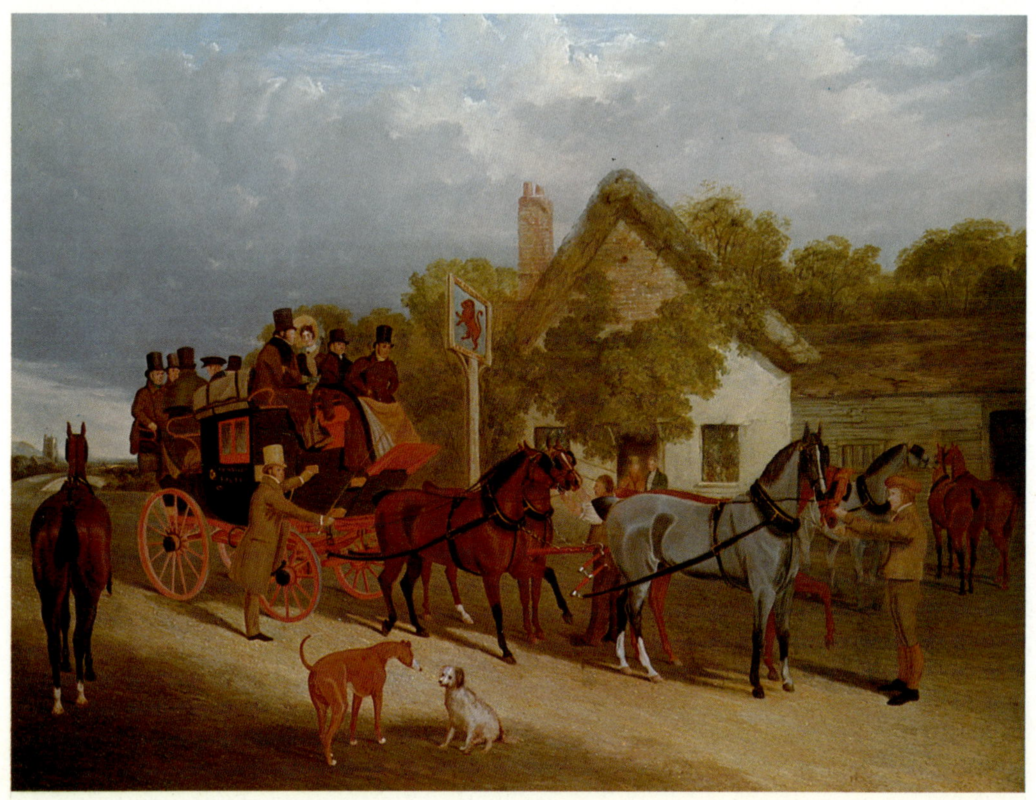

38

Coaching Scene. The Red Lion on Cambridge Road. Signed. 28 × 36 ins.

Courtesy:
Richard Green Gallery

List No 136

From the historical point of view his middle-period pictures have interest as they reflect the changing fashions of the times, and the increasing participation of ladies in the sport. In the earlier pictures the master is sometimes wearing a topper, whereas later, it was *de rigeur* for him to wear a cap, which has become the usual practice. Nowadays, almost any member of the hunt sees fit to wear a cap, on some shibboleth of safety, when a bowler or top hat would be appropriate – except for farmers.

But for all his expertise in sporting pastimes, Herring felt the need to reach a different (buying?) public, one that liked horses about the place to be sure, but not necessarily stars of the racing world as such. So titles began to appear such as 'Mares and Foals', 'A Mail-coach of George IV's Time', 'The Straw-yard' and 'The Timber Carriage'; in fact his first exhibit at the Society of British Artists in 1836, was of a 'Gothic Church at Lewisham'.

The Society had been formed in the previous century, partly as an answer to the Royal Academy's monopoly – the Academy had its critics even then; when Stubbs had fallen out with the RA he had joined the Society, James Ward had had a similar experience.

Herring, after a tentative beginning (one picture in 1836; three in 1837 and one in 1838) was elected a member in 1841 and became a constant exhibitor. (He too, had not been pleased with the hanging of one of his pictures by the RA). In 1841 he was represented by three works, and in 1842, on being elected vice-president, by nine. In 1843 he showed eleven, in 1844 eleven, in 1845 nine, and so on. He gave up exhibiting in the galleries in Suffolk Street in 1852, when he ceased to be a member, when his last batch of five pictures included an historical piece of Cromwell's soldiers in Arundel Church.

The British Institution was another outlet for painters in search of buyers, too. His first exhibit there had been, suitably enough: 'The Race', shown in 1830. He next exhibited in 1834, 1837 and 1838 with one picture apiece, and after that several were shown each year except for a gap of seven years from 1853, when he moved to Kent.

Although the critics did not give as much space to the BI shows as the Academy's, they did write them up, and Herring continued to exhibit there until the year of his death (1865). The chorus of praise from the sporting press that he was accustomed to, may not have prepared him for the comments made by one writer, who was more of a connoisseur than a loyal 'Turfite', and not over-generous with his superlatives.

Referring to his 'Timber-Carriage' exhibited in 1840, the critic wrote: 'The landscape here is certainly the most successfully designed and executed composition of the kind that we have ever seen from the pencil of this artist. Nothing can be more natural than the green glade leading to the cottage nestled among the monarchs of the forest. All the other details are cleverly managed, but did Mr Herring ever see such horses as he has given us tacked to a country timber wain? If so, he has had better luck than ever fell to our share. Why, the leader of that team, that magnificent grey, would do honour to Count D'Orsay's cab. Any dealer would jump at him for an investment at a couple of hundred guineas.'

And he went on to say – in a more jocose vein – about his picture of 'The Straw-yard': 'Here all is worthy of praise; the horses are drawn with great skill, and the pigs would warrant Moses never to omit a chine with his turkey. Morland never accomplished more undeniable porkers.'

Herring and his family moved from Park Street to 9 Cottage Green, in Camberwell in 1840. His reputation at this time was no longer confined to the English aristocracy, and had gone before him to France; it was in the year 1840–41 that he went to Paris at the invitation of the popular heir to the throne, the Duc d'Orleans, to paint portraits of five of his own horses. These were later to be engraved by the indefatigable Charles Hunt, and published by J. Moore in England, simultaneously with publication in Paris by Rittner & Goupil, with particulars in French and English.

The Duke paid Herring a great compliment in giving him such a big commission, for he was in a position to command the best, and therefore by implication, there was no French artist at that time who could measure up to the task.

Theodore Géricault had died young in 1824, but his known admiration expressed for English sporting painters, combined with the effect of his picture of the Derby (now in the Louvre), may have prompted the decision.

The delightfully elegant portrayal by Eugene Lami of the Duke in full fig as a Marshal of France astride a curvetting grey Arab (in the collection of the Duc de Guise) dated 1842, was a charming work, but Lami was not necessarily the man for a true racing picture. Strangely enough, a large number of the Duke's father's collection had found their way into our Royal collection during the Revolution, in 1792.

An interesting point about this series is that the particulars printed show that the horses which ran in these important races were mostly bred from imported English sires and ridden by English jockeys. The Duke's Beggarman, for instance, being by Zinganee out of Adeline, was bred by the Earl of Stradbroke, and ridden by James Robinson. He was a prolific and much-travelled winner, counting the Goodwood Shield, the Boulogne Gold Cup, the Brussels Gold Cup and a Versailles Sweepstake amongst his successes.

Two pairs of pictures were done of the two main races of the year, in which Herring collaborated with the French artist, G. B. Campion, Herring painting the horses and Campion the background. One race was the Special Prize of 5,000 francs given by the Royal Studs, in which the Duke's Roquencourt had a tough battle. It was run in three heats over 2½ miles, including a stiff hill, and four of the best horses in France took part. Roquencourt won two out of three heats in record times of 4min. 47sec., and 4min. 43sec.

The other pair of pictures show the Chantilly Derby, 'They're Off' and 'Preparing to Start'. Here the Duke's Tragedy was beaten by Lord Henry Seymour's Poetess over a course 'Once and a distance round'. It was noteworthy that the colts carried only 8st 9lb and fillies 8st 6lb, whereas the accepted weights for the Classics today are of course, 9st and 8st 9lb respectively. Herring, never one to let the grass grow under his easel, promptly engaged with Lord Henry for a portrait of his Poetess, which I believe is still owned by the French Jockey Club. He also painted Baron A. de Rothschild's Anatole, winner of the French St Leger at Chantilly.

Herring's unsleeping powers of observation and his ever-active pencil were clearly at work on this trip, for apart from the racing pictures, he exhibited shortly afterwards at the BI and the SBA, pictures of a 'French Blacksmith's Shop', a 'French Inn Yard', and in 1844, a 'French Coast-scene' at the SBA, and a 'French Road-side Inn' at the BI.

In 1845 another honour had come Herring's way, when he was appointed animal painter to HRH the Duchess of Kent (Queen Victoria's mother). For the Duchess he painted one of his most charming pictures, still in the Royal Collection, of two of the Queen's favourite riding-horses, with side-saddles on, Tajar (or Tagar) and Hammon, waiting with a groom at the foot of a flight of steps at Osborne (or Windsor Castle?). This was given to Her Majesty as a birthday present. The Queen was so pleased with it that she commanded Herring to paint a favourite hack horse of her own, to present to Prince Albert on his birthday. (Afterwards engraved and published in the *Art Journal* in June 1856.)

Reading Sir Oliver Millar's encyclopaedic volume, *The Queen's Pictures*, it is pleasant to learn how often, one or other member of the Royal family – particularly the Queen herself and Prince Albert, planned nice little surprises for their relatives, of a picture as an anniversary present of some sort: a habit which could admirably be revived amongst the general public, in place of the never-ending supply of second-rate photographic reproductions of Constable's 'Corn-field' or Vincent's 'Sunflowers'.

In Mr Muir's memoir, it is recounted how Herring got the better of no less a personage than J. M. W. Turner, RA, at an Exhibition of the BI, as follows:

'It was upon varnishing day of one of the Exhibitions of the British Institution that Mr F. R. Lee (afterwards RA) exhibited a picture the colours of which he had some trouble to properly balance. Appealing to Mr. J. M. W. Turner, RA, who was present, to give him a hint as to what the picture wanted to correct the deficiency, Mr Turner looked over his spectacles, and catching the idea, instantly fetched a piece of white upon his palette knife, and dabbed it upon the roadway in the picture, saying, "That's what it wants," meaning a piece of white. This merciless treatment did not commend itself to Mr Lee, who scraped the white off the picture and appealed to Mr Herring as to what he would advise, suggesting at the same time he should paint a white horse over the part Mr Turner had dabbed with white. As time was limited for much to be done, the horse was very quickly painted by Mr Herring, and upon the following day, when the Gallery was opened, Mr Gambart, the well-known publisher of his day, saw the picture, and in reply to a query as to what he thought of it, said, shaking his head, "Yes, it is a very good picture, but it smells very fishy".'

Since his debut at the RA in 1818 only a few horse pictures had been accepted, and his two canvases hung in 1830 of 'Interior of a Stable' and 'Velocipede' elicited the following discouraging note from a critic who wrote: 'Of the former [*the Stable*] we think there is not sufficient diversity of colour to constitute it a pleasing picture. If we may infer from its situation, we should say the committee considered it endowed with lofty pretensions. 'Velocipede' is cleverly painted, but it wants effect; the background has not been sufficiently attended to."

After that rather cold douche he did not show again until seven years later – 'A Favourite Cob'. Then he had two horses in the exhibition of 1838. By 1840 he must have

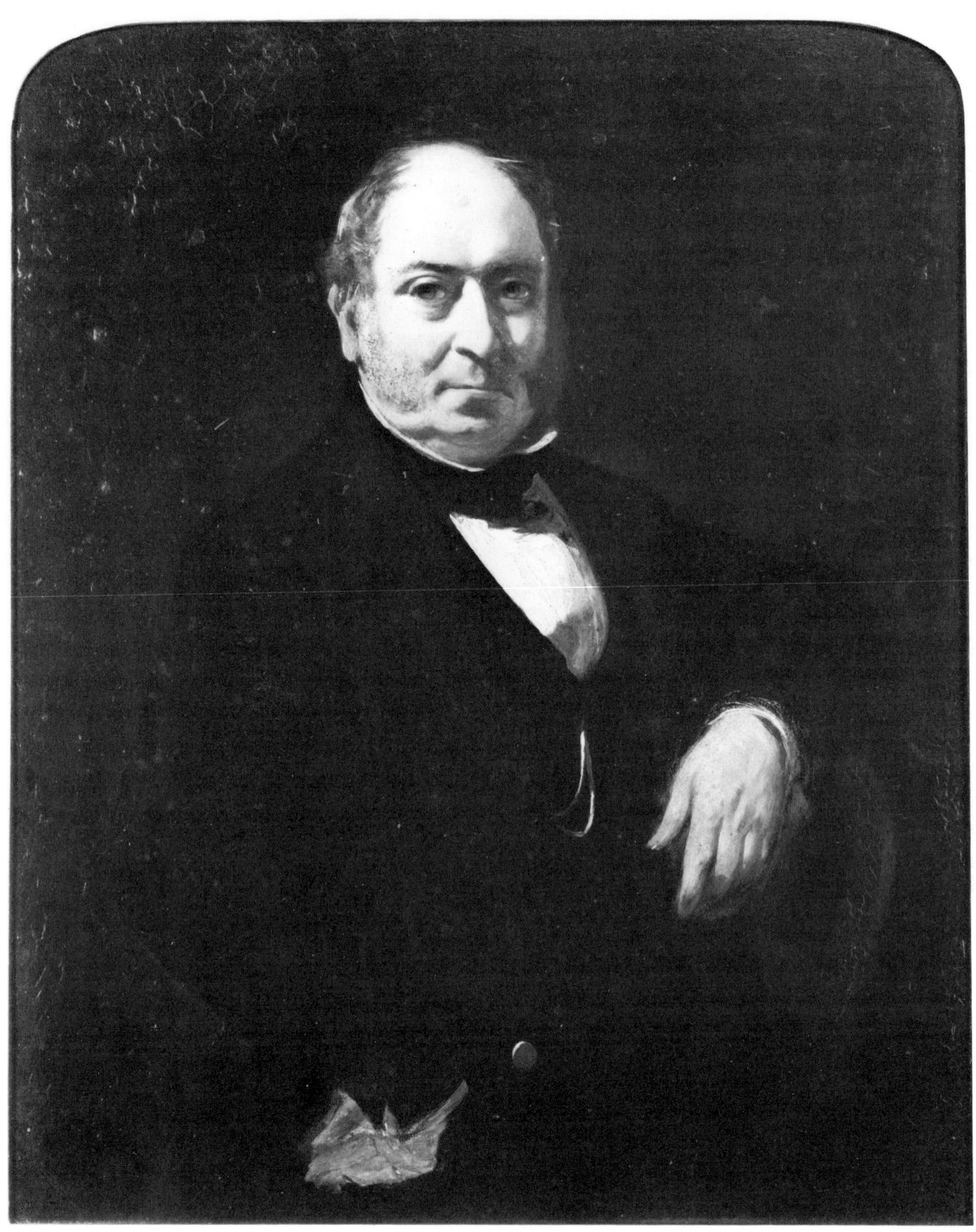

39

J. F. Herring senr (aged 52)
by Alfred Corbould
1847. 11½ × 9½ ins. Courtesy: Mr John Warner

seen that there was a prejudice against horse-portraits as not befitting the dignity of the Academy, and his entries were more generalised under such titles as 'Going to Plough'. Between 1845 and 1863 none of his works was hung, whether any were submitted we do not know.

He was still busy with his St Leger and Derby series, and other works; portraits of Nutwith, Gladiator and Slane being much admired. He also branched out into 'subject' pictures such as 'Mazeppa' (from Byron) and 'Waiting for the ferry-boat'. Here Mrs Stirling goes wrong in her memoir because when she says Herring's son, Charles, had a hand in the design of 'Waiting for the Ferry-boat' – and increasingly in others, Charles would only have been fourteen years old. So, although he was very talented and did help his father later on, it could hardly have been at this stage.

Herring's chief 'assistant' in fact, in the Mazeppa picture (SBA 1842) was his beautiful white Arab, Imaum, who features in so many of his canvases; now by a cottage door, or waiting for some boisterous Cavalier outside an Inn. Imaum came into Herring's possession through an odd combination of circumstances.

He was one of the first four Arabs presented to Queen Victoria by the Imaum of Muscat. The Queen, however, gave him to the Clerk of the Royal Stables, who as Sparrow says, 'was not a fine courtier', for he sold the gift-horse at Tattersall's, and Herring was lucky enough to be the last bidder.

This intelligent creature served as a model for Herring's most moving and poetical composition of the end of the hapless Mazeppa's[1] torturous ride as recounted in Byron's famous poem of that name. It had been published in 1813, and was one of a series of Tales which, it has been said, acted like a heady wine on his public. Herring made copies of two pictures – apart from his own version – of the subject painted by that admirable French artist, Horace Vernet, and these are now in the Tate Gallery, having been presented to the British Sporting Art Trust by Mr Paul Mellon. They illustrate two episodes in the story told by Mazeppa in his seventieth year to Charles of Sweden, as they rested in camp after the disastrous defeat of Pultowa.

As Byron put it so well:

The Ukraine's hetman, calm and bold:
But first, outspent with his long course,
The Cossack prince rubbed down his horse,
And made for him a leafy bed
And smoothed his fetlocks and his mane,
And slacked the girths and stripped his rein,
And joyed to see how well he fed;
For until now he had the dread
His wearied courser might refuse
To browse beneath the midnight dews;
But he was hardy as his lord
And little cared for bed and board . . .
    That steed from sunset until dawn
    His chief would follow like a fawn.

[1] Not the race horse, Mazeppa, painted by Lambert Marshall

Mazeppa then told his story, of how, as a young page, he had wooed and won the young wife of proud Count Casimir, had been found out and punished. He was seized and bound – 'with many a thong', to the back of an unbroken 'Tartar of the Ukraine breed, wild as the wild deer and untaught, with spur and bridle undefiled, T'was but a day he had been caught', which was then lashed with a whip and let loose.

Byron's vivid lines convey the terror of the furious gallop across the plains and through the forests, carried 'Upon the pinions of the wind, All human dwellings left behind', and tell how, when at last, his poor steed sinks exhausted to the ground, 'With gasps and glazing eyes he lay, And reeking limbs immoveable, His first and last career is done', – a vast herd of wild horses surround the dying horse and his all but dead burden still tied with bloody thongs.

It is this dramatic moment that Herring chose for his version of the subject, and how well has he captured the feeling in Byron's stanzas:

"On came the troop – they saw him stoop. . . .
They stop – they start – they snuff the air,
Gallop a moment here and there,
Approach, retire, wheel round and round,
Then plunging back with sudden bound,
Headed by one black mighty steed,
Who seemed the patriarch of his breed,
  Without a single speck or hair
Of white upon his shaggy hide;
They snort – they foam – neigh – swerve aside,
And backward to the forest fly,
By instinct, from a human eye
  They left me there to my despair. . . .
I little deemed another day
  Would see my houseless, hopeless head."

Herring included the black raven of ill omen, flying out of the wood on the left. The poem ends with the rescue of Mazeppa by a Cossack maiden who nurses him back to health, to fight again another day, still bearing the scars of his horrific adventure.

Incidentally, it is quite untrue that *all* the white horses in the picture resemble Imaum, which Mrs Stirling maintains in her purple passage on the subject, in her book, *Painter of Dreams*.

Later on, in about 1848 or 49, when he wanted a model for the dead horses he was to introduce into a picture of The Battle of Waterloo, at the old Gallery of Illustrations, according to 'The Druid' (H. H. Dixon), Herring sent for Pedro, 'a black man from Batty's Circus, who taught Imaum to lie down in a few lessons . . . and he became so complete a trick-horse that Pedro declared he wanted nothing but youth to beat the other time-honoured pets of the Horse Ballet quite out of the field.'

According to Shaw Sparrow this picture was part of a large panoramic scheme intended to represent all the principal places between Southampton and Calcutta, and carried out in tempera. So whether 'The Battle of Waterloo' was a part of that scheme or some other is in doubt. Anyway, Herring we know was required to paint nearly life-size, the Arabs and Barbs in 'The Overland Route to India' diorama. This was designed by two well-known scene painters, William Telbin and Thomas Greives who did the landscape, aided by John Absolon, who painted the figures, and Herring's son-in-law, the well-known animal illustrator Harrison Weir.

Herring, in a letter to Charles Stanhope, said he had quite knocked himself up painting fifteen horses, nearly the size of life, as many camels, sheep, fowls, vultures and pigeons, but from not having been used to working standing on planks etc, and no sitting down, was forced to take a rest at home.

This exploit with the distemper brush must have been an abrupt departure from Herring's usual fine sables, but the result was so appreciated by Messrs Greives, Telbin and Absalon that, on completion of the task, they presented him with a silver tea-pot, coffee-pot, cream ewer and sugar-basin, suitably inscribed, 'as an acknowledgment of the very eminent services rendered,' dated April 1850. Harrison Weir received a silver bread-basket. Unfortunately, the Gallery of Illustrations has long since vanished, but Shaw Sparrow mentions that a friend of his well remembered it in the 80s. The silver service mentioned is still in the possession of the Warner family.

This system of collaboration between artists is so foreign to the modernist's attitude of extreme individualism, that it deserves some explanation. The mere fact that more than one hand has been responsible for a picture does not necessarily invalidate it from the artistic point of view; it was common practice in Renaissance studios, for the master to design the work, and allocate some portions of it to his assistants – and who would disdain the services of an apprentice like Botticelli?

But to come to more recent times. Great portrait painters like Sir Antony Van Dyck and Sir Peter Lely in the 17th century, who were of course, much more than 'face and hands' painters, did employ helpers in the matters of dress and background, as did the Kneller factory. The Flemish school did the same: Rubens collaborating with Snyders, Paulus Potter with Wouwermanns, Hackaer with Berchem.

In the 18th century, the division of labour was frankly admitted, and it may be of interest to list some of the works produced in this way in the field of sporting art.

Sawrey Gilpin, for instance, is known to have produced pictures where he painted the horses, George Barrett, RA, the landscape, and Zoffany the figures. On other occasions, Wm Hogarth painted in no fewer than six faces for a painting by John Wootton; James Ward, RA painted the horse in John Phillips' painting of the Russian commander, Platoff; H. B. Chalon added a dog to a picture by Ben Marshall in 1813; and in 1824, a Yorkshire collector, Colonel Thornton, commissioned Philip Reinagle, RA, to paint himself, and Ben Marshall to paint his grey mount, in a picture called 'Breaking Cover', to hang as a companion piece to a picture of 'Death of a Fox'.

So, for Herring to do the same is really nothing out of the way. His best-known contribution to another's work, is probably the race-horses he painted in water-colour for Wm Frith's picture of Derby Day. As we have seen, he collaborated with G. B. Campion in France, and also with another French painter, E. Boutibonne, in pictures of the Queen, Prince Albert, and the Emperor Louis Napoleon and Empress Eugenie of France.

One of the most successful 'co-operative' ventures is the one of the 'Blacksmith's

Force' (owned by Lord Leith); here the hound and the smith is by Sir Edwin Landseer PRA, the woman (naturally looking very Spanish) is by John Phillips, and the rest of the picture, including our old friend, Imaum, is by Herring himself. So similar, moreover, are the various parts of the picture in technique, that it is hard to distinguish which are by whom – that is the result of tradition rather than revolution in art. The nearest parallel in that century would be the close resemblance in technique between Sisley, Monet and Pissaro, amongst the Impressionists. Landseer himself, who was not too good at 'likeness' according to Queen Victoria, had help from Winterhalter in some of his portraiture – where he did not blatantly use photographs, but that is a different story. The degree of collaboration between Herring and his sons will be dealt with in a later chapter, as it deserves special consideration.

As regards his method of work, which was very painstaking, we have the authority of Mr Muir in saying that Charles did assist his father with the preparation of the materials – which he could well have done in his 'teens. He it was who prepared the colours supplied by Mr Robson, the colourman of Covent Garden, grinding them himself and mixing them with twenty-year-old oil, using sugar of lead as a drier. The purity of his colours must have been obtained by painting over a prepared white ground. He did not fall prey to the prevalent vice of using too much bitumen in the shadows, which has caused many a good picture to crack badly – even Sir Joshua's, and his careful varnishing has preserved his tints for the most part in all their pristine clarity. Such well-made pictures withstand the ravages of time, and cleaning them presents few problems.

Herring used to sit to his work, unlike James Ward or John Constable, and from a letter written from Camberwell in 1848 we learn that once he had a stable studio built light and large enough for his equine models, 'he went ahead'. He owned two 'clever horses' at the time, which he drove in double harness, and one that one of his sons used as a hack.

From 'The Druid's' account it appears that, 'Leading lines were always his great guide for perspective and he invariably worked from left to right.' It is not quite clear what is meant by 'leading lines' – but then 'The Druid' was no great art critic.

Different sporting artists have had different methods of composition: Francis Barlow 'Paynts the ayre first then the chief thing of his quadro afterwards', whereas Stubbs and Tillemans painted in animals and figures first then worked up the sky and landscape to them. It seems probable that Herring followed Stubbs in painting the animals first, and a small sketch owned by Lady Macfadyen seems to bear this out.

'The Druid' adds that his great racing pictures were usually got by the aid of a sketch-book with ideal horses and jockeys, which a 'few strokes from life' at the post converted into portraits. He also says that Herring never saw the mare, 'Vision', but sketched her years after her death merely from the description of William Beresford, who pronounced 'the likeness perfect'. No mean feat of visual imagination.

With all this ability, however, Herring was morbidly sensitive to criticism. In a letter to his old friend and patron, Charles Spencer Stanhope (1848) quoted by Shaw Sparrow, he confessed this weakness of 'former days'. . . . 'If you will have the goodness to look coolly on what is called a critic,' he wrote, 'I am sure your sound good sense will tell you

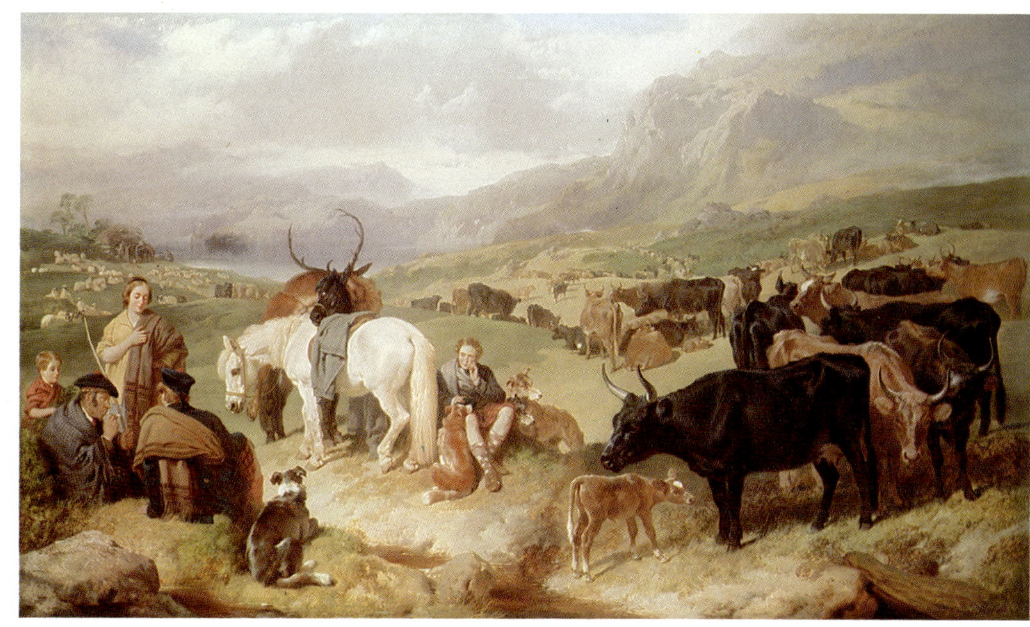

40

A Meeting of Deer Stalkers
Signed J. F. Herring 1852 and H. Bright 1858. 42 × 72 ins.

Courtesy:
Richard Green Gallery

List No 247

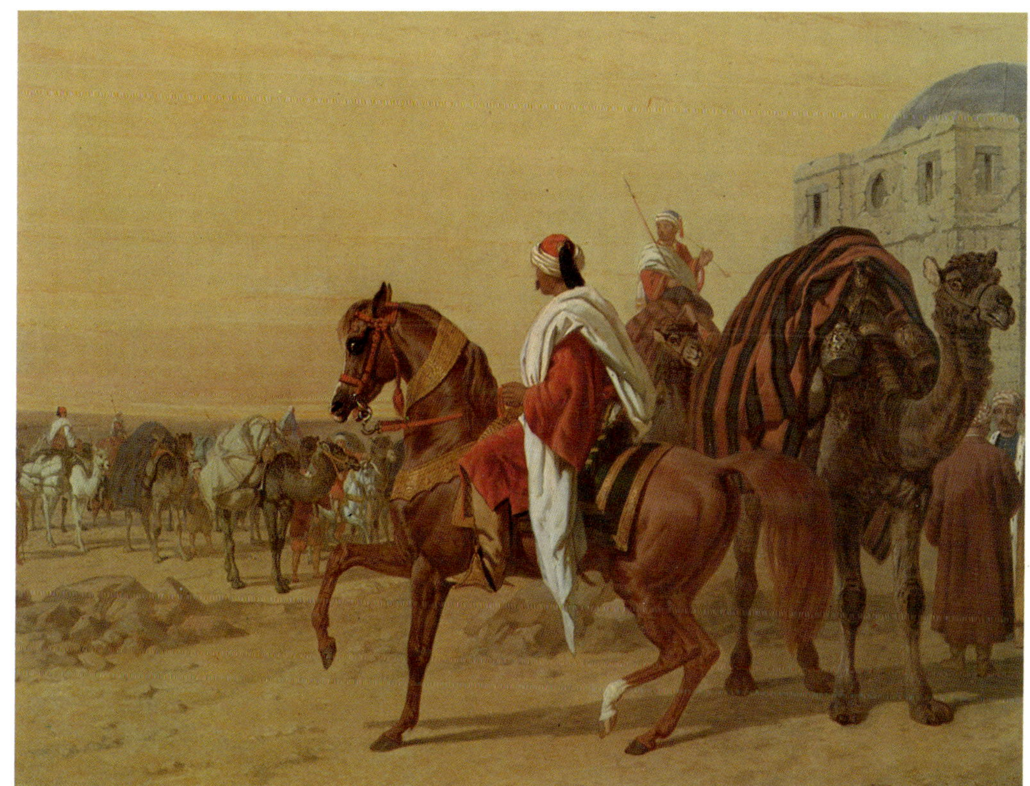

41

Arab Caravan (study for 'The Overland Route'). Signed and dated 1852–55.

Courtesy: Mr John Warner

List No 248

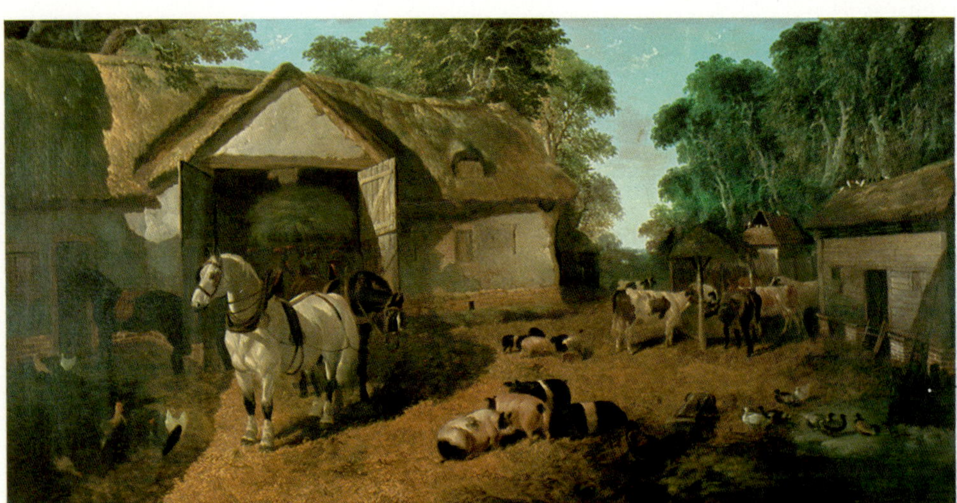

42

Meopham Farmyard. Signed and dated 1857. 26 × 52 ins.

Courtesy: Lady Violet Macfadyen

List No 283

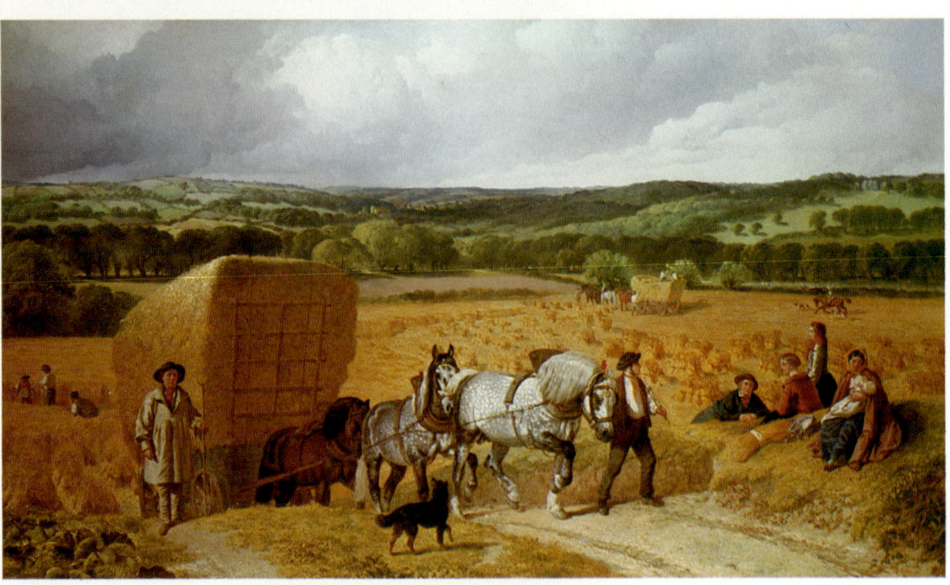

43

Harvest Time. Signed and dated 1859. 42 × 72 ins.

Courtesy: Richard Green Gallery

List No 288

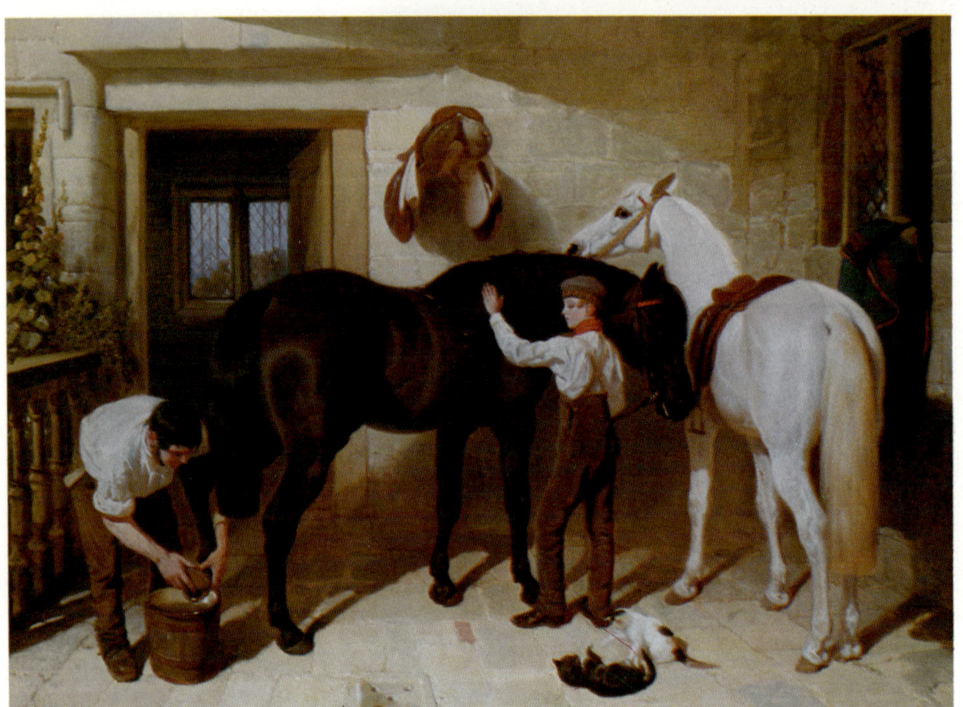

44

Outside a stable. Two grooms preparing horses for hunting. Signed and dated 1849. 27 × 36 ins.

Courtesy: Richard Green Gallery

List No 208

45

End of the Day's Shoot.
Signed and dated 1829.
22 × 30¼ ins.

Courtesy: Sotheby's

List No 47

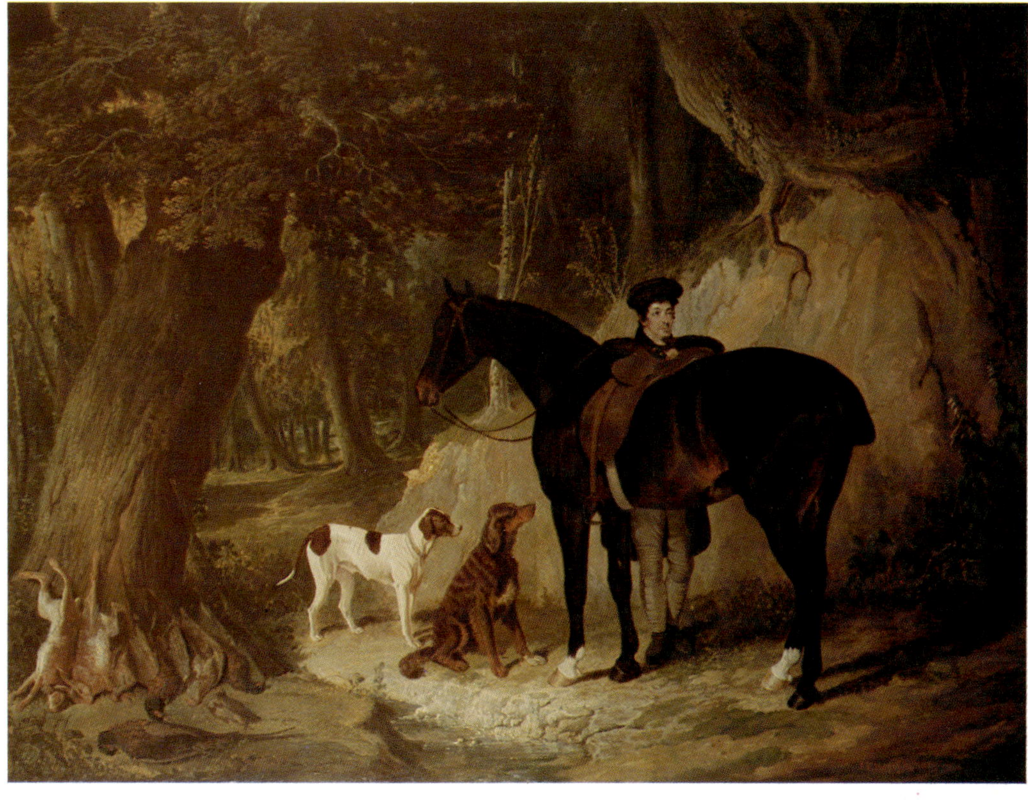

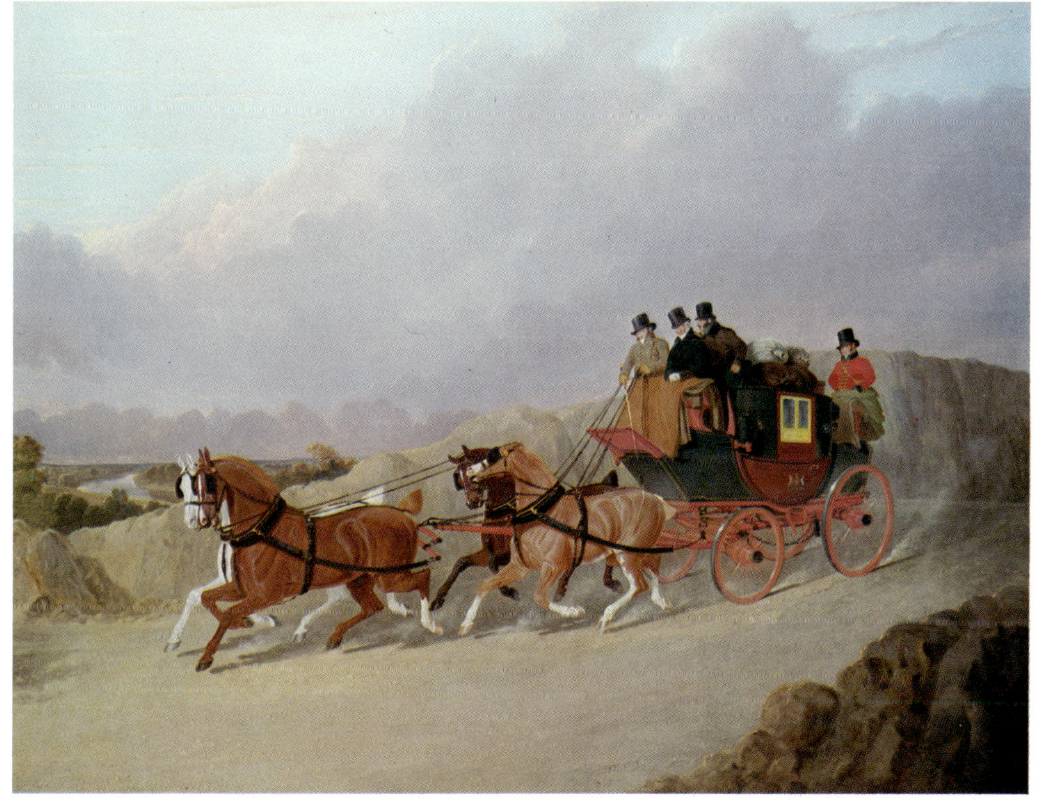

46

London–Edinburgh Royal Mail Coach. Signed and dated 1853. 27½ × 35½ ins.

Courtesy:
Richard Green Gallery

List No 252

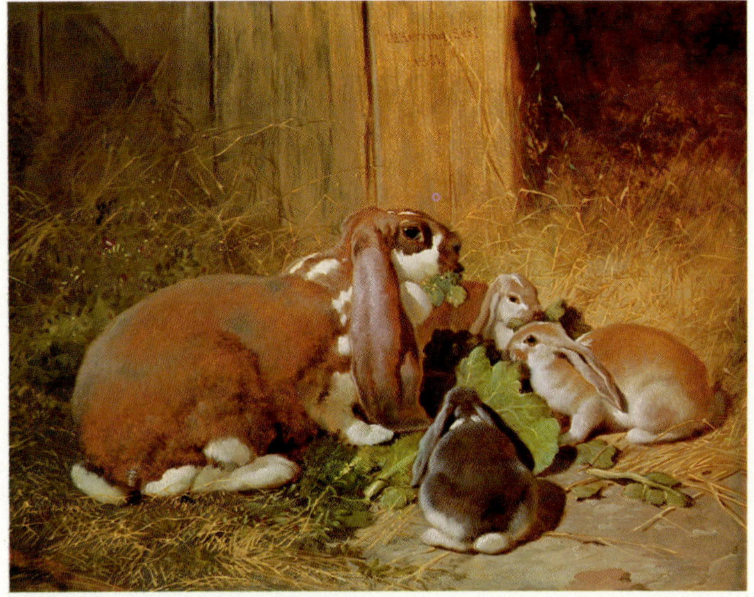

47

Lop-eared Doe and Young. *c.*1850. 14 × 18 ins.

Courtesy: Richard Green Gallery

List No 218

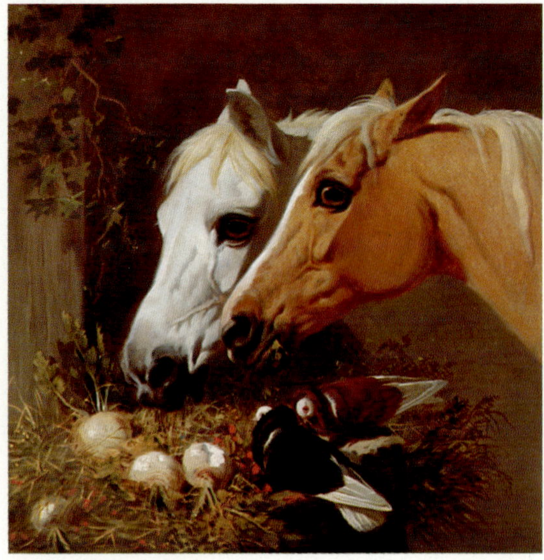

48

Favourites. Signed and dated 1848. Panel 13 × 13 ins.

Courtesy: Richard Green Gallery

List No 200

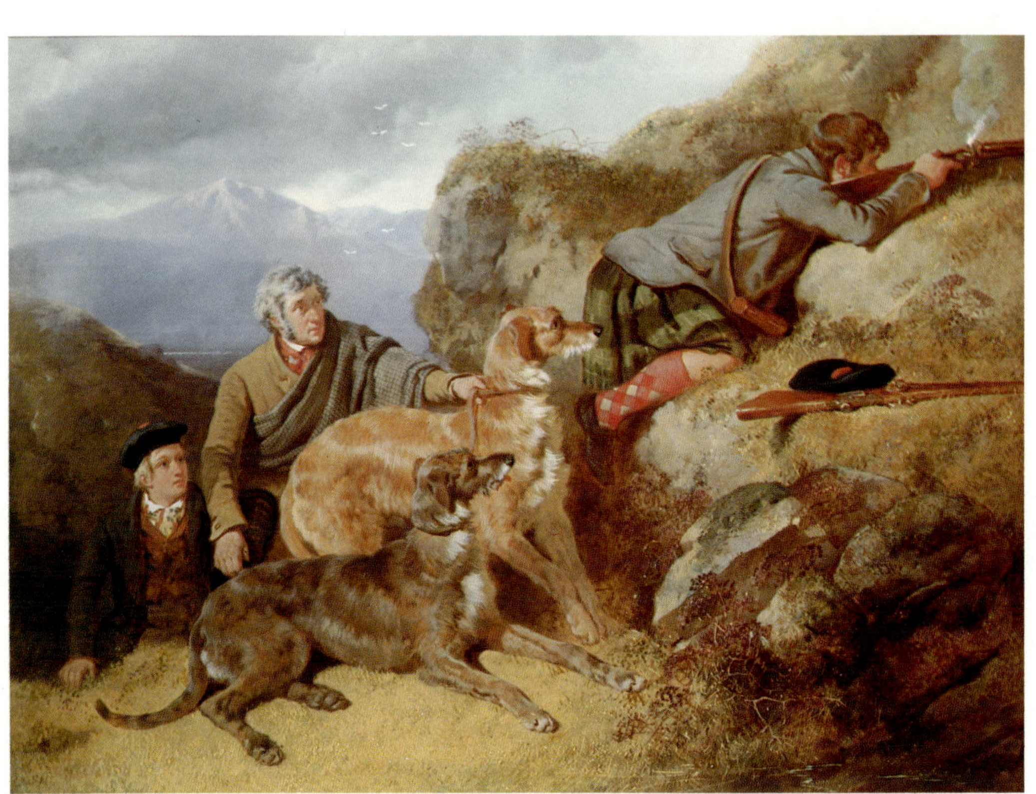

49

In the Highlands. Signed with initials. 20 × 30 ins.

Courtesy:
Richard Green Gallery

List No 193

they are the most dangerous of all persons who may enter a Young Artist's studio. Their talent for criticism is often over-rated, and they go from one Artist's house to another, chilling every attempt that thought and industry dictates; and with their harsh remarks, throw such a check that the Artist's spirits become depressed, and what might, perhaps, with a little encouragement, have been a work, when finished, of considerable skill, is put down with disgust, never more to be looked upon.'

Shaw Sparrow treats these obviously heart-felt complaints with some derision, but in expressing them, Herring was showing no more resentment than is usual amongst artists, who mistakenly imagine that all criticism is pejorative, whereas it has often revealed the arrival of a new and exciting talent. Moreover, by omitting the first part of this letter, he is guilty of a selective quotation that gives quite the wrong impression. The whole text is given in Mrs Stirling's memoir, and it makes clear that Herring, so far from resenting the obligation he was under to Charles Stanhope for his encouragement in his early days, was actually afraid that any adverse criticism from someone as knowledgeable and well thought of in society circles as he, might blight his chances of success, at a time when he had a wife and an increasing family to support.

Herring continues by consoling himself with the thought that he was now (1848) 'out of the pale of that sort of thing', and happy to say that his pictures were no sooner seen than purchased. In fact he had just sold a picture for £157 10s. which was re-sold for 250 gns and sold again for 500 gns – a price far beyond his most sanguine expectations when he was labouring at Doncaster.

He heartily denied any dislike for his patron, and freely confessed that it was a feeling – however unjustifiable – of dread of his judgment that had perhaps caused a distance between them over the years, after Herring's 'extremely uphill beginning'. (See Appendix A1.) He concluded with a warm invitation to call at his house whenever agreeable; an invitation which his old friend evidently accepted.

His other *bête noire* was a fear of being copied. Again in a letter to Stanhope in 1849, he says that he mixes up very little with Art and artists. 'And why? you would ask. Both myself and Landseer find it will not do to let artists visit your studio, for as sure as you do, when you have half finished a picture, to your great annoyance you find that there are two or three of the same subject in the field with you. Such was the case with Landseer's "Lady Godiva",[1] in consequence of which he has not finished the picture.'

This is a grave slur on his fellow artists, if true; if not, we can only assume that his friend, Landseer's experience made this notion of his something of a mania. The actual copying of his pictures which went on in the 1920s, according to David Livingstone-Learmonth,[2] would no doubt have made his hair stand on end with horror.

Herring became so worried about forgeries of his work, that according to the *Art Journal* of 1849, p. 327, he is reported as having appealed to the magistrates at the Guildhall; he was told that, according to a legal decision on record, a signature on *Linen*

[1] Landseer made a second attempt at this subject with 'Lady Godiva's Prayer' in 1866, which, although one of his admirers called it 'unfortunate', was sold at Christie's in the posthumous sale of 1874, for £3,360.
[2] *The Horse in Art*

(i.e. canvas) to a Deed was not binding, but that the party who sold the pictures might be prosecuted for obtaining money by false pretenses. There is no record of his taking the matter any further.

His son-in-law, Mr Harrison Weir, tells a nice story about Herring's open-hearted ways at this time. It seems that a carpenter had made some rabbit hutches with mahogany fronts, with which Herring was very pleased. When the man told Herring he was giving up his trade to take over a beer-shop in the Triangle – not far from Cottage Green, he set to and painted a large picture of the Flying Dutchman for him on an oil-cloth, about 6ft x 4ft in size. It was subsequently removed to Hildenborough in Kent, and while there was seen and purchased by Mr Henry Graves of Pall Mall. The sign was afterwards sold for over £700 and sent to Australia.

There is an inn called the Flying Dutchman that still stands opposite the turning into Powder Mill Lane, Hildenborough, but – most inappropriately – it now bears a sign with a square-rigged sailing ship, instead of the great horse.

Harrison Weir also says that Herring painted a sign for the 'Yorkshire Grey' in the Borough market for his brother Charles, who was writer to Messrs Barclay Perkins & Co, the brewers of Southwark. When it got damaged by the weather, it was again worked upon by Herring, and after his death was re-touched by Weir himself.

Yet another sign of the Dutchman was painted by Herring and presented to a Frant brewer called Mr Ware. This showed a fore-shortened view of jockey and horse.

It is amusing to think that Herring, who had started so nervously with just such commissions, should gamely take on similar ones when he was established as a leading artist.

He was now 58 years old, and had been living in London for nearly 20 years, long enough to establish his ascendancy in his chosen speciality; his next move speaks of someone who – perhaps unconsciously – feels the urge to return to his roots in the country.

6

Last Years in Kent

1853–1865

The decision that took Herring from his comfortable home in Cottage Green, Camberwell, to the Weald of Kent, was almost as impulsive as his sudden departure – so many years before – for Yorkshire, but a deal more rational. In a letter to a friend of the family in the United States, he tells us that the stink from a manure factory recently erected nearby upset him so much on a walk to the stables that he could hardly breathe, and he determined there and then to quit London. 'I cannot,' said he, 'neither will I, live here any longer. Send someone for *The Times*.' A property was there found advertised – 'To let with immediate possession at the neighbourhood of Tonbridge etc, etc.' So he set off the next morning by rail, saw the place, was delighted with it, came to an agreement, signed the lease for 7, 14 or 21 years, and was installed in about a fortnight. A conclusion of unheard of rapidity in these days. But his judgment, though precipitate, was sound; Meopham (pronounced: Meffam) Park seemed ideal.

Three miles from Tonbridge on a pleasant rise about half-way between the North and South Downs, facing south-west, it was a Georgian mansion, built on the site of a much older house. Its rooms were spacious, and it offered all in the way of fresh air and facilities that he required both for the relief of his asthma, and the peace and quiet for his work.

Taken together with a Park of 30 acres, there were walled kitchen gardens, pleasure grounds, a five-acre orchard, lodge, granaries, brewing-house, farm-yard, piggeries, cow-houses, and a 'very pretty saddle-room', – and a room to paint in, 21ft square; just what he needed, and all for £180 a year.

He adds a characteristic touch of the careful house-keeper, that although only one and a half hours from London by rail, 'no droppers-in' made the journey and had to be entertained. 'At Camberwell', he writes, 'I have known sixteen sit down to supper, *not one expected*, and nine bottles of wine, besides beer drank after eight.'

And it is indeed a most charming place still. It has been the home of Lady Violet Macfadyen and her late husband, Sir Eric Macfadyen, MP, for over 40 years, but the farm is now let off. Unfortunately, a fine old barn was burnt down some years ago that figured in several of Herring's pictures, but the other buildings are much the same as in his day. Sir Edwin Lutyens extended the house at each end, in the 1900's, and designed an elaborate portico over what was the front door (which is now at the South end), otherwise it remains a monument to Herring's good taste with its sunny, panelled rooms overlooking lawns embellished with magnificent cedar and chestnut trees.

Lady Macfadyen has long been a most devoted and knowledgeable admirer of the painter, and has collected a number of excellent examples of his work which hang in the house. It was here that a special centenary celebration took place in 1965, when many of his descendants and their friends gathered together to do him honour.

And indeed one can easily imagine him, hale and hearty, though well into his sixties, driving a smart gig along the high road from Tonbridge, and then turning into Power Mill Lane, from whence a winding drive of exactly two furlongs, leads up to the house. The name commemorates one of the ordnance factories where a terrible explosion took place in 1855, which shook the house to its foundations, and scared the family into rushing into the garden to enquire what had happened. His coachman told Herring that no one was hurt, but in another five minutes the men would have entered the mills to remove the two charges that had just exploded: to which he piously observed, it was another of the interpositions of Providence. The mill was moved to Scotland before World War II.

Anyway, with 'hay enough to pay the rent, and corn enough to keep the horses', and his family about him, he had everything he liked and needed about him: models, both human and equine, beautiful countryside and a snug studio. 'Rural figures,' he wrote, 'we can command by a call or a whistle.' He noted that 'in England, everything depends on a name (which he had), and judging by the superiority of his books, his pictures were enhanced at least 50 per cent in the market, since coming to Meopham.'

As a tangible instance of his good fortune he mentioned that he had received a commission for twelve farming subjects to be engraved, which he did not think he would have obtained, had he remained in Camberwell.

The move, in fact, ushered in what was to prove a most prosperous period of his life; he only had to send a letter or two to London, saying he had something to show, and 'down would come the dealers and clear the deck'.

His son Charles added his encomium on the Garden of England, when writing to the same family friend in America, and in a charmingly whimsical manner evokes the pleasant life they led, the picnics, the boating on the Medway and the absurdities of fashionable bonnets and boots, which he illustrated with vivid sketches.

His devotion to his parents comes out too: 'My father looks like a jolly old Governor – which he is, and Mama looks like his wife – which she is, and they both together look like an old married couple – which they are.' Again, 'My father and I trudge on jollily together – our two noddles or in other words heads – do wonderful things in the World of Art. We devote certain hours every day to painting, just enough not to fatigue or make us tired of which we are about – and the rest of the day we devote to anything, sometimes one thing, sometimes another.'

No hint here of any animosity or disagreement between himself and his father, with whom he obviously worked in close harmony on their pictures together. Relations between Herring and his son-in-law, William Biggerstaff, Emma's husband, were very strained, however, in consequence of a family tiff that severed all contact for three years. Biggerstaff had tried to take the head of the table at Meopham, while Herring, Mrs Herring and Charles were out at Hastings, and when Ben and Jennie did not allow it, he took offence. 'He is a great beast,' said Herring, 'and would drink the sea dry, at least he would try if it happened to be wine'.

His younger son, Benjamin, was married by this time, 'and quite tired of his wife – a very industrious woman'. Ben married twice, and his father thought he was a man who 'wouldn't stick at anything, fond of making mischief and no good to himself or anyone else'. He nevertheless painted some attractive pictures, (of which four are in Lady Macfadyen's collection). They do not have the detailed precision of his father's draughtsmanship, but have a pastel charm of their own.

He was afraid, Fred (John Frederick), his eldest son, would lose his sight. The doctors attributed his malady to excessive smoking, for he would smoke six pipes of tobacco at a time. But he lived to be 92 so he seems to have recovered alright. He married a Miss Kate Rolfe, who was the daughter of the landscape artist, A. F. Rolfe, and was herself something of a painter. She was a member of the Society of Women Artists, and exhibited at the Royal Academy in 1852, a picture of 'The children of the late George Templer, Esq of Sandford Orleigh'. Her address then was 45 Robert Street, Hampstead Road. She also exhibited at the RBA in 1866, 'The Old Lodge', priced at £10. Her address then was 31 Nicholas Lane, Lombard Street. Of course the artists concerned do not always live at the addresses given in the catalogues, as it may only be the address of a dealer handling the delivery of pictures, so the couple may well have been living at Meopham, on those dates.

Anyway, with a groom, a coachman and a gardener at his disposal and livestock of every description to hand, a new phase opens up for Herring.

Gone are the race-horse portraits, gone the coaches and four, he now addresses himself to the depiction of rural life. He concentrates on the farmyard – and romanticises it unblushingly. No mud and manure for him, everywhere fresh straw, clean piglets and blue skies. The tall trees sway in a gentle breeze, and white doves are cooing atop the thatched roofs of barn and stable; hens cluck over their chicks, and ducks anxiously pursue their ducklings – and if a dog should break the rustic spell by barking, one feels he'll be sent to his kennel in disgrace.

When the cold fingers of winter draw icicles on the water butts, and snow mantles the fodder-racks, the animals shelter from the elements and forage from the well-filled mangers.

How idyllic it all seems! and a trifle monotonous. For that reason it has hardly seemed worth-while to list as many of them as are believed to exist, apart from those that were exhibited at the time. The titles are the same, only the dimensions vary. There are usually three or four horses, one of which is almost invariably a grey. John Frederick, junr also painted a number of farm yard scenes, but it is not too difficult, generally speaking to

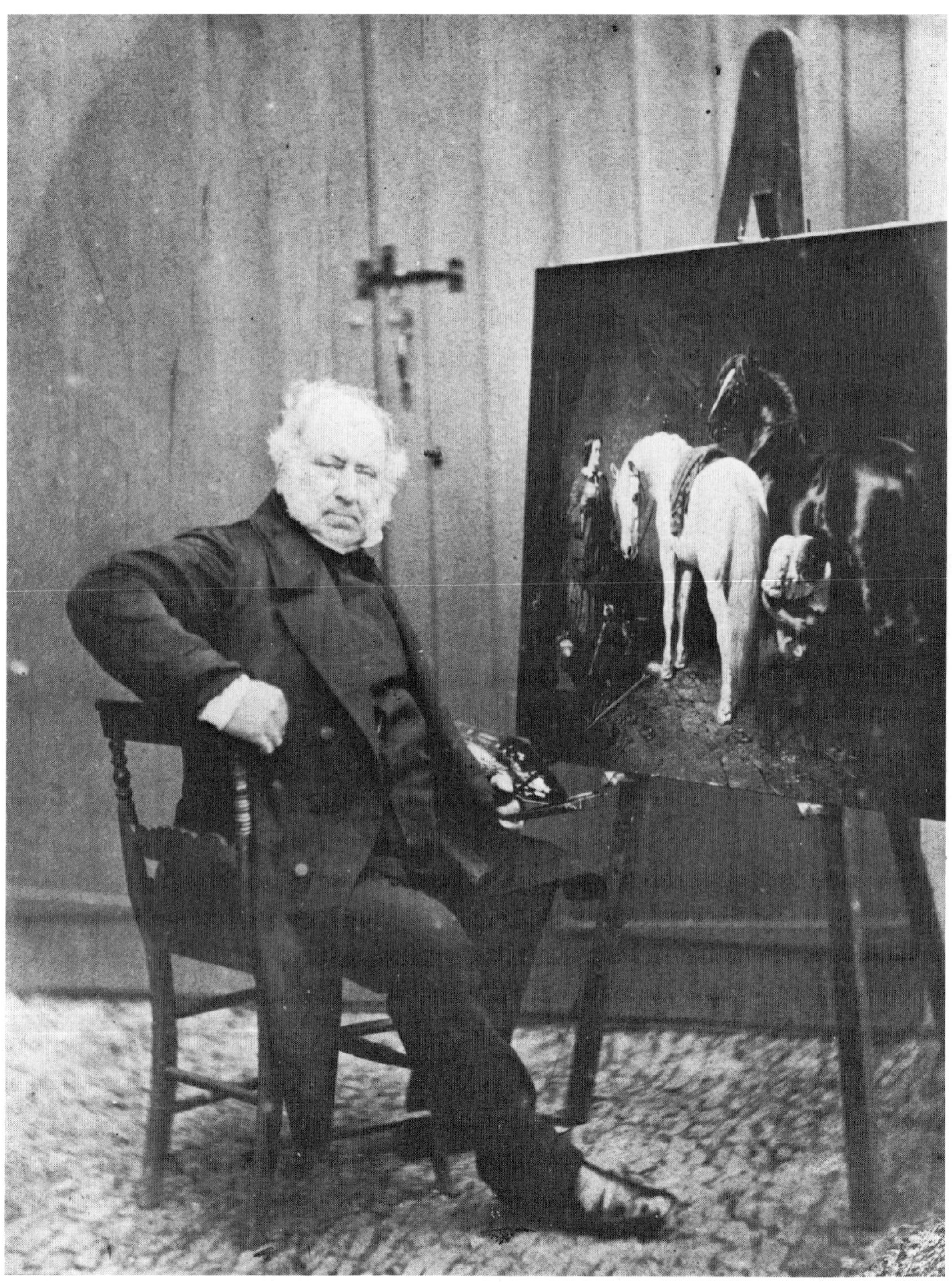

50

J. F. Herring senr in his studio at Meopham Park, aged *c.*65
(See monochrome No. 83, page 119)
Courtesy: Mr John Warner

differentiate one from the other. We have mentioned, therefore, only some of the best ones of this subject that we have actually inspected.

If, as Herring states, his productions were eagerly taken up, there must have been a good market for them. The new middle class in the suburban villas of Twickenham and Bedford Park must have greatly desired these evocations of the simple life – as indeed, did a previous generation who bought up the rustic felicities of George Morland. For Herring was not so simple as to ignore the public. And though Victorian sentiment played a part in his use of rather coy titles, such as 'The Temperance Society' for horses drinking water, there was never anything of the limpid gaze of human affections in his animals' eyes, nor anything slipshod in his careful portrayal of fur and feather, which he still observed with the clinical detachment of a Dutchman's scrutiny.

He adopted, too, at this time, circular-framed canvases of about 16ins diameter for charming little studies of long-eared fancy rabbits, poultry and farming scenes, in which his son Charles often had a hand.

It is pleasant, the way he always throws in – for free as it were – hens and ducks, donkeys and goats, into his large farm yard pictures. A nice contrast to the swept and garnished, concrete jungle of the modern farmstead, where the chickens are mutilated and isolated in batteries, sacrificed on the altar of 'efficiency'.

Wherever possible he also introduced water into his pictures, either horses standing in a stream, or cattle drinking, up to their hocks in a village pond. There is too, a refined quality of light, reminiscent of Cuyp, in many of the morning and evening views, most of which were engraved, and sustain their appeal in the process.

But although he had left the racing world behind him – his last Derby winner was of Teddington in 1851 – his long-established reputation as a horse painter lived on. And when William Powell Frith was working on his famous picture of 'Derby Day' in 1857, he appealed to Herring to help him with the horses, although they were a very insignificant part of the composition.

Herring showed his generous nature over this request by providing Frith with detailed notes on how a jockey holds the reins, how his legs are angled and the action of a racehorse. He went so far as to paint a most exquisite water colour sketch in a letter to Frith, with his suggestion for fitting the distant horses into the picture above the frieze of humanity in the foreground. (See No. 64, page 74.)

He also painted a picture of 'The Return from the Derby, Clapham Common', a print of which was engraved by J. Harris, in 1862, and is in the BM – and was recently exhibited at the RA Exhibition, Derby 200. As the catalogue noted: 'this major example illustrates vividly the various modes of transport which crowded the turnpike road on Derby Day . . . before the railways relieved the pressure, this road, winding through Clapham and Mitcham was the only available route for the sixteen-mile journey from London to Epsom.' Herring, typically, resisted the temptation to fill his picture with drunken revellers, and gloomy losers sporting souvenir dolls, paste-board noses and comic hats, and his innate sense of decorum prevented him from portraying overturned post-chaises and importunate tinkers – a temptation the Alkens and others could never resist.

The top hats are as glossy and the turnouts as perfect as when leaving St James's that morning, but if that is a limitation, then Herring made the most of it, and the picture is no less true for being less roystering than others.

Queen Victoria too, when she heard that he was disabled with gout and asthma, showed her consideration for him, by sending down three of her Arabs to be painted at Meopham, rather than bother him to go to Windsor.

These horses were, Bagdad, Krosaid – a charger that had belonged to the Prince Consort, and Said – the horse on which the Royal children had been taught to ride. The portrait of the last, Said, which was painted in an Eastern landscape, was subsequently placed in the royal collection at Osborne, in the Isle of Wight. The pictures of Bagdad and Said are still in the collection, and of course the very attractive canvas of 'Tajar and Hammon', which he had done some years before for the Queen's mother, the Duchess of Kent, which used to hang at Osborne.

Herring's style by this time, showed a greater suavity of brushwork; the veins and tendons of his horses' limbs were suggested rather than anatomised. And he clearly had benefited from his contact with Landseer in the ability to render atmospheric perspective in the mountains and glens of Scotland, or the hills of Wales. There is a new breadth and spaciousness in his approach to landscape which produced some of his finest work.

Two of these, dated 1854, were exhibited in the Centenary show at Ackermanns in 1965. The passion for wild, windswept crags and rocky ravines which obsessed Turner, with Herring provided a *mise-en-scène* for herds of Highland ponies; if there was a strain of poetry in his make-up, it shows itself here in the flickering shadows from clouds scudding across the sky, to match the mood of a helter-skelter gallop of alarm, whereas when the mares and foals are quietly grazing, rounded static cumulus clouds are piled on the horizon, and the scene is bathed in an even light.

How much more naturally are these animals grouped and posed in contrast to the frozen action of two race-horses, galloping '*ventre-à-terre*', legs extended before and behind, being whipped past the winning-post, as in his earlier work.

But there was a dark cloud menacing the happiness of the family at this time, which was Charles's illness. When Herring was writing to his friend in the States in November 1855, he mentions that 'Charles is laid up and has been for 10 weeks with something of rheumatic gout in his ancles (sic), but he bears it very patiently and keeps his spirits well.' Later he goes on: 'I am sorry to say that since I began this letter, Charlie has got the Rheumatism in both his ancles and is obliged to use crutches, crawls on his knees to bed, and has scarcely any use in his legs. He unfortunately wont be told. He has been wearing a very thin pair of slippers, and the cold and damp have now fixed in his ancles, and I fear he will be some time before he gets well, for at present he is getting worse and his ancles swell frightfully.'

Charles himself, writing at much the same time, gallantly makes light of his malady. 'I am quite the countryman, you should see me in the winter, very rough clothing – Breeches and gaiters and other garments to match – this you will say is rather different from the Exquisite you used to know at Camberwell. I begin to find dress rather ridic-

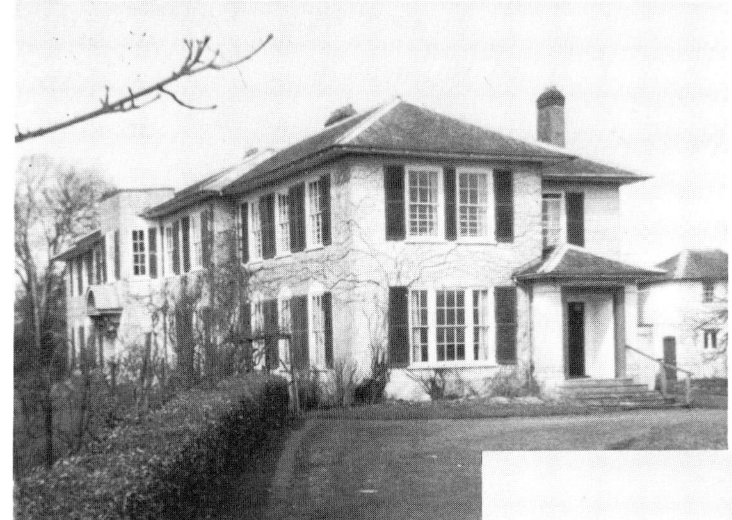

MEOPHAM

PARK

MARCH 1979

Photos by the author
Courtesy: Lady Macfadyen

51

The entrance

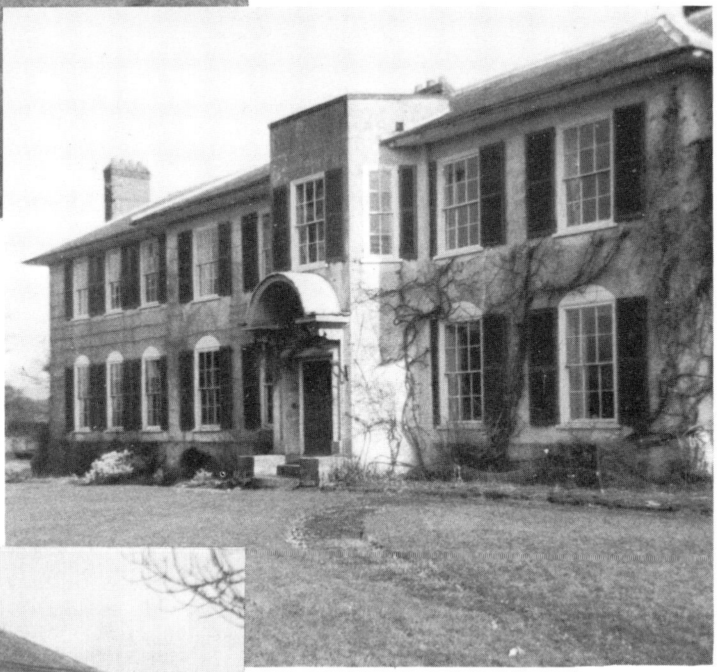

52

The South-West front with the Lutyens porch

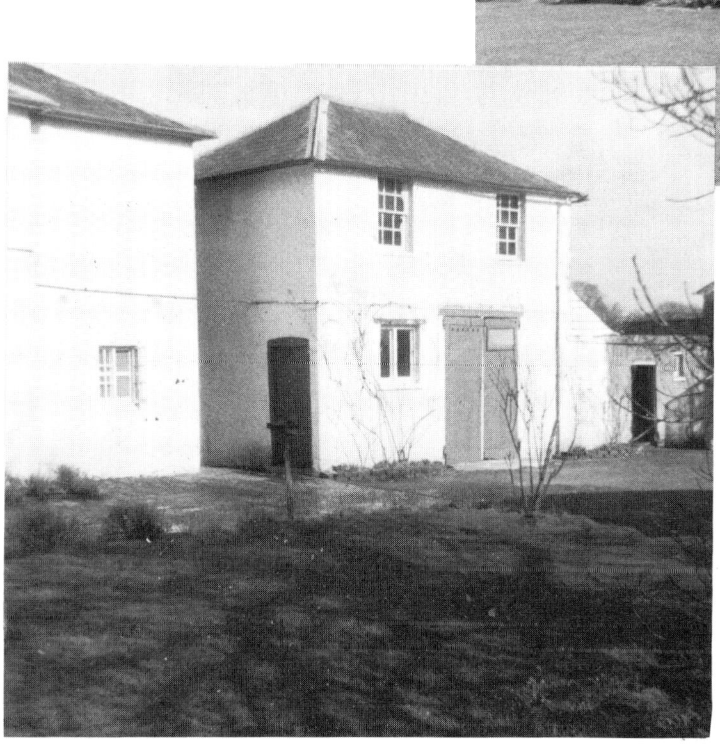

J. F. Herring's studio

53

ulous – Friends think just as much of you in shabby or coarse clothes, it is not dress that is only necessary to happiness . . . at this present moment I have my left leg elevated at about 90 degrees – don't you think it looks very like years creeping on when a Handsome young Bachelor is troubled with gout – it is aristocratic – what an empty consolation is it not? I am saying a great deal of myself, don't think me egotistical . . . it is very strange (joking apart) that I am considered very like Louis Napoleon and Jenny is considered like the Empress. I think there is some resemblance as we have had a very good opportunity of judging, we have just put two horses into two pictures, one of the Emperor and one of the Empress which are to be published.'

This comment refers to the pictures in which Herring and Charles collaborated with the French artist, E. Boutibonne. This – to us – bizarre arrangement also, included pictures of the Queen and Prince Albert, which were exhibited at the RA in 1855 and 1857.

But between these dates, those walks of 8 miles a day – 'pretty good for a Cockney' were over, and poor Charles's life was suddenly ended on 1 June 1856, by an attack of malignant scarlet fever. By his death, the family lost someone whose humorous self-mockery must have much eased their squabbles, and his father lost a faithful friend and collaborator. So moved was the old man, that he laid the front drive down with sea-shells, and never more rode over it. Charles was buried at Hildenborough churchyard.

It seems probable that Herring's third child, Sarah, died about this time too, so including the second son, who had been christened Benjamin, and died as an infant at Doncaster in 1821, it left John Frederick, junr, Ann who had married the animal painter, Harrison Weir, Emma, aforementioned, who was married to Wm Biggerstaff, young Benjamin and Jane or Jenny who married a Mr Warner, who was a solicitor in Tunbridge Wells in the late 1850's. It is from this branch that the present Mr John Warner, himself a solicitor in the same old firm in the same town, and his family are descended, some of whose pictures he has kindly allowed us to reproduce.

Despite his grief, Herring was indefatigable, but he recalls that when he was a night coachman of only 19 years old in a very cold bleak country, bordering on Scotland, the rough work he wasn't use to, must have opened up his lungs, as he had been shut up in a hot work-room for years, and now he could not face a fog or an East wind. All the more creditable then is the fact that in the following year, 1857–58, he produced such an impressive work as his 'Horse Fair on Southborough Common'. This has all the vigour, the sure touch and the colourful detail of a much younger man. It shows a great gathering of farm horses, ponies and country folk at the local summer event, and into it he introduced a marvellous portrait of himself, on the extreme left. (*See plate 20.*)

It was at this time that Herring first exhibited some pictures painted in collaboration with the landscape painter called 'Rolfe', – Alexander Rolfe – at the Portland Gallery. He had taken up exhibiting there since 1854 (when one of his works – 'Interior of a Stable' – was priced at 250gns), and he had had two pictures painted with Rolfe, in the years 1857–58, and three in 1859 (priced between 15 and 60gns) – seven in all. The remaining seven works shown in 1860 and 1861, were ascribed solely to him.

Rolfe was an artist noted for his landscapes and fishing subjects, and the father of J. F. Junr's wife, Kate. Kate was herself an able artist, but she and her husband were then living at great Wilbraham, near Cambridge, so some way from Meopham. There must have been a serious rift between Herring and his eldest son, because he is not mentioned, nor is any provision made for him in Herring's will, as I have said.

In June 1861, Herring again wrote a friendly, chatty letter to Stanhope (Appendix A4) in which he claimed that 'his faculties were yet unimpaired, and his hands as steady as when he first knew him,' but, significantly, he also admitted that he had been laid up with influenza and bronchitis and was totally unable, though willing, to pay his compliments to Stanhope in London.

It seems that he had not visited London for six years, and for the past year had not been able to wear a shoe or a boot, as an attack of erysipelas had 'settled in his ancles, just at the gartering place, below the knee it was 23½ins round,' and he thought the skin must have given way.

He also asks for Stanhope's opinion on two recent pictures which were then at his agent's in Duke Street, Manchester Square; 'Market Day' and 'A Village Horse Fair', the latter, by the dating probably the Southborough Fair mentioned above.

His comments show that for all his 66 years, he was as busy as ever, with twenty pictures on hand at home which he felt Stanhope would like, and that these had been written up in the *Sporting Magazine*.

He again asks Stanhope to come down by train from London Bridge to visit him, and – with a touch of pride – adds that his carriage would meet him at Tonbridge Station.

Imaum, his dear faithful old friend, he says, was now broken-winded and retired, but still made a good model for a study of an old white horse, which was exhibited at the BI.

By some quaint conceit, he headed this letter – 'Born 14 August 1795' – as if to emphasise the inexorable passage of time; his memory was at fault in any case, as he was born on 12 August 1795.

The splendid photograph of him in the studio at Meopham (Plate 50), must have therefore been taken before this erysipelas had set in as it shows him, august, white-haired, dressed in a beautifully cut dark suit and wearing highly polished boots. The artists among my readers will note that he is using two very fine brushes and a mahl stick, and is holding a small, rectangular palette: this is still a treasured memento of the old man in the possession of Mr John Warner. On the easel is one of his charming stable compositions (Plate 83) showing his daughter, Emma, bringing out a bowl of soup to the 'blacksmith'.

According to Mr Muir's memoir, this figure of the blacksmith was modelled by his man, William Terry, who had been with him for seventeen years – until 1856. He it was who often sat for his master as the 'chalk' jockey in many of his racehorse pictures. He also posed with Herring's daughter in 'Market Morning', where the horses belonged to a neighbouring market-gardener. In 'Feeding the Arab', Herring's cook is represented holding the Arab, Imaum, while William Terry, sitting down, is holding the sieve from which the black horse is feeding.

These two horses were mentioned by Druid in his account of a visit to Meopham to see Herring in 1862.

He said that Imaum looked 'peaky and worn', and past doing tricks, but, 'in his prime, Mr Herring was followed by a gentleman into a yard in Piccadilly and had 200gns bid for him there and then.' Needless to say, Herring turned down this quick profit.

But he was no longer a young horse when Herring drove him and the black a few years before in the phaeton from Camberwell to Stevenage and back in a day – a matter of seventy-five miles. He had been to see the Earl of Strathmore who was a leading steeple-chase rider, about painting his horse 'Switcher' (in HM The Queen Mother's collection), and to take studies for his famous work: 'Steeplechase Cracks' (Plate 14). Apparently, Imaum was 'wonderfully stout' for an Arab, and ended the hard day fresher than the English black who had never shirked his work by comparison before.

This amazing old horse was reputed to sleep, leaning against his stall, and had not been seen to lie down for at least eight years. Another equine character of the establish-ment was a pony called Snowball. He used to walk into the drawing-room for gingerbread, and upon one occasion nothing would tempt him to be removed through the door, so he had to be got out through the window. Herring was also proud of a miniature pony he had, called Jack, only 37ins high. He too had the run of the place and used to walk gravely up the front steps in search of his gingerbread, or to enquire if he was wanted for the market basket that day.

What a delightful way of life is suggested by these memories! Every anecdote tells us something of the great painter's simplicity and good nature. The somewhat stern expres-sion in his photograph, one feels, would melt into a gracious amiability just as soon as the snap was taken. Or to show his pleasure at the delight evinced by Druid at seeing versions

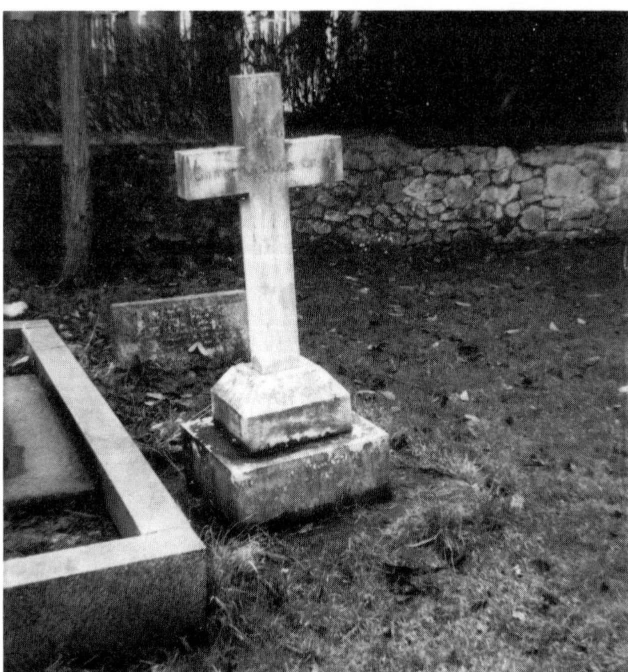

54

J. F. Herring's resting place in the churchyard of St John the Evangelist, Hildenborough, Kent

of paintings of some of his famous horses like Sultan, 'with his beautiful Arab head and dish nose', Attila, Langar, Dr Syntax, Mameluke, Partisan and Venison. These may have been included in the sale after his death. His eyesight seems to be as good as ever as he is not wearing spectacles – unless of course he took them off for the occasion.

But, as with most mortals, with age came infirmity, and in his later years, plagued as he was with asthma, and trouble in his feet, he had to be pushed around his little estate in a wheel-chair. Even so, he found an original diversion to amuse himself with. This consisted of lining up a row of bottles on a fence, some yards from where he was sitting, and then proceeding to knock their tops off with a flourish of his whip.

If he had had modern drugs to ease his asthma, he would no doubt have lived longer. As we now know, this affliction – for it is not a disease – is really caused by stress, and it takes hold at an early age, as it did with him; partly as a consequence of his tough days and nights 'on the box', but also possibly because of his acrimonious relationship with his father. His extraordinary dedication to his art, also argues a nervous disposition that makes tremendous demands on the system – perhaps to prove to the world and himself, that his chosen vocation was the right one. His almost excessive love for detail, only overcome in his late work, but still there, is another sign of an obsessive – if not neurotic compulsion, from which few Victorian painters were free – and look how the public now adores these very Victorians, once so despised!

But he had had a good life; he had come from nowhere, a rank outsider, had finished full of running, and well ahead of the field.

He had brought up a large family, by his own unaided efforts, and earned the respect of the connoisseur and the devotion of his friends and acquaintances, by his fair dealing and hard work.

If his landscape painting harks back to Wouwermann, de Loutherbourg and the Dutch school, rather than John Constable, his portraiture to Anthony Devis rather than Tom Gainsborough, his mediaevalism to the Tower of London rather than Florence – he was in good company, and he had earned for himself a place – at any rate in British art history, that is unique.

After him came the photograph and the Pre-Raphaelites, and a general decline in sporting art until his admirer, Sir Alfred Munnings, PRA, took up the torch and proved himself equal to the task of marrying the demands of modern technique to the love of horses.

Now it was all over, and he lies buried in the churchyard of St John the Evangelist, in the parish of Hildenborough, alongside his dearest son, Charles. He died on 23 September 1865, and his will was proved at only £4,000, but it sufficed for his widow, Sarah, who later was buried beside him, too.

7

The Problems of Attribution

It must be apparent by now, that 'J. F. Herring & Sons' was very definitely a family firm, and to refer merely to a 'Herring' is misleading, as it may be a 'red one' – or a Harry Hall. But as the value of a John Frederick senr may be worth as much as ten times more than a John Frederick junr, it is worth making an attempt to sort out clues to their authorship, and to at least indicate the more obvious differences between them, and other members of his family.

Researching such a prolific painter as Herring, one immediately comes up against the problem that there are numerous versions, of different dimensions, of pictures of the same horse, facing right, facing left, with or without jockeys or attendants. This does not apply to his predecessors like Sawrey Gilpin or Ben Marshall.

The Wm Woodward Collection catalogue (Baltimore Museum, USA) for instance, states that there are five other paintings of Jack Spigot, apart from their own, five of Memnon, six of Beeswing, nine of Maltilda, no fewer than fourteen of Touchstone, signed and dated at various times between 1833 and 1846, including one of 1837 owned by the English Jockey Club, and one of 1846 owned by the American Jockey Club, and so on. Considering there are only half a dozen of such a famous animal as The Flying Dutchman, it is hard to see why there should be so many of Touchstone, who was a lovely little horse, but no more distinguished than the 'Dutchman'.

Are they all genuine, that is the question?

There has always been talk about the number of fake Herrings on the market in the 1920's, but one must doubt whether many of these would deceive a really knowledgeable eye. There are fewer painters today with his extraordinary skill than there were in his own day, when copying was more the word for what went on, than faking. Also, was it really worth the risk, when Woodward himself could purchase five pictures from Messrs Fores for only £1,000 in 1924? When Shaw Sparrow's book came out, 'Old Herring', as he called him, was not even very popular. Somebody called A. Festing, was known to fake some Herrings, but that was in his later manner.

Since his prices have soared in recent years, the temptation must be greater, but the public is correspondingly more wary – or should be, after the Keating scandal, and the discovery that a certain number of works attributed to John Constable for many years, are in fact by his son Richard.

Although several kind people have written to inform me that they own a Herring picture, I have still been unable to trace some of his known pictures of Derby, Oaks and St Leger winners, and it would be the greatest possible interest to know where they are – and if they are 'right'.

To find them would not only complete the record, but would also be a boon to students of turf history and breeding.

Before examining the question of signatures, it may be of some use to elucidate some of the questions which arise when any picture is in doubt, not only a Herring.

The expert of course, always looks at the back of a picture first. This is to check whether the stretcher is old or new, and whether the canvas, visibly nailed round the edges, is original or has been re-lined at some time. Herring generally used a Winsor and Newton canvas, but he painted his smaller pictures on wooden panels.

Our expert will then consult the catalogue of sale for the 'provenance' i.e. the history of ownership where known, and details of its previous exhibition. There are pitfalls here for the amateur in the descriptions in some catalogues. For instance, a picture described as by 'J. F. Herring senr', signed and dated, is considered a warranty of authorship, but just 'J. F. Herring', implies that it might be by father or son. Merely the one word 'Herring' conveys that the particular picture is thought to be one of his in the absence of further corroborative evidence. This convention, by the way, applies to non-sporting artists such as Romney or Gainsborough, so once the jargon is understood, it need deceive no one.

The best London galleries and auctioneers with a reputation to lose are very careful, in their attributions, but mistakes can be made, and in fact a picture can 'acquire' a provenance of blameless virtue because a former attribution has been incorrect.

So, in the absence of such information, how are the 'real' Herrings to be distinguished from the others? The puzzle is made no easier for the fact that Herring and his eldest son shared the same initials and there is no law compelling one or other to inscribe his works with the words Senior or Junior. One can't help wishing Herring had christened Junior with any other names rather than his own – what a lot of confusion would have been avoided, particularly as JF Junr set to work to paint as much like his sire as he could.

Numbers of authentic pictures by Herring senr are unsigned or undated, on the other hand, there must be a few 'in'-authentic ones that have just possibly had a signature added. So, an examination of the signature is essential.

As far as the racehorse pictures are concerned, the dates of foaling and winning races can be checked, and its likeness compared to other pictures of the same horse, and such features as a white sock on the off-fore, or blaze down the nose will help to identify it. Mameluke, for instance, was painted by Abraham Cooper, Ben Marshall and James Ward, as well as Herring, so the matter is simplified.

One of the snags here is that, as we have seen, Herring often made copies of his early pictures, perhaps ten years later, and is believed to have over-painted others with which he was not satisfied, bearing in mind Marshall's advice not to leave early, uncharacteristic, works lying about to discredit a hard-won reputation.

Another way of checking on a painting is to compare it with an engraving made from it – and this applies to his hunting and farmyard pictures as well as his racehorses. The mere existence of such prints argues that he painted the originals from which the engravings were taken, as his name appears on the legend with that of the engraver and publisher, though not always on the picture itself. But even here, minor variations may occur in the print that are the responsibility of the engraver. And where men of the calibre of a J. Harris or a C. Reeve are involved, as they worked for other artists such as Hancock and Hall, their prints bear more of a family resemblance to one another than do the actual pictures, where the method of painting varies quite considerably.

All these caveats, however, come under the heading of 'external' evidence: what matters in the long run is the 'internal' evidence, and this concerns, firstly, the style, and secondly the signature.

As regard his style, Herring was something of a phenomenon. He seems to have sprung, fully equipped into his mature style, which remained meticulously fine all his life. His drawing improved, his perspective became more atmospheric and his composition more sophisticated, but his love for detail – even the smallest weed in a hedge-row, and his devotion to sporting and rural pursuits stayed with him. This is all the more remarkable as he did not come from an artistic family, like Landseer, and he did not attend any arts school, such as the Academy. There are, however, broad distinctions to be made in dating his undated pictures, that correspond roughly with the chapters in this book. In other words, the first phase, when he was in Doncaster, features especially, race-horses, hunters and dogs, and a few coaching and hunting pictures, and continues through the three years at Newmarket. In London, he endeavours to widen his appeal, and the first smithy and forge pictures, and some stable and farming scenes appear. The last phase, at Meopham in Kent, he paints fewer and fewer horses on their own, and no more Derby winners, and concentrates on the agricultural and domestic genre scenes, with his son Charles, and views of the Highlands. Of course, hunting and coaching pictures are scattered through his *oeuvre*, and in fact, one of his finest sets of the Chase, was published after his death (1865).

The earliest drawings I have seen are the three pen and wash sketches reproduced in Mrs Stirling's book. These show a pointer, a fox, and a greyhound in pursuit, and they are such as any apprentice hand might have scribbled in a note-book; in fact the turning body of the greyhound is – anatomically – quite incorrect. We know he was always drawing in his youth, and this assiduous study must have brought him along apace. It may not be insignificant too, that a copy of Stubbs's 'Anatomy' was found in his studio after his death. His first patron, Charles Spencer-Stanhope, knew what he was talking about, when he commended his early efforts at Doncaster in about 1818, for, by 1826 he had already produced a masterly work (Plate 4) a picture of Mr Richard Watts's brood mare, Manuella, recently presented to the Tate, for the British Sporting Trust by Mr Paul Mellon.

J. F. HERRING Jnr

55

Horses, pigs and chicken. Signed. 11 × 17 ins.

Courtesy:
Richard Green Gallery

List No 298

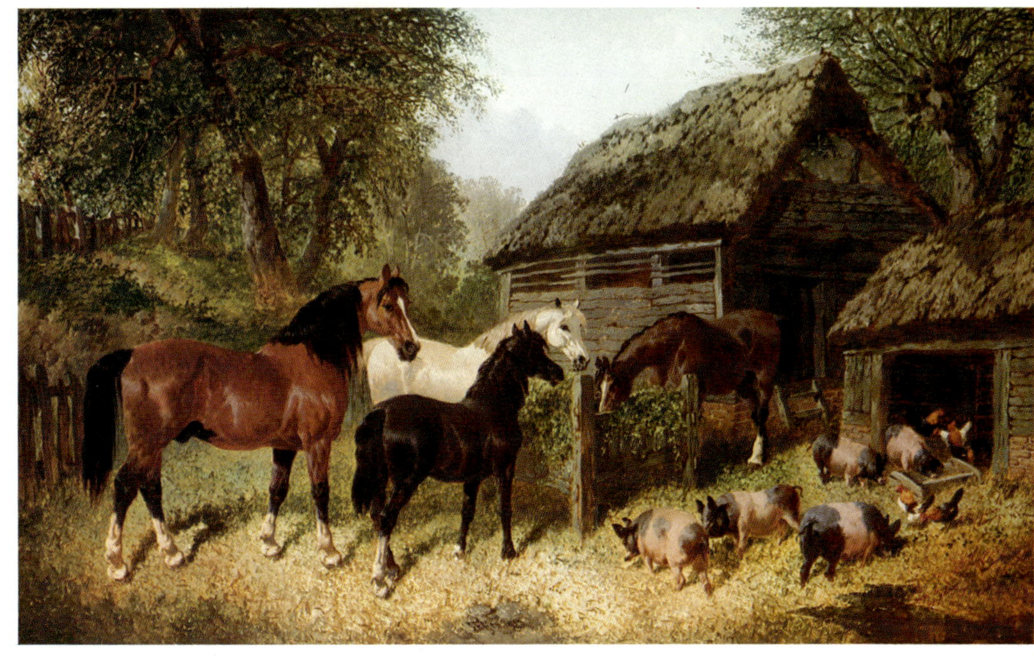

J. F. HERRING Jnr

56

Horses and pigs disturbed in a Field. Signed. 12 × 18 ins.

Courtesy:
Richard Green Gallery

List No 299

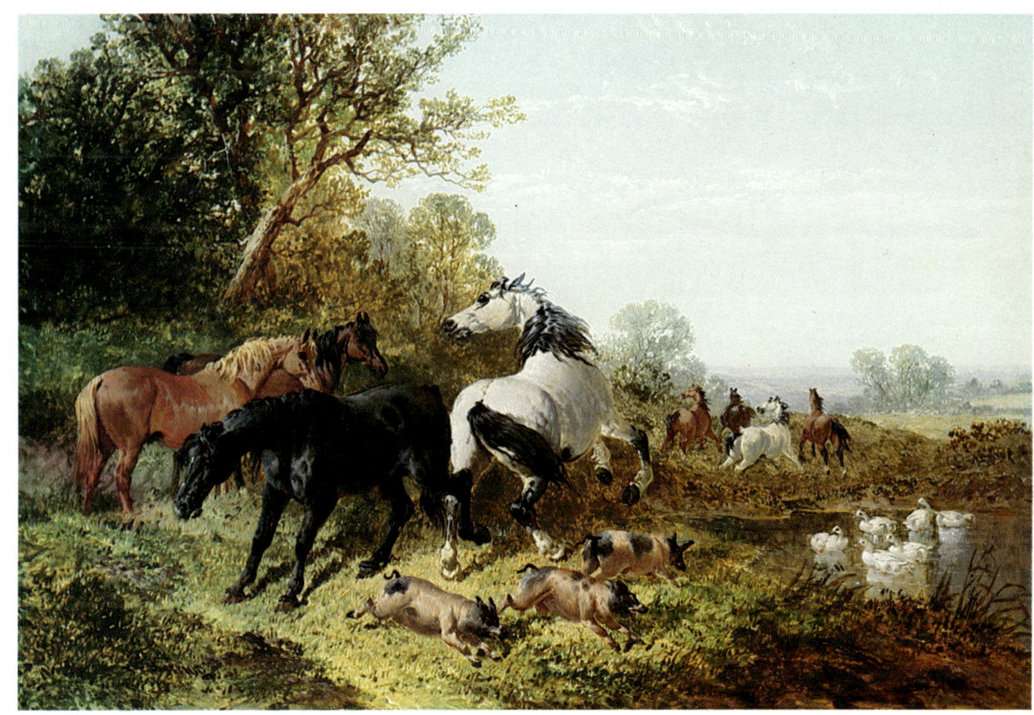

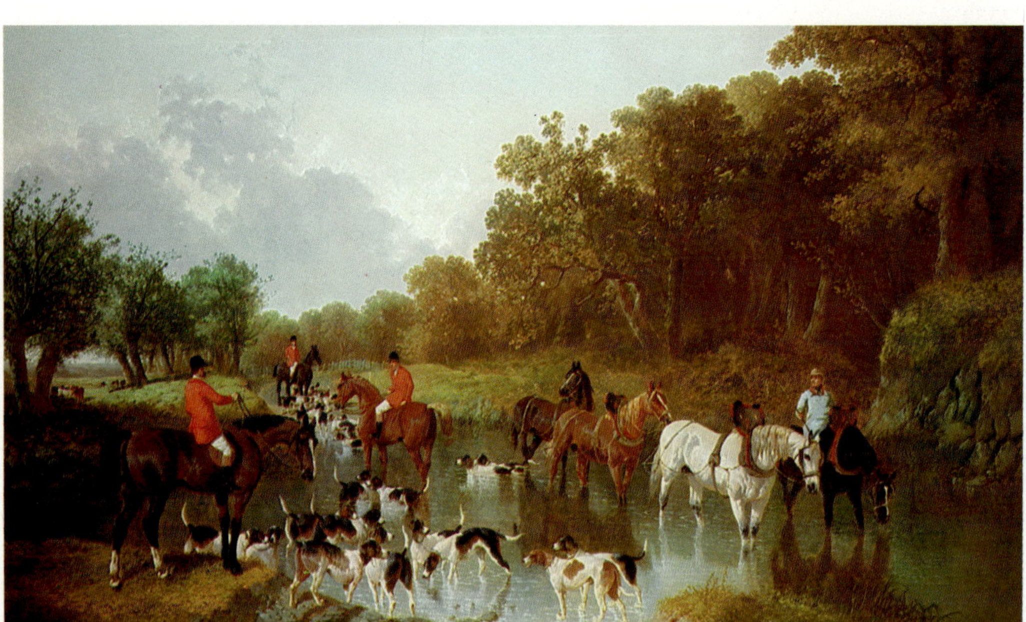

J. F. HERRING Jnr

57

Huntsmen and Hounds at a Ford. 29½ × 49½ ins.

Courtesy:
Richard Green Gallery

List No 300

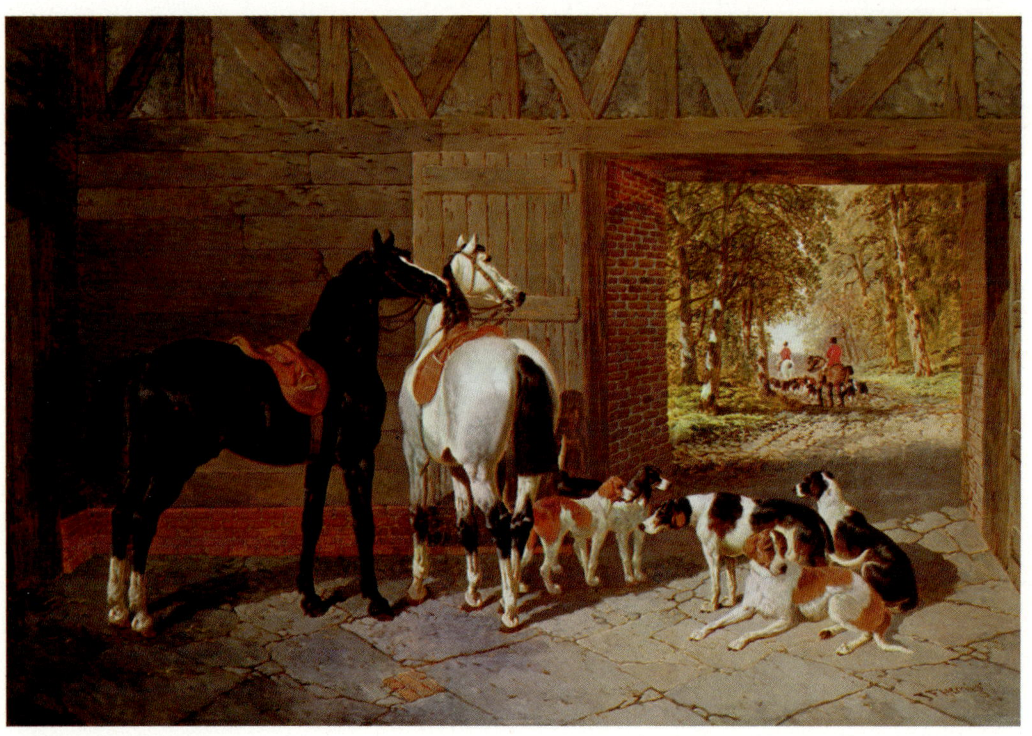

J. F. HERRING Jnr

58

Off to the Meet. Signed. 24 × 36 ins.

Courtesy:
Richard Green Gallery

List No 301

J. F. HERRING Jnr

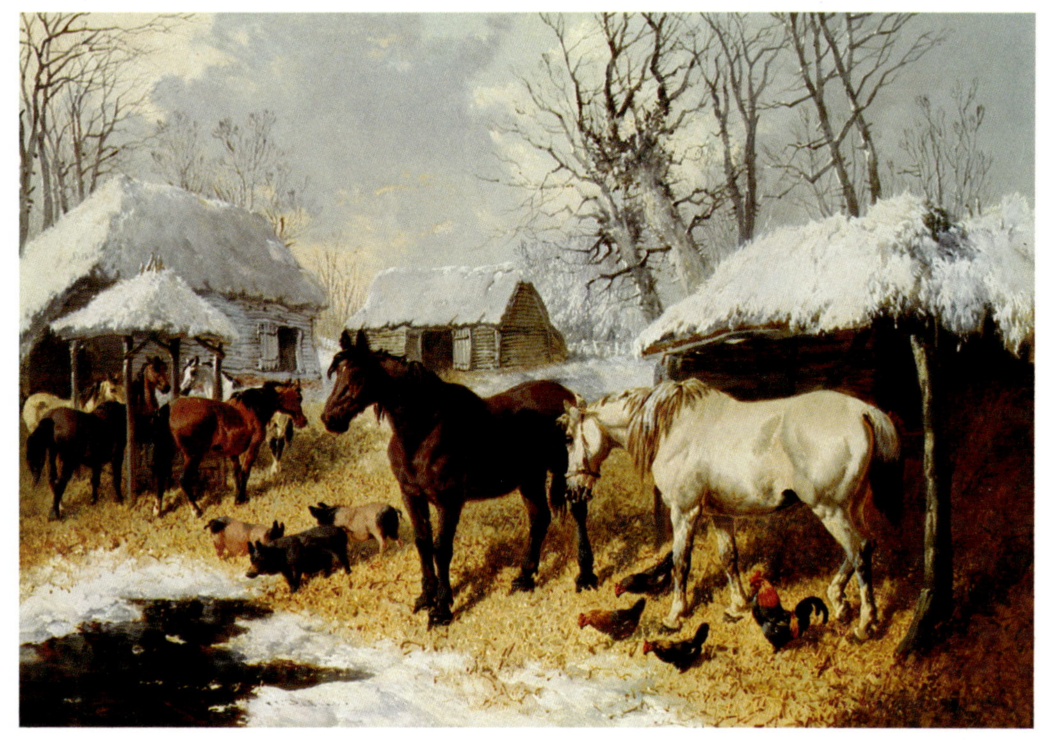

59

A Farmyard Scene in Winter. Signed. 14 × 20 ins.

Courtesy:
Richard Green Gallery

List No 302

BENJAMIN HERRING Senr

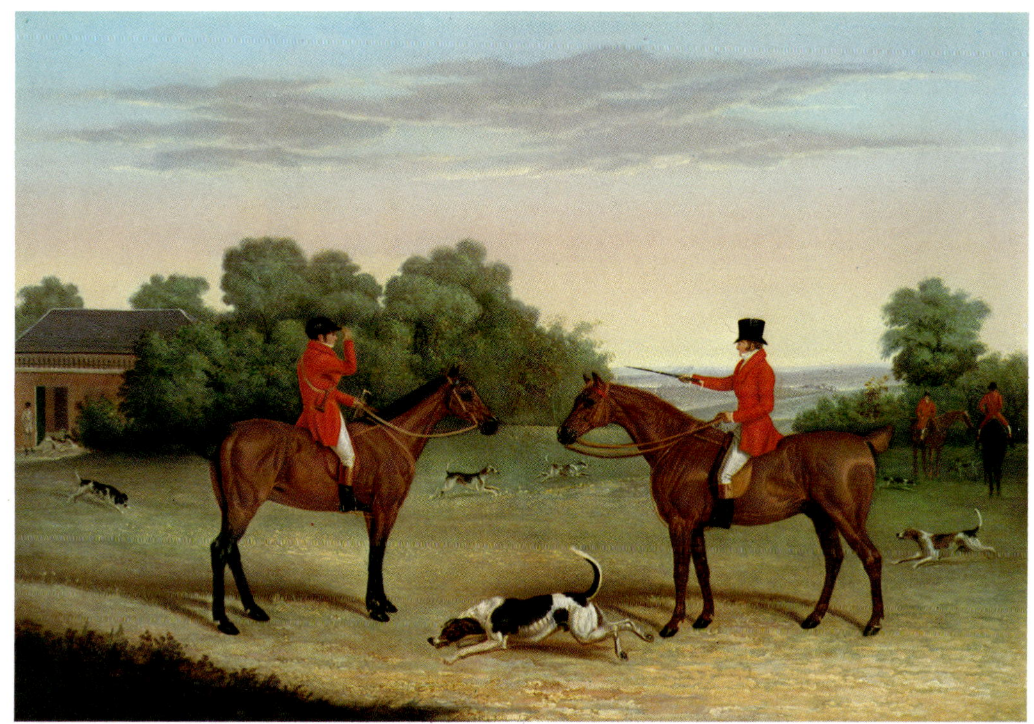

60

A Master and Huntsman outside kennels. Signed and dated 1826. 21 × 30 ins.

Courtesy:
Richard Green Gallery

List No 294

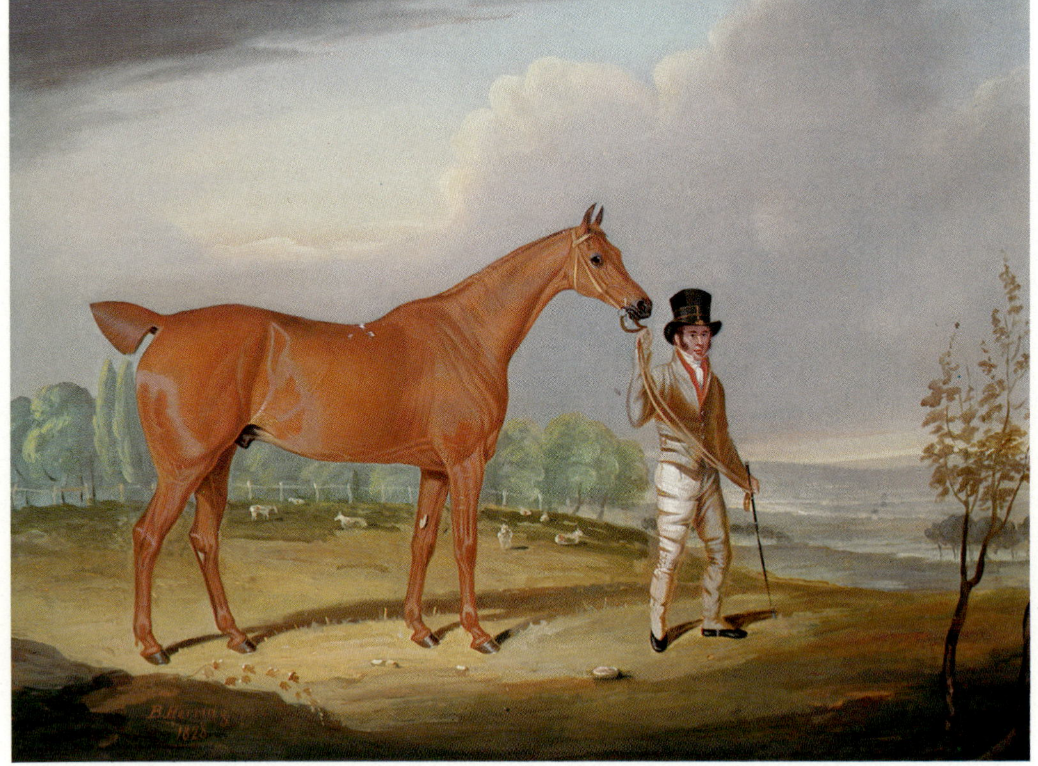

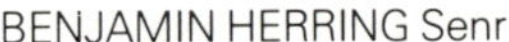

BENJAMIN HERRING Senr

61

A Chestnut Hunter with Groom. Signed and dated 1828. 12½ × 17 ins.

Courtesy:
Richard Green Gallery

List No 296

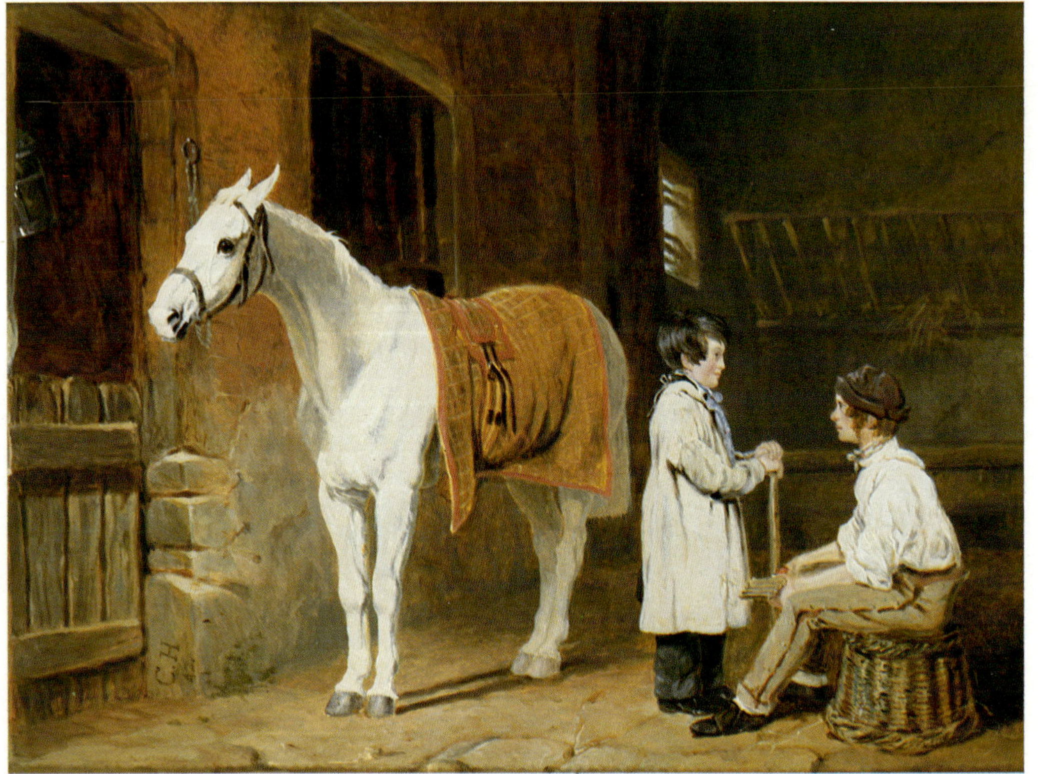

CHARLES HERRING

62

Stable boys with a grey cob. Signed with initials and dated '43. Panel 8¾ × 12 ins.

Courtesy:
Arthur Ackermann & Son Ltd

List No 306

It shows this lovely mare, bending an enquiring gaze on the spectator, in an elaborate landscape, with stables and a lake in the distance, upon which are reflected some white swans swimming. The tree foliage on the right of the canvas is rendered with a confidence that loses nothing because it is so faithfully defined; it still has more life than a typical tree by, say, Zoffany, generally considered his superior. The sky, so often such an attractive feature of Herring's work, is here rendered with the most delicate of touches. The 'provenance' of the picture, by the way, is faultless, to confound the doubters, coming down from the original owner who commissioned it.

He had, by this time, got well into his stride with his series of St Leger stars, and Manuella shows a distinct advance on his conception of Jerry, in the year 1824, when he triumphed in the York and Doncaster St Legers.

It is instructive to compare his version of Jerry, with that by the popular Yorkshire painter, David Dalby. This handsome black horse, without a trace of white about him, is shown by Herring with his hocks fairly well tucked under him, and his beautifully painted head is set on a real swan neck. His quarters look bigger, and his legs longer, than in the Dalby version. One feels there is an element of flattery here, because Dalby shows his hocks as 'running away into the next county' – as the saying goes, but his frame is more close-coupled with the fore-arms and cannon bones shorter than in Herring's picture. Also Herring painted the jockey, Ben Smith, with far too small a head, which is out of all proportion, whereas Dalby has drawn his haggard features correctly. Although Herring's version is enlivened with a view of horses at exercise in the background, and the sweep of blue sky contrasts with the overcast sky in the Dalby, it seems that the Dalby is more true to life, if not so fashionably slick as the Herring.

One wonders who commissioned these pictures as there was a major scandal concerned with the Doncaster St Leger of that year, that bears repeating, and shows Ben Smith to have been the 'most quiet and simple-minded creature that ever trod Yorkshire ground'.

It seems that a crooked owner, one Mr Robert Ridsdale, had bribed Harry Edwards to pull the favourite, Jerry. He then laid heavily against the horse, but the plot was discovered and Edwards was replaced on the day by Smith. Ridsdale and his friends were unable to hedge their bets in time, and lost a packet when Jerry won.

Time and again his truthfulness in equine portraiture was commended, and it speaks well of Herring's inborn ability and perseverance, to have achieved such a level of competence in such a short time, without professional tuition of any kind. It has occurred to me that he may, however, have had a few hints along the way from the successful, Charles Schwanfelder, who only lived a few miles away at Leeds, but there is no hard evidence to support this idea, as I mentioned before.

This was the time when he travelled round Yorkshire, from one country seat to another, painting the dogs and hunters of the sporting gentry such as Sir Richard Bellingham Graham, Sir Mark Milbank and others, apart from making his connection with the Hon. Edward Petre, the Zetland, Sykes and Searborough families, John Scott, John Bowes and others, who provided him with model winners of the St Leger. There were by the way,

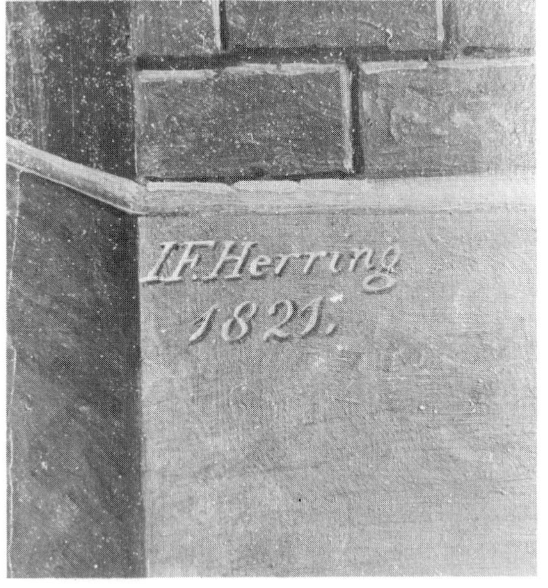

63

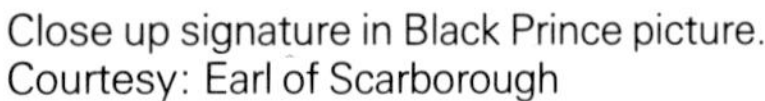

Close up signature in Black Prince picture.
Courtesy: Earl of Scarborough

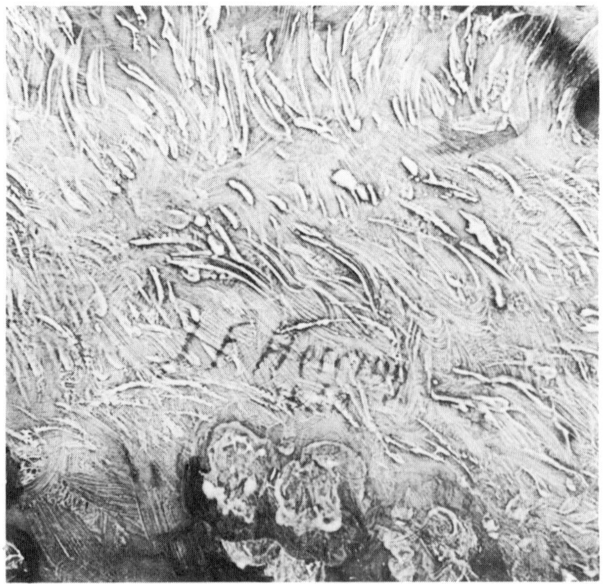

64

Close up of fake signature.

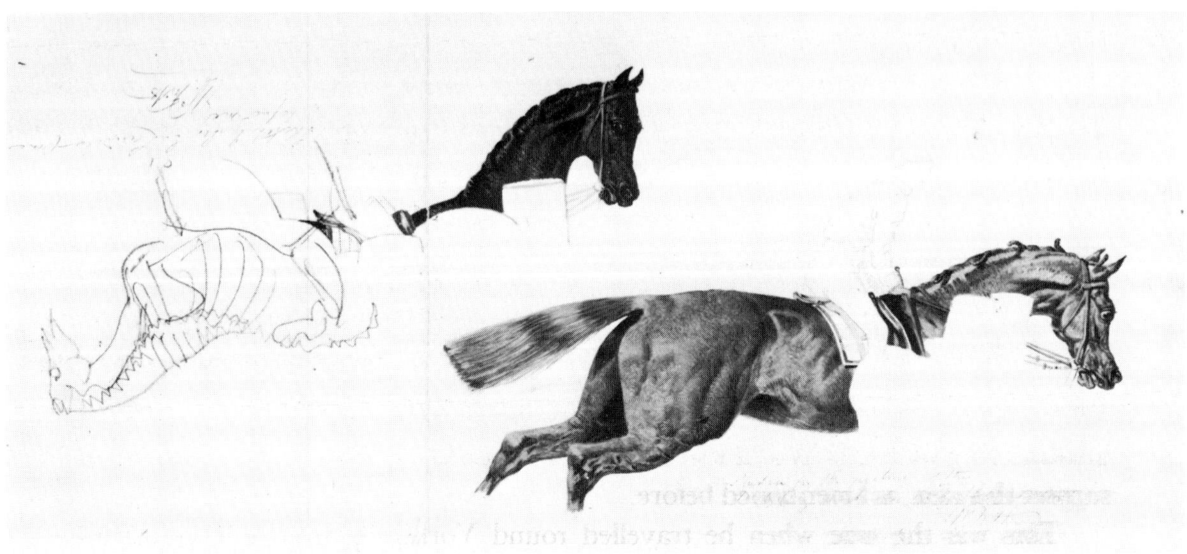

65

Herrings sketches for Wm P. Frith's 'Derby Day' and a sketch of a horse's skeleton by Sir E. Landseer.
Courtesy: The British Museum

several races known as 'St Legers' at that time, principally at York and Preston, but it was the Doncaster event that became known as the Great St Leger Stakes, and eventually consolidated its position as the last Classic of the year.

At this period, his brother Benjamin (*See Plate 17*) painted one or two rare studies of heavy horses, typical of their breed, such as Lord Bolton's 'Pride of England', a Shire (1829) and the Duke of Beaufort's Suffolk punch, 'Captain' (1815). Herring did paint a picture of a white-faced longhorn steer in store at the Tate, otherwise he left what might be called, 'breed propaganda' pictures to others such as Thomas Weaver and H. B. Chalon.

He also tried his hand at mounted riders, with a rather quaint group of the Sorby family of Bruton Hall, Sheffield (1828), and the podgy-faced young George Campbell, later Duke of Argyll, clad in Highland dress, perched on his pony in a landscape. These pictures are however, almost 'primitive' compared with his accomplished later works of Mad Jack Mytton and Mr Haigh of the Surrey foxhounds. The Squire Mytton, at full gallop, waving on hounds with his top hat, has more than a flavour of Ferneley's approach – which perhaps is not surprising as Ferneley was such a favourite artist of the hunting 'bloods'.

Perhaps the most pleasing of his group pictures of this period 1833 is the picture of Sir Mark Wood and Vespa – and of this there are two versions, fractionally different in size.

In one the signature is painted over the canopy of the stable door, and in the other under the step. In both the top-hatted Baronet stands holding Vespa, with his trainer leaning over the stable door, and a groom holds a shining white hack on the left. The poses, the frieze-like arrangement and the colouring are exactly alike in both versions, except for a difference in the skies. In one a slightly mauve, thundery sky grades off to a lighter tone on the left, whilst in the other, bright sunlight breaks through high-flying clouds overhead.

This must be an instance of Herring himself painting two versions, and varying the sky to his taste – although the shadows do not vary, which perhaps they should. A copyist would surely have painted the skies in a similar manner, whereas the artist himself felt free to change them. There is another typical instance of a small variation in two similar pictures in a much later work of Meopham stable.

How he found the time to paint such perfect copies of his own work when he had so many commissions on his hands is a mystery. He often painted a single portrait of a winner, then a view of the start with other horses, and also the finish of the race as well. At this time, moreover, his sons were too young to be of any assistance. One has to remember, too, that most commissions involved considerable travelling to accomplish, in the days when there were no 'inter-City' expresses.

It was not uncommon, in those days, for artists to paint versions of their more important pictures: James Ward did three of his famous group of an Alderney bull, cows, goats and sheep, called 'Protection' at the Victoria and Albert Museum, with slight variations in the sky too. In more recent times, Sir Alfred Munnings painted two versions of his great picture of Hyperion, but that was because Lord Derby was not satisfied with it. Munnings also copied his own composition of his wife and himself on the terrace outside

Castle House, merely substituting a different horse in the second, for the one his wife was riding in the first.

At this juncture, it is appropriate to consider the question of the form of Herring's signature, to which we have alluded.

In the early work the signature slopes to the right, and is filled in with a shadow line, e.g. brown and yellow or red and brown. The Earl of Scarbrough has a charming work of 1821 which shows this characteristic, and it is also painted into the brickwork of a wall – a favourite device. But Herring soon settled for a backward-sloping hand, which remained constant for the rest of his career. As his hand-writing – which was very beautiful – exhibits a pronounced slope to the right, this seems to have been a deliberate choice, perhaps to give the effect of being in the same plane as the ground.

His pictures of horses were signed on the left, or the right, with the horse's name sometimes inscribed in the centre. Usually done in brown paint, the 'J', 'F', and 'H', were drawn with serifs, the final 'g' showing a hint of a flourish. In some pictures, he seemed to take a delight in hiding the signature amongst the foliage, along a wall in the background, or even up the side of a stable-door post, and it often requires a glass to discover it.

The earliest date the writer has been able to find when he added 'Senr' to his work, is in an attractive small panel of the Earl of Lichfield's chestnut colt, Elis, the St Leger winner of 1836. His eldest son, John Frederick, was not born until 1815, so it rather looks as though he was already afraid of competition although JF Junr would only have been 21 at the time!

Nevertheless, it is possible to distinguish the two. For a start, many of JF Junr's pictures are signed, 'J Fred Herring', which, as he was known as 'Fred', points surely to his authorship. Also the actual writing of the name, lacks the characteristic care, serifs and backward slope of his father's. It was often inscribed with a peculiar convex curve, too. I don't personally think he would ever have added 'Senr' to his own signature. This solves the problem of all those pictures assigned to JF Junr, but of horses dating from long before he was in action, which he must have copied from his father's work, or even from the engravings from them, if the originals were not available. In most cases, the horse's name is followed by the date it won a race, or was painted by his father, with the additional date of when JF Junr painted it.

Apart from these considerations, JF Junr completely lacked the anatomical knowledge and sheer painterly expertise of his parent. His hunting or 'chasing scenes for instances, are brushed in, in a careless, almost impressionistic manner, totally at variance with Herring's 'facture'. Later in the 50's and 60's, when he was exhibiting on his own he painted numerous farmyard scenes, which, like his father's, contain groups of horses, cattle and poultry, but are more fussily detailed, and have herbage and foliage enriched with spots of colour. That is not to say that he did not assist his father in various pictures of such scenes, where Herring did not scruple to append his own signature.

There is no fear of ascribing any of the great classic winners to Herring's youngest son, Benjamin, for although he had a pretty talent, he was only born in 1830, so would not have been competent until the 1850's, by which time the family had moved to Kent, and other subjects were in vogue. Benjamin usually signed in red paint, backward sloping, and his palette tends to be much more pastel than the rest of the family's. Lady Macfadyen has a hunting scene and a most intriguing little picture of a village labourers' procession by Benjamin, which repay study.

When we come to Charles, Herring's favourite son, however, the plot thickens, for he was a clever and sensitive artist. His letters testify to the fact that he worked with his father – if not for him, and received £500 a year to do so. He was, therefore unassuming enough to allow his father to take the credit for their joint efforts. Only one of his own works, of a horse in a stable, signed unmistakably with his initials, CH, has come to light in recent years, and this was painted when he was only 17.

It already demonstrates his remarkable precocity in handling paint, and indeed this fluid technique, much more in Landseer's manner, became the predominant feature of Herring's later works. Charles was born in 1828, and died at the age of 28, in 1856, so for about ten years it is hard to separate the work of father and son. Charles did exhibit on his own account at the Royal Society of British Artists, so there must be a number of his own works somewhere to be found. I am inclined to think that the prevalence of rabbits, ducks and hens in this period, points to Charles's fondness for the family animals.

But Herring did not only paint in collaboration with his own family, he also carried out commissions with other artists.

As we have seen, he painted the race-horses in pictures for the Duc D'Orleans of racing at Chantilly, with the French artist, G. Campion; the horses in the picture of the Doncaster Gold Cup with James Pollard; the horses for a charming work, 'Barney will ye no let the girls alone?' (York Art Gallery), with Thos Faed, the Scottish painter. He also put in, or at least provided the models for, W. P. Frith's race-horses in his Derby Day picture. He – and Charles – created the horses on which the Royal personages are mounted, in the pictures in the Queen's collection, of the Prince Consort, Queen Victoria, The Emperor Louis Napoleon and his Empress of France. He also collaborated with Henry Bright and Baxter in some history pictures of Cavaliers and Roundheads. He, Sir Edwin Landseer and J. Phillips combined in a picture of a smith at work in his forge (which used to belong to Lord Leith and has been stolen). Lastly, several joint works with a landscape painter called 'Rolfe' are listed in the catalogue of the British Institution. This could have been Alexander Rolfe, noted for his country fishing landscapes, who was the father of his daughter-in-law, JF's wife, and a relative of his brother, Charles's wife.

The other great co-operative venture in which he took part was the panorama of the 'Overland Route to India', mentioned previously, where the overall design was carried out by two scenic artists, Telbin and Greives, and he and his son-in-law, Harrison Weir, who married his daughter Ann, were responsible for the camels and horses and other beasts, painted life-size. A sketch of one of these panels, or a preparatory study reminiscent of a J. H. Laporte, fortunately still survives in the collection of a direct descendant of his youngest daughter, Jennie, Mr John Warner (Plate 41).

What puzzles one rather about these arrangements, is that Herring himself, in most cases, could just as well have painted the figures in the paintings as his collaborator. All this activity though, surely points to the general acceptance and acknowledgment of his pre-eminence in painting horses, when there were, after all, a number of excellent equestrian painters active at the same time. The name of Sir Francis Grant springs to mind. He was a favourite at Court, had painted the Royal couple (and also Sir Tatton Sykes), and yet it was Herring that Boutibonne turned to, and it was the French artist who signed the paintings.

There are a few indications of his method of painting. He always had a sketch-book by him, dozens, of all different sizes were sold from his studio after his death – but few survive.

His water-colours show that he drew in his composition in pencil. A small oil in Lady Macfadyen's collection shows a background painted in, with signs of pencil marks round the study of a horse, apparently painted over the background.

One thing is sure, that is that his methods were sound enough to survive the years, and all the 'restoration' needful in most of his works, which are after all over 100 years old, is a careful cleaning off of old varnish and a re-varnishing. This is in contrast to so many of Stubbs's works that have come to auction in recent years, which have been heavily over-painted, when damaged by the passage of time or accident.

The water-colours I have seen are usually painted on a grey paper, where the flickering touches of colour outline the forms, and much of the paper is left bare.

I have said that for someone wishing to possess a Herring, but with a limited purse, a good engraving is sometimes an agreeable substitute, and even here, prices vary widely, according to the state of the print. Reference to the catalogue of prints will give an enquiring buyer a key to what is required, but caution should be exercised.

Modern prints are on sale, which, though from the old plates, are sometimes very worn and unsatisfactory. Moreover, they are clumsily painted in water-colour, and the colours of the jockeys and other features are not always correct. The 19th century prints that were aquatinted are much more desirable – and costly.

Lowest in the scale come modern photographic reproductions on modern creamy paper, that have an indentation as of a plate mark round the picture, but are only worth a few pounds. These are the objects usually displayed in betting-shops to lend a sporting ambience to the punters.

It is pointless to suggest prices as they seem to go up all the time, but an attempt has been made in Appendix E to list some of the more important sales of recent years.

The enduring popularity of every form of racing picture must be because they strike a chord in the breast of the least 'horsey' of men. They can be found all over the world, too.

Now that a national collection of sporting pictures is at last being assembled by the British Sporting Trust for permanent exhibition at the Tate Gallery and the York City Art Museum, perhaps the fresh charm of these painters will come to be better appreciated. And not least among them will figure the name of John Frederick Herring, senr.

Appendix A

From Mrs A. M. W. Stirling's book

I

A LETTER WRITTEN IN RESPONSE TO ONE FROM MR CHARLES STANHOPE:

Stanhope wrote expressing a wish to see Herring again and regretting any apparent rift in their relationship that may have been caused by Stanhope's friendly criticism in the past.

Cottage Green,
Camberwell. Feb 28th 1848

(My Dear Sir) There are many men who are free from crime, but few free from Error. I was, I can assure you, delighted to receive a letter from you, the whole of which I read with delight, *except* the part where you say you could see I did not like you because you did not praise me. Before you made this observation, having so good a recollection of all circumstances connected with my extremely uphill beginning, you might have borne in mind at the time you allude to, you were considered one, if not the best, judge in the Neighbourhood, and moving in the best society for patronage, and every syllable you might utter derogatory to my then small ability, although not ill-meant, was like the Fable of the boys and the frogs, *death to me* – but I will not do you the injustice to say – *sport to you*. Forgive my using a familiar expression, viz: 'As it was in the beginning,' etc.

I don't think either praise or censure had anything at the time you speak of, to do with what you think was – dislike towards you. (It) was (I am now ready to acknowledge) *actual fear*. I then had a wife and an increasing family. I frequently heard 'Mr Charles Stanhope had said this,' 'Mr Charles Stanhope had said that,' I could not help myself; your judgment was consulted and you gave it frequently against me. Therefore, instead of dislike, mine was *dread*. I dreaded your seeing what I was doing, feeling you might speak against it the first time Art was mentioned where you might chance to be of the party.

Years have rolled on since we last met, and therefore I don't mind giving you a true version of what I formerly felt. And if you will have the goodness to look coolly on what is called a critic, I am sure your good sense will tell you they are the most dangerous of all persons who may enter a Young Artist's studio.

Their talent for criticism is often over-rated, & they go from one Artist's house to another chilling every attempt that thought and industry dictates; and with their harsh remarks, throw such a check, that the Artist's spirits become depressed, and what might, perhaps, with a little encouragement, have been a work, when finished, of considerable skill, is put down with disgust, never more to be look'd upon.

I am now, I am happy to say, completely out of the pale of this sort of thing, and am happy to say that my pictures are no sooner seen than purchased. I sold a picture last year for which I received £157 10, it was re-sold for 250 gns, and since for 500 gns. Certainly a price far beyond my most sanguine expectations when I was labouring at Doncaster.

I have quite given up painting simple portraits of Horses, unless allow'd to make them into subjects. I produced a painting a short time since in 15 hours which I refused 150 gns for. I'll tell you why – I did not chuse (sic) to let the copyright go with it. It is now in the British Institution. You will see Mr Vernon is a purchaser of one of my pictures, and which is chosen for the National Gallery.

I have now a stable which I have built wherein I paint all my animals, and I have 3 very clever horses in it, 2 I use in double harness, and the other, one of my sons uses as a hack. The carriage horses are both white, one of them is one of the 4 the Imaum of Muscat sent over as a present to our Queen. He is a pure Arab & one of the most elegant animals *in action* I ever saw. The hack is a black one.

I met Mr Collingwood some years ago at Brighton, and he spent at least a couple of hours with me talking over old times.

I am quite convinced to be an artist of any note, good models and a good light are most essential auxiliaries. As soon as I came to London I got both, and immediately went ahead.

What I have written, I hope you will not take in other light than a letter written from one friend to another. Had I thought otherwise, I should not have said what I did in the short account of my Early Life.[1]

I shall conclude by saying I shall be most happy to see you at my house whenever agreeable to you to favour me with a call, but should like to know a few hours beforehand in order to be at home to receive you.

My wife, you know, died in 1838. I am again married to a woman of the same age, for they were both born May 12th, 1795.

(Yours etc etc JFH)

2

LETTER TO MR STANHOPE FEBRUARY 17th, 1849

re engravings being made from his pictures

There are two new ones in mezzotint just out call'd 'The Society of Friends' & the other 'Pharoah's Chariot Horses', both circulars, the latter's the best that has appeared from any of my productions, it is 3 heads of White Horses & was exhibited in the British Institution last year.

3

LETTER TO MR STANHOPE MARCH 5th, 1850,

then a vicar living in Cheshire, thanking him for the gift of a Cheshire cheese, and describing his toil with the Panorama for the 'Overland Route to India'.

Ere this you must imagine I am the most ungrateful person you have for some time met with, but if so, perhaps a few lines will explain that away. I had accomplished the whole of my Exhibition pictures, viz: 3 for the British Institution & 10 for the Society of British Artists of which I am now a Member.

There is now far advanced a Panorama or Diorama, entitled the Gallery of Illustration, i.e. any subject is to be illustrated through the means of paintings *in distemper*, with occasional transparent and moving effects, & the subject now in hand is the overland route to India. As a matter of course, there are a considerable number of Animals introduced, & I was selected as the most popular artist for the purpose. Stanfield [*Clarkson Stanfield, a popular scenic designer?*] & Roberts [*David Roberts, a clever topographical artist, favoured by Turner?*] promised their aid and names, but up to this day have not got one step further. I promised & have *perform'd.* I have painted about 15 horses, nearly the size of life, as many camels, sheep, fowls, vultures & pigeons, but from not have (sic) been used to standing on planks, etc. & no setting down, have quite knocked myself up & have been from home to recruit. That is why your kind present has not before been acknowledged. My folk did not like to write for me, so it has been left undone. I have no less than 27 letters to answer. (I shall esteem your offering no less as coming from you. We *do* now and then like a *Toast*, with a glass of Burton and Welsh ale.)

You ask if Graves' print is finished. *No*, but very nearly. It looked beautiful when last I saw a proof. I find I have sold 2 out of 3 of the pictures I sent to the British Institution. I sold one this Nov. for 80 gns – a farmyard – snow.

[1] Herring evidently wrote an account of his early struggles for Mr Stanhope, which has unfortunately been lost.

I am glad to hear your Barnsley man gets on so well, I did not like quite his notions of grouping in his Game pictures last year; however it had redeeming qualities about it, & I shall expect to see something better this season. I have an invitation to go to Sheffield and should I go shall perhaps see him and his work.

With the kindest regards from my family and Self, etc. etc.

4

LETTER TO CHARLES SPENCER-STANHOPE, 9 June, 1861, from JFH

Headed – in jest – 'Born 14th August, 1795'
(Discrepancy, In records as 12th August, *1795)*

'It is really quite refreshing to see a letter from so old and respected a friend as yourself.

I am sorry to say that I am totally unable, though thoroughly willing, to pay my compliments to you in London. I am still too much an invalid to venture from home.

I have not been in London for nearly six years, and since last August have not had on a shoe or a boot. I was suddenly attacked with influenza which brought on bronchitis and then erysipelas which settled in my ancles (sic) just at the gartering place, below the knee it was 23½″ round – I thought the skin must have given way . . .

If you can make it convenient to call at Mr Jennings, 16 Duke St, Manchester Square, you will see two of my recent productions, 'Market Day', and 'A Village Horse Fair,' Indeed I should much like your opinion on them.

I have about 20 pieces here, *all* of which I think you would like. There is a short account of them in the Sporting Magazine for the present month, in a paper called the Omnibus, the first article in the number.

I have all my faculties yet unimpaired; my hands are as steady as when first you knew me.

It would be too much I fear, to ask you to run down here. Could you do so, by sending me word what train you would leave London Bridge, my carriage should meet you at E Tonbridge Station, as I live three miles on the London side of Tonbridge. If you should feel inclined to pass a night here, I have a bed at your service.

My children are all married, two of the daughters have families, the 3rd has not.

I have one small picture in the British Institute of an old white horse – by the bye, one of the two who took you to town from Camberwell, an 'Arabian'.[1] He never does anything, being sadly broken-winded, but he still makes a good model and I am very fond of him . . . I have a pony only 37 inches high.'

5

COPY OF A LETTER FROM JFH TO AN OLD FAMILY FRIEND, ROSALIE, THEN MARRIED AND LIVING IN AMERICA

(Lady Macfadyen's original)

Near Tonbridge Kent. Nov 11 1855
Meopham Park.

My dear Rosalie,
I must first beg you to forgive my seeming neglect in not answering your kind letter sooner. I have not got over your leaving England yet. 'Tis difficult to part with our friends and more especially when there seems but little chance of our ever seeing them again. Such I seem to think will be the case with you.

[1] Imaum.

When you left England you were but like a delicate plant, requiring every possible care; tho' it gives one much pleasure to hear of your welfare and happiness, I am scarcely able to believe it. Writing to you does not give me the pleasure I should wish; it may appear selfish, but so it is.

I cannot forget your skill in everything you undertook, and now Annie can sing very nicely, how glad I would I have been to see you sitting together. However we must all submit to our fate be it what it may! I cannot but wish you had the *same Husband* . . . and all the comforts you possess, but should like you to be within a day's ride of your old Friends.

You would be I am sure highly delighted with the place we now reside at. The Misses Gail (?) calculate upon their summer and winter visits as a restorative. They come down here for a fortnight and return quite other beings from what they were when they first arrived.

I must try and describe Meopham Park. It is pronounced Meffam. It was enclosed and the house built by Sherriff Kirby, a celebrated pin merchant in the City. It is distant from London by the Rail 41 miles to Tonbridge which is 3 miles to Meopham, by the road from Cornhill to our Lodge Gates rather short of 30 miles, but as we can get to London – including the ride to Tonbridge in an hour and ½ we prefer the Rail.

The Park is 30 acres, the Gardens, pleasure ground and orchards 5 acres and a half. From the lodge gates (which is where my coachman lives and whose wife attends to it) it is a drive of exactly a ¼ of a mile and up Hill.

The Dining-room is 30ft by 19 and looks into a conservatory. The Library and drawing Room are on each side of a good-sized entrance hall and are both (a) little in size being 20ft by 18. We have two fine kitchens, a butler's pantry and china closet, nine bedrooms 18ft by 11, a Granary over the Brew-House, 2 stables, and 2 coach-houses, over the Stables, hay chambers, and over the Coach Houses apple rooms. Piggerys, Cow-house, Farm-yard and cowshed, a very pretty Saddle Room, and a room to paint in 21ft square. We have also a field about 4 acres. We have 5 horses. An open and a close carriage, 10 cows, pigs, 2 donkeys, Geese, Peacock and hen, lots of Fowls and Ducks and 2 Dogs.

I fancy I hear you say whatever could make you leave the place where everything seemed so comfortable? (Cottage Green, Camberwell) It was as follows.

My former life has I fancy in a great measure acted on my general system. I was but 19 when I was a night coachman, in a very Cold bleak country, bordering on Scotland, and having been for years shut up in hot work-shops and not regularly inured to such rough work, consequently (at least I imagine so) it opened out my lungs and now I cannot face a fog or an east wind, in either of which I can scarcely breathe.

One day I left the house not very well, to go down the garden to the stables. I had scarcely got ½ way when I was obliged to return.

There had been a Manure manufactory erected by the Canal, on the London side, and to cause the decomposition they put acids, as vitriol, onto bones, and other animal substances, and the stench all round the neighbourhood is quite intolerable. It was this I met when I got into the House, the drains were as bad inside as the nuisance outside.

I said I cannot, neither will I, live here any longer. Send some one for the Times. The first thing I saw was 'to let with immediate possession at the neighbourhood of Tonbridge etc etc.' I set off the next morning by rail, saw the place, was delighted with it, came to an agreement, signed the lease for 7, 14 or 21 years, and was here installed in about a fortnight. Now for its advantages . . . we grow Hay enough to pay the rent, £180 per annum. Then we grow Corn enough to keep the Horses, the Gardens supply us with vegetables, and the orchard with fruit, but that is not the (greatest) advantage, 'tis this. When at Camberwell I have known 16 sit down at supper, *not one expected*, and I have known 9 bottles of wine, besides beer, drank after 8. Now here we have no droppers in, without a special invite. No loss of time and get rid of them for others.

You know in England everything depends on a name. I have one, and as such from the superiority of our Books in consequence of the light and facilities in landscape, Rural figures etc which we can command by a call or a whistle, that the pictures are enhanced at least 50 per cent in the Market, since we have been here.

In proof of which . . BANG . . . BANG, 'What's that'. Father, Father, the powder mills have blown up, and so they have. We live only a straight ½ mile from some powder mills, and we have just had five shocks that shook the house to the foundations. 'tis ½ Past 8 and very dark. When I sent out to look, to the gate that enters the pleasure ground, there were great flakes of Fire lying on the grass. I have sent down to hear if any lives are lost, for though tis Sunday, I believe they are always at work. The last explosion broke 3 panes of a Glass in the Entrance Hall door, that was about 4 years ago, two men were blown to Atoms. My coachman has just come back he says no-one is hurt, but in another 5 minutes the Men would have entered the Mills to remove the 2 Charges that have just exploded, another of the interpositions of providence. . . . I have only to send a Letter or two to London and say I have something to show, and down come the dealers, and clear the deck.

Have just now, one commission that I *certainly* should *not* have had, had I resided in London. Viz 12 pictures, of farming and agricultural subjects, various. The 12 are to be engraved, and bring out 11 as a work.

We shall have lived here next March 3 years, and the place, as Mr Saml. Gale said the other day when he and Eliza came down must be seen to be duly appreciated, it is always kept in beautiful order. We stand on a hill call'd Meopham Bank and have a panoramic view all round the profile of the Ground is thus

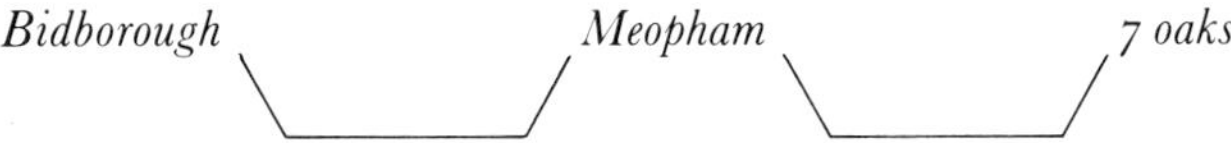

We are but 5 miles from the pretty little town of Sevenoaks, and 9 miles from Tunbridge Wells, and our Tonbridge Station is 3 miles short of ½ way from London to Dover where we can get in 1½ hours. The air is most salubrious. Where I used to walk at Camberwell a Mile I now walk 60 (?).

Mrs H. is as fat as one of my pigs. Jennie is full of life and spirits, they have the carriage every day at 12 for 2 hours ride, and go to Tonbridge for the letters. I am sorry to say Nancy is very unwell, and has been even worse since her last confinement. She has 4 children, 2 Boys and 2 Girls. Charlie is laid up and has been for 10 weeks with something of Rheumatic gout in his ancles (sic), but he bears it very patiently and keeps his spirits well. Fred (JFH Junr?) it is thought will lose his sight, which the doctors attribute to excessive smoking. He would smoke 6 pipes of Tobacco at a time. Ben is married and *quite tired* of his wife. She is a very industrious Woman, and always in her business, he wont stick to anything, and will always be in hot water, fond of making mischief, and no good to himself or anyone else.

Emma's husband is a great beast, and will not allow her to see even Nancy, so that for the last 3 Years none of us have even seen her. She has been very ill which no-one wonders at. The cause of the dissension was, that when Ma, Charlie and I were at Hastings, Mr Biggerstaff wish'd when he came to dinner on the Sunday to be Master of the Ceremonies, and take the head of the table, have the key of the Wine cellar, and beer and do just as he liked which *I* had told Ben and Jennie not to allow, at which they took tiff and have never spoken to any of the family (except Fred) since. He would drink the Sea dry, at least he would try if it happened to be wine. 'tis impossible in a letter of this description to help its being a disjointed affair, 'tis not like writing an Article which generally speaking is written several times over, and perhaps when revised scarcely an original sentence is made use of. In this I am obliged to write as my thoughts arise.

I am happy to say Miss Gale is carrying her years remarkably well, she is just the same Miss Gale she has been the past 48 years – which is the time I have known her – *behind* she looks only 2 or 3 and twenty. Her most failing point is her eyes, she is not safe out by herself, for she does scarcely see an object 'til she touches it. Mary is just the same as ever. Always ill, but when she sets her mind on anything, away she goes. Says nothing as to where she is going to any one, and comes back *for her? too late.* Yet she will do it, remonstrance is of no use. I shall never be at all surprised at her being run over.

Rebecca sticks to her hard work from 5 in the morn. till 11 at night wearing herself completely out. yet she looks better than usual. I do really think the short stays here have been very beneficial to her.

You may perceive by the writing I am tiring, but, I am anxious to make what I write interesting, how far I shall succeed, I cannot say. I send you a Memoir. The Portrait (? Corbould's?) I never considered good, that you must judge for yourself about. We have just now a N.E. wind blowing keenly, a sudden Change which does not agree with me. I generally keep pretty much in doors.

I am sorry to say that since I began this, Charlie has got the Rheumatism in both his ancles and is obliged to use crutches, crawls on his knees to bed, and has scarcely any use (in) his legs. He unfortunate(ly) wont be (told?). He has been wearing a very thin pair of slippers, and the cold and damp have now fixed in his ancles (sic), and I fear he will be some time before he gets well, for at present he is getting worse, his ancles swell frightfully. I mention'd this in the beginning of this epistle but then he could get about.

Jennie's music and Singing Mistress is a Mrs Hutchings, has been the round of England before she was married in the name of Miss Sinclair, her real name being considered by (?) not being sufficiently Aristocratic. *Carmen.* She has a charming voice, sings glees at sight and power enough to be heard at Church (for she is engaged there) when Organ is at full power. She is something like this (Drawing) very amiable. Much to be pitied, She had been married 8 years and no appearance of any family when she (?) aborted and Strong symptoms that she was likely to be a Mother. She has one boy and when she had been confessed at most a month, her husband after going into her room to say goodnight – dropt down dead on entering the room he slept in. She is dark with Raven black hair (?).

With kind regards from all here to yourself and Husband etc.

Remain My dear Rosalie etc.
JFH.

6

LETTER FROM CHARLES HERRING TO 'ROSALIE'

– a friend of the family then resident in the US

Dated: November 12th (Written from Meopham Park)
[*c.* 1855]

My dear Rosalie,
I dare say you think it very unkind of us not to have written to you before this – forgive us – you are not forgot tho' absent. I mean to write what little news I can muster – of course it cant be expected there is very much in the short space of years to relate. Let me see – I am very pleased and delighted that our old sister Rose is so comfortably settled and happy, for you know you were always considered one of our family. We missed you very much after your first absence – and do now, sometimes. I should like very much to see you and yours – you may perhaps come to old England again, if so you will find old faces to welcome you, as tho only a short time had elapsed since you left us.

Jenny and my Father have told you between them of our little family feuds, is it not a pity that we should not all be at peace with one another. We have one great consolation, however, *we* don't make the quarrels. An Uncle of my father's used to make a very terrible remark about dissension, he said – 'This life is too short for us to quarrel, my dear John'. This observation was to my father – I hope (have?) never forgotten – It was relative (?) (endemic) in some of my uncles, you know their love of bickering – I think my father's description of this place makes it unnecessary for me to say a word about it – only to corroborate what he says. It is a lovely spot, and in the Garden of England – Kent – It is one of England's noted beautiful counties. How I love the country, I hardly ever go to London, in fact I have only been there five times in three years, and each time only for a day – so you see I dont show much affection for the Metropolis.

I am quite the countryman you should see me in the Winter, very rough clothing – Breeches and gaiters and other garments to match – this you will say is rather different from the *Exquisite* you used to know at Camberwell.

I begin to find *dress* rather ridiculous – Friends think just as much of you in shabby or coarse clothes – it is not dress that is only necessary to our Happiness – I find that – My father and I trudge on jollily together – our two noddles or in other words Heads – do wonderful things in the world of art – we devote certain hours every day to painting, just enough not to fatigue or make us tired of which we are about – and the rest of the day we devote to anything – sometimes one thing sometimes another.

I like gardening (ie) Superintending the Gardeners' movements, I am fond of flowers, and I think I may say that we generally have as good a show as most small people – we are noted for Geraniums and Calceolarias – very great with the latter.

I wish you could just have a peep at us in the summer, you would think we lived in a juvenile fairyland, but I am not quite sure whether you would take our small family for Fairies –

Jenny says that perhaps I am the most 'H-airial' – I suppose she alludes to my enormous Moustaches. The above is a rough sketch of we rough country Faries, we have no wings, or we might pay you a visit.

At this present moment I have my left leg elevated to about 90 degrees – dont you think it looks very like years creeping on when a Handsome young Bachelor is troubled with gout or something very like it. There is one comfort, so I am told – it is aristocratic – what an empty consolation is it not? I am saying a great deal of myself, dont think me egotistical, for really I cannot think anything else, am I not vain? I dont ride Horseback now, it did not suit me, but I dare say when I am well that I walk on average 8 miles a day, pretty good exercise for a halfbred cockney.

You must recollect my pretty little Black mare, we have her still, she is as beautiful as ever but does no work. The Arabian we have still also, he is also a pensioner, we only use them for models, they are immortalised.

Poor Glaucus, the Italian greyhound is dead, he died here. We have a wonderful lot of pets here, I would tell you their names but that would be too much, they would fill a sheet by themselves. *My* particular pet is a Dog, he has a world of names himself, and what is most singular he answers to all of them. I will enumerate them, dont laugh, – Richard Turpin, Dick, Turps, Turpentine, Dickey, and Turpin, now I think this is enough for a little bit of dog. I will give you a sketch of him, some say he's ugly and other people Differ, you must give your opinion. When he is in motion he looks like an animated lump of rough black hair, for black is his colour.

We have another dog – a House dog, such a brute, very savage, he is a mastif – such a mouth.

We have become acquainted with some very nice families at Tonbridge. We make little picnics in the summer which go off very well. Tonbridge picnics are noted for one thing – they never forget the *salt*, which is generally the case at other places. Also in the summer there is a great deal of boating – the River Medway runs from Tonbridge to about half way to our house, all thro the meadows. I go, of course, at the proper time always to meet these little Parties, Principally Ladies, which is very interesting and exceedingly Pleasant and soothing to one's feelings.

I dare say you would like to know a little about the fashions – they are getting very Peculiar down here; straw hats with very broad Brims for young and old – in the former they are very becoming but in the latter very much t'other.

The Ridiculous is the way Bonnets are worn now – Bonnets – they are no such thing. I consider it nothing more than a little bit of coloured silk saturated with artificial flowers and then pinned onto the top knot. Boots are boots in England now – the Ladies will soon dress exactly like the Gentlemen, but speaking of boots, Ladies' Boots, they are all leather stitched with white toe-caps, thick soles, high heels lace up the front with brass eyelet holes, there is one very sensible thing about them, they do keep the feet nice and dry –

– that is something new for English Ladies to consider. I have said a great deal about your brother Charley, but before I finish this long rigmarole I will give you a sketch of myself, one that would be recognised by any individual with the slightest knowledge of me.

It is very strange (joking apart) that I am considered very like Louis Napoleon and Jenny is considered like the Empress.

I think certainly there is some resemblance as we have had a very good opportunity of judging, we having just put two horses into two pictures, one of the Emperor and one of the Empress, which are to be published. (ED: engraved) Do you think this like me, –

or do you think I am altered? Jenny is very like me and wears her hair turned back off the fore-head, some people think she is a little 'gone', I suppose they mean mad, well perhaps she is, we consider it a very pleasant madness, and are rather pleased she is not sane. She is very domesticated, as are cats – she has turned quite a dress maker, so are tailors. Her principal hobby is sleeves – she comes out wonderfully in that part of her 'Habiliment' – Excuse my bad French. My father looks like a jolly old Governor – which he is, and Mamma looks like his wife, – which she is, and they both together look like an old married couple – which they are.

I hope you will be able to make this out, I am not a first-rate writer – lost it all at Mrs Austin's – I cant write like my Paternal – never could and never shall.

I hope your mother is well, and Charlie and Anne, give my love to them. I must begin to draw in now, you'll (be) very tired reading this 'sea sarpint' of a letter. I am getting tired writing it as I am obliged to sit very awkwardly on account of my crippled ankle – not tired of writing to you for I could keep on telling you little bits of news for a considerable time.

Now goodbye, Dear sister Rosely (sic) – give my kindest regards and wishes to your husband and tell him I hope we may one day be acquainted.

Love to yourself and a kiss to each of your *little* ones,

from yours ever sincerely,
Charley.

Appendix B

I

J. F. HERRING'S LAST WILL AND TESTAMENT

THIS IS THE LAST WILL AND TESTAMENT of me JOHN FREDERICK HERRING of Meophan Park Tonbridge in the County of Kent artist I appoint my dear Wife Sarah Herring my brother Francis Herring of Globe Wharf Kent Road London Gentleman and George Daniel Warner of Tonbridge in the said County of Kent Gentlemen to be Trustees and EXECUTORS of this my Will.

I give and bequeath ALL MY PERSONAL ESTATE AND EFFECTS of which I may die possessed of what nature or kind soever unto my said Wife the said Francis Herring and George Daniel Warner upon Trust as soon as conveniently may be after my decease to sell get in and convert such part thereof as shall not consist of money or securities for money and to stand possessed of all monies to arise from such sale and conversion and also of such part of my said personal estate as shall at the time of my death consist of money or securities for money upon trust after payment thereout of any just debts funeral and testamentary expences to invest the residue thereof in the names or name of the trustees or trustee for the time being of my Will in or upon any of the Public Works funds or securities of the United Kingdom or any real securities in England with liberty for the said trustees or trustee with the consent in writing of my said Wife and after her decease with the consent in writing of my daughter Jane Herring hereinafter mentioned whilst she shall continue unmarried to vary and transpose the investments from time to time for any other investments of the description aforesaid and upon further trust to pay to or permit and empower my said Wife to receive the annual income of the said monies or the stocks funds and securities whereon the same shall be invested during her natural life to be applied by her to and for her own use and the use of my said daughter Jane equally so long as my said daughter shall live and remain unmarried.

But should my said daughter Jane die in the lifetime of my said Wife or be previously married then I direct that my said Wife shall receive and enjoy the whole of such interest dividend and annual income to and for her own use absolutely during her natural life and from and after the decease of my said Wife leaving my said daughter Jane surviving her and unmarried then I direct my said trustees or trustee to pay to or permit my said daughter Jane to receive the whole of such interest dividends and annual income during the term of her natural life or until she shall be married for her own use and benefit absolutely and from and after the decease of my said Wife and the decease or marriage of my said daughter Jane upon trust to pay and divide the whole of the said principal monies trust funds and securities equally between and amongst my daughters Anne the Wife of Harrison Weir of Peckham in the County of Surrey Artist Emma the Wife of William Biggerstaff of Camberwell in the County of Surrey Banker my said daughter Jane she being then alive and having been married and my son Benjamin Herring of Tonbridge aforesaid Artist share and share alike the share of each of my said daughters respectively to be paid to her to and for her own separate use free from the debts control or engagements of her then present or any future husband and her receipt alone to be a sufficient discharge for the same and in any case any of my said children shall have departed this life previous to the time of the payment and distribution of the said principal monies trust funds and securities then I direct that the share or shares of such of my said children so dying as aforesaid shall be equally divided between and amongst the survivors and survivor of them.

I devise to my trustees all real estates if any vested in me as trustee or mortgagee subject to the equities affecting the same respectively I empower my trustees to give receipts for all monies and effects to be paid or delivered to them by virtue of my Will and declare that such receipts shall exonerate the persons taking the same from all liability to see the application or disposition of the money or effects therein mentioned I declare that if my said trustees or trustee or any of them or any person or persons to be appointed under this clause shall die or disclaim or be unwilling or incompetent to execute the trusts of my Will it shall be lawful for my said Wife and after her death for the competent trustees or trustee for the time being if any whether

refusing or retiring from the office of trustee or not or if none for the executors or administrators of the last surviving trustee to substitute by any writing under her his or their hand or hands any fit person or persons in whom alone or as the case may be jointly with the surviving or continuing trustee or trustees my trust estate shall be vested and the trustees or trustee for the time being of my Will shall be competent to exercise the powers and directions given to the trustees herein named
And I exempt every trustee of my Will from liability for losses occurring without her or his own wilful default and authorize her or him to retain and allow to his or her Cotrustees or trustee all expences incidental to the trustee ship
Lastly I revoke all former and other Wills In witness whereof I have to this my Will contained in three sheets of paper set my hand to each sheet thereof this seventeenth day of June in the year of our Lord one thousand eight hundred and fifty six
JOHN FREDERICK HERRING Signed by the Testator as and for his last Will and Testament in the presence of us present at the same time who in his presence at his request and in the presence of each other have hereunto subscribed our names as witnesses – I Richardson residing at Meopham Park Tonbridge Kent – Sarah Rees of Meopham Park Cook

PROVED at London 13th Novr 1865 by the Oaths of Sarah Herring Widow the Relict and ffrancis Herring the Brother and George Daniel Warner the Executors to whom Admon was granted.

Effects under £4,000.

2

Obituary from the Art Journal *p 328, 1865*

Mr John Frederick Herring

This artist, known through a long course of years as a most successful animal painter, died, at his residence, Meopham Park, near Tonbridge, on the 23rd of September, in the seventy-first year of his age.

Though we call Mr Herring an 'Animal painter', the term takes in a wider significance than his works have generally shown, for he made horses his speciality more than the stock which frequent the pastures and the farmer's straw-yard; yet these, accompanied by the stragglers from the poultry-yard and dove-cot, are to be seen associated in some of his pictures. Like another veteran artist of the same kind, Mr Abraham Cooper, RA, Herring was self-taught, and traced back his love of the horse, and the desire to become its 'portrait-painter', to the fact of the 'professional' engagement with the animal in his early life. It is now nearly half a century ago since he left the metropolis – he was born in the county of Surrey – for Yorkshire, without any other special object in view, we believe, than to see the 'St Leger' run for at Doncaster, and seek employment as a 'whip'.

For several years after this he drove a stage-coach between Wakefield and Lincoln, and finished his career on the box as driver of the London and York 'Highflyer', a celebrated coach in its day. When not occupied on the road he was engaged in painting the portraits of favourite horses for the owners, and also races and racing scenes. During thirty years in succession, the winners of the St Leger 'stood' to him for their portraits, and when he had entirely relinquished the coach-box, Mr Herring devoted himself solely to that branch of Art in which he subsequently became distinguished.

Among the works by which this artist is distinguished – and so many of them have been engraved on a large scale, and have had a wide circulation, that they are well known both here and in America – are: 'The Baron's Charger', 'Members of the Temperance Society', 'Feeding Time', 'The Farmer's Pet', 'Duncan's Horses', 'Pharaoh's Chariot Horses', four agricultural scenes, entitled respectively 'Spring', 'Summer', 'Autumn', and 'Winter', 'The Country Bait', 'Quietude', 'Returning from Epsom', 'Market Day', 'The Derby Day', 'The Horse Fair'.

He also painted the portraits of several favourite horses belonging to her Majesty; one of these works was engraved in the *Art Journal* for 1856, as a portion of our 'Royal Gallery'.

Mr Herring was an old and valuable member of the Society of British Artists.

Appendix C

I

CHRISTIE, MANSON & WOOD SALE: 5 MAY 1864

16 Herring pictures owned by Messrs Fores, obtained direct from the artist

(to be sold in one lot)

1. THE START FOR THE DERBY – including 29 horses. 'Herring's chef d'oeuvre' (*Note in the catalogue that this was bought in for 1,450 gns*)

2. THE BLUE RIBBON OF THE TURF
(1) Saddling. (2) A False Start. (3) The Run In. (4) Returning to Weigh.

3. THE FLYING DUTCHMAN AND VOLTIGEUR running the Great Match at York for 1,000 sovs a side (The properties of the Earl of Eglinton and the Earl of Zetland, each horse having won both Derby and St Leger)

4. THE FLYING DUTCHMAN with Fobert, the trainer, and Marlow, the jockey.
('Mr Herring's portrait shows a colt remarkably well furnished for its years. As in a racer, they should be, the hind limbs are powerful, but not in that conspicuous degree which throws the forehand into comparitive insignificance. There is strength displayed in every part, and rarely do we see an animal more compact. All the parts are balanced, and in the perfection of the whole, rather than in the preponderance of any one, the favourite seems to derive his extraordinary capabilities.' – *Morning Post.*)

5. THE BRITISH STUD. Portraits of celebrated thoroughbred stallions and mares whose performances and produce are well known, being the progenitors of many of the celebrated winners of the day.
(1) Touchstone and Emma, (2) Pantaloon and Languish, (3) Camel and Banter,
(4) Muley Moloch and Rebecca, (5) Lanercost and Crucifix, (6) Bay Middleton and Barbelle
('This matchless series of thoroughbreds makes the blood dance through ones veins to think of the deeds of these favoured of the seraglio, while to votaries of the Turf – apart from the merit of these pictures as works of art, they are of great importance as preserving the portraits of the most celebrated blood of the present era' – *Sporting Magazine.*)

6. STABLE SCENES, Race-horses, Hunters and Cart-horses.
(1) Race-horses ('The scene is the interior of the saddling stable at Newmarket and its tenants are four cracks of the day; the effect of grouping and the variety of expression given, is admirable.' – *The Era.*)
(2) The Hunting Stud
('Represents the interior of the hunting stable with four stalls, in which there are four perfect pictures of what every hunting man would like to possess, bone and muscle – and symmetry of the most perfect cast, three of the animals are under the hands of grooms in workmanlike attitudes, while the fourth stands the admiration of his master and his friend' – *Bell's Life.*)
(3) Teams of cart-horses, baiting (eating)
('Shows the interior of the roadside stable, in which waggon teams are congregated, after and during bait – the positions of all are natural and varied, while the symmetry and useful characteristics are truthfully and admirable preserved' – *Bell's Life.*)

2

CHRISTIE, MANSON & WOOD SALE: 3 FEB 1866

of finished pictures and sketches in oil and water-colours,

by order of the Executors.

1. DRAWINGS – framed and glazed. 42 works of horses, mares and foals, smithies, stables, goats, horse fairs, ploughing etc. Studies for The Frugal Meal, Return from the Chase, Cavaliers, ducks and poultry.

Sold for sums from 1 gn (A Poultry Seller) up to 5 gns (Horses and Ducks. Top price: £8 for The Horse Fair drawing in pencil.

2. COLOURED SKETCHES (framed). 15, ranging from 3 gns Sportsman in a Landscape to £21 10s 6d for a Mail Coach.

3. SKETCH BOOKS. 24 sketch books of varying sizes, with numerous pencil drawings and some 'highly finished'. – also sketches of buildings and for the Overland Route from 1 gn up to £5 10s.

4. COLOURED SKETCHES (unframed). 8, mostly of horses: 6s. up to £3 7s 6d.

5. SKETCHES IN OILS. 48 horses heads, horses, dogs and cows from 1 gn up to £28 7s for a group of finished sketches in *oil on paper* of Priam, Blacklock, Bay Middleton, Queen of Trumps and Orville. Also a sheet of *outlines* of Priam, Orlando, Venison, Touchstone, Partisan and The Baron for £3 10s.

6. UNFINISHED PICTURES. 24, of Cavaliers and Cromwell's soldiers, mail-coach and hunt, bull and cow, and a design for a hawking picture etc. Top price £157 10s for Deer-stalking.

7. FINISHED PICTURES. 10, top prices £199 10s for Market Day, £189 for Horse Fair, £100 for An Interior with Horses, £73 for Shoeing.

8. FINISHED PORTRAITS OF HORSES. Out of 32 pictures, 23 of subjects of his series of Derby and St Leger winners, and other outstanding racewinners; two of Faugh-a-Ballagh (one unframed), two of Sultan (one, unframed), two of Whalebone. Also pictures of Arabians, sheep, a dog etc, (apparently not sold by artist.)

Lord Falmouth bought 5 – including the two Faugh-a-Ballaghs at prices varying between £6 10s to £15. The lowest price in the group was 6 gns and the highest £29 paid for Dr Syntax. *(NOTE – did he keep the originals of ones that were engraved, unless the owners bought them, or were these copies of his own?)*

Subjects as follows: Sultan, Bay Middleton, Flying Dutchman, Glencoe, Irish Bird-catcher, Stockwell, Faugh-a-Ballagh, The Baron, Orville, Emilius, Teddington, Whalebone, Touchstone, Camel, Surplice, Dr Syntax, Newminster, Beeswing, Gladiator, Grey Momus and Attila.

9. ARTISTIC ACCESSORIES. Several easels of mahogany, a female lay figure, an articulated lay figure of a horse, six plaster models of animals, drawing boxes, a camera, prepared drawing-paper – and a copy of Stubbs's *Anatomy of the Horse*.

10. FRAMES – 8 gilt, dimensions 11½ × 9½ ins; 29½ × 21 ins, 23¾ × 17½ ins; 33½ × 23½ ins.

Appendix D

THE HERRING FAMILY TREE

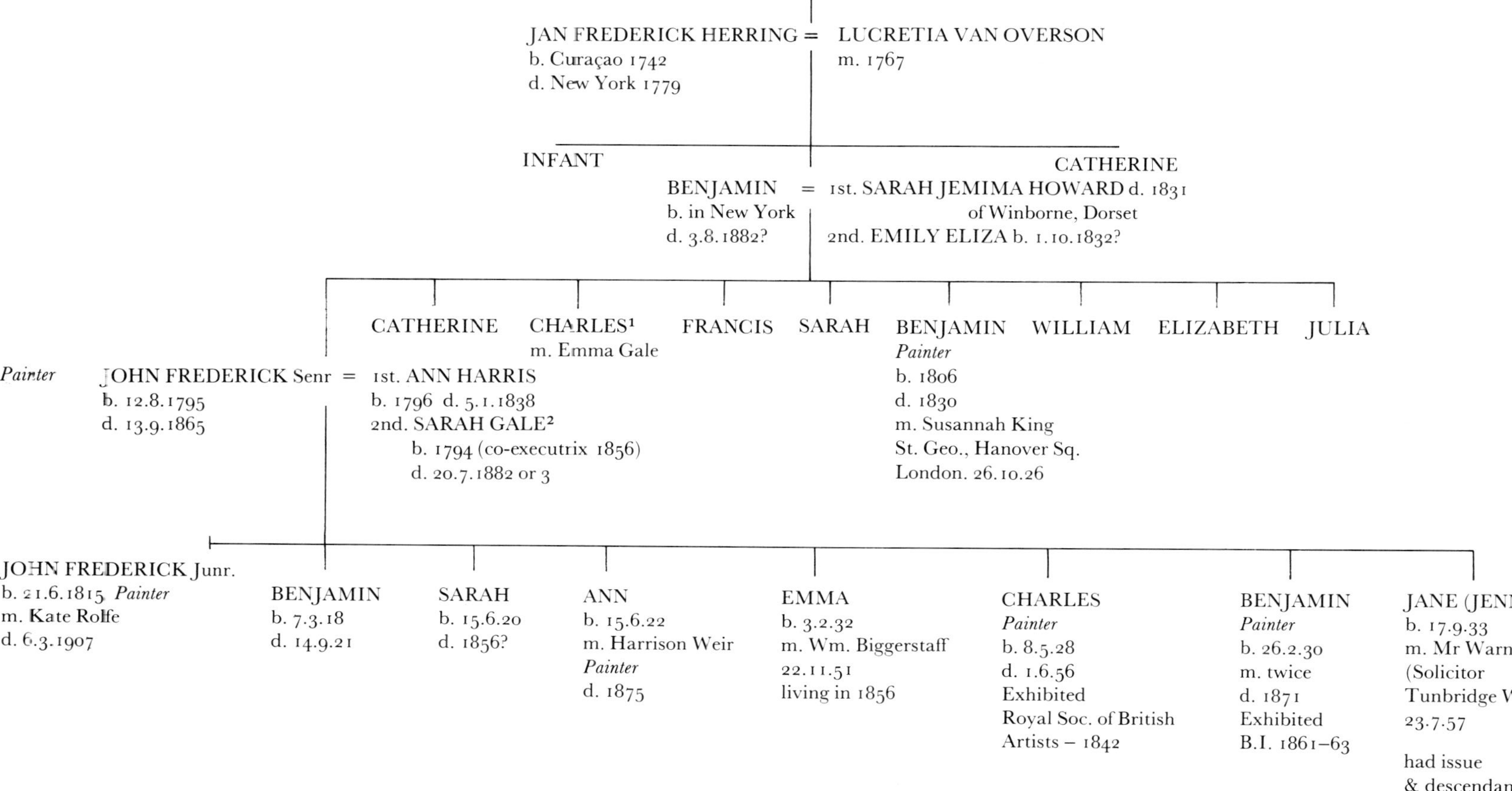

1 JFH Senr's brother Charles, m. Emma Gale in 1822, and had 10 children. His eldest son Charles, m. Louisa Hughes and had 9 children. His son, Leonard, m. Martha Anne Webster in 1884, and had 2 children, the elder his son, Ernest Leonard m. Irene Margaret Whittingham in 1913 and had 3 children, issue still living. His daughter Mildred Ethel m. John Douglas Halewood MRCVS and had issue still living.

2 See Appendix A1: JFH states he has married again a woman born on the same day and year as his first wife, i.e. May 12th, 1795, thus differing from this family information. Sarah's birth-date on the tomb-stone gives the year 1794.

Appendix E

I

COMPARISON OF PRICES AT TEN-YEAR INTERVALS

from: 'Art Prices Current', 1931–32; 1941–42; 1951–52; 1961–62; 1971–72
with some prices obtained by Stubbs pictures in the same period.

1931–32

J. F. HERRING Senr
At Home, £16; Ducks and Drakes, £12; Farmyard, £7; Gamekeeper's Cob, £19; Horses in a barnyard, $110; Three hunters chased by a lion, £5 (35 × 50 ins); Matilda, $1,500 (22 × 30 ins) chestnut mare, plaited mane, Jem Robinson up and John Scott, trainer, dated 1828; Pig in sty, £6; Racehorse, Beeswing (27½ × 35½ ins) in a loose box, signed, £26; Six-Mile-Bottom, Huntsmen in full cry (21 × 26 ins) to Lepper, £50.

NOT SIGNED: Farmyards, various, £6–£21; racehorse, Little Driver, jockey up, on Downs (21½ × 29½ ins) to Fores, £115; Mundig, jockey up, on Downs with other horses (8½ × 11½ ins) to Leggatt, £31; Over the green $50; Stratton Hunt, nr Bicester (15½ × 23½ ins) to Crisp, £11; Lord Middleton, portrait of, in hunting costume on horseback with hounds outside a mansion (Birdsall?) (11 × 13 ins) to Sabin.

J. F. HERRING Junr
Farmyard, $60 (22 × 36 ins).

Prices obtained by George Stubbs in same year: Dogs, £57; Dogs in a landscape, £57; Sir John Ramsden on a chestnut horse (40½ × 59½ ins) £21; Hunter and groom, £787; Waiting for master, $60.

1942–42

Coaching scene, £11 to Ackermanns; Grey horse, £15 (21½ × 28½ ins) to Goffs; Horses and pigs, £13; The Day's Bag and Feeding Time (a pair) (22½ × 33½ ins) dated 1850. £14.

Stubbs's prices: Fox-hunting (40 × 50 ins) £20; Four shooting subjects (29½ × 24½ ins) £304 to Gooden & Fox; Sportsman in scarlet (34½ × 46 ins) £162.

1951–52

From the collection of Edward Hulton – Charles XII galloping, won St Leger 1839, owned by Major Yarborough (27 × 35 ins) £399; Don John and other horses, won St Leger 1838, owned by Lord Chesterfield (26½ × 35 ins) £546 to Dunedin Art Gallery; Faugh-a-Ballagh in a box, won St Leger 1844 (27 × 35 ins) to Walter Hutchinson, £168; Industry and another horse, won Oaks 1838, owed by Lord Chesterfield (27½ × 35½ ins) to Gates *£546*; Merry Monarch in a box, won Derby 1845 (27 × 35 ins) £52. Other owners' prices – Van Tromp signed 1847, $350; Morning, £183; End of Day's shooting, £84; Farmyard scene, £33; another $300.

Stubbs's prices: Baronet, Sam Chifney up, £630; Farmer's wife and Raven, £304; Gimcrack, £12,600; Molly Longlegs, £1,050; Three broodmares at grass, £1,050; Turf, jockey up, £5,250.

1961–62

Beeswing in a stable, £150; Clydesdale stallion, £120; Squire Osbaldeston on Tranby, £99; Cotherstone, signed and dated 1843 (8¾ × 12 ins) £80; Doncaster Gold Cup 1826, $2,000; Firefly, £80; Flying Dutchman, black horse galloping, Chas Marlow up, signed and inscribed Derby and St Leger winner (41 × 72 ins), £1,732; Fortuna as fire screen (9½ × 12), £273; Jack Spigot and Fortuna – £787 signed 1824 (39½ × 39½ ins) from Mrs T. Orde-Powlett to Tryon; Leamington Hunt two whippers-in and hounds (35 × 50 ins) to Frost and Reed, £2,800; Lord Chesterfield's Industry, *£2,310*; Whisker, £840.

Stubbs's prices: Leaping Horse, £170; Racehorse in action, £230.

1971–72

By Benjamin Herring junr (dated 1871) Chestnut hunter and groom £460 to Richard Green.
By John Frederick Herring junr (dated 1907) Full Cry, £950.
By John Frederick Herring senr: Stableyard in Winter, signed and dated 1847 (27¾ × 37½ ins) £2,600; Cavalier and Lady on grey horses in Castle courtyard, signed and dated 1861 (49½ × 49½ ins) £1,200; Dr Syntax, a bay racehorse, £577 to Ackermanns; Ducks and ducklings by a stream (9½ × 11½ ins) £1,100 to R. Green; Happy Family, signed and dated (19½ × 26½) £3,400; Little Wonder, signed and dated 1840 (13½ × 17 ins) £504; Orville, a bay horse, winner of St Leger 1802, signed, dated and inscribed 1817 (13½ × 18 ins) on panel, £577; London–York carrier's wagon and London–Leeds Royal Mail, signed and dated on reverse (23½ × 35½ ins) £4,410 to Bailey; London–York Wagon outside Swan Inn, Grantham, signed and dated 1860 on reverse (23½ × 35½ ins) property of J. Rodney M. Vaughan, £3,150 to Allsopp.

Stubbs's prices: Brown and white dog in a landscape, £10,000.

2

PAINTINGS BY JOHN FREDERICK HERRING Senr

sold 1973–76 through Sotheby's

£70,000
Coach awaiting the change on the Great North Road between Newmarket and Lincoln. 48 × 73 ins. Signed and dated 1838. Sold on 31.10.73, lot 20.

£62,000
Vespa, Dark Bay Racehorse. 28 in × 36 in. Signed and dated 1833. Sold on 31.10.73, lot 15.

£37,000
Mr Richard Watts' Memnon, Light Bay. 30 in × 40 in. Signed and dated 1826. Sold on 28.4.76, lot 159.

£36,000
Sorby Family of Button Hall, Sheffield. 27 in × 39 in. Signed and dated 1828. Sold on 31.10.73, lot 23.

(This list excludes the Richmondshire Militia painting £40,000, see Plate 22)

Whilst every effort has been made to identify as many of Herring's pictures as possible, the list that follows is necessarily incomplete. Those numbered under their year's date (1–293) are known to be in private collections, or to have been sold by dealers or through the auction-rooms within recent years. They may, of course, include some listed as exhibited at the RA or elsewhere, where the few details preclude double-checking. Forty-two pictures in the Wm Woodward collection, USA, are listed separately. Since going to press, a number of his excellent works have come to light which, unfortunately it has not been possible to include at this stage. The Author and the Publisher would be grateful for any further information on the whereabouts of other pictures not included.

Even so, the total of 503, not allowing for duplication but adding works exhibited at the various Societies, is a respectable one for a working life (say, 1815–1865) of 50 years. Add to this the originals painted for the 167 engravings, 13 sets lithographed and 2 autotypes – making 182, and giving a total of 685 in all, again, not allowing for duplication, but considering that a possible four or more pictures may make up a set, it can readily be appreciated that such an output was the fruit of an exceedingly prolific career.

It is regretted that limitations of space have made it impossible to print more than a token representation of the works of JF jnr, Charles and Benjamin jnr.

General List of Paintings

IN CHRONOLOGICAL ORDER

1815

1 **Filho da Puta**. Won St Leger 1815. 34.5 × 45 cm. Signed. Brown horse standing against a wall, facing left jockey up. Doncaster Art Gallery.

1819

2 **Walton**. Sir John Shelley's bay colt in a stable-yard. Signed, inscribed and dated 1819. 18 × 24 ins. Bred by Sir Hedworth Williamson, by Sir Peter Teazle out of Arethusa in 1799. Won the King's Plate, Newmarket, 1803, and after running second in the Craven Stakes, was sold to Sir John Shelley in 1804. Altogether he won three races in 1803, seven races in 1804 and five races in 1805, all under Sir Hedworth Williamson's name. He became a very famous sire.
Exhibited: Richard Green Gallery, 1978.

1820

3 **St Patrick**. Chestnut facing left, judge's box in background. Won St Leger 1820. Signed and dated 1820. 34 × 44 cm. Doncaster Art Gallery.

4 **Jack**. Mr Edwin Sorby's favourite hack by river at Button Hall, Sheffield. (By descent.) Signed and dated 1820. 21½ × 29 ins. Sold at Sotheby's.

5 **The Richmondshire Yeomanry on manoeuvres**. Signed and dated 1820. 41 × 53¾ ins. Inscribed on stretcher: 'Mr Herring at Gore Hartley Esq. Middleton Tyass, to be left at Scotch Corner'. Exhibited: Sotheby's. *(See Plate 22.)*

1821

6 **Mare and Foal** in a landscape. Signed and dated 1821. Oils on panel, 21½ × 29½ ins.
Sold through Spink & Son. *(See Plate 67.)*

7 **Black Prince** held by his trainer. Signed and dated 1821. Owned by The Earl of Scarbrough. *(See Plate 66.)*

8 **Terriers in a Stable**. Signed and dated 1821.
Sold at Sotheby's for £500.

9 **Magistrate**. Signed and dated 1821.
Ex collection: Walter Hutchinson.

1822

10 **The London–Edinburgh Royal Mail Coach**, at the Blue Bell Inn, Barnby Moor, Yorks. Signed and dated 1822, 28 × 36 ins. The Blue Bell Inn, one of the largest posting establishments in the North, was owned by Mr George Clark, an early patron of Herring's.

Private collection. Exhibited: Arthur Ackermann & Son Ltd 1965.

11 **Dick** – a black and white winning greyhound, in a landscape. Signed and dated 1822. 30½ × 42 ins. Painted for Mr George Clark (see above), by descent.
Private collection. Exhibited: Arthur Ackermann & Son Ltd 1965. *(See Plate 78.)*

12 **Theodore**, with John Jackson up and his lad at Doncaster, facing left. Won St Leger 1822. Signed, inscribed Theodore and dated 1822. 30½ × 44 ins. Bay colt by Woful ex Rosalind foaled 1819, owned by the Hon. E. Petre, trained by John Croft. Won a race at Richmond as a two-year-old, the St Leger and three other races, 1822, Gold Cup at Manchester, 1824; sold to Mr Carleton and won the Gold Cup and the Member's Plate, Edinburgh 1825. Theodore was tried a few days before the St Leger with his stable companions, but owing to the bad state of his feet he was beaten in a few hundred yards. So great a cripple was he, that when brought to the post for the race, it is said that Jackson burst into tears exclaiming: 'What! ride such a cripple as that?' He won at 100-1. *(See Plate 1.)*

1823

13 **The Duchess's Ponies**. Signed and dated 1823. 66 × 90.2 cm. A pair of ponies harnessed for a carriage, with the initials E.D. (Elizabeth Darlington) on the harness, led by a coachman in livery, in the stable yard at Raby Castle.
Collection: The Late Lord Barnard. Exhibited British Sporting Paintings 1975.

14 **Portrait of Miss Drabwell**. Signed and dated 1823. 31½ × 26½ ins. Small full-length, standing with a black hunter by a pillar, and spaniel with his paw on her straw hat.
Sold at Christies.

15 **Barefoot**, a chestnut horse with T. Goodisson up wearing harlequin silks and striped cap, a groom to the right, standing on a race-course. Won St Leger 1823. Signed and dated 1823. 14½ × 19 ins. Subject engraved by T. Sutherland and published by Sheardown, Doncaster, 1823. Barefoot, foaled in 1820 by Tramp ex Rosamond, bred by Mr Richard Watt.
JD Sale at Sotheby's, Part Three.[1] Exhibited: Arthur Ackermann & Son Ltd 1965.

16 **Little Driver**, with W. Clift up, facing right. Signed, inscribed and dated 1823. 22 × 30 ins. Brown gelding by Ardrossan foaled 1819, owned by Mr Cleaver and subsequently by W. Hepworth, 1823, then by Capt Berkeley, Capt Locke, Mr Williams and Sir William Lumley. Between 1823 and 1827 Little Driver won 15 races including the King's Plate at Doncaster, 1823.
Exhibited: Arthur Ackermann & Son Ltd 1971. *(See Plate 69.)*

1824

17 **Jack Spigot**, dark bay in extensive landscape, stables right, facing right. Won St Leger 1821. Signed and dated 1824. 40 × 50 ins.
Ex collection: Lord Bolton. Sold for £14,700 Christies 1964.

18 **Jerry**, Ben Smith up and trainer at Doncaster. Owned by Mr Gascoigne. Won York St Leger and Great St Leger, 1824. Signed and dated 1824. 21½ × 29½ ins. Black colt by Smolensko. *(Plate 2.)*

19 **Don Antonio**, held by a groom on Newmarket Heath, the owner, Mr Ferguson and trainer standing by, taking snuff. Signed, inscribed and dated 1824. 22 × 30 ins. Foaled in 1821, Don Antonio was by Octavian and bred by Mr Ferguson, who sold him in 1825 to Mr Bell. He was bought by Mr Skipsey in 1826 when he won four races. In 1827 he won five races, including the Winyard Stakes at Stockton and the Silver Cup at Durham.
Ex collections: Charles Sweeny Esq., Mr and Mrs Jack Dick. Exhibited: Arthur Ackermann & Son Ltd 1965 and Richard Green Gallery 1974. *(See dust jacket.)*

1825

20 **Figaro** with J. Lye up. Signed and dated 1825. 22 × 30 ins. By Haphazard out of a mare by Selim, bred in 1818 by Mr Joseph Rogers. Sold at Ascot 1822 to the Hon. Orde Powlett. Second in Derby

[1] 'JD Sale' refers to the sale by Mr & Mrs Jack R. Dick conducted in four parts by Sotheby & Co in 1973, '74, '75 and 1976.

J. F. HERRING Senr

66

Black Prince held by his trainer. Signed and dated 1821. 45 × 56 ins.

Courtesy:
The Earl of Scarbrough

List No 7

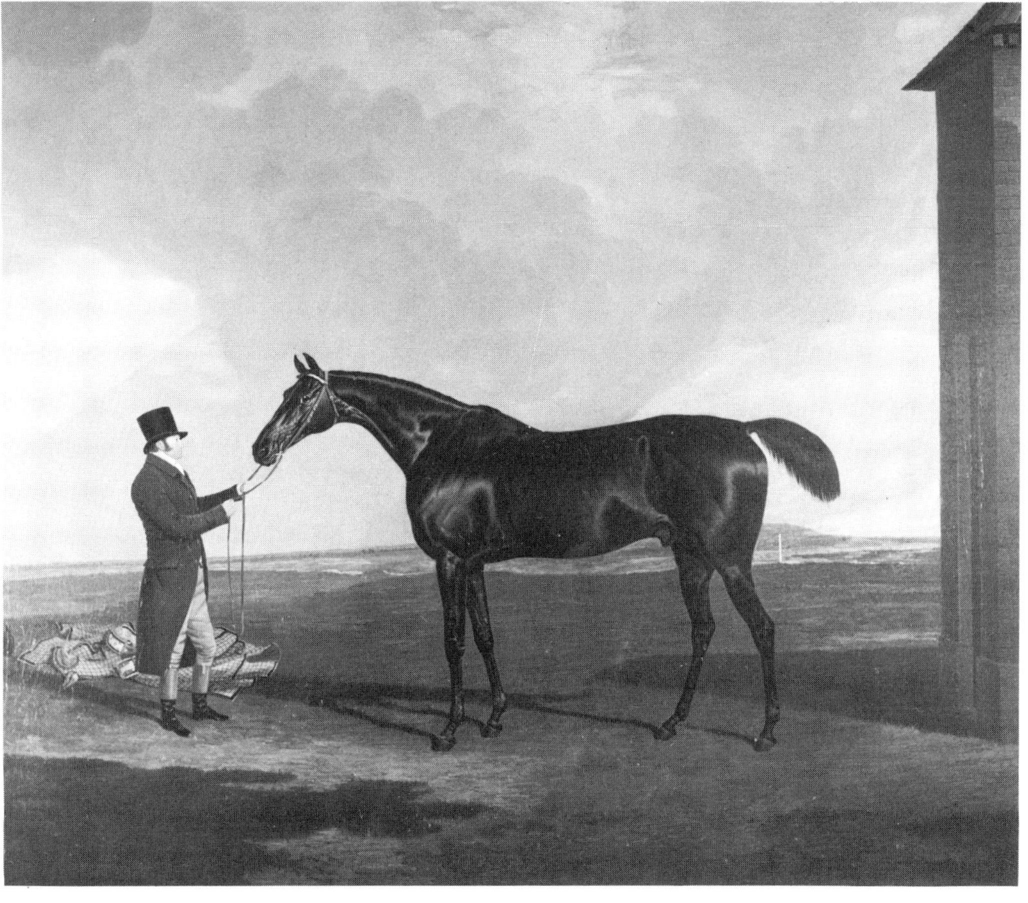

67

Mare and Foal. Oils on panel. Signed and dated 1821. 21½ × 29½ ins.

Courtesy: Spink & Son Ltd

List No 6

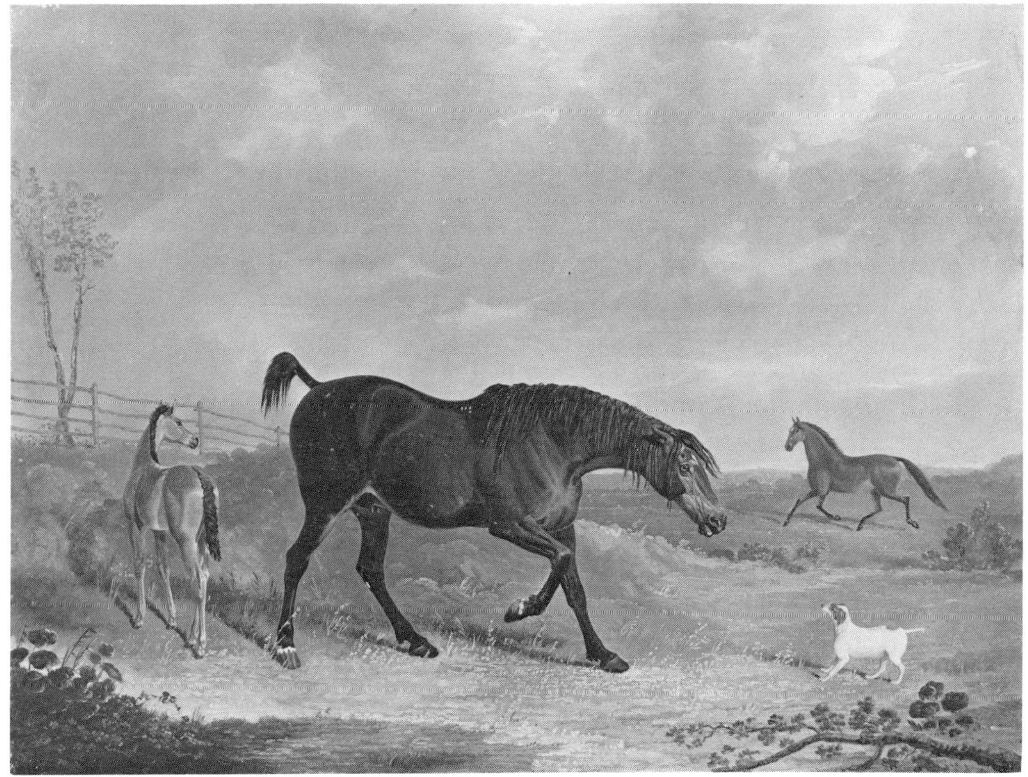

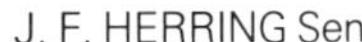

J. F. HERRING Senr

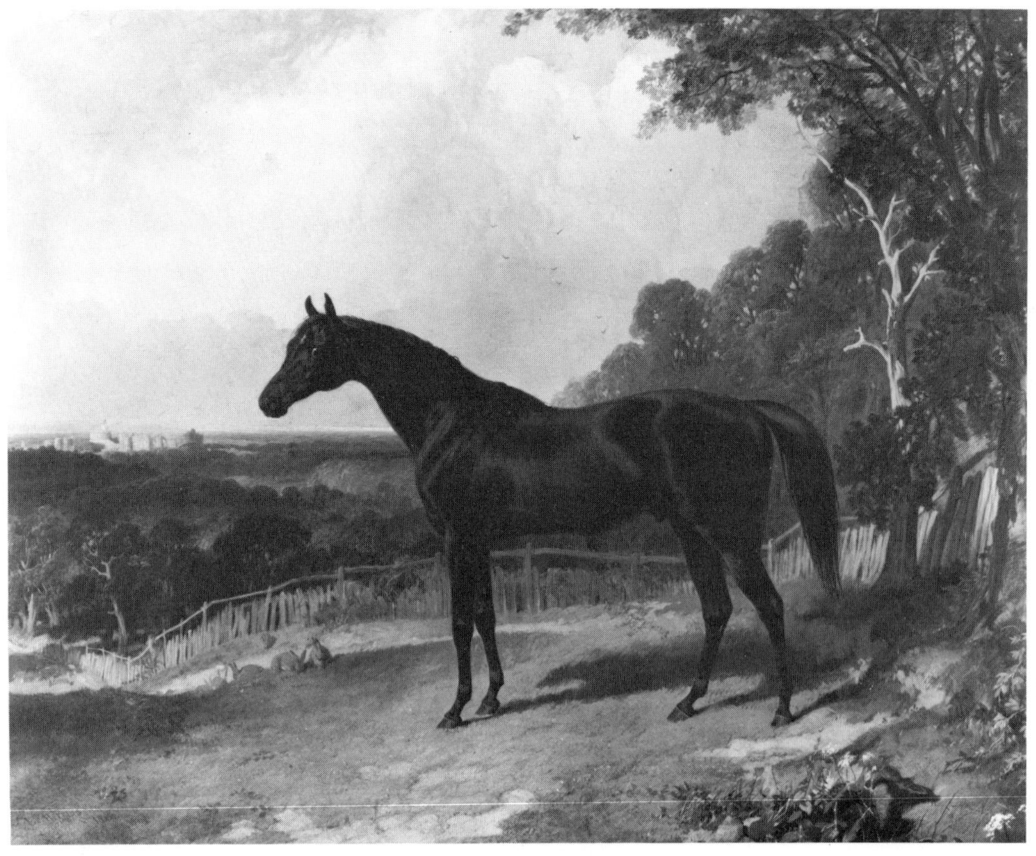

68

Said – Black Arab Stallion. Signed and dated 1846. 21½ × 29½ ins.

Courtesy: HM the Queen

List No 174

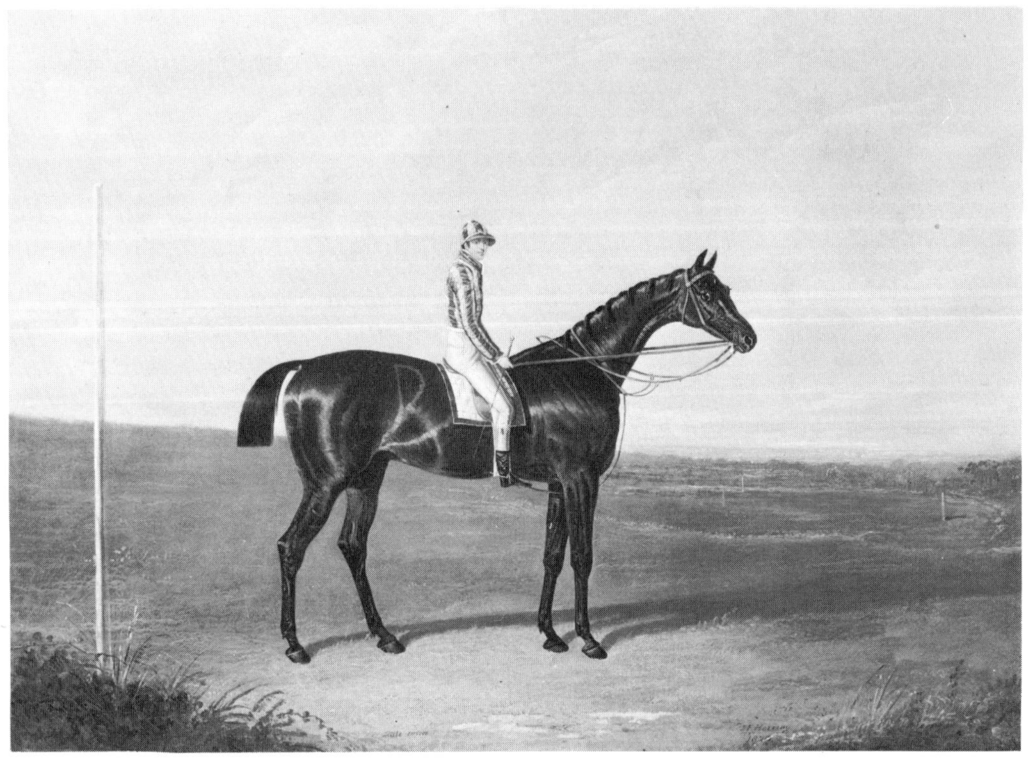

69

Little Driver. Signed, inscribed and dated 1823. 22 × 30 ins.

Courtesy: Arthur Ackermann & Son Ltd

List No 16

1822, won Oatlands Stakes at Newmarket and the Doncaster Stakes in 1823. Exhibited: Arthur Ackermann & Son Ltd. *(See Plate 3.)*

21 **Manuella**, a mare at Mr Richard Watt's stud, Bishop Burton, Yorks. Tree-trunk right, extensive landscape beyond and lake with swans; in the railed paddocks, view of shelter stables in distance. Signed, inscribed and dated 1825. 40 × 50 ins. This lovely mare, foaled 1809, was by Dick Andrews ex Mundane, and owned by Mr W. N. W. Hewett. Won the Oaks 1812 and two other races same year. April 1814 was sold to Lord Sackville, and shortly afterwards to Mr R. Watt, for whom painted and by family descent to 1976.
Collection: Paul Mellon. Exhibited: Arthur Ackermann & Son Ltd. *(See Plate 4.)*

and

22 **Manuella**, dam of Memnon (no trees in picture, see above). Signed, inscribed and dated 1825. 27¾ × 38 ins.
Witt Library.

24 **A Groom on a Chestnut** leading a bay with side-saddle in a park, to right the steps of a terrace. Signed and dated 1825. 26¾ × 39 ins.
Collection: Lt.-Col. A. Heywood Lonsdale. JD Sale at Sotheby's, Part Two.

1826

25 **Grey Arab** stallion in Windsor Great Park, facing left. This magnificent animal was bred by Mr George Clark, and afterwards sold to the Prince Regent. Painted for Mr Clark and thence by descent. Signed and dated 1826. 21½ × 29½ ins.
Private collection. *(See Plate 11.)*

26 **Tarrare**, George Nelson up. Won Derby 1826, owned by Earl of Scarborough. 19 × 14½ ins.

and

27 **Tarrare** against a wooden fence. Signed. 32 × 41¾ ins.
Exhibited: Arthur Ackermann & Son Ltd.

28 **The Match between Actaeon and Memnon**, Lord Kelburn's chestnut colt, Actaeon, H. Edwards up, beating Lord Darlington's colt, Memnon, S. Chifney up, in the Great Subscription Purse at York in 1826. Signed and dated 1826. 24 × 36 ins. Actaeon, by Scud ex Diana, was bred by Mr R. Milnes in 1822, and bought by Lord Kelburn in 1826. Besides this race he won the Doncaster Racing Club Stakes and the Richmond Gold Cup in 1826.

29 **Memnon**, light bay horse, W. Scott up, wearing the harlequin silks of Lord Darlington. Signed and dated 1826. 30 × 40 ins. Memnon, by Whisker ex Manuella (see above) was bred by Mr R. Milnes in 1822. Won Champagne Stakes, Doncaster, 1824; York St Leger and Great St Leger, the Gold Cup at Grimsby and the Gascoigne Stakes in a walk-over in 1825, and the Ascot Gold Cup in 1827.
Result of 1825 St Leger was first ever to be carried by pigeon, while a bird took the message to London, a specially trained dog took it to Manchester.
JD Sale at Sotheby's Final.

30 **Doncaster Gold Cup – 1826**. Race in progress, inscriptions under the horses from left to right: Fleur de Lis, Mulatto, Humphrey Clinker, Helenus, Jerry, and is also inscribed, Doncaster Gold Cup, 1826. Signed and dated 1826. 17¾ × 35¾ ins.
Collection: Paul Mellon.

31 **Bay Pony** in a yard, cropped ears and tail, near a pump, hay stacks beyond and dog. Signed and dated 1826. 21½ × 29 ins. Exhibited: Arthur Ackermann & Son Ltd.

1827

32 **Mameluke**, held by trainer in a landscape. Won Derby 1827, J. Robinson up. Signed and dated 1827. 14 × 18 ins. Bay colt owned by Lord Jersey, by Partisan ex Miss Sophia.
Engraved by R. G. Reeve. Literature: T. H. Taunton's *Portraits of Celebrated Racehorses*, 1886, vol LL, p. 281 illus.
Exhibited: Richard Green Gallery 1975.

33 **Finish of Doncaster Gold Cup**. Mulatto, Memnon, Fleur de Lis, Longwaist, Tarrare, racing to left. Signed and dated 1827. 49 × 89.5 cm.
Doncaster Art Gallery.

34 **Fleur de Lis**. Signed and dated 1827. 21 × 29 ins.
Sold Leggatt Bros.

35 **Matilda**, J. Robinson up on Doncaster Racecourse. Won St Leger 1827, by Comus ex Juliana, bred and owned by Hon E. Petre. 28 × 35½ ins.
Collection: Jockey Club. (See also a version 9½ × 12½ ins. Signed initials and dated 1827, with Elis, Rowton and The Colonel, and below.)

36 **Duplicate** – a bay stallion and groom in a stableyard, facing left. Signed and dated 1827. 21 × 29 ins.
Private collection.

37 **Chestnut Hunter** standing in a riverside meadow, extensive landscape beyond. Owned by Mr John Wilkinson, Levitt Hagg, nr Doncaster. Signed and dated 1827. 15½ × 20 ins.
Collections: John Wilkinson, 1827, Doncaster and Edward Crawshaw, Warmsworth. JD Sale, Sotheby's Part Three.

1828

38 **Matilda** in a stable. Won St Leger 1827. Signed and dated 1828. Panel 10 × 12 ins. Bay filly by Comus ex Juliana. Bred 1824 and owned by Hon. E. Petre. Won also Two Sweepstakes at York and Doncaster, 1826, and Sweepstake at York.
Exhibited: Arthur Ackermann & Son Ltd 1978.

39 **John Mytton Esq**, of Halston, Salop. Dated 1828. 61 × 73.7 cm. Squire 'Jack' Mytton (1796–1834), a celebrated eccentric of his time, who squandered a fortune and came to an early death. The handsome rake is here seen riding a useful cock-tailed hunter with a touch of 'blood' about him, facing the spectator and waving his top hat, while hounds are running.
Exhibited: Arthur Ackermann & Son Ltd 1965.

40 **The Sorby Family** of Button Hall, Sheffield. Signed and dated 1828. 27 × 39 ins. The family, all mounted, seen in a field on the edge of a wood. In the centre John Sorby, Esq aged 73, wearing a dark coat, buff breeches and gaiters and top hat, on a chestnut hunter; to the right standing holding a gun, his son Edwin Sorby, aged 36, wearing a brown velvet coat, buff breeches and black cap; to the left Horatio Sorby aged 9, dark blue coat on a dapple grey pony, two setters accompanying them.
Collections: John Sorby and J. R. Waterhouse, a descendant. JD Sale Sotheby's Part One.

41 **The Colonel**, chestnut colt, William Scott up and the owner, Hon. E. Petre and groom. Won St Leger 1828. 28 × 36 ins. cf. *The Horse in Art*, where it is reproduced (p. 73), by David Livingstone-Learmonth who writes: 'A good example of Herring's portraits of racehorses. The sky is good and the painting of the clothing, particularly the rider's breeches excellent. Perhaps the artist has given too much bosom to the owner's hack, the position chosen is at a difficult angle to depict correctly; but the racehorse looks a careful study and a good likeness. Notice the knee-rolls on Mr Petre's saddle. They must have just been coming into fashion about this time, for, in a hunting picture by F. C. Turner dated two years later, they are absent. 'Eddard' Petre however, had been one of the 'legs' in Regency days and would have the latest innovation'. Foaled in 1825, Colonel was by Whisker ex May Lady's dam. Won the Champagne Stakes, 1827. Narrowly failed to win the Derby of 1828 in which he was just beaten by the Duke of Rutland's Cadland by a short head. After winning the St Leger he was sold to King George IV for £4,000. Won the Craven Stakes 1830 and 1831.
Collection: Mrs J. Lockwood.

and

42 **The Colonel**. Chestnut, white blaze facing left in a stable.
Doncaster Art Gallery from Collection: Earl of Dalhousie.

and

43 **The Colonel**, William Scott up. Signed and dated 1828. 19¼ × 25¼ ins.
Collection: Sir Harold Parkinson. Literature: P. Willett, *The Thoroughbred*, illustration, p. 53.

Also another version, one of a set of four St Leger winners.

44 **The Colonel**, facing left, W. Scott up and his trainer, right. Signed initials and dated 1828. 9½ × 12½ ins. (See also Elis, Rowton and Matilda.)

45 **Start of St Leger 1828**. Including the horses Cambridge, Velocipede, Bessy Bedlam, Colonel, Jour de Noces, Belinda and Ballad Singer, the Grand Stand in the background.
Owned by Messrs Fores. W. Shaw-Sparrow, p. 83. British Sporting Artists.

46 **J. F. Herring senr and his brother Benjamin** in a neo-classical landscape. *c.*1828, 20 × 24 ins (by J. F. Herring senr.)
Collection: Mrs Gould, USA.
Courtesy: Arthur Ackermann & Son Ltd. *(See Plate 17.)*

1829

47 **The End of the Day's Shoot**, signed and dated 1829. 22 × 30¼ ins. Man in a wood standing behind his horse with a Pointer and Setter by his side, his bag and shot gun resting against a tree to the left.
Collections: Walter Hutchinson and Mr and Mrs Jack R. Dick. Exhibited: Richard Green 1976. Literature: *Burlington Magazine*, March 1967, p. 180. *(See Plate 45.)*

48 **Rowton**, chestnut colt with W. Scott up, facing left on a racecourse, black jacket and cap, pink sleeves. Won St Leger 1829. Signed initials and dated 1829. 9½ × 12½ ins. By Oiseau ex Katherina, owned by the Hon. E. Petre. Also won the Oatlands Stakes in 1832. (One of a set of four, same dimensions, see also, Elis, The Colonel and Matilda.)

1830

49 **Vanish** with Sam Darling up. Owned by Mr J. Houldsworth. Signed and dated 1830. 22 × 30 ins. Chestnut colt by Phantom out of Treasure, bred in 1825. Winner of 22 races between 1827 and 1831 including the Craven Stakes and St Leger Stakes at Manchester 1828, the Cleveland Stakes and the Gold Cup at Heaton Park in 1831.
Exhibited: Arthur Ackermann & Son Ltd. *(See Plate 5.)*

50 **Chorister**, J. Day up, on York racecourse, facing right. Signed and dated 1830. 22 × 30 ins. By Lottery ex a mare by Chorus. Won Sweepstakes at York as a two-year-old, and the St Leger and two other races in 1831. Bred by Marquis of Cleveland.

1832

51 **Margrave**. Won St Leger 1832. 26 × 38 ins.
Collection: Paul Mellon.

52 **Vestris** facing left with trainer. Signed and dated 1832. 28 × 36 ins.
Exhibited: Richard Green Gallery.

53 **Whalebone** in a paddock, stable right and distant landscape. Signed and dated 1832. 30 × 22 ins.
Exhibited: Knoedler.

54 **Archibald**, bay racehorse with A. Pavis up, wearing the navy blue silks and orange cap of Col. Peel, standing outside a rubbing house. Signed and dated 1832. 28 × 36 ins. Foaled in 1829, by Paulowitz ex Garcia, owned and bred by Col. J. Peel. Won a sweepstakes at Ascot and the Cockboat stakes at Newmarket in 1831. In 1832 he won the Two Thousand Guineas, the Shirley Stakes at Epsom and the Newmarket St Leger.
Collections: Col. J. Peel, for whom the subject was painted and by descent, to Major P. Peel MC. JR Dick Sale Sotheby's Part Two. Literature: P. Willett, *The Thoroughbred*, illustration p. 52.

55 **Lord George Campbell**, afterwards 8th Duke of Argyll, as a young boy in tartan dress on a pony in a deer park. Signed and dated 1832. 22 × 28 ins. The 8th Duke (1823–1900) held several important Government posts including Lord Privy Seal.
Collection: J. Wentworth Donahue, NY. JD Sale Sotheby's Final.

1833

56 **Lucetta**, brown filly in a stable, facing left. Dated 1833. 8 × 10 ins. By Reveller ex Luss, foaled by Mr Stanlake Batson Cambridge in 1826, sold to Sir Mark Wood, Bt. in 1828 for 2,000 gns. Won four races and dead-heated at Newmarket in 1829, won six races including The Ascot Gold Cup in 1830, four races in 1831 including the Audley Sweepstakes, eight races in 1832 including the Jockey Club Plate and three races in 1833, when she was retired to Hare Park Paddocks.
Exhibited: Arthur Ackermann & Co Ltd 1975.

57 **Rockingham**, facing left. Won St Leger 1833. Signed and dated 1833. 10 × 11 ins.
Sold Sotheby's.

58 **Rockingham**, a bay colt held by his trainer, Mr Forth, with jockey Sam Darling on a racecourse.

Signed and dated 1833. 10½ × 12½ ins. Rockingham, by Humphrey Clinker, out of Medora, purchased by Mr Richard Watt of Bishop Burton, October, 1832 for 1,000 gns. Winner of St Leger 1833 and Goodwood Cup 1835. Sold Christies. *(See Plate 6.)*

59 **St Giles**, with Wm. Scott up, on training gallops. Won the Derby 1833. Signed and dated 1833. 28 × 36 ins. Foaled in 1829 by Tramp ex Arcot and was jointly owned by Messrs Ridsdale and Gully. In 1832 he won at Newmarket, and in 1835 he won the Craven Stakes at Catterick and a Purse of £50 at the York Spring Meeting.
Collections: C. V. Whitney and Mrs C. J. Tippett, USA. JD Sale Sotheby's Part One.

60 **Vespa**, with owner Sir Mark Wood, Bt. holding the mare's bridle, trainer leaning over stable door right, and lad with white hack and groom, in a landscape, possibly the gallops or a race-course. Won the Oaks 1833, J. Chapple up. Signed and dated 1833. 28 × 36 ins. Foaled 1830 by Muley ex Miss Wasp. Also won four races in 1834, Oatlands Handicap, King's Plate and Jockey Club Plate at Newmarket and Kings Guineas, Chelmsford. Sold to Count Hunyady of Hungary, end 1834. There are two versions of this important picture, practically identical, except for a small variation in the dimensions, in one the sky is overcast with signature over the door, in the other a brighter sky and rounded clouds with signature at bottom of stable door.
Collections: C. V. Whitney and Mrs C. J. Tippett, USA. One sold from JD Sale Sotheby's to Richard Green Gallery for £62,000 (Part One). *(See Plate 7.)* One exhibited: Arthur Ackermann & Son Ltd 1975 (27½ × 36 ins).

61 **Three Horses** in a stream. Signed and dated 1833. 9 × 12 ins.
Exhibited: Arthur Ackermann & Son Ltd.

62 **Margrave**, with J. Robinson up. Won St Leger 1832. Signed and dated 1833. 26 × 38 ins. Dark chestnut by Muley, ex a mare bred at Hampton Court by Election, foaled 1829. Bred by Mr Nowell of Underlay and sold as a yearling to Mr Wareford, who sold him to Messrs Gulley and Ridsdale at end of 1831. Won three races as a two-year-old, and the Gascoigne Stakes and Grand Duke Michael Stakes and St Leger in 1832. Retired to stud in 1834 and sent to Virginia, USA, in 1835. See *Taunton* vol III, illustration p. 120.
Collection: Paul Mellon. Exhibited: Arthur Ackermann & Sons Ltd 1962, illus.

63 **Rubini, Whale and Beiram**, Goodwood Cup 1833 (one of a pair, other is The Start). Signed and dated 1833. 28¼ × 42 ins. Collection: The Jockey Club. *(See Plates 70 and 71.)*

also

64 **Rubini**, owned by the trainer, Mr John Kent as a 5-year-old. Signed and dated 1834.
Collection: The Jockey Club.

65 **The Running of the Goodwood Cup 1833**. Rubini, Whale and Beiram. Signed initials, dated indistinctly. Panel 5½ × 11½ ins.
Exhibited: Richard Green Gallery.

66 **Dark Bay Hunter**, side-saddled and bridled in a landscape. Inscribed and dated 1833. 17¼ × 23½ ins.
Exhibited: Richard Green Gallery. *(See Plate 15.)*

67 **Mazeppa** bound to a grey horse, pursued by wolves. Signed and dated 1833 – after Horace Vernet. *(See Plate 72.)*

and

68 **Mazeppa** lying by his fallen steed, surrounded by frightened horses. Signed and dated 1833 – after Horace Vernet.
Collection: Paul Mellon. Exhibited: Tate Gallery. *(See Plate 73.)*

69 **Mazeppa and Wolves**.
Exhibited: Pawsey & Payne.

1834

70 **Glaucus** in a paddock. Signed and dated 1834. 28½ × 36½ ins. Owned by the Earl of Chesterfield. Bay colt by Partisan out of Nanine bred by General Grosvenor in 1830. Won Ascot Gold Cup

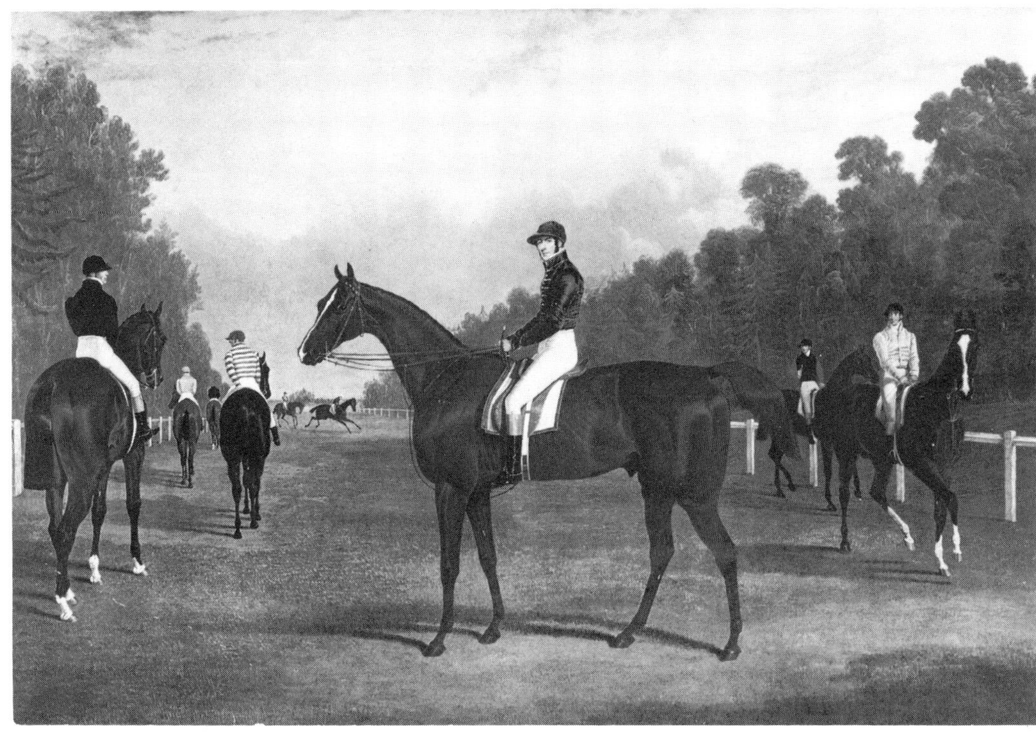

70

Rubini before the start of the Goodwood Gold Cup 1833. Signed and dated 1833. 27¼ × 41¼ ins.

Courtesy: The Tryon Gallery

List No 63

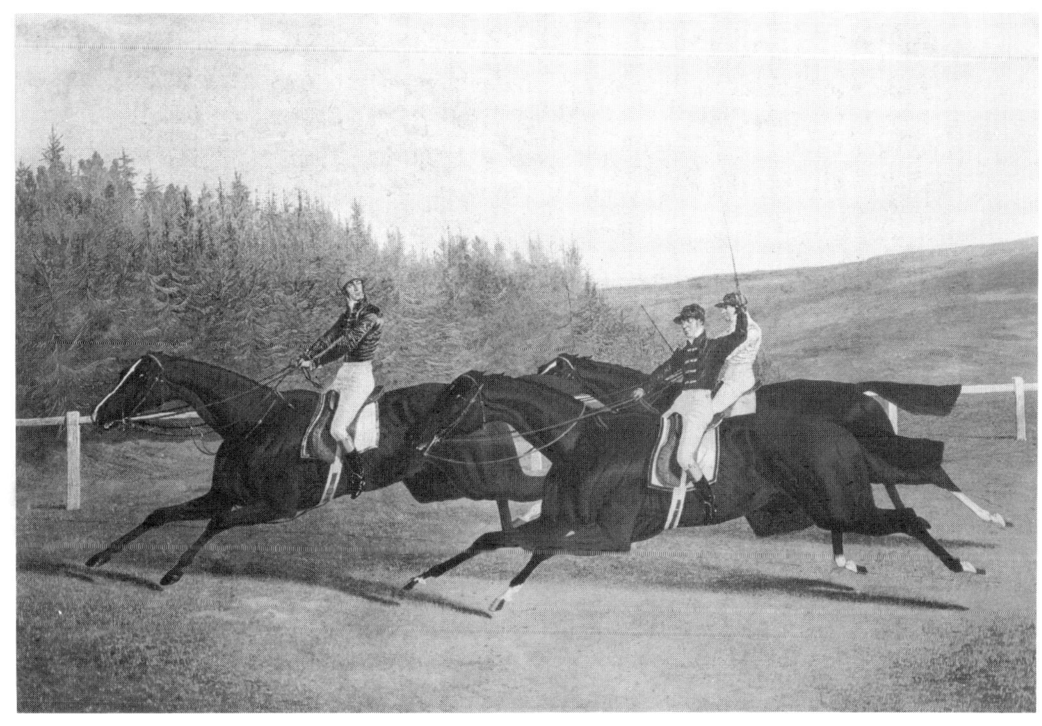

71

Rubini, Whale and **Beiram**, Goodwood Cup 1833. Signed and dated 1833. 28½ × 42 ins.

Courtesy: The Tryon Gallery

List No 63

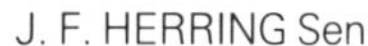
J. F. HERRING Senr

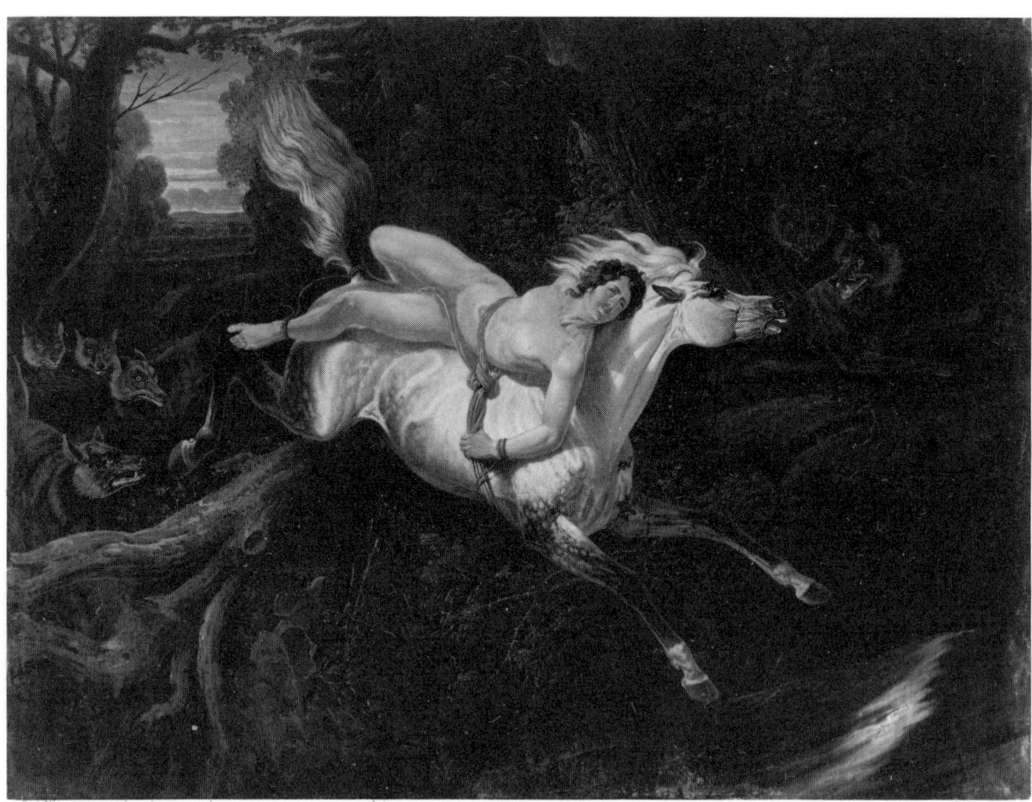

72

Mazeppa pursued by Wolves
One of a pair with 73.
Dated 1833.
(after Horace Vernet)

Courtesy: The Tate Gallery

List No 67

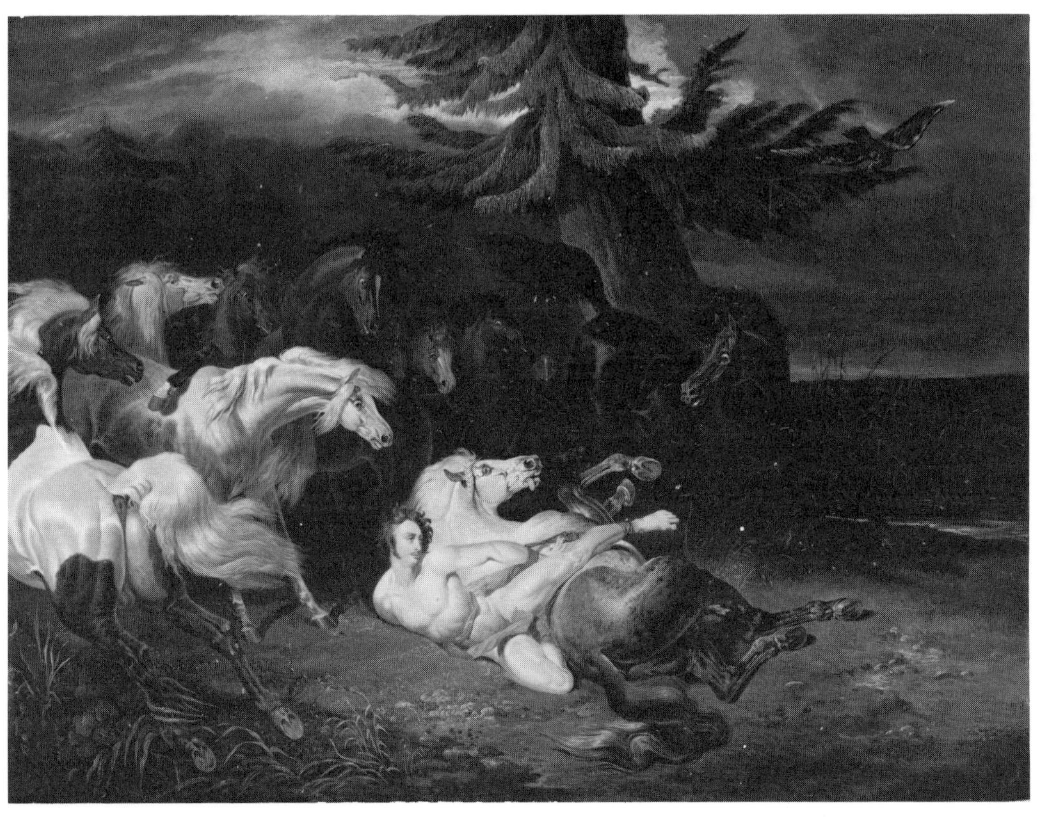

73

Mazeppa surrounded by horses. One of a pair with 72.
Dated 1833.
(after Horace Vernet)

Courtesy: The Tate Gallery

List No 68

in 1834, Goodwood Stakes 1835 and six other races, walked over three races.
Exhibited: Arthur Ackermann & Son Ltd. *(See Plate 74.)*

71 **Portrait of Mr Daniel Haigh** on a hunter, facing right. He was Master of the Old Surrey Hunt. Signed and dated 1834. 28 × 36 ins.
Collection: Mr E. Cooper-Bland.
cf. David Livingstone-Learmonth, *The Horse in Art*, who writes: 'Considered by many to be the finest Herring in existence. The setting, overlooking his county, is noble. The horse is a magnificent type of weight-carrying hunter, a horse which one would associate more with the Shires than with a provincial county bordering on London, a county in which, if we are to believe Mr Jorrocks, a 'swell' was a rarity. There is no reason to doubt that Mr Haigh rode such a horse for the portrait rings true. Note the beautiful painting of the herbage in the right foreground . . . a really good Herring like this one speaks for itself'

72 **Plenipotentiary**, chestnut colt with P. Conolly up. Won the Derby 1834. Owned by Mr Stanlake Batson, by Emilius ex Harriet. Also won a race at Newmarket. Signed and dated 1834. 22 × 30 ins.
Exhibited: Richard Green Gallery 1975.

73 **Fox Hunting** – full cry. Signed and dated 1834. 14 × 32 ins.
Collections: Miss Diana Cartmell. Exhibited: Richard Green Gallery 1977. *(See Plate 27.)*

74 **The Suffolk Hunt in Full Cry**. Signed and dated 1834. 14 × 32 ins. The gentleman on the chestnut hunter clearing the brook is George Mure, who was Master between 1827 and 1845.
Collections: Sir Walter Gilbey, Bt. 1910, J. A. Fielder, 1843 and H. J. Joel. Exhibited: Arthur Ackermann & Son Ltd 1978.

75 **Highland Scene**. Drover's repast, Highland cattle, sheep etc. Signed and dated 1834. 23 × 34 ins.
Collection: Colonel John Warner. *(See Plate 85.)*

76 **Touchstone**. Won St Leger 1834 and twelve other races. Bred and owned by the Marquis of Westminster. Brown colt by Camel ex Banter by Master Henry. Also won Ascot Gold Gup twice, the Doncaster Cup and Dee Stakes, the best stayer of his time. 'Somewhat peculiar horse with fleshy legs and hocks which turned out so wide when he gallopped that a barrel might have been placed between them. Extremely lazy at home, he pulled hard in his races and had a habit of swerving away from the whip. Outstanding sire – his stock included Derby winners Cotherstone, Orlando, Surplice and Newminster who also won the St Leger and carried on the Touchstone line. His mares were extremely successful at stud and includes The dam of West Australian – the first horse to win the Triple Crown.' While being ridden by the Earl of Wilton he also won a Gold Cup at Heaton Park.

Several Versions
(1) Signed, inscription 'Touchstone' and dated 1834. Panel 9 × 12 ins. Collection: The Jockey Club.

(2) in a stable, on panel facing right, 24 × 36 ins. Collection: The Jockey Club.

(3) in the paddock, Wm. Scott up and Colonel Peel's Slane in background. 9 × 12 ins. Collection: The Jockey Club.

(4) another, 14 × 19 ins. Collection: The Jockey Club. Exhibited: Ackermanns.

(5) with jockey up, facing right. Signed and dated. 39.5 × 49.5 cm. Doncaster Art Gallery.

(6) in a stable, facing right. 12 × 16 ins. Signed and dated 1839. Collection: Mrs E. Huxley. JD Sale Sotheby's Part One (£11,000).

77 **Matilda**, Wm. Scott up, with Hon. E. Petre, the owner and young Lord Derby on a cob. Signed and dated 1834. 11¾ × 15¾ ins. Matilda won the St Leger in 1827 beating Mameluke, so, as the mare would have been ten years old at this time, this canvas must be partly from an earlier picture of the subject by Herring, painted in 1828. *(See Plate 38.)* Private collection.

78 **Major Henry Bullock on his Bay Hunter**, a meet in the distance. Signed and dated 1834. 14½ × 19 ins. Major Bullock, as a cornet in the 11th

Light Dragoon Guards, fought at Quatre Bras, where his horse was shot under him, and at Waterloo. He subsequently transferred to the Life Guards.
Collection: Major H. R. Bullock, Dumfriesshire.
Exhibited: Arthur Ackermann & Son Ltd 1976.

79 **A Bay Hunter** held by a groom wearing a red waistcoat in a stable yard. Signed and dated 1834. Panel 14 × 18 ins.
Collection: P. O. Brocklehurst. JD Sale Sotheby's Final.

1835

80 **Clearwell, Rosalie and Plenipotentiary** racing at Newmarket, Craven Meeting. Signed and dated 1835. 9 × 12 ins. The race was won by Mr Stanlake Batson's chestnut colt, Plenipotentiary, P. Conolly up, with the grey, Clearwell, owned by Lord Orford, second and Colonel Peel's bay filly, Rosalie, third. Clearwell also won the 2,000 gns at Newmarket, Robinson up, the Wokingham Stakes, Ascot, and the Ewell Stakes at Epsom, all in 1834. Rosalie won the Prendergast Stakes, Newmarket in 1833.
Exhibited: Richard Green Gallery 1975.

81 **The Finish of the Derby Stakes**, 1835. Mr Bowes's Mundig winning from Lord Orford's Ascot in the run up to the finishing post, followed by the rest of the field. Over a hundred mounted spectators are seen galloping from the hill on the left towards the crowd on their horses standing near the post. Signed, inscribed with horse's names and dated 1835. 18 × 40¼ ins.
Names of the runners and riders: (Right to left) Mundig, Ascot, Duke of Rutland's Florestan (W. Wheatley); Mr Ridsdale's Luck's All (G. Edwards); Mr J. Peel's Trim (J. Chapple); Mr J. Robinson's Stockport (S. Darling); Sir G. Heathcote's Valentissimo (F. Buckle); Mr Pettit's Ibrahim (E. Wright); Mr Ridsdale's Coriolanus (P. Conolly); Duke of Cleveland's colt by Memnon (S. Chifney junr); Duke of Richmond's Elizondo (F. Boyce); Lord Jersey's Silenus (E. Edwards); Lord Jersey's Ibrahim (J. Robinson); Lord Warwick's Pelops (G. Galloway).
Betting: Ibrahim 2-1, Ascot 3-1, Mundig 6-1, Elizondo 10-1, Coriolanus 12-1, colt by Memnon 20-1, Trim and Valentissimo 50-1, Pelops 100-1. After four false starts Silenus led the field from Mundig, Ascot, Ibrahim and Pelops to Tattenham Corner, when Mundig prevailed.
Collections: Bryan Jenks Esq, Astbury Hall, Shropshire; Medmenham Abbey Sale, Sotheby's 24 June 1942. Literature: P. Willett, *The Thoroughbred*, illustration p. 54. JD Sale Sotheby's Part Two.

82 **Mundig**, chestnut colt. Winner Derby 1835 with other runners going left. Signed. Mundig, by Catton ex Emma, was trained by John Scott at Malton and had not run until the 1835 Derby. However, he was thought to have been trained enough to have a good chance in a moderate year. In the same year he won a £100 Foal Stakes at Doncaster and the following year he won three King's Plates as well as suffering many defeats.
Doncaster Art Gallery.

83 **Dangerous** with J. Chapple up. Won Derby 1833. Signed and dated 1835. 8½ × 11½ ins. Owned by Mr Isaac Sadler.
Exhibited: Richard Green Gallery 1973.

84 **Plenipotentiary** with P. Conolly up. Won Derby 1834. Signed and dated 1835. 8½ × 11½ ins. Owned by Mr S. Batson.

85 **Priam** with S. Day up. Won Derby 1830. Signed, inscribed and dated 1835. 8¾ × 11¾ ins. Owned by Mr Sam Chifney. Won fifteen races including the Derby, the Craven Stakes 1831 and the Goodwood Cup 1832.
Exhibited: Arthur Ackermann & Son Ltd 1979.

86 **Miss Letty** in a stable. Won the Oaks 1837. Signed and dated 1835. 14 × 17½ ins. Owned by the Hon. T. Orde Powlett.
Collection: Lady Bird. Exhibited: Arthur Ackermann & Son Ltd 1979.

87 **Lucetta**. Signed, inscribed and dated 1835. Sold at Sotheby's.

88 **Preserve**. Owned by Mr Greville. Unsigned. 20½ × 24¾ ins. The filly Preserve won the 1,000 Guineas in 1835, and was also the favourite for the Oaks that year, but was beaten. She was in fact owned by Lord George Bentinck, whose early enthusiasm for racing and betting did not meet with the approval of his father, the Duke of Portland. To deceive his father, he frequently entered

his horses under other names, including that of his cousin, Charles Greville.
Collection: Mr Victor Morley Lawson, on loan to the Tate Gallery through the British Sporting Art Trust.

1836

89 **Bees-wing**, bay mare standing in a stable. Signed and dated 1836. 15½ × 20½ ins. Foaled in 1833, Bees-wing was by Dr Syntax ex a mare by Ardrossan and bred by Ralph Riddell. She won the Doncaster Cup three years running in 1840, 1841 and 1842, and also the Ascot Gold Cup in 1842. She was a highly successful brood mare at stud, one of her offspring being Newminster, the 1851 St Leger winner. Several other versions.
JD Sale Sotheby's Part Three.

90 **Elis**. Won the St Leger 1836. Signed, inscribed Elis and dated 1836. 10 × 12 ins. A light chestnut colt, Elis was by Langar ex Olympia, and owned by the Earl of Lichfield and Lord George Bentinck, who had her conveyed from Goodwood to Doncaster by the first horse box, and pulled off a coup.
Collection: Mrs E. M. Wheeler. Exhibited: Richard Green Gallery.

and

91 **Elis**, with J. Day up. *c.*1836. 31 × 41 ins.

and

91A **Elis** in a stable. 4 × 5 ins.
Collection: The Jockey Club.

92 **Cyprian** in a stable. Signed and dated 1836. 8 × 10 ins. Exhibited Richard Green Gallery.

93 **Bay Middleton**, with J. Robinson up in Lord Jersey's blue and gold stripes, mile post on the right, pawing the ground. 27½ × 33¾ ins. By Sultan ex Cobweb, bred and owned by the Earl of Jersey. Won the 2,000 Gns, the Derby, Buckhurst Stakes at Ascot, and Grand Duke Michael Stakes, Newmarket 1836. Ran only as a three-year-old, never beaten. 7 races won.
Illustrated in *Taunton* Vol III. Presented by Lord Wavertree to the Jockey Club.

94 **Mameluke**. Won Derby 1827. Signed and dated 1836. 8½ × 11½ ins. By Partisan ex Miss Sophia, bred by Mr R. C. Elwes, owned by Earl of Jersey, who also owned the second in the Derby, Glenartney, who had previously beaten him in the Riddlesworth Stakes. It was rumoured that Harry Edwards on Glenartney had not exerted himself to the utmost as he had had a substantial bet on Mameluke. Mr John Gulley bought Mameluke for 4,000 gns to run in the St Leger, but here a conspiracy by Messrs Crockford and Ridsdale effectually put him out of the race after a series of false starts – in which the starter was implicated – had upset him, and the Hon. E. Petre's Matilda won the race after a hard struggle. In 1828 he won the Oatlands Stakes and the Portland Stakes, but was beaten in the Doncaster Cup. In 1829 he won three more races, when Gully sold him to Mr Theobald to go to stud. Eventually he was exported to America, but he was not a success there.
Exhibited: Richard Green Gallery 1973.

95 **Whisker**. Signed, dated and inscribed 1836. 36 × 48 ins.
Collections: Countess of Halifax, Duke of Grafton. Sold Christie's, 1960.

1837

96 **Mango**. Won St Leger, Ascot Derby and Newmarket St Leger 1837. Signed and dated 1837. 10 × 12 ins. By Emilius ex Mustard, bred by Mr Thornhill, owned by C. C. Greville. Later exported to America.
Collections: Mrs E. M. Wheeler, Earl of Rosebery. Exhibited: Richard Green Gallery 1978.

97 **Black Carriage Horse** and white dog in a stableyard. Signed and dated 1837. 22¼ × 32¼ ins.
Collection: Frank Wootton. Exhibited: Arthur Ackermann & Son Ltd.

98 **The Meet Near Harrold, Beds**. 22 × 27 ins. One of a pair with, *(See Plate 23.)*

99 **The Hunt in Full Cry**. Signed and dated 1837. Both exhibited by Richard Green Gallery. *(See Plate 24.)*

1838

100 **Grey Momus** with J. Day up wearing yellow silks and cap in a landscape. Signed and dated

1838. 14 × 18 ins. By Comus ex a mare by Cervantes, was bred by Sir Tatton Sykes and sold to Lord George Bentinck for whom he won the 2,000 gns, Ascot Cup, Grand Duke Michael Stakes and Newmarket St Leger in 1838. He won the Port Stakes and three other races in 1839.
Collection: Mrs K. Faure. Exhibited: Arthur Ackermann & Son 1965. JD Sale Sotheby's Part Three. *(See Plate 8.)*

101 **Team of Coach Horses** awaiting the change on the Great North Road between Newark and Lincoln; the Royal Mail is seen approaching on a road to the left. Signed and dated 1838. 48 × 73 ins.
Collections: General Oglander, Isle of Wight, Major D. Oglander by descent. JD Sale Sotheby's Part One.

102 **A Chestnut Hunter** standing in a lakeside meadow, a distant landscape to the left, the property of Sir Wm. Erle. Signed and dated 1838. 24½ × 29½ ins.
Collection: Sir Wm. Erle (afterwards Lord Erle, Lord Chief Justice). JD Sale Sotheby's Part Two.

103 **Don John** with Wm. Scott up before the start of the St Leger. Won St Leger 1838. Signed and dated. 12 × 16¾ ins. Bay colt by Tramp (or Waverley) ex Lepanto's dam, foaled 1835. He won six other races between 1837–39. Owned by the Earl of Chesterfield. Five other versions, one with Lord Chesterfield and trainer on horseback, right. (Sotheby's 1959.)
Exhibited: Arthur Ackermann & Son Ltd 1978.

104 **Amato** with J. Chapple up, in a landscape. Won the Derby 1838. Signed, inscribed and dated 1838/9. 12½ × 16½ ins. Brown colt by Velocipede ex Jane Shore, bred by Sir Gilbert Heathcote and trained by Ralph Sherwood at the Durdans, adjoining Epsom racecourse. Although the 15 hand Amato had never raced before his performance on the gallops created a lot of confidence in the betting, but a few days before the race he developed a cough. When this was known, the odds drifted to 30-1. On the day, despite three false starts, he won easily from Ion, and the 5-2 favourite, Grey Momus.
Literature: *Taunton* 1888 Vol III p. 231. Exhibited: Richard Green Gallery 1976.

105 **The Two Favourite Hunters of John Scott**, on Langton Wolds above his training stables at Malton, Yorks. Signed and dated 1838. 27½ × 35 ins. John Scott, 'the Wizard of the North' (1794–1871) was one of the leading trainers of the day. Between 1827 and 1864 he trained six winners of the Derby, eight of the Oaks, sixteen of the St Leger and eight of the Two Thousand Guineas.
Collections: John Scott, for whom the picture was painted, Miss Chute, his step-daughter, Mrs Robert Pearson, grand-daughter of John Scott, Colonel W. E. Pearson, CBE, by descent. Sold for £23,000, JD Sale Sotheby's Part Two. *(See Plate 19.)*

106 **Mr Sowerby's Grey Carriage Horses** in stableyard, at Putteridge Bury. Signed and dated 1838. 40 × 50 ins.
Collections: The Sowerby family, Luton, until 1950 by descent, Paul Mellon 1971. Exhibited: Arthur Ackermann & Son Ltd.

107 **Harkaway**, a chestnut with jockey up. Signed and dated 1838. 11½ × 16 ins. Foaled in 1834 by Economist ex Nabocklish, owned and bred by Mr Ferguson. Won Wolverhampton and Goodwood Cups and Queen's Plate at Doncaster in 1838, and Cheltenham and Goodwood Cups in 1839.
Sold Christies.

1839

108 **Barcarole**, Lord Albemarle's racehorse in a landscape, facing left. Signed and dated 1839. 22 × 30 ins. By Emilius ex Bravura, foaled 1833. Won the 1,000 Guineas in 1838 (also five-year-old?)
Exhibited: Arthur Ackermann & Son Ltd 1975.

109 **The Doncaster Gold Cup 1838**. The Earl of Chesterfield's three-year-old bay colt, Don John, carrying 7st 3 lbs, is beating Beeswing, The Doctor and Melbourne. Signed and dated 1839. 111.8 × 205.7 cms. This picture is a result of collaboration between Herring and James Pollard, Herring doing the horses in the foreground and Pollard the crowded stands and coaches with passengers and grooms at rear, and the Judge's Box on the left. Exaggerated poses give an exact record of the scene at the post, not an impression of rapid movement.
Private collection. Exhibited: British Sporting Paintings 1975.

74

Glaucus. Signed and dated 1834. 28½ × 36½ ins.

Courtesy:
Arthur Ackermann & Son Ltd

List No 70

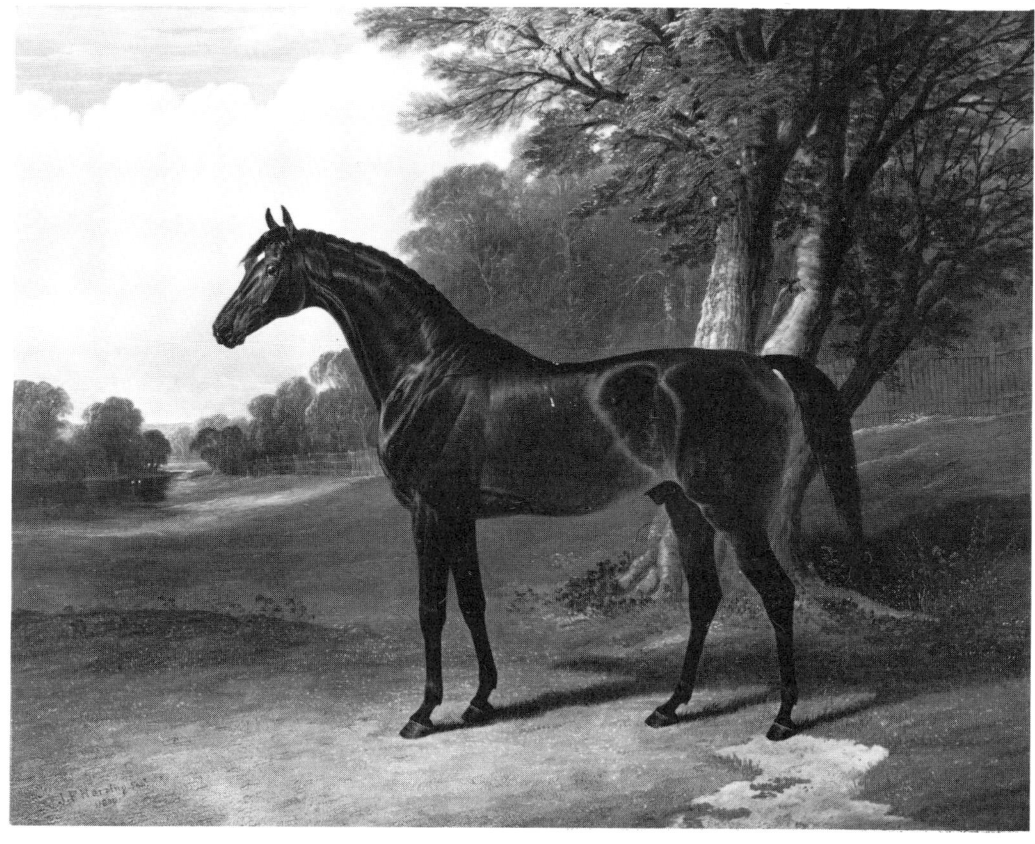

75

Four Horses in a Large Barn. Signed and dated 1844. 27 × 35½ ins.

Courtesy: J. D. D'Arcy Clark

List No 155

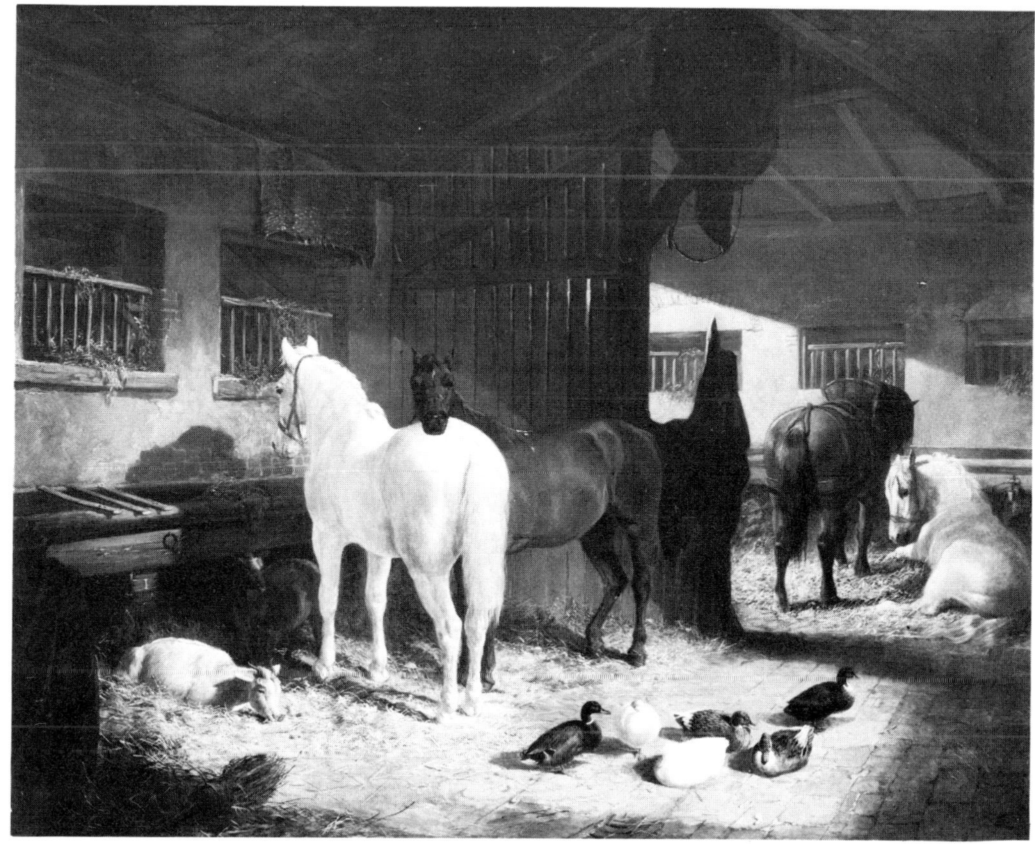

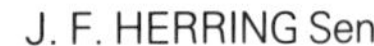

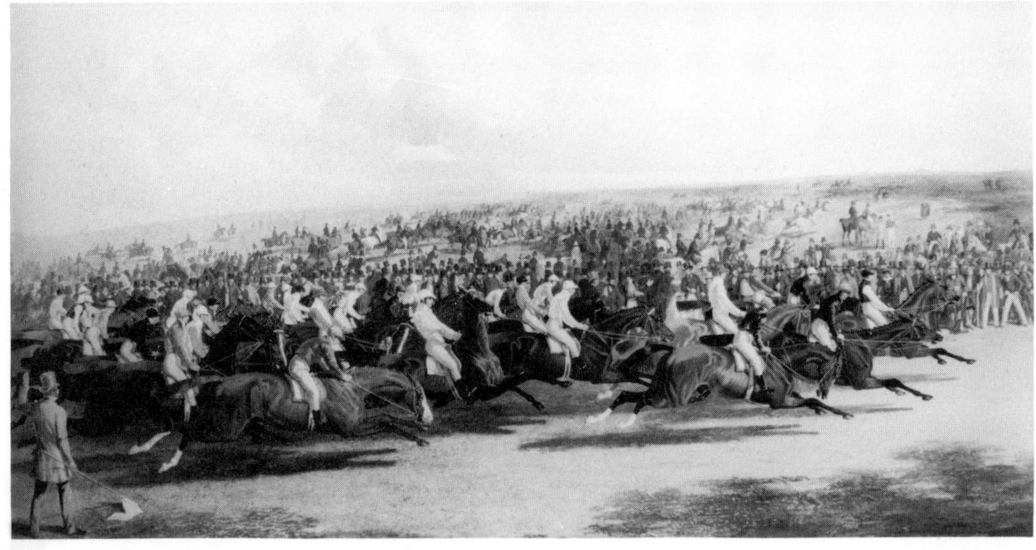

76

Start of the 1844 Derby.
Signed and dated 1844.
40½ × 82½ ins.

Courtesy:
National Trust of Scotland

List No 164

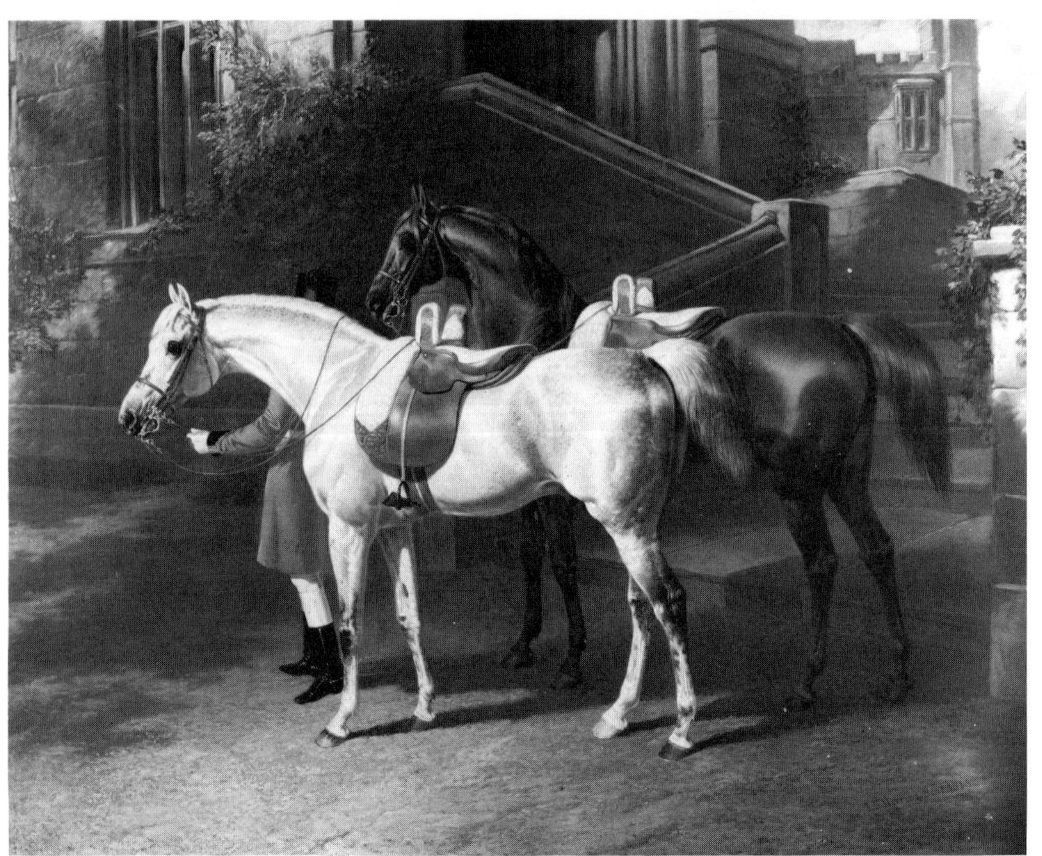

77

Hammon and Tajar. Signed and dated 1845. 28 × 36 ins.

Courtesy: HM the Queen

List No 165

110 **Charles XII** with William Scott up, and **Euclid** with P. Conolly up at Doncaster. Charles XII won St Leger 1839. Signed and dated 1839. 12 × 16¾ ins. Charles XII, a brown colt by Voltaire ex Wagtail, won The Cup at Liverpool and St Leger 1839. He won a further fifteen races between 1840–43. Euclid, a chestnut colt by Emilius ex Maria, dead-heated with Charles XII in St Leger but was beaten in the re-run. He won four other races in 1839 and three in 1840.
Exhibited: Arthur Ackermann & Son Ltd 1978.

111 **Charles XII**, in front, and **Euclid**, both mounted facing right. 33 × 40 cms.
Doncaster Art Gallery.

112 **Euclid** with Pettit, his trainer and the jockey Patrick Conolly. Signed J. F. Herring 1839 lower right. 15½ × 19½ ins. Euclid, owned by Thomas Thornhill of Riddlesworth, Norfolk, was favourite for the Derby in 1839, in which he was ridden by Conolly, but came third. The same year he ran a dead heat with Charles XII for the St Leger, but lost the deciding heat by a head.
Collection: Mr Victor Morley Lawson, on loan to the Tate Gallery through the British Sporting Art Trust.

113 **Vandeau**, a white greyhound by Park Gate in a landscape, facing left. Signed and dated 1839. 25 × 30 ins.

114 **Full Cry** – huntsmen and hounds in an open landscape approaching a fence, a windmill and pond in the distance. Signed and dated 1839. 28 × 36 ins.
Collections: Lord Woolavington (Catalogue p. 97), Major Sir Reginald and Lady Macdonald-Buchanan. Exhibited: Arthur Ackermann & Son Ltd 1967. JD Sale Sotheby's Final.

115 **Ascot: Gold Cup Day**. Signed J. F. Herring 1839 lower left. 20 × 30 ins. This shows the field for the 1839 race. In the centre foreground, the winner, Mr Isaac Day's Caravan (by Camel out of Wings) waits to be saddled by Jem Robinson, with the favourite, St Francis (second) left, Ion (third) beyond and the Bey of Algiers (last) on the right. The Royal Standard flying above the smaller grandstand indicates the presence of the young Queen Victoria and Prince Albert. The larger grandstand had been newly completed; its foundations had been laid by Lord Errol, Master of the Royal Buckhounds, whose servants are seen on the right. Also engraved.
Private collection, on loan to the Tate Gallery, by arrangement with Leggatt Brothers, through the British Sporting Art Trust.

116 **Two Brown Coach Horses** in a stableyard, with groom and two greyhounds. Signed and dated 1839. 27 × 30 ins. Private collection.

117 **London–Edinburgh Royal Mail** on the road, head on. Signed and dated 1839. 35¾ × 28 ins.
Exhibited: Arthur Ackermann & Son Ltd.

1840

118 **Launcelot**, a black racehorse with a black cat in a stall. Won St Leger 1840. Signed and dated 1840. Panel 12 × 16 ins. Bred by the First Marquis of Westminster by Camel ex Banter – a full brother to Touchstone.
Collection: Mrs E. Huxley. JD Sale Sotheby's Part One. Also a version 11½ × 15 ins, signed and dated 1840, in the collection of the Duke of Westminster.

119 **The Finish of the Doncaster St Leger** 1840. Launcelot, a black colt with Wm. Scott up, narrowly winning from the bay, Maroon, both owned by the Marquis of Westminster and running in his colours of yellow silks and black cap. Signed and dated 1840. 27¼ × 40¼ ins. Launcelot was by Camel ex Banter, by Master Henry, by Orville who won the St Leger in 1802, who was by Beningborough who won the St Leger 1794. In the closing stages of the race, it seemed to lie between Launcelot and Maroon, but Nat Flatman brought up Gibraltar to challenge Maroon, who then menaced Launcelot. But Scott urged on Launcelot who broke down but ran on gamely to win.
Collections: Lord Woolavington, Bretby Heirlooms 1918, Viscountess D'Abernon 1955. JD Sale Sotheby's Part Two. *(See Plate 9.)*

120 **Chestnut Stallion** in a walled paddock by a stable facing left. Signed and dated 1840. 21 × 29 ins. Private collection.

121 **Mail Coach** horses awaiting the change by a cottage, greyhounds etc., coach approaching left. Signed and dated 1840.
Exhibited: Arthur Ackermann & Son Ltd.

122 **Grey Hunter** in a stable facing left. Signed and dated 1840. 27½ × 35½ ins. Sold Christie's.

123 **Chestnut Hunter** held by a groom in a stable-yard. Signed and dated 1840. 28 × 36 ins. The horse, a weight carrier with white blaze, held by groom in a tamoshanter and light coat.
Exhibited: Arthur Ackermann & Son Ltd 1978.

124 **Sunrise**, a team of horses and two farm-hands. Signed and dated 1840. 27 × 35 ins. [These horses are neither cart nor hunters – *Author's note.*]
Collection: Lady Violet Macfadyen.

125 **A Wooded Landscape**, with 'squire' on a horse talking to peasant with donkey and panniers, right, cows resting left. Signed and dated 1840. 55 × 76 cm. Sold Christie's.

126 **Farming Scenes**, set of four circulars. Signed and dated 1840. *c.* 12 ins in diameter.
Collection: Lady Violet Macfadyen.

127 **Sunset**, a cart horse drinking. Signed and dated 1840. 28 × 30 ins.
Exhibited: Arthur Ackermann & Son Ltd.

128 **Fido**, a chestnut hunter standing by a stream, a country house beyond. Signed and dated 1840. 27¼ × 35¼ ins. JD Sale, Sotheby's Part Two.

129 **The Pocket Hercules** beating Auburn for the Bibury Handicap Plate, June 1840. 9 × 11¾ ins. Mr W. Ley's The Pocket Hercules won twelve races between 1836 and 1840, and was originally owned by Squire Osbaldestone, owner of Auburn, before he sold it to Mr Ley.
Exhibited: Arthur Ackermann & Son Ltd 1979.

130 **Crucifix**, a bay racehorse with J. Day up in Lord Bentinck's colours in an extensive landscape. Won the Oaks 1840. Signed, inscribed Crucifix, Oaks, 1840. 39½ × 49½ ins. Crucifix. by Priam ex Octavian, bred by Lord George Bentinck.
Private collection: Earl of Halifax.

1841

131 **Coronation**, P. Conolly up, facing right. Won The Derby, 1841. Signed and dated 1841. 13¼ × 17¼ ins. Bay colt by Sir Hercules ex Ruby, bred by Mr A. Rawlinson of Chadlington, Chipping Norton in 1838. Won two races as a two-year-old, and the Derby, Oxford Cup and two other races.

132 **Ghuznee**, a bay filly. Won the Oaks 1841. Signed, inscribed 'Oaks' and dated 1841. 12½ × 15¾ ins. Engraver: C. Hunt. By Pantaloon ex Languish, owned by The Marquis of Westminster, also won Coronation Stakes, Ascot, 1841, walk-over, W. Scott up.
Collections: Mrs E. Huxley, Mr and Mrs Jack R. Dick. Also a version 13½ × 17½ ins, signed and dated 1841, in the collection of the Duke of West-minster.

133 **Jennie Herring** and a man holding Imaum in a stable. Signed and dated 1841. 30 × 25 ins.
Exhibited: Arthur Ackermann & Son Ltd 1965.

134 **Beggarman**, a bay racehorse, J. Robinson up. Signed and dated 1841.
Sold Sotheby's.

135 **Waiting the Return of the Ferryboat**. Signed and dated 1841. 39½ × 51½ ins.
Exhibited: Royal Society of British Artists, 1841. No 577; Richard Green Gallery 1978.

136 **The Royal Mail**. Signed and dated 1841. Two versions: (a) Changing horses outside the Swan Inn, Bottisham, Cambridge (Sold Sotheby's £21,000). (b) Changing horses outside the Red Lion (Sold Sotheby's £2,200). *(See Plate 38.)*
These two pictures are almost identical except for the Inn sign, and the perspective of the buildings in the background is different, but the greyhound and terrier, rear view of change horse on the left and posture of the harnessed horses, ostlers and passengers are all the same. It seems likely that picture (b) was a copy of picture (a), but probably by Herring.

137 **Plenipotentiary**, **Touchstone**, **Priam** and **Grey Momus** pictured with jockeys up racing on Epsom racehorse. Signed and inscribed with names of horses and dated 1841. 24 × 42 ins. Mr Batson's Plenipotentiary won the 1834 Derby, P. Conolly up; the Marquis of Westminster's Touch-stone won the 1834 St Leger, S. Calloway up; Mr E. Chifney's Priam won the 1830 Derby, S. Day up; Lord George Bentinck's Grey Momus won the 2,000 Guineas in 1838, J. Day up.
Collection: The Holford family. Exhibited: Arthur Ackermann 1975.

1842

138 **Bees-wing**, bay filly with Cartwright up. Signed and dated 1842. 22 × 30 ins. Owned by Mr William Orde, by Dr Syntax. Won Doncaster Cup 1840 and Ascot Gold Cup 1842.
Exhibited: Richard Green Gallery 1978.

139 **Diamond**, bay colt in a loose box. Signed, inscribed and dated 1842. 28 × 36 ins. Owned by Mr Francis Lovell.
Exhibited: Richard Green Gallery 1977.

140 **Phenomenon**. Signed and dated 1842.
Exhibited: Richard Green Gallery.

141 **Chestnut Mare**, dam of Phenomenon with stallion and two foals. Signed and dated 1842. 13½ × 17½ ins. Sold at Christie's for £5,000.

142 **Attila**. Signed and dated 1842. 13½ × 17½ ins. Sold Christie's.

143 **Confidence**, celebrated trotting horse, driven by a gentleman (right to left). Signed, inscribed and dated 1842. 40 × 50 ins. 'Confidence' was purchased in New York by Louis Buonaparte for 750 gns and presented by him to the Duke of Richmond. In an unbeaten career he won his last match over two miles of Sunbury Common on 18th October, 1839, for £100 a side, the time being 5 mins 39 secs. He was allowed by all judges to be the most complete trotter in existence.
Collections: Mrs William Murray, Mrs J. Lockwood. Exhibited: Arthur Ackermann & Son Ltd 1965.

144 **Caroline Elvina**, J. Holmes up, in a landscape. *c.*1842. 23½ × 29½ ins. Foaled 1835, by Tramp ex Babel, bred by Lord Chesterfield. Sold to Tsar of Russia, 1842. Collection: The Jockey Club.

145 **Blue Bonnett**, bay racehorse in a stable. Won St Leger 1842. Signed, inscribed and dated 1842. Sold Sotheby's.

146 **Bay Hunter in a Meadow**. Signed and dated 1842. Sold Sotheby's.

146a **Etonian**, a brown hunter in a stable. Signed and dated J. F. Herring 1842. 27½ × 28½ ins. On the back is written: 'Etonian by Herring Senr, bred at Badminton 1834'.
Collection: The Duke of Beaufort.

1843

147 **Cotherstone**, bay racehorse (a composite picture) inscribed. Won the Derby and Two Thousand Guineas 1843 with W. Scott up in the colours of John Bowes Esq of Streatlam, MP for Co. Durham who bred the horse. Signed J. F. Herring Snr 1843. 34 × 44 ins. Also included in rococo frame: Top left, Gibside Fairy, grand-dam; top right, Whalebone, grandsire; middle left, Whisker, grandsire; centre, Cotherstone; middle right, Camel, grandsire; Bottom left Emma, dam; bottom right, Touchstone – sire. Collection: HM Queen Elizabeth The Queen Mother.

147a **Cotherstone**, in a stable. W. Scott up. Signed and inscribed. Panel 8 × 10 ins. Owned by Mr J. Bowes, by Touchstone, by Camel ex Banter, by Master Henry who won the St Leger in 1802, who was by Beningborough who won the St Leger in 1794. JD Sale Sotheby's Part Two.

148 **Nutwith**. Won St Leger 1843. (No details available.) Witt collection.

149 **Bluebeard**, bay racehorse in a stable. Initials on rug 'FL'. Signed, inscribed and dated 1843. 28 × 36 ins. Owned by Mr Francis Lovell.
Exhibited: Richard Green Gallery 1973.

150 **Charles XII** in a stable. Signed and dated 1843. 28 × 36 ins. Owned by Mr A. Johnston. By Voltaire out of Wagtail, bred by Major Yarborough in 1836. Won 17 races including the Great St Leger and Doncaster Cup and Liverpool Cup in 1839, the Craven Stakes and Goodwood Cup in 1841 and the Craven Stakes again in 1843.
Exhibited: Arthur Ackermann & Son Ltd. *(See Plate 10.)*

151 **William Scott**, the jockey. *c.*1843. Signed JFH. 29½ × 24 ins. William Scott (1797–1848) was one of the foremost jockeys of his generation, and, it was said, if not the best, the most honest. He won the St Leger nine times (including a run of four wins from 1838 to 1841), the Derby four times and the Oaks on three occasions. In this picture, head to waist, he wears the colours of the prominent Northern owner, Mr J. Bowes, Streatlam Castle, Durham. Mr Bowes won the St Leger twice, in 1835 with Mundig, and again in 1843 with Cotherstone (see above), which leads one to

believe that the likeness was taken on one of these dates, probably the last.
Collection: Mr Paul Mellon.

1844

152 **Faugh-a-Ballagh** with his owner, Mr Irwin and trainer and Bell, the jockey in a stable. Signed, inscribed and dated 1844. 34 × 44 ins. Won the St Leger 1844, Bell up, and Grand Duke Michael Stakes and the Cesarewitch, Bell up. By Sir Hercules ex Guiccioli.
Exhibited: Richard Green Gallery 1975. *(See Plate 12.)*

153 **The London to York Carriers** outside the King's Arms. Signed and dated 1844. 28 × 48 ins.
Collection: Mr H. J. Joel. Exhibited: Richard Green Gallery 1978.

154 **The York to London Mail Change** at the Horse and Jockey. Signed and dated 1844. 28 × 48 ins.
Collection: Mr H. J. Joel. Exhibited: Richard Green Gallery 1978.

155 **Four Horses in a Large Barn**, two goats and ducks etc. Signed and dated 1844. 27 × 35½ ins.
Private collection. *(See Plate 75.)*

156 **Alice Hawthorn** – A race-mare saddled in a stable facing right, held by a groom. 27½ × 35½ ins. Signed J. F. Herring senr and dated 1844. Alice Hawthorn by Muley Moloch out of Rebecca, winner of the Chester Cup and Stakes 1842, Doncaster Cup 1843, and Goodwood Cup 1844 etc.
Collection: Sir Noel Murless.

157 **Camel**, owned by the Earl of Egremont, and **Banter**, owned by Lord Grosvenor, in a paddock. Signed and dated 1844. 18 × 27½ ins. Camel and Banter were the sire and dam of the 1834 and 1840 St Leger winners, Touchstone and Launcelot.
Exhibited: Arthur Ackermann & Son Ltd, 1979.

158 **Two Cart-Horses** in stalls. Signed and dated 1844. 11 × 15 ins.
Exhibited: Arthur Ackermann & Son Ltd.

159 **The Broken Pipe**, hunters with grooms at a trough, dog playing with pipe. Signed and dated 1844. 28 × 36 ins.
Exhibited: Richard Green Gallery. *(See Plate 33.)*

160 **Boy on a White Pony** and goat. Signed and dated 1844. 36 × 28 ins.
Exhibited: Arthur Ackermann & Son Ltd.

161 **Pacolet, Lady Julia** and **Baronet's Lady**, three thoroughbreds to pasture with a groom. Signed and dated 1844 (indistinct). 27¾ × 47¾ ins. Provenance: from Mr Steuart Wardell for whom it was painted.
Sold Christies.

162 **Touchstone**. Signed and dated 1844 – facing left.
Exhibited: Richard Green Gallery.

163 **A Happy Family**, ducks and ducklings. Signed and dated 1844. 19½ × 26½ ins.
Exhibited. Richard Green Gallery. *(See Plate 32.)*

164 **Start of the 1844 Derby** (the 'Dirty Derby'). Signed and dated 1844. 40½ × 82½ ins. The 'dirtiest Derby in history' was run on 22 May 1844, after four false starts. It was won by a four-year-old, Maccabaeus competing under the name of Running Rein, a real three-year-old, with Orlando second. Maccabaeus had been switched to win as the two-year-old, Running Rein, the year before. Another horse, Leander, who was a six-year-old was also entered, but fell and was destroyed after the race. In addition, Ratan, the second favourite was 'pulled' as was The Ugly Buck. Colonel Peel, owner of Orlando brought an action against the innocent owner of Maccabaeus/Running Rein, and Orlando was awarded the race. Much stricter rules resulted from the scandal.
Herring has painted the true colours of the horse's jockeys including, Leander, green, white sleeves; The Ugly Buck, black, orange cap; Orlando, purple, orange cap; Running Rein/Maccabaeus, all white; Ratan, white, red cap.
H.M. Treasury on loan to The National Trust of Scotland, Brodick Castle. *(See Plate 76.)*

1845

165 **Hammon and Tajar**. HRH The Duchess of Kent's saddle horses by Windsor Castle steps. Signed and dated 1845. 28 × 36 ins.

78

Dick – a champion greyhound.
Signed and dated 1822.
30½ × 42 ins.

Courtesy: J. D. D'Arcy Clark

List No 11

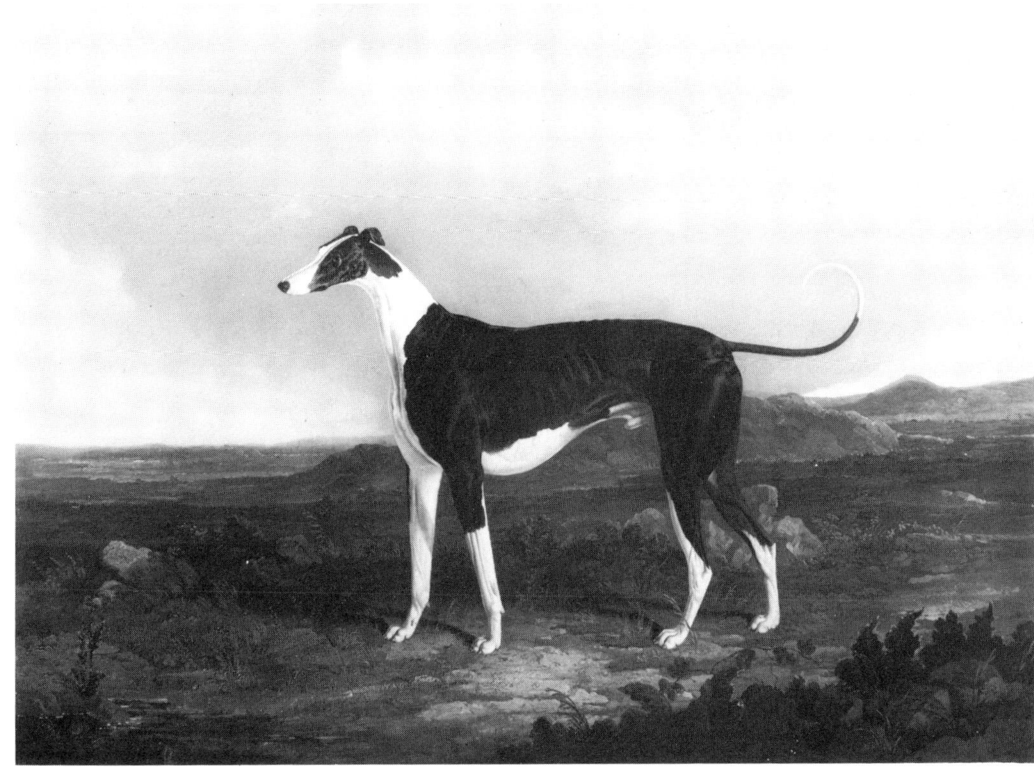

79

The Frugal Meal. Not signed or dated. 21½ × 29½ ins.

Courtesy: The Tate Gallery

List No 191

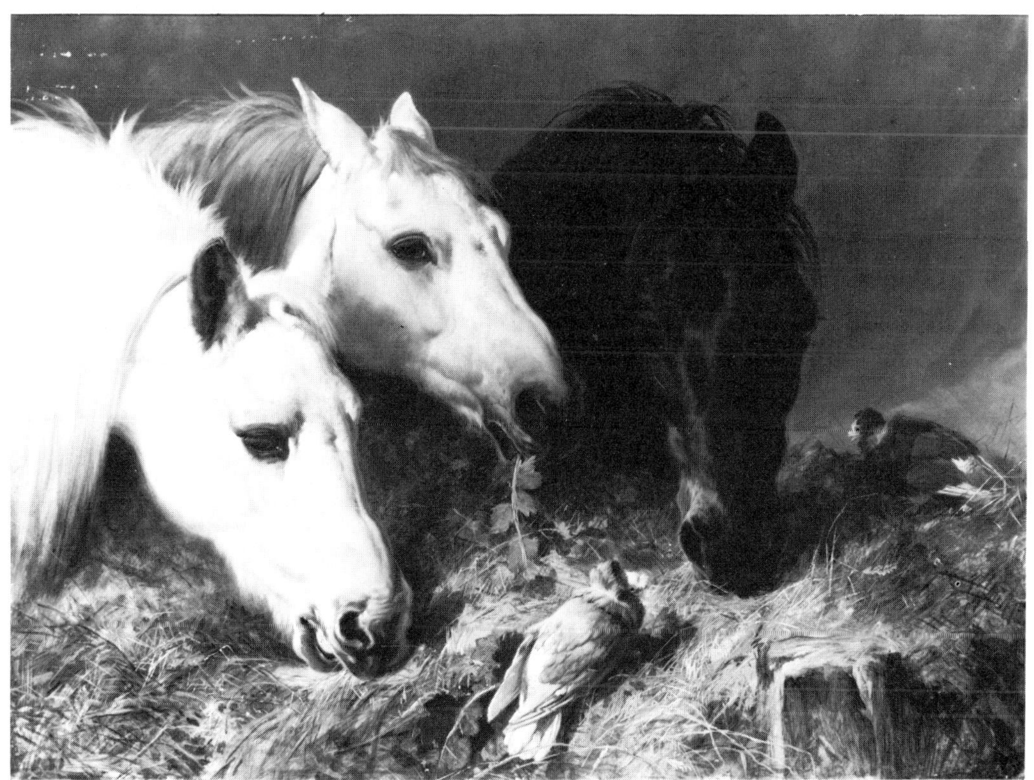

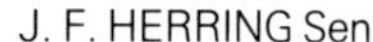
J. F. HERRING Senr

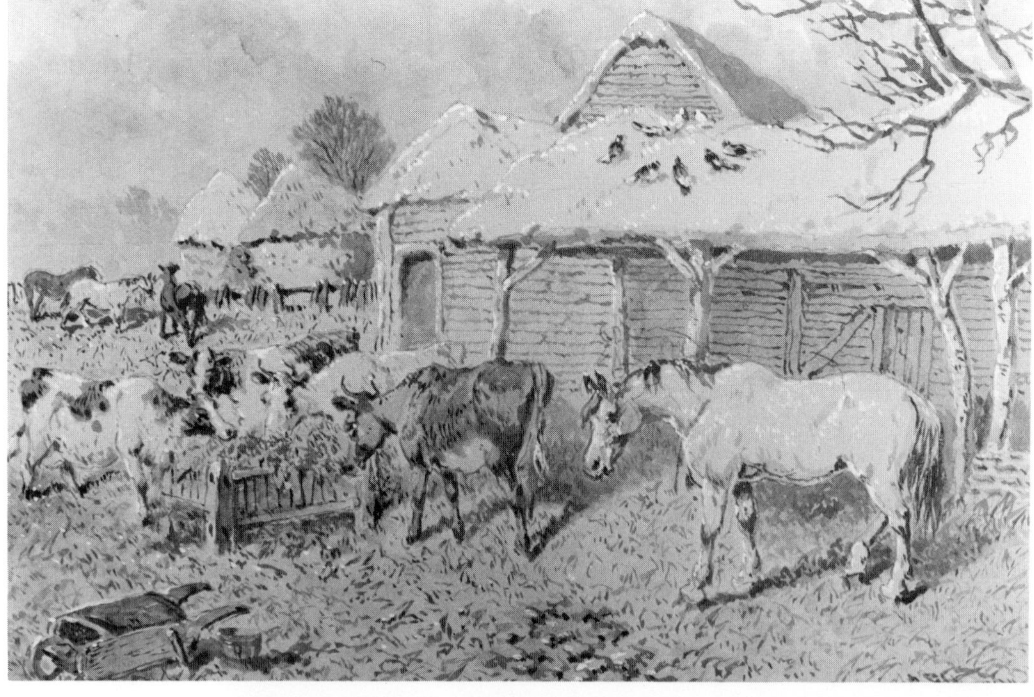

80

Farmyard Scene (water colour)

Courtesy: York City Art Gallery

List No 220

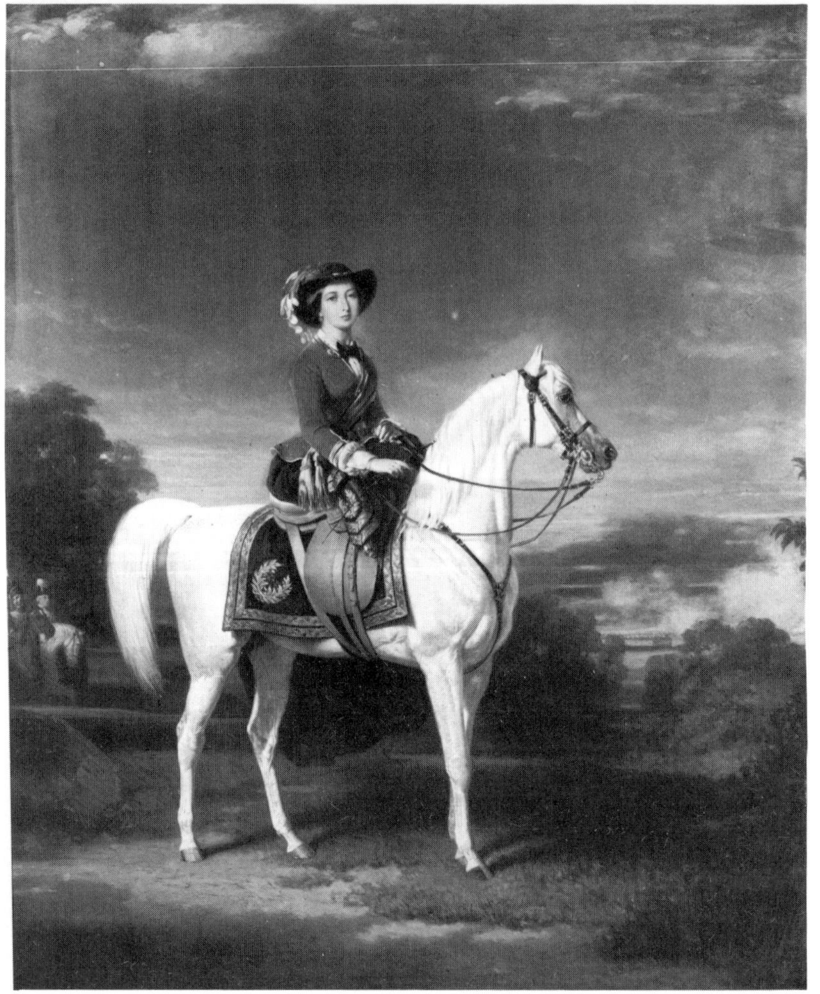

81

Queen Victoria on a white Arab. Signed E. Boutibonne and dated 1858 (with J. F. Herring senr). 43½ × 36½ ins.

Courtesy: HM the Queen

List No 286

Collection: Her Majesty Queen Elizabeth II. *(See Plate 77.)*

166 **The London–Glasgow Royal Mail** on the road. Signed and dated 1845. 23½ × 32½ ins. Collection: Sir A. Mortimer Singer, 1930; Alfred H. Caspary 1940; Mrs James Donahue, New York. Exhibited: Arthur Ackermann & Son Ltd 1976.

167 **The Kicker**. Signed and dated 1845, inscribed.
Sold Sotheby's.

168 **Cambridgeshire Hunt**, set of four, 1 The Meet near Foxton. 2 Gone Away. 3 Full Cry. 4 The Death. Signed and dated 1845. All 21½ × 29½ ins.
Exhibited: Richard Green Gallery.

169 **St James's**

and

170 **St Giles**. A pair of contrasting coach horses, one with a smart top-hatted coachman, and the other a ragged driver. Signed and dated 1845. 15 × 20 ins.
Exhibited: Richard Green Gallery 1976.

171 **Watering Horses outside Bell Inn**, rustic and girl, sheep on right. Signed and dated 1845. 28 × 26 ins.
Exhibited: Arthur Ackermann & Son Ltd.

172 **Long-Horned White Face Bull**. Signed and dated 1845. 18 × 24 ins.
Exhibited: Arthur Ackermann & Son Ltd.

173 **A Drake and Ducks**. Signed and dated 1845. 21 × 30 ins (rounded top corners).
Collection: Lady Violet Macfadyen.

1846

174 **Said**, black Arab stallion in Windsor Great Park. Signed and dated 1846. 21½ × 29½ ins.
Collection: Her Majesty, Queen Elizabeth II. *(See Plate 68.)*

175 **Pantaloon**, spotted stallion in a paddock. Signed and dated 1846. 28 × 36 ins.
Exhibited: Richard Green Gallery. *(See Plate 16.)*

176 **Traverser** in a stable. Signed and dated 1846. 18 × 24 ins.
Witt collection. Exhibited: Knoedler.

177 **Elis and Bay Middleton**, racing to the right. Signed and dated 1846. 42 × 26 ins.
Collection: Sir Tatton Sykes.

178 **Sir Tatton Sykes**, a bay horse held by Sir Tatton Sykes in a stable, rug lying over manger (lop-eared horse). Signed and dated 1846. 30 × 22 ins.
Collection: Sir Tatton Sykes.

179 **Pyrrhus the first** (two versions). Signed and dated 1846.
Sold Sotheby's.

180 **Mendicant**. Signed and dated 1846.
Sold Sotheby's.

181 **Steeplechase Cracks**. Signed J. F. Herring senr lower right. Not dated. 24 × 44 ins. The field of twelve taking a jump in a point-to-point includes portraits of three famous steeplechase riders, Jem Mason in the foreground on the right and Alan McDonough and Tom Oliver in the centre of the group. The title is taken from the engraving by J. Harris published by Messrs Fores in 1852 as No 2 of the National Sports series.
Collection: Her Majesty, Queen Elizabeth the Queen Mother. Exhibited: British Sporting Paintings, 1975. No 107. *(See Plate 14.)*

182 **James 'Jem' Mason on Lottery**. First winner of the Grand National and other races. Signed, inscribed and dated '46. 25 × 19 ins. Owned by Mr H. John Elmore.
Collection: C. M. W. Cartwright, RN. Exhibited: RA Winter 1956/7. Portraits No. 458.
(Not to be confused with the 'Lottery' who won Doncaster Gold Cup 1825.)

1847

183 **Chestnut Horse in a Landscape**. Signed and dated 1847. 34 × 44 ins. Horse is trotting hard from right to left, dog chasing, two labourers by fence right, extensive landscape beyond with castle tower to right with standard flying.
Collection: Lotherton Hall, Aberford, nr Tadcaster, Yorks.

184 **Ducks and Fancy Pigeons** and white dove. Signed and dated 1847. Circular 23½ ins.
Private collection.

185 **Farm-Yard in Winter**, horses, pigs etc. Signed and dated 1847. 28 × 36 ins.
Exhibited: Arthur Ackermann & Son Ltd.

186 **Farm-Yard**, three horses, cock on a water butt, pigs etc. Signed and dated 1847. 27 × 36 ins.
Exhibited: Arthur Ackermann & Son Ltd.

187 **Spring**, a white pony in a stable, facing left. Signed and dated. 36 × 28 ins.
Collection: Sir Tatton Sykes.

188 **Study of Chestnut Horse, Cossack**, in a stable. *c.*1847. 6¾ × 8¾ ins. Oil on panel with traces of pencil outlines.
Collection: Lady Violet Macfadyen.

189 **Stableyard in Winter**. Horses, pigs, ducks. Signed and dated 1847. 28 × 36 ins. Exhibited Richard Green Gallery. *(See Plate 37.)*

190 **Group of Three Steeplechasers and Riders** (unfinished) *c.* 1847. Allan McDonough on Brunette, won many races in Ireland and finished fourth in Grand National in 1847; Tom Oliver on Discount, won the Grand National in 1844, and Jem Mason on Lottery won many races including the Grand National of 1839.
Exhibited: Arthur Ackermann & Son Ltd. *(See Plate 13.)*

191 **The Frugal Meal**, three horses' heads at a sparse manger, two doves. Exhibited: Royal Academy, 1847. Not signed or dated.
Collection: Tate Gallery. *(See Plate 79.)*

192 **Grey Orville**. Signed and dated 1847.
Collection: Sir William Worsley from G. C. Bower.

193 **In the Highlands**, a ghillie and a boy with two deer hounds, a gun taking aim. 20 × 30 ins. Signed with initials. *c.*1847–52.
Courtesy: Richard Green Gallery. *(See Plate 49.)*

1848

194 **Beeswing and Foal**, Newminster (by Touchstone) facing right. Signed and dated 1848. 19½ × 23¼ ins.
Collection: The Jockey Club.

and

195 **Beeswing** in a stable. *c.*1848. 14½ × 19½ ins.
Collection: The Jockey Club.

196 **Friends.** Signed and dated 1848, circular 13 ins. Exhibited Richard Green Gallery 1975. *(See Plate 26.)*

197 **The Artist's Daughter**, Jennie, with Imaum. Signed and dated 1848. 22 × 22 ins.
Exhibited: Richard Green Gallery 1975.

198 **Bay Carthorse** with goats and chickens in a stable-yard. Signed and dated 1848. 30 × 40 ins.
Exhibited: Richard Green Gallery.

199 **Carthorses in a Farmyard**. Signed and dated 1948.
Exhibited: Arthur Ackermann & Son Ltd.

200 **Favourites**. Heads of two horses at a manger with two fancy pigeons. Signed and dated 1848. Panel 13 × 13 ins.
Exhibited: Richard Green Gallery. *(See Plate 48.)*

201 **Interior of a Smithy**, blacksmith shoeing a grey, chestnut Shire horse behind. Signed and dated 1848. 34 × 44 ins.
Exhibited: Arthur Ackermann & Son Ltd.

202 **Grey Working Horse** and ducklings. Signed and dated 1848.
Exhibited: Arthur Ackermann & Son Ltd.

203 **Horse, Pony and Donkey Heads**. Signed and dated 1848. 30 × 24 ins.
Exhibited: Arthur Ackermann & Son Ltd.

204 **Sunset**, horses going home. Signed and dated 1848. 28¼ × 18¼ ins.
Exhibited: Arthur Ackermann & Son Ltd.

205 **Farmyard**, group of horses right, two goats and ducks. Signed and dated 1848. 28 × 38¼ ins.
Collection: Mrs R. Hollins, USA. Exhibited: Arthur Ackermann & Son Ltd.

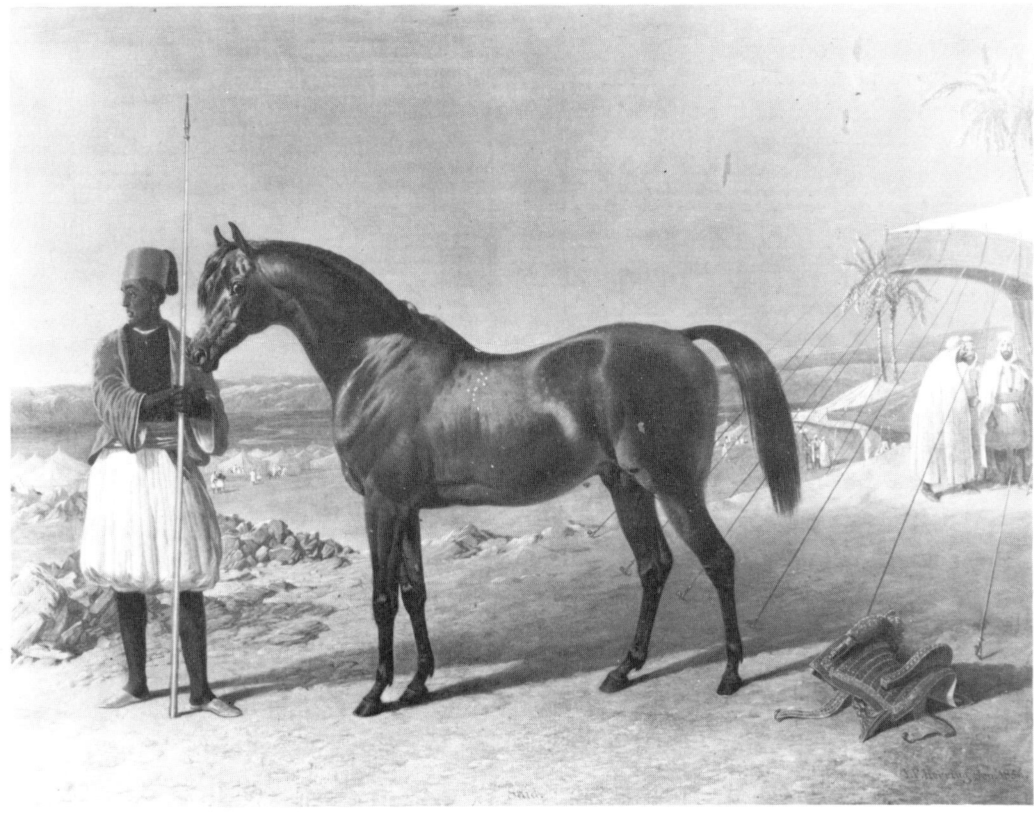

82

An Arab in a landscape.
Signed and dated 1856.
21½ × 29½ ins.

Courtesy: HM the Queen

List No 281

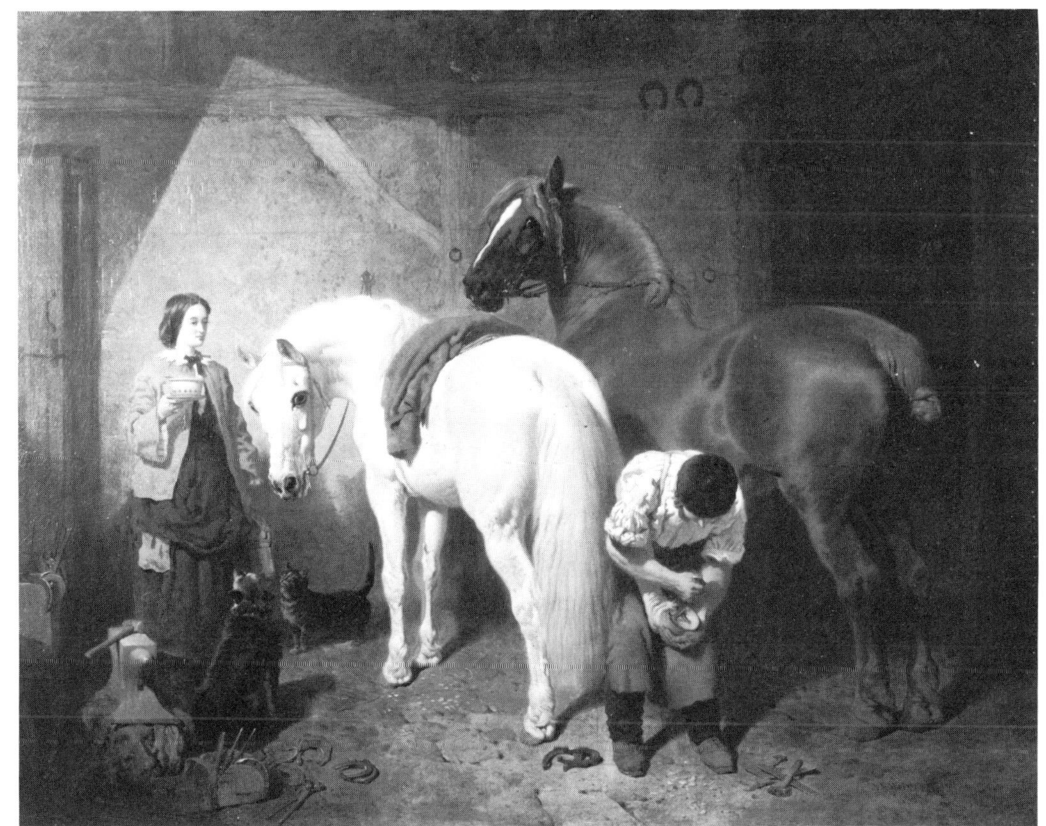

83

Shoeing Imaum with Jennie Herring. Signed and dated 1856. 33 × 43 ins.
This is the same picture on the easel in the photograph of Herring in his studio, page 62.

Courtesy: Mr John Warner

List No 279

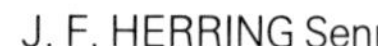

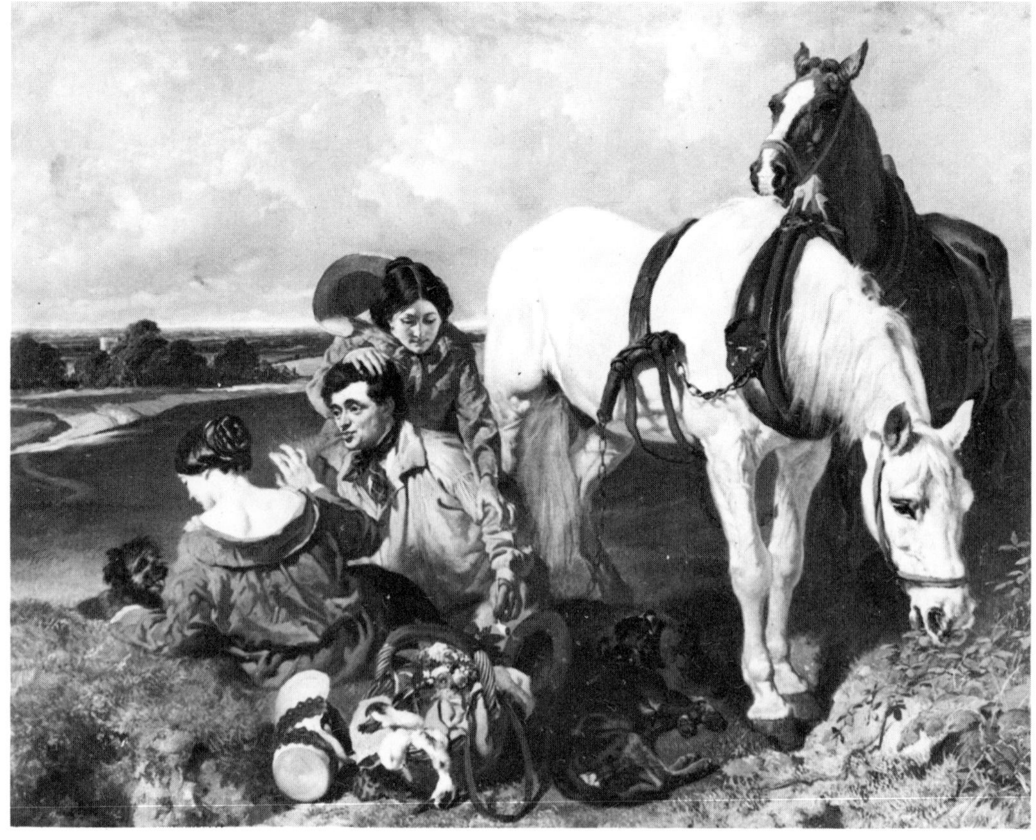

84

'Barney will ye no let the girls alone!' Signed and dated 1850 J F H *and* Thos Faed.

Courtesy: York City Art Gallery

List No 219

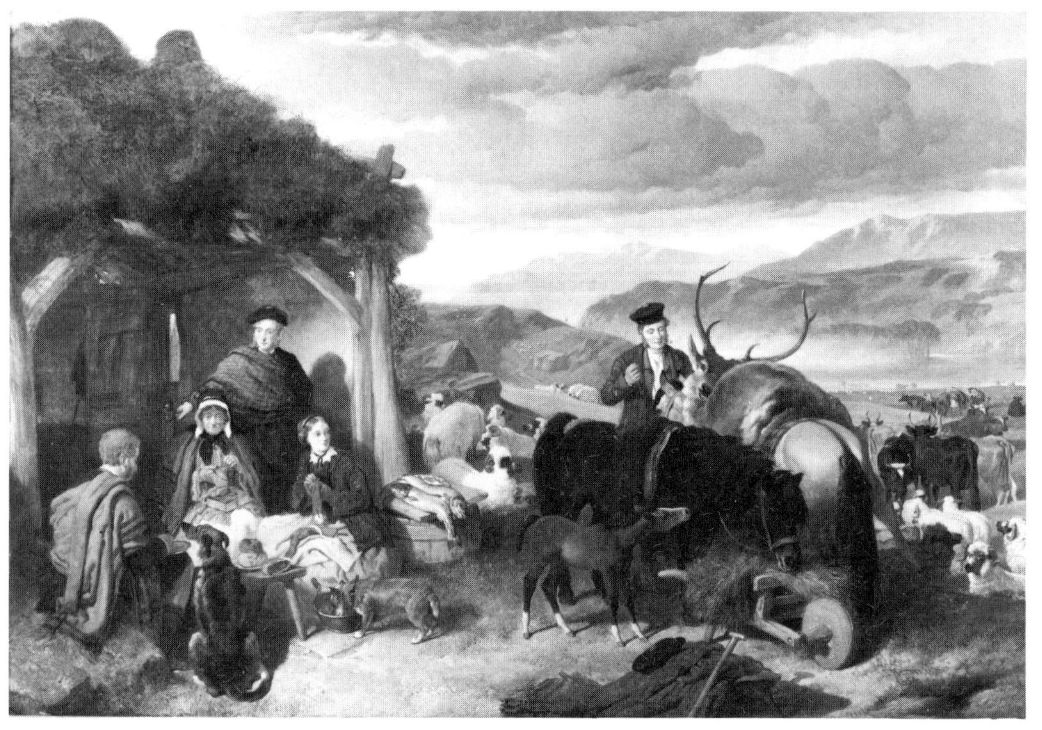

85

Highland Scene. Drover's Repast. Signed and dated 1834. 23 × 34 ins.

Courtesy: Mr John Warner

List No 75

206 **Sow, Boar and Piglets**. Signed and dated 1848. Circular 14 ins.
Collection: Mr Eric Fawcett.

207 **Calico**. Signed, inscribed and dated 1848.
Sold Sotheby's.

1849

208 **Outside a Stable**, two grooms preparing horses for hunting. Signed and dated 1849. 27 × 36 ins.
Exhibited: Richard Green Gallery. *(See Plate 44.)*

209 **Irish Water Spaniel** retrieving a mallard duck. Signed and dated 1849.
Sold Sotheby's £900.

210 **Stable Companions**. Signed and dated 1849. 14 × 14 ins.
Exhibited: Richard Green Gallery 1974.

211 **Grooms and Horses** in a stableyard. Signed and dated 1849. 27 × 37 ins.
Exhibited: Arthur Ackermann & Son Ltd.

212 **Head of Flying Dutchman** – a sketch. Inscribed on reverse stretcher.
Exhibited: Arthur Ackermann & Son Ltd.

213 **Chestnut, Grey and Bay Horses** being watered by a farm-hand in a stable. Signed and dated 1849. 28 × 36 ins.
Exhibited: Arthur Ackermann & Son Ltd.

214 **Flying Dutchman** with his owner, Lord Eglinton and jockey in tartan jacket yellow sleeves. Signed. 19½ × 31½ ins.
Collection: Lady Violet Macfadyen.

215 **Bay Hunter** in a landscape facing left. Signed and dated 1849. 14½ × 18 ins.
Exhibited: Richard Green Gallery.

216 **All My Eye**. Signed, inscribed and dated 1849.
Sold Sotheby's.

c. 1849

217 **Hen and Chicks** beside a pool. 13½ ins circular.
Collection: Lady Violet Macfadyen.

1850

218 **Lop-Eared doe and young**. 14 × 18 ins. *c.* 1850.
Exhibited: Richard Green Gallery. *(See Plate 47.)*

219 **'Barney! Leave the Girls Alone!'** Signed and dated 1850 (re-lined 1973). 34 × 44 ins. In a rolling landscape, a young man blows pipe-smoke into a girl's face but is restrained by a second girl; two harnessed cart-horses stand to the right. In 1883 the picture was exhibited in York as 'Paddy, leave the girls alone.' The figures have traditionally been attributed to Thos Faed and a note exists in Faed's record book (MS in National Gallery of Scotland archive) to the effect that he painted in the figures on Herring's 'picture' for Mr Lloyd in 1852; he possibly mistook the date, since the record book was compiled at the end of his life.
Literature: *York Catalogue*, 1907, No 111, as Herring; Preview, 76, 1966, p. 707, illus; C. Wood, *Dictionary of Victorian Painters 1971*, p. 65.
Exhibited: Suffolk Street 1851 (431) as Herring. Burton Bequest, 1882, York City Art Gallery. *(See Plate 84.)*

also

220 **Farm Horses and Cattle** in a snowy farmyard, in water colour on grey Whatman paper. Signed J. F. Herring.
York City Art Gallery. *(See Plate 80.)*

221 **Three Horses at a field entrance** and roller. Signed and dated 1850. Circular 15¼ ins.
Collection: Lady Violet Macfadyen.

222 **The Baron's Charger**, with attendant, young woman and spaniel begging by an archway. 36 × 45 ins. *c.* 1850.
Courtesy: Richard Green Gallery. *(See Plate 30.)*

223 **Busy Farmyard Scene** with horses, pigs, cattle and 'pyramid' fodder rack, at Meopham Bank farm buildings and trees. *c.* 1850. 26½ × 50 ins.
Collection: Lady Violet Macfadyen.

224 **Two horses in a stable**, poultry etc. A pair, both 15½ ins circular.
Collection: Lady Violet Macfadyen.

225 **A pair of farmyard scenes**. (1) Horses and

other animals in a farmyard. (2) Horses beside a stream. Signed and dated 1850 and 1851. Circular 16 ins.

226 **Farmyard in winter**. Signed and dated 1850. 40 × 50 ins.
Exhibited: Richard Green Gallery 1974.

227 **Three Horses beside a River**. Signed and dated 1850. 16 × 16 ins circular.
Exhibited: Arthur Ackermann & Son Ltd 1978.

228 **Rustic watering his Horse** at a pump, dog barking at a donkey. Signed and dated 1850. 14½ × 19½ ins.
Exhibited: Arthur Ackermann & Son Ltd.

229 **Sir Joseph Hawley** in a gig drawn by a champion trotter, Red Bonnet, going left at speed. *c.* late 1850s. 24¾ × 29½ ins. Sir Joseph won four Derby's with Teddington, Beadsman, Musjid, and Blue Gown, and was most successful owner of the day; although he looks amiable in the picture, he was actually a secretive and misanthropic man, who ran his own secret trials without even telling his trainer the weights, and he made a fortune out of betting.
Collection: The Jockey Club. *(See Plate 31.)*

230 **Flying Dutchman Beating Voltigeur at York**, Judge's box left. *c.*1851. 27 × 39 ins. Lord Egremont's Flying Dutchman by Bay Middleton, 5 years old, carrying 8st 8½lbs, Marlow up, finishing ahead of Lord Zetland's Voltigeur, 4 years old, 8st, Nat Flatman up, in the celebrated match over 2 miles of the old course for 1,000 Guineas. Flying Dutchman won by a 'short length' at evens.
Collection: The Jockey Club.

231 **Rhode Island Red Hen** and chicks. 11¾ × 9½ ins. Signed and dated on a panel.
Collection: Mr Eric Fawcett.

232 **Henry Willis**, aged 10, astride his pony. Signed 1851. 36 × 28 ins.
Exhibited: Richard Green Gallery. *(See Plate 35.)*

233 **The Hunter's Return**, barefoot girl and ghillie with white pony bearing a dead stag, and two lurchers. Signed and dated 1851–52. 40 × 50 ins.
Provenance: James F. Graham and Sons, New York. Geraldine Rockefeller Dodge, New York.

234 **Nancy**. John Osborn up, owner and trainer, York Minster in background. Signed and dated 1851.
Exhibited: M. Bernard, 1953.

235 **The Green Grocer's Cob** and man and woman in a stable. Signed and dated 1851. 22 × 30 ins.
Collections: The Hon. Mrs W. J. Hanna, Mr and Mrs Lyall Smith. Exhibited: The British Institution, 1851, No 249; Richard Green Gallery 1978.

236 **Lop-eared Doe and Young**. Signed and dated 1851. Panel 10 × 12 ins.
Sold by Richard Green, 1976, £1,700.

237 **Hunters at Grass**, Haddon Hall. Signed and dated 1851. 40½ × 51 ins.
Collection: Mr John Haynes, New York. Exhibited: Richard Green Gallery 1974. *(See Plate 21.)*

238 **Muscovy Ducks** and ducklings. Signed and dated 1851. 13½ × 17½ ins.
Sold at Sotheby's, £2,200.

239 **Study of the Head of an Arab**. Signed with initials and dated 1851. 9¼ × 12 ins.
Exhibited: Richard Green Gallery 1973.

1852

240 **Horses and Figures** and livestock in a barn at Meopham. Signed and dated 1852. 23 × 35 ins.
Exhibited: Richard Green Gallery. *(See Plate 36.)*

241 **Goat and Kids**. Signed and dated 1852. 16¼ × 16¼ ins.
Exhibited: Richard Green Gallery. *(See Plate 25.)*

242 **Cattle by a Stream**.

and

243 **Two Horses Watering**. A pair signed and dated 1852. Circular 16 ins.
Exhibited: Arthur Ackermann & Son Ltd.

244 **Cattle Watering at a River**. Signed and dated 1852. 13½ × 17½ ins.
Sold by Sotheby's for £700.

245 **Ducks and Ducklings**. Signed and dated. 14 × 18 ins. – a pair.
Exhibited: Richard Green Gallery 1976.

246 **Ducks and Ducklings** on a river bank. Signed and dated 1852. Panel 14 x 18 ins.
Exhibited: Richard Green Gallery 1976.

247 **A Meeting of Deer Stalkers**, ponies, cattle and sheep in Highlands. Signed J. F. Herring 1852 and H. Bright 1858. 42 × 72 ins.
Provenance: L. V. Flatou engraved, sold at Christie's 1861 for £153, and 1973 for 5,000 gns. *(See Plate 40.)*

248 **Arab Caravan**, Arab mounted on a prancing steed, foreground, other figures, camels, etc. and fortress in background of desert landscape (Study for 'The Overland Route'). Signed and dated 1852–55. 17 × 23 ins.
Collection: Mr John Warner, by descent. *(See Plate 41.)*

249 **White Drake and Duck** with ducklings beside a pool. Signed and dated 1852. 9½ × 11¼ ins.
Collection: Lady Violet Macfadyen.

250 **Ducks and Ducklings** and **The Foster Mother**. Signed and dated 1852 and 1850. A pair, panel 10 × 12 ins.
Exhibited: Richard Green Gallery 1976.

1853

251 **Two Harnessed Cart Horses** by a barn, wheelbarrow and ducks. Signed and dated 1853. 27½ × 35½ ins.
Sold Christie's.

252 **London–Edinburgh Royal Mail Coach**. Signed and dated 1853. 27½ × 35½ ins.
Exhibited: Richard Green Gallery. *(See Plate 46.)*

253 **The Flying Dutchman**, brown colt being saddled by two grooms, his owner, the 13th Earl of Eglinton is seen conversing to the right with jockey, Charles Marlow. Signed and dated 1853. 18 × 24 ins.
Engraved by J. Harris & C. Quentery for Fores' National Sports series Racing Plate 1, Saddling. This is the right horse in the composition 'The Flying Dutchman', published 13 May, 1856.
Won the Derby and St Leger 1849. By Bay Middleton ex Barbelle, by Sandbeck, bred by Colonel Vansittart and sold to Lord Eglinton for 1,000 gns. As a two-year-old he won all the five races he entered, including the July Stakes, Newmarket and the Champagne Stakes, Doncaster.
After several successful races in 1850 The Flying Dutchman was defeated in the Doncaster Cup by Voltigeur, who had won the Derby and St Leger in the same year.
After the Match with Voltigeur, the 'Dutchman' never raced again and was retired to stud. In 1858 he was sold for £4,000 and exported to France where he was a successful stallion.
Collections: Mr Edwin Martin, for whom the subject was painted, Mr J. L. Martin by descent. Sold Christie's, 22 November 1968, with artist's receipt for £36 15s., and at JD Sale Sotheby's Part Three for £10,000. Literature: P. Willett, *The Thoroughbred*, illus p. 132.

254 **Three Horses**, one white, by pyramid fodder rack. Signed and dated 1853. 17 × 20 ins.
Exhibited: Arthur Ackermann & Son Ltd.

255 **Mare and Foal** at a water trough, stables in the background. Signed and dated 1853. Panel 10 × 12 ins.
Exhibited: Richard Green Gallery 1975.

256 **A Lop-Eared Doe** and litter eating vegetables on a grassy bank. Signed and dated 1853. Panel 10 × 12 ins.
Sold JD Sale Sotheby's for £3,500.

257 **In the Stable-Yard**. Signed and dated 1853. 18 × 24 ins.
Collection: J. D. Hodgson, USA. Exhibited: Richard Green Gallery 1974.

1854

258 **Black Horse**, saddled and bridled, drinking from a trough. Signed J. F. Herring senr and dated 1854. 12¾ × 17½ ins. Presented to National Gallery of Ireland by Dr Barry, 1873.

259 **Repose**

and

260 **Alarm**, ponies and mares in a mountainous

landscape. Signed and dated 1854. Each 24 × 36 ins. 'Repose' shows the ponies calmly grazing, the horizon bounded by static cumulus clouds; 'Alarm' the ponies galloping about, scudding clouds and shadows.
Collections: Mr J. J. Quelch, Mr and Mrs J. B. Sumner. Exhibited: Birkenhead 1931. Exhibited: Arthur Ackermann & Son Ltd 1965.

261 **Clydesdale** in a stable. Signed and dated 1854. 28 × 36 ins.
Collection: Mrs R. Hollins, USA.

262 **Three Horses** (mares) by a fence. Signed and dated 1854.
Exhibited: Arthur Ackermann & Son Ltd.

263 **Tajar** in a stable (owned by the Duchess of Kent). Signed and dated 1854. 22½ × 27 ins.
Exhibited: Richard Green Gallery.

264 **Highland Scene**, dead stag on a pony, pony mare and foal, sheep, cattle in distance right. Left under a shelter, family group in Scottish garb (possibly Charles Herring and Mrs J. F. Herring) with a sheep dog, fresh salmon on a tub, mountains and loch in distance. Signed and dated 1854. 23 × 34 ins.
Collection: Mr J. Warner, by descent.

265 **Hop Pickers** in an extensive landscape of hop vines being harvested. 'Druid' states that the farmer in a straw hat on a cob is Herring himself 'notably unconcerned with Mr Gladstone's policies.' Signed and dated 1854–60. 25 × 43 ins.
Sold Christies.

266 **The Deer Stalker**. Signed and dated 1854, with Henry Bright.
Exhibited: Richard Green Gallery.

267 **The Game-Keeper's Shack in the Highlands**, figures having a meal, left, pony and foal and dead stag, right. Signed and dated 1854. 41 × 67 ins. Similar to Mr Warner's canvas, see above.
Sold Christie's for £1,200.

268 **Finish of St Leger 1854**. Mr J. B. Morris's Knight of St George beating Lord Zetland's Iran (unfinished). 13½ × 17½ ins.
Sold Sotheby's for £800.

269 **A Flat Race**, set of four scenes with well known horses. (1) Saddling. Signed and dated 1854. (2) A False Start. Signed and dated 1853–54. (3) Run In. Signed and dated 1854. (4) Returning to Weigh. Signed and dated 1854. Each picture 20¾ × 41½ ins. This picture does not represent any particular race, and brings together eight horses, Flying Dutchman, Voltigeur, West Australian, Stockwell, King Tom, Teddington, Surplice and Lady Evelyn, all of which had won Classic races, excepting King Tom, between 1848 and 1853.
Collection: the Earl of Halifax.

1855

270 **Waiting for the Master**, a groom and saddled bay hunter by the steps of a mansion. Signed and dated 1855, stamped with the artist's initials on the stretcher.

271 **A Rustic Courtship**. Signed and dated 1855. 13¾ × 17¾ ins.
Sold Sotheby's for £2,200.

272 **Noonday Rest**, rustic scene. Signed and dated 1855. 49½ × 39½ ins.
Sold Christie's. *(See Plate 34.)*

273 **Rataplan and Wild Dayrell** in the Doncaster Cup 1855. Rataplan won from Dayrell who broke down. Previously, Dayrell, a brown colt bred by Lord Zetland and owned by Mr F. Popham, after a chequered career when he won a Sweepstake at races, excepting King Tom, between 1848 and 1853.
Collection: the Earl of Halifax.

274 **In the Stables at Meopham**, a white horse, Imaum, with the artist's daughter, Jennie, in doorway left, with a stable hand, two dogs and ducks. Signed and dated 1855. 33 × 43 ins.
Collection: Lady Violet Macfadyen.

See also a similar picture of the same subject:

275 **Stable Interior, Meopham Park, Kent**. 34 × 45½ ins (unsigned).
Collection: The Hon. P. J. Fairfax. Exhibited: Arthur Ackermann & Son Ltd 1961 and 1965.

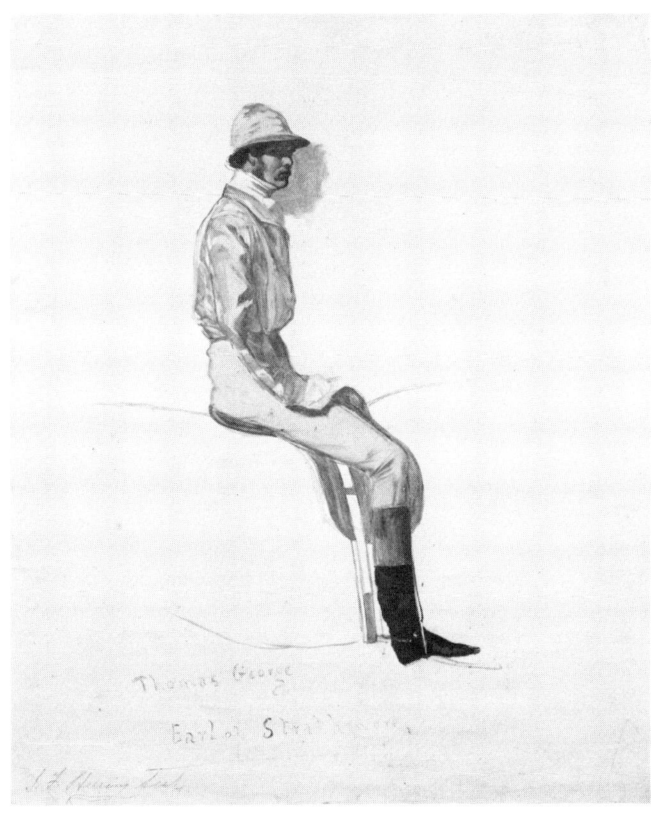

86

Thomas George, Earl of Strathmore
Water colour sketch astride horse.

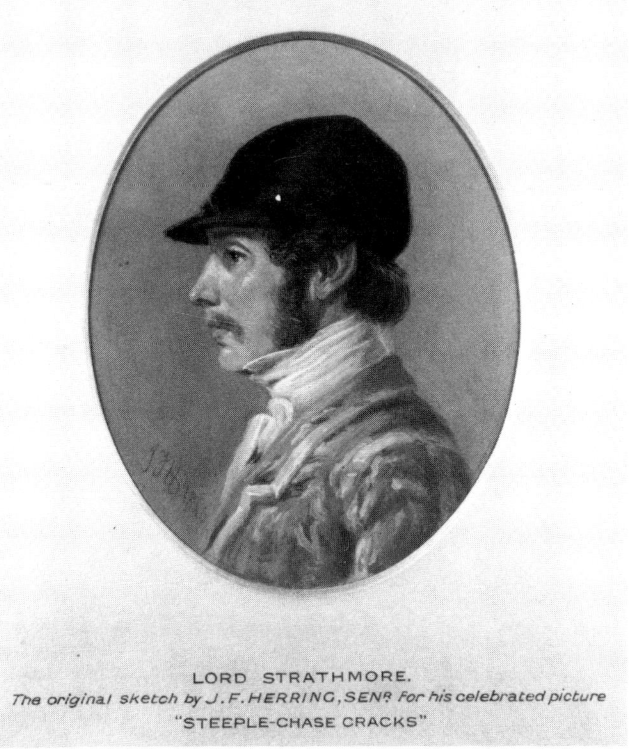

87

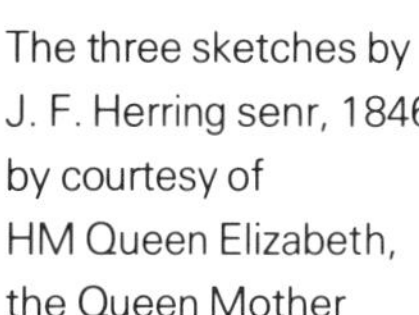

The three sketches by
J. F. Herring senr, 1846
by courtesy of
HM Queen Elizabeth,
the Queen Mother

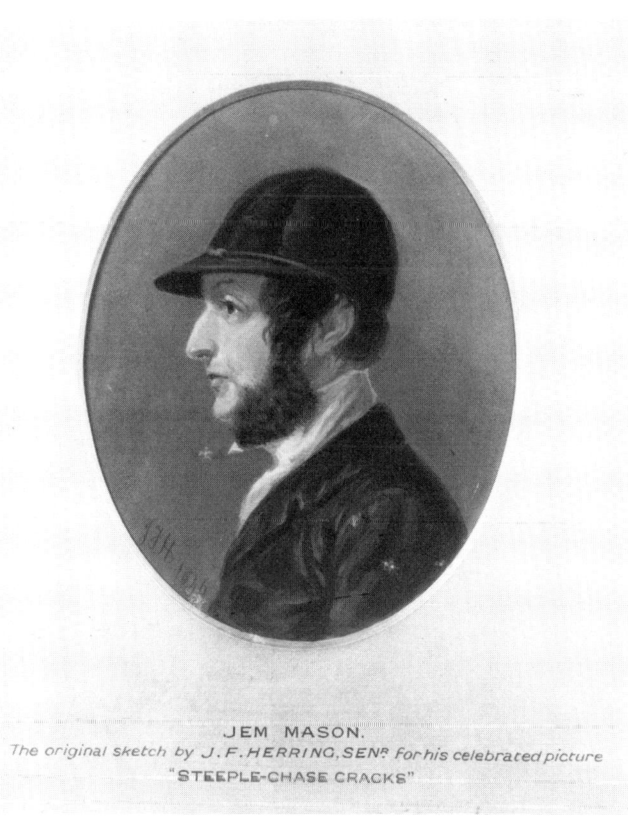

88

276 **A Cavalier's Visit**. By Herring, Bright and Baxter. Signed by each and inscribed and dated 1855. 49½ × 39½ ins.
Exhibited: Richard Green Gallery.

277 **White Greyhound in a Landscape**, park gates to right. Signed and dated 1855.
Sold Sotheby's.

278 **Watering Horses at a Well**. Signed and dated 1855. Panel 14 × 18 ins.
Exhibited: Richard Green Gallery.

1856

279 **Shoeing Imaum**, Suffolk Punch on right, with dog and cat, artist's daughter, Jennie, left (man holding up Imaum's hind leg probably William Terry). Signed and dated 1856. 33 × 43 ins. This is the same picture seen on Herring's easel in the photograph p. 62.
Collection: Mr J. Warner, by descent. *(See Plate 83.)*

280 **Jennie**, skewbald and ducks. Signed and dated 1856.
Exhibited: Arthur Ackermann & Son Ltd.

281 **The Arab Said**, in a landscape. The horse on which the Royal children were taught to ride. Signed and dated 1856. 21½ × 29½ ins.
Collection: Her Majesty, Queen Elizabeth II. *(See Plate 82.)*

1857

282 **Horse Fair, Southborough Common**. Signed and dated 1857–8. 39 × 69½ ins. Self portrait of the artist standing left in buff top hat. Sold with a receipt from the artist, 24 April 1858, for £300, and cushion cut signet gypsy ring given by the artist to the owner.
Exhibited: Richard Green Gallery. *(See Plate 20.)*

283 **Meopham Farm Yard**. Signed and dated 1857. 26 × 52 ins.
Collection: Lady Violet Macfadyen. *(See Plate 42.)*

1858

284 **Boroughbridge Horse Fair**, church on left. Signed and dated 1858. 31¾ × 72¼ ins.
Witt collection.

285 **Meopham Farm Yard**. Signed and dated 1858. 24¼ × 36¼ ins.
Witt collection.

286 **Queen Victoria** on a white Arab. Signed E. Boutibonne and dated 1858 (with J. F. Herring senr).
Collection: HM The Queen. *(See Plate 81.)*

1859

287 **Rural Scene**, cattle and ducks by a stream and a fine Channel Island bull on right, woods behind. Signed and dated 1859. 39½ × 49 ins.
Sold Christie's.

288 **Harvest Time**, wide landscape of waggons loaded with sheaves of corn approaching up a rise left, drawn by dappled greys, with various figures. Signed? 42 × 72 ins.
Provenance: From Mr Edward Shayer to whom it was sold by the artist in July 1859, on stretcher.
Sold Christie's. *(See Plate 43.)*

1860

289 **Timber Waggon and Four Horses** by a river, boy on a pony, right. Signed and dated 1860. 35 × 59 ins.
Private collection.

290 **The Forge**, grey working horse, blacksmith and goat. Signed and dated 1860. 9½ × 12 ins.
Exhibited: Richard Green Gallery.

291 **Two Men in a Gig**. Monogram 1860.
Exhibited: Richard Green Gallery.

1861

292 **Spacious Farm Yard**, barns right, cow-stalls left, church in distance, horse, cattle, pigs and poultry. Signed and dated 1861. 26 × 44 ins.
Exhibited: Richard Green Gallery.

293 **Grey Mare and Foal**.
Exhibited: Richard Green Gallery.

Paintings by Benjamin Herring senr

294 **A Master and Huntsman** outside kennels. Signed and dated 1826. 21 × 30 ins.
Exhibited: Richard Green Gallery. *(See Plate 60.)*

295 **Longwaist**, with the owner, Mr Fulmer Craven and trainer, Mr Dilly, Sam Day up, facing left, rubbing house right. Signed, inscribed Longwaist and dated 1827. 29½ × 37 ins. Bay colt by Whalebone ex Nancy, foaled 1821, bred by Mr Craven. Between 1824 and 1828 he won 27 races, including the Craven Stakes 1825 and 15 Gold Cups. He was sold to Squire John Mytton at the end of 1825 for 3,000 gns. At the Mytton Stud sale he was purchased by Mr Alexander Nowell of Underley at whose stud he died in 1835.
Collections: Miss Tracey, Bournemouth; Charles H. Theriot, New York.
Literature: *British Sporting Painters*, Walter Shaw Sparrow, p. 218; the *Theriot Catalogue*, New York 1940, illus p. 29.

296 **A Chestnut Hunter** and groom. Signed and dated 1828. 12½ × 17 ins.
Exhibited: Richard Green Gallery. *(See Plate 61.)*

J. F. Herring junr

297 **A Farmyard Scene** with cattle, poultry, horses and pigs. Signed. 22 × 44 ins.
Exhibited: Richard Green Gallery.

298 **Horses, Pigs and Chickens** by a farmyard pond. Signed. 11 × 17 ins.
Exhibited: Richard Green Gallery. *(See Plate 55.)*

299 **Horses and Pigs** disturbed in a field. Signed. 12 × 18 ins.
Exhibited: Richard Green Gallery. *(See Plate 56.)*

300 **Huntsmen and Hounds** at a ford. 29½ × 49½ ins.
Exhibited: Richard Green Gallery. *(See Plate 57.)*

301 **Off to the Meet**, two saddled horses and hounds in a stableyard, huntsman and hounds in distance. Signed. 24 × 36 ins.
Exhibited: Richard Green Gallery. *(See Plate 58.)*

302 **A Farmyard Scene in Winter**. Signed. 14 × 20 ins.
Exhibited: Richard Green Gallery. *(See Plate 59.)*

303 **Shooting Duck at Six-Mile-Bottom**. Signed and dated 1832. 22 × 30 ins.
Private collection. *(See Plate 28.)*

304 **A View of Six-Mile-Bottom**. Signed and dated 1836. 15½ × 12½ ins.
The Witt collection. *(See Plate 29.)*

304a **Lucetta**, brown mare owned by Sir Mark Wood. Won at Ascot 1830 and Goodwood Stakes 1832. Initials 'M.W.' on blanket. Signed Fred Herring 1836. 8¾ × 11¾ ins.
Collection: The Marquess of Exeter.

305 **Three Horses Harnessed to a Farm Wagon** in a ford, in a landscape. Attributed to J. F. Herring junr. 12 × 18 ins. *c.*1850.
Collection: Mrs Peggy Robinson.

Charles Herring

306 **Grey Cob** and two lads in a stable. Signed with initials and dated '43. Panel 8¾ × 12 ins.
Exhibited: Arthur Ackermann & Son Ltd. *(See Plate 62.)*

Benjamin Herring junr

307 **Timber Waggons** and horses in a glade, and other examples in Lady Macfadyen's collection.

Paintings by J. F. Herring senr in The William Woodward Collection of English Sporting Art, Baltimore Museum of Art, Maryland, USA

The late Mr William Woodward made his great collection of sporting pictures from about the year 1922 until 1929, and his interest in the British thoroughbred influenced his choice mainly towards pictures of race-horses. There are three by Stubbs, four by J. N. Sartorius and two by Harry Hall in the collection now housed at the Baltimore Museum, Maryland, USA. By far the greatest number however are by J. F. Herring senior, with no fewer than 42.

These were practically all purchased from Messrs Fores in London, a firm with connections going right back to Herring himself, at prices which look absurd today.

For instance, he bought eight pictures of the St Leger winners between the years 1815 (Filho da Puta) and 1825 (Memnon) for a mere £2,500. These, it is true, are mostly the small signed portraits Herring made for the engraver soon after the race, and measure about 14 × 19 ins each. Later, others were added, Jack Spigot, 1821; Barefoot, 1823; Jerry, 1824; Matilda, 1827; Touchstone, 1834; Queen of Trumps, 1835; and Faugh-a-Ballagh, 1844 – making an unique set of fifteen in all.

Mr Woodward also bought a picture of Voltigeur with three others for £1,000 from Fores in 1924; the highest single price recorded is thought to be the £735 paid for a large picture of Touchstone (signed and dated 1843), 27¾ × 36 ins, in 1928. For ease of reference, it has been thought better to list this collection separately in alphabetical order, although space does not allow of the inclusion of all the very full details given in the excellent and well-researched catalogue, which makes the information available to the researcher in this country look meagre indeed.

Alarm. Signed J. F. Herring senr, inscribed Alarm 4 Years Old. Horse facing right in stall. 18 × 24 ins.

Antonio. Signed J. F. Herring, horse with jockey and owner in courtyard. Winner St Leger 1819. 14½ × 19 ins.

Barefoot. Signed and dated 1823, horse facing right with mounted jockey. Winner St Leger 1823. 14½ × 19 ins. Four other versions.

Bay Middleton. Signed, oil on panel, horse facing right in stall. Winner Derby 1836. 8½ × 9¾ ins.

Beeswing. Signed and dated 1843, horse facing left in stall. Famous mare and winner of fifty-one races. 14 × 18 ins. Six other verions with varying stall backgrounds. (See also Jockey Club's Collection). One of Doncaster Cup with background by James Pollard, 1838.

Blacklock. Signed. Horse facing right in stall. Oil on panel 10 × 12 ins. One other version, signed and dated 1817, 24½ × 29½ ins. Sold Sotheby's 1965.

Camel. Signed, horse in landscape. 28 × 36 ins. Two other versions of horse alone, prancing, also included in composite picture of ancestors of

Cotherstone owned by the Queen Mother, and with Banter in a landscape, see below.

Camel and Banter. Signed J. F. Herring senr. 22½ × 28 ins. Purchased from Fores for £500, 1928. Part of a lot of sixteen pictures put on sale by Christie, Manson and Woods in 1864 which Fores had obtained from the artist over the years. Withdrawn as did not fetch reserve of 1,450 gns. Another version exhibited Ackermanns 1979.

Catton. Signed J. F. Herring 1830, inscribed Catton. Horse in a landscape. 27¾ × 35¾ ins. Bred by Earl of Scarborough, also in Famous Sires series.

Cobweb and her foal, Bay Middleton. Signed and dated 1833, mare and grazing foal. Oil on panel 10 × 11 ins.

Crucifix. Signed and dated 1840. Horse with jockey facing right. Winner Oaks 1840. 20 × 24 ins.

Dangerous. Signed J. F. Herring – inscribed Dangerous Horse. Jockey mounted running to left. Oil on panel. 9½ × 11¼ ins. This painting was purchased from Herring by Thomas Dawson in about 1833. Three other versions mentioned.

The Duchess. Signed J. F. Herring. Horse, jockey mounted trotting to left. Winner St Leger 1816. 14½ × 19 ins. Another version lent to Doncaster Art Museum by Parker Gallery 1958.

Ebor. Signed J. F. Herring. Horse, jockey mounted facing left, robed horses in background left. Winner St Leger 1817. 14½ × 19 ins.

Faugh-a-Ballagh. Signed J. F. Herring senr 1844, inscribed Faugh-a-Ballagh. Horse facing left in stall. Winner St Leger 1844. Other versions, one sold Sotheby's 1973.

Filho-da-Puta. Signed J. F. Herring. Horse mounted jockey walking to right. Winner St Leger 1815. 14 × 19 ins. See also two versions in Doncaster Museum.

Flying Dutchman. Signed J. F. Herring senr, inscribed 'Flying Dutchman. Derby & St Leger 1849'. 14 × 18 ins. At least four other depictions of this famous racehorse.

Gustavus and Tommy. Signed J. F. Herring 1839. Two horses drawing large-wheeled coach to right in The Extraordinary Trotting Match Against Time. Oil on panel. 20 × 29½ ins.

Jack Spigot. Signed J. F. Herring, inscribed Jack Spigot 1821. Horse with jockey mounted facing right. Winner St Leger 1821. 14½ × 18¾ ins. Five other versions.

Jerry. Signed J. F. Herring, inscribed Jerry 1824. Horse, jockey mounted facing left. Winner St Leger 1824. 14½ × ½9 ins. Three other versions.

Lady Hampton. Signed J. F. Herring senr 1842. Trotting horse drawing large-wheeled coach to left. 21½ × 29½ ins.

Matilda. Signed J. F. Herring, inscribed Matilda 1827. Horse facing left in stall. Winner St Leger 1827. Oil on panel. 10 × 12 ins. Nine other depictions mentioned.

Melbourne. Signed J. F. Herring senr 1853, inscribed Melbourne. Horse facing right outside stable-door. 28¾ × 36¼ ins. Most noted Sire of his day, winning Sire three times, 1846, 1853 and 1857. He died in 1856 aged 22.

Memnon. Signed J. F. Herring, horse, jockey mounted facing right running horse in far background. Winner St Leger 1825. 14½ × 19 ins. Four other depictions, and one of Actaeon beating Memnon. Exhibited: Richard Green Gallery, London.

Orville. Signed J. F. Herring S-, inscribed Orville, St Leger 1802. Horse facing right in walled courtyard. 14½ × 18¼ ins. Similar portrait but with wall in background sold at Christies June 1970.

Pocahontas and Stockwell. Signed and dated 1819. Three mares and three foals in landscape. 24¾ × 30 ins.

Queen of Trumps.* Signed J Fred. Herring. Six Mile Bottom 1835. Horse, jockey mounted facing right. 9¼ × 12 ins. Winner St Leger 1835. Three other versions mentioned.

*The inscription suggests that this is a copy by J. F. Herring junr of one of his father's works.

Queen Mary and Blink Bonny. Signed and dated 1854. Mare and foal in landscape. 23 × 30 ins.

Reveller. Signed J. F. Herring. Horse with jockey mounted facing left, attendant kneeling right. Winner St Leger 1818. 14½ × 19 ins.

Saint Patrick. Signed J. F. Herring. Horse with jockey mounted facing left. Winner St Leger 1820. 14½ × 19 ins. Another sketchy version Doncaster Museum.

Stockwell. Signed J. F. Herring 18–. Horse in landscape facing left. 22 × 30 ins. Another version, facing left against a rough board fence.

Sultan. Signed J. F. Herring senr 1843, inscribed Sultan. Horse in stall facing right. 14 × 18 ins.

Surplice. Signed twice, on wall – J. F. Herring senr, on blanket J. F. Herring, inscribed Surplice. Horse in stall facing right. Winner Derby 1848. 13¾ × 18 ins.

Theodore. Signed J. F. Herring. Horse with jockey mounted walking left. Winner St Leger 1822. 14½ × 19 ins. Two other versions.

Touchstone. Signed J. F. Herring senr 1843. Horse in landscape facing left. Winner St Leger 1834, Doncaster Cup 1835, Ascot Gold Cup twice and other races. 27¾ × 36 ins. Fourteen other portrayals mentioned and numerous engravings.

Velocipede. Signed J. F. Herring 1829, inscribed under left horse – Velocipede, under right horse – The Colonel. Both mounted on race-course, one from rear, other facing left. 28 × 36 ins. Eight related paintings show the horses together and individually in different sizes and poses.

Voltaire. Signed J. F. Herring 1830, horse with jockey mounted facing left. 22 × 30 ins.

Voltigeur. Signed J. F. Herring senr, inscribed Voltigeur. Horse facing left in a stall. Winner St Leger and Derby 1850. 18 ×24 ins. Two or three other depictions including those of his famous match with Flying Dutchman. (See below.)

Whalebone. Signed J. F. Herring 18– (indistinct), horse in landscape facing left. Was bred by Duke of Grafton in 1807, so resemblance must be suspect. 22 × 30 ins. Three other depictions.

The Doncaster Cup 1824. Fleur-de-lis, Mulatto, Humphrey Clinker and two others racing to left with captions. Signed J. F. Herring 1827 and inscribed. 18½ × 30 ins. Two similar versions of different sizes.

The Match at York between Voltigeur and Flying Dutchman. 17½ × 27½ ins.

Racing Cracks of the Day. Signed and dated 1845, The Baron, Refraction, Sweetmeat and Alarm in stables. 18 × 27½ ins.

List of Exhibited Paintings by J. F. Herring senr

THE ROYAL ACADEMY

Year	*Subject*	*Cat. No.*	*Address*
1818	Portrait of a dog.	231	From Newgate Street.
1826	Thyroes (a hunter).	281	
1830	Interior of a stable.	508	Doncaster and 34 Rathbone Place.
	Velocipede, the property of W. Armitage Esq. (A critic in speaking of these two pictures observes: 'Of the former we think there is not sufficient diversity of colour to constitute it a pleasing picture. If we may infer from its situation, we should say the committee considered it endowed with lofty pretensions. 'Velocipede' is cleverly painted, but it wants affect; the background has not been sufficiently attended to'.	549	
1837	Favourite Cob, the property of a gentleman, called T F H.	416	31 Park Street, Camberwell.
1838	Rockingham. J. Theobald Esq.	487	34 Rathbone Place.
	Slane. Colonel Peel.	1122	
1840	The Farm-Yard.	726	9 Cottage Green, Camberwell.
	Going to Plough.	32	
1845	Favourites.	670	
1863	The Farm, Autumn.	51	4 Haymarket.
	Watering the Team.[1]	223	
1864	Farm-Yard.	76	
	Horses and Poultry.	91	
	Horses, Pigs etc.	248	
1865	The Old Lodge.	201	212 Piccadilly.
	Horses Feeding.	437	
1866[1]	Watering the Team.	291	
	The Farmer's Friend.	161	
	Horses Feeding.	525	
1868	Horses and Poultry.	99	
	Dangerous Play.	220	

N.B. – 22 pictures in all, 3 re-exhibited.

[1] Herring died in 1865, so the above works being exhibited posthumously probably include three already exhibited e.g. Watering the Team, Horses Feeding and Horses and Poultry, although it is possible the titles were repeated for different pictures.

THE SOCIETY OF BRITISH ARTISTS, SUFFOLK STREET
83 in all

Year	*Subject*	*Cat. No.*	*Address*
1836	Gothic Church at Lewisham.	509	9 Newman Street W1.
1837	A Horse.	98	Fuller's Rathbone Place.
	Horses.	349	
	Horse.	499	
1838	Partisans (Lord Lowther's).	41	31 Park Street, Camberwell.
	ELECTED MEMBER		
1841	A Mail-Coach, George IV's Reign.	349	9 Cottage Green, Camberwell.
	Crucifix (winner of the Oaks, 1840).	540	
	Waiting for the Ferry-Boat.	577	
	ELECTED VICE-PRESIDENT (President was F. V. HURLSTONE)		
1842	Duncan's Horses.	4	9 Cottage Green, Camberwell.
	Duncan's Horses.	16	
	Going to the Fair.	240	
	Countess of Derby's departure from Martindale.	401	
	'Charger' (deerhound of Caledon Alexander, Esq.)	448	
	'Mazeppa'.	521	
	A French blacksmith's Shop.	607	
	Stable-yard.	702	
	Cattle.	703	
1843	The Country Bait Stable.	6	
	Interior of a Country Stable.	77	
	Trotting Cob, 'Silvertail'.	224	
	Our Nell (winner of Oaks, 1842.)	226	
	Scene on Cannock Chase.	342	
	Dr Syntax, Sire of Beeswing.	390	
	Charles Twelfth XII (dead-heated with Euclid St Leger 1839.)	395	
	A Country-Inn-Yard.	568	
	'Please, Measter, don't want a lad'.	524	
	Dinner-time.	525	
	Beeswing.	537	
1844	Ducks.	62	
	Hydrobibists.	162	
	Ducks.	176	
	The Straw-Yard.	204	
	Interior of cow-house.	258	
	The Watering-Place.	269	
	The Timber-Carriers.	306	
	Winter.	374	
	French Coast Scene.	472	
	The Farmer's Stable.	497	
	The Blue Bell.	523	

1845	Faugh-a-Ballagh (winner of the St Leger, 1844).	121	9 Cottage Green, Camberwell.
	Vulcan and Hebe.	171	
	Ducks.	224	
	Orlando (winner of the Derby 1844).	321	
	Waiting to be shod.	353	
	Taking it Coolly.	396	
	The Farmer's Pet.	551	
	The Straw-Yard.	559	
1846	The Ferry.	72	
	The Gamekeeper's Cob.	156	
	The Oaks, 1845 – a False Start.	334	
	Gossip.	453	
	Labour.	518	
	Rest.	525	
1847	Quietude.	34	
1849	Nanny.	23	
	A Study.	45	
	Winter.	99	
	Happiness.	115	
	Market-gardeners.	148	
	Horses' Heads.	293	
	Farm, Stubble-yard.	338	
	Horses' Heads.	415	
1850	Watering-place.	7	
	Interior of a stable.	19	
	Poulterer and Dealer in Game.	75	
	Young goats and pigeons.	114	
	Pigs.	157	
	The Stirrup-cup.	184	
	Straw-yard.	279	
	Miss and her young charge.	367	
	A Farm-yard.	437	
	Landscape and sheep.	440	
1851	Popping the question.	33	
	Cavaliers regaling.	72	
	Duck Hawkers.	289	
	Seven for sixpence.	412	
	'Barney, leave the girls alone!' – (at York with Thos Faed).	431	
	Farm-yard, Winter.	485	
1852	Horses feeding.	24	
	Arab and Favourite.	38	
	Cromwell's soldiers in Arundel Church.	191	
	Farm-yard, St Rudagore's Abbey.	272	
	Farm-yard.	441	

THE BRITISH INSTITUTION
44 in all

Year	*Subject*	*Cat. No.*	*Address*
1830	The Race.	359	34 Rathbone Place. (Fuller's Shop)
	Preparing to start.	373	
1834	Dray-Horses (Barclay, Perkins & Cos).	301	
1837	Mares and Foals.	255	
1838	Preparing for the start of the Derby.	313	
1839	Mail-coach Horses ready for changing.	192	9 Cottage Green, Camberwell.
	Mail-coach descending a hill.	317	
1840	The Straw-yard. (See p. 49.)	106	
	The Timber-Carriage.	201	
1841	Returning from the plough.	72	
	A Village scene.	91	
	A French Inn-yard.	316	
	A Farm-yard.	318	
	A farm-yard.	364	
1842	The Ferry.	106	
1844	French roadside Inn.	345	
	A farm-yard.	358	
1845	Tranquillity (Animal-Painter to HRH the Duchess of Kent).	501	
1846	Interior, two horses, four fowls.	235	
1847	A straw-yard.	146	
	The Frugal meal.	259	
1848	A study.	268	
1849	Ducks.	154	
1850	A farm-yard.	3	
	Study for kids.	22	
	Ducks.	81	
1851	The rabbit fancier.	94	
	The greengrocer's cob.	249	
1852	The watering-place (Dumfries).	128	
	An Arab and his favourite.	382	
1853	Ducks.	103	
	Ducks.	121	
1860	The Farm-pond (100 gns).	521	Meopham Park, Tonbridge.
1861	An old horse, ducks (£35).	112	
1862	Ducks (£35).	138	
	A horse fair (80 gns).	582	
1863	The mid-day meal (10 gns).	16	
	The end of the course (30 gns).	26	
	Ploughing (10 gns).	33	
	Ducks.	131	
	The road anterior to rails (100 gns).	489	
1864	Fancy rabbits (£30).	108	
	Ducks (£30).	123	
1865	Mares and foals (£25).	573	

THE PORTLAND GALLERY
19 in all

Year	*Subject*	*Cat. No.*	*Address*
1854	Ducks and ducklings (30 gns).	214	Meopham Park, Tonbridge.
	Rabbits (30 gns).	220	
	Interior of a stable (250 gns).	223	
	Mare and foal (Winter scene) (30 gns).	276	
	Mare and foal (30 gns).	278	
1857	The watering-place, No 1, (painted with Alexander I. Rolfe) (20 gns).	106	
	Farm team going out (painted with Rolfe) (60 gns).	106	
1858	Farm-yard (painted with Rolfe) (60 gns).	73	
	The Homestead (painted with Rolfe) (20 gns).	88	
1859	Farm-yard (painted with Rolfe) (60 gns).	105	
	The watering-place No 2, (painted with Rolfe) (20 gns).	108	
	The Homestead (painted with Rolfe) (£15).	182	
1860	From nature.	245	4 Haymarket.
	English farm-yard – Summertime.	249	
1861	Stormy weather.	9	
	Horse and pony.	266	
	Study from nature.	289	
	The farmer's best friends.	536	
	We are all frozen out.	543	

We are indebted to the privately printed and very rare memoir by Mr J. B. Muir for this catalogue of Herring's engraved works, which appeared only some 28 years after the artist's death, and is unlikely ever to be improved upon.

This list of the engravings is printed here therefore, in the hope that it may be useful to collectors as a source of ready reference, and the author claims no credit for the abundant information contained therein, except where an editor's note indicates some additional material.

General List of Engravings

IN ORDER OF PUBLICATION

1824

308 **Dr Syntax**. 20 × 16 ins – in mezzotint by William Ward junr, engraver to HRH the Duke of Clarence. Doncaster: published September 1824. Dedicated by permission to Ralph Riddell Esq, by his obedient servant J. F. Herring. Dr Syntax was got by Paynator, his dam by Beningborough, grandam Jenny Mole by Carbuncle, Prince T'Quassaw, Regulus, Partner. Dr Syntax won twenty gold cups, seven at Preston, five at Lancaster, five at Richmond (Yorks), one at Middleham, one at Northallerton, and one at Pontefract, besides winning sixteen other engagements, beating all the best horses of the day. Price £1, or £1 10s. for proofs.
"The anatomical precision of Herring is well brought out by the engraver . . ." *Annals of Sporting*. 1 November 1824.

1828

309 **Bessie Bedlam**. 17 × 13 ins. Engraved by H. T. Pyall. 'To Col. King of Ashby House, in the county of Lincoln, a most honourable and distinguished supporter of the turf, and a truly splendid specimen of an old English gentleman, this print is most respectfully inscribed by his obliged and obedient humble servant, Rees Davies.' London: published 1 July 1828, by Moon, Boys & Graves, 6 Pall Mall, and Rees Davies, Hull.

310 **Bessie Bedlam**. 16½ × 12 ins. Engraved by R. G. Reeve. The property of Col. King, to whom the print is dedicated by J. F. Herring and S. & J. Fuller. London: published 15 September 1828, by S. & J. Fuller at their Sporting Gallery, 34 Rathbone Place.

*c.*1832

311 **Christopher Wilson**, 'FATHER OF THE TURF'. Particulars not known.

20 × 17¾ ins. Another portrait of this gentleman (in a landscape) was painted and engraved by Mr R. Woodman senr, 5 Great College Street, Camden Town. Published October 1842 by R. H. Woodman, 118 Jermyn Street, St James. Upon the right hand side of the plate is printed: 'The horse is from a painting by J. F. Herring.'

312 **Orville**. 14¾ × 10¾ ins. Charles Hunt sculpt. Bred by the Earl of Fitzwilliam. The property of his late Majesty George IV. London: published by S. & J. Fuller at their Sporting Gallery, 34 Rathbone Place, W.

1834

313 **Tramp**. 14¾ × 10¾ ins. Charles Hunt sculpt. Newmarket. Bred by Mr R. Watt in 1810. The property of Mr Ridsdale. London: published 29

May 1834, by S. & J. Fuller at their Sporting Gallery, 34 Rathbone Place, W.

314 **Emilius**. 14¾ × 10¾ ins. Charles Hunt sculpt. Newmarket. The property of Mr Thomas Thornhill. London: published in 1834 by S. & J. Fuller at their Sporting Gallery, 34 Rathbone Place, W.

1838

315 **Grey Momus**. 16¾ × 12¼ ins. Engraved by C. Hunt. The property of Lord George Bentinck, to whom the plate is dedicated. London: published July 1838 by S. & J. Fuller at their Sporting Gallery, 34 Rathbone Place, W.

1839

316 **Grand Stand, Ascot, Gold Cup Day, 1939**. 29½ × 20¼ ins. Engraved by Charles Hunt. Showing the starters Caravan, Ion, Dey (Bey?) of Algiers, and St Francis, with trainers and jockeys preparing for the race opposite the Royal Stand. Published: June 1839, by J. Watson, Vere Street, W. 'To Her Most Gracious Majesty, Queen Victoria, this print is dedicated by Her Majesty's loyal and devoted servant, J. Watson.' Re-issued in September 1839 with the name and address of John Moore at his wholesale looking-glass and picture-frame manufactory, corner of West Street, Upper St Martin's Lane, established 1794 [sic] with the dedication line altered accordingly to J. Moore.
The Plate was again issued by Messrs Barnett, Moss & Co, of Leman Street, Whitechapel, September 1852, bearing their name and address upon the publication line. *(See Plate 89.)*

317 **Harkaway**. 16¾ × 12½ ins. Engraved by Charles Hunt. Winner of the Gold Cup at Goodwood in 1838, rode by Wakefield. Forty subscribers, eight started. Bred in 1834 by Mr Ferguson. London: published July 1839, by John Moore at his wholesale looking-glass and picture-frame manufactory. Corner of West Street, Upper St Martins Lane.

318 **Extraordinary Trotting Match Against Time**. 29½ × 20¼ ins. Engraved by C. Hunt. Published 1 November 1839, by R. Ackermann, at his 'Eclipse' Sporting Gallery, 101 Regent Street, London. This match made against time for £100, in which Mr Burke of Hereford notoriety undertook to drive two horses in the same vehicle alternately forty-five miles in three successive hours, was decided on Tuesday 25 June 1839, over five miles on Sunbury Common, from the Staines End to the five milestone towards Hampton, which was completed in 2 hrs 55½ minutes.
The wheeler, Tommy, trotted twenty miles in harness two months previously to the above match on the West Bromwich Road in 1 hour and 18 minutes with the greatest ease. The leader, Gustavus, formerly the property of the Duke of Gordon, a most extraordinary animal, twenty-four years old, completed his twenty miles in 1 hour and 14 minutes, and is now the property of C. Edwards Esq.
Mr Burke also in March 1837, for a great stake, undertook with his two ponies to go from the Bolt-in-Tun, Fleet Street, to Mr Bosley's Hotel, Hereford, against the Mazeppa coach, of 137 miles. Mr Burke reached the above hotel 12½ minutes before the coach, the distance being completed in 14 hours and 11 minutes.
Up to the above performance on Sunbury Common, Mr Burke, out of thirty-five most extraordinary matches, won thirty-two, and now for any sum to the amount of £1,000, Mr Burke challenges the distance of the train from Birmingham to London, and give half an hour's start. And the money is ready at Mr Dowling's, Editor of Bell's Life, in London.

319 **Charles XII and Euclid**. Meeting for the decider after the dead heat. 16¾ × 12¼ ins. Engraved by Mr Charles Hunt. Published November 1839 by Messrs S. & J. Fuller, Rathbone Place, W.

320 **Beeswing with Jockey mounted galloping**. 16½ × 12½ ins. Engraved by C. Hunt. Bred and owned by Mr W. Orde. A famous mare and winner of many races and cups. Published 25 November 1839, by J. Moore, Nos 1 and 2 corner of West Street, Upper St Martin's Lane.
A subsequent issue of this plate was made with the date of publication line as above altered to June 20 1842, giving the full details of the races and cups won by this celebrated mare to the end of her career. 'Winner of the Ascot Gold Cup, 1842' is inserted upon the same line, in open letters, as the title.

1840

321 **Euclid**. 16¾ × 12¼ ins. Engraved by C. Hunt. Bred by Mr Thomas Thornhill. London: published 6 April 1840, by S. & J. Fuller at their Sporting Gallery, 34 Rathbone Place.

322 **Doncaster Great St Leger, 1839**. 29½ × 18¼ ins. Engraved by C. Hunt. Published 6 May 1840, by John Moore, at his wholesale looking-glass and picture-frame manufactory, Nos 1 and 2 Corner of West Street, Upper St Martins Lane. Established 1694. The dead heat between Charles XII and Euclid, and eleven others that contested the race. Charles XII, W. Scott up, blue red cap, Euclid, P. Connolly up, white, scarlet sleeves, white cap. The other horses and their jockeys and colours also listed. *(See Plate 90.)*

323 **Charles XII and Euclid**. The finish after the dead heat, Charles XII winning by a head. 17 × 12½ ins. Engraved by C. Hunt. London: published 19 May 1840, by J. Moore at his wholesale picture-frame and looking-glass manufactory, Nos 1 and 2 Corner of West Street, Upper St Martin's Lane. Established 1694.

324 **Beggarman**. 17¼ × 12¾ ins. Engraved by C. Hunt. The property of HRH the Duke of Orleans, to whom the print is dedicated by special permission by the publisher, J. Moore. Particulars in French and English, separated by a Ducal coronet. London: 21 September 1840. Published by J. Moore, West Street, Upper St Martin's Lane, and Paris par Rittner & Goupil, Boulevard Montmartre, No 15.

Winner of the Goodwood Shield, 1840, value 500 sovs, with 880 sovs added. Rode by James Robinson. Forty-four subscribers; nine started, beating Lanercost, Platoff, Bey of Algiers. Bred by the Earl of Stradbroke, by Zinganee out of Adeline, 1835. Won Boulogne Gold Cup, 1839. Beat Primefit in a match for 200 gns at Champs de Mars; at Versailles won a sweepstake beating Anthony; at Chantilly received forfeit from Barberina.

The first state of this print is the best, but 'entirely wrong' in the spelling and grammar, and almost incomprehensible in the French text; this has the arms of the Orleans family surmounted by a Duke's coronet. In a subsequent issue the French text is corrected and the coronet altered, probably to that of a Duke of royal blood.

*c.*1840

325 **James Nunn on his favourite old hack** (foreman for many years to W. Chaplin Esq). 22¼ × 17¼ ins. Engraved by G. & C. Hunt. London: published by J. Moore, 1 West Street, St Martin's Lane. No date. Printed by S. H. Hawkins.

1841

326 **Anatole**. 17 × 12¾ ins. Engraved by C. Hunt. Winner of the Great St Leger stakes at Chantilly, 1840. Rode by E. Flatman. Thirteen subscribers; nine started. Bred in 1837 by Mr Bernard, by Royal Oak out of Waverley mare by Waverley. The property of Baron A. de Rothschild, to whom this print is by permission respectfully dedicated by J. Moore. Particulars in French and English, separated by a baron's coronet. The publication line is at the top of the title: London, January 6, 1841, published by J. Moore, 1 and 2 West Street, Upper St Martin's Lane (printseller to HRH the Duke of Orleans); at Paris, Goupil & Co, Boulevard Montmartre, No 15.

327 **Poetess**. 17¾ × 13 ins. Engraved by C. Hunt. Winner of the Derby at Chantilly, 1841. Rode by W. Boyce. Thirty subscribers; ten started. Bred in 1834 by Royal Oak out of Ada. The property of Lord Henry Seymour, to whom this print, by his Lordship's permission, is respectfully dedicated by J. Moore. Particulars in French and English, separated by a coronet. The publication line is above the title, surrounded by a thicker line, forming a kind of frame around the print, between which is printed: London, August 7, 1841. Published by J. Moore, 1 and 2 Upper St Martin's Lane, printseller by special appointment to HRH the Duke of Orleans; et Paris, Goupil & Co, Boulevard Montmartre, No 15. The original oil painting is the property of the French Jockey Club.

328 **Chantilly Races**. A pair. 27 × 17 ins. Engraved by C. Hunt. Special prize of 5,000 francs. Run May 1841. (By G. B. Campion and J. F. Herring). London: published 1 October 1841, by J. Moore, at his wholesale looking-glass and picture-framing manufactory, 1 and 2 Corner of West Street, Upper St Martin's Lane, by special appointment printseller to HRH the Duke of Orleans; et Paris, Goupil & Co, Boulevard Montmartre, No

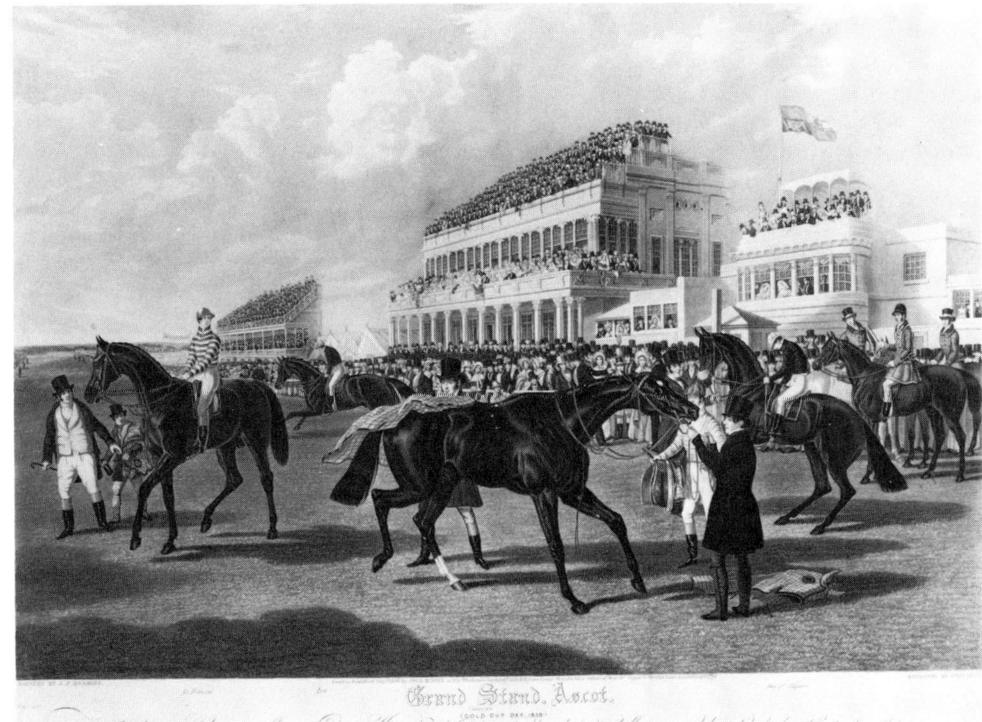

89 **Grand Stand, Ascot.** Gold Cup Day 1839. 29½ × 20¼ ins.
Engraved by Charles Hunt. *List No 316*

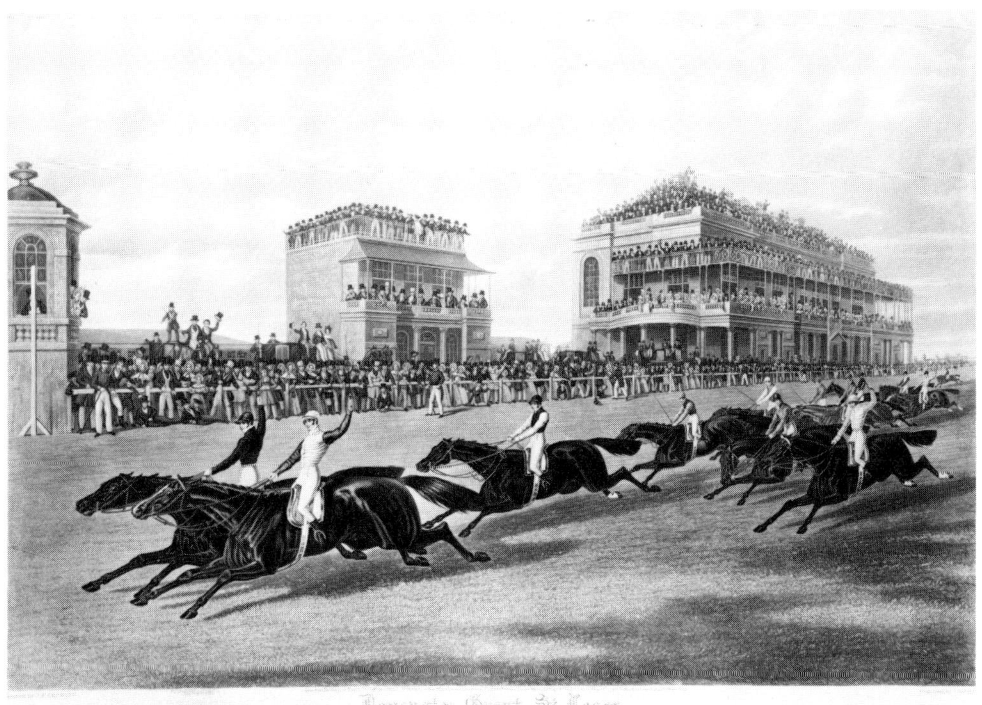

90 **Doncaster Great St Leger 1839.** 29½ × 18¼ ins.
Engraved by Charles Hunt. *List No 322.*

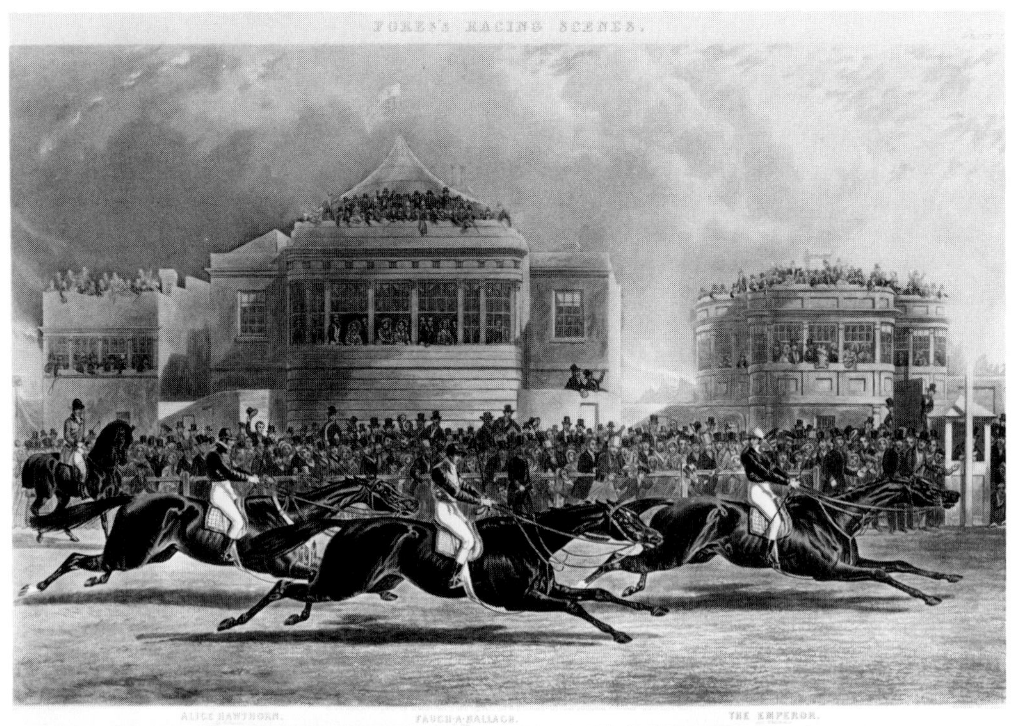

91 **The Race for the Emperor's Cup 1845.** 27½ × 17¾ ins.
Engraved by J. Harris. *List No 334*

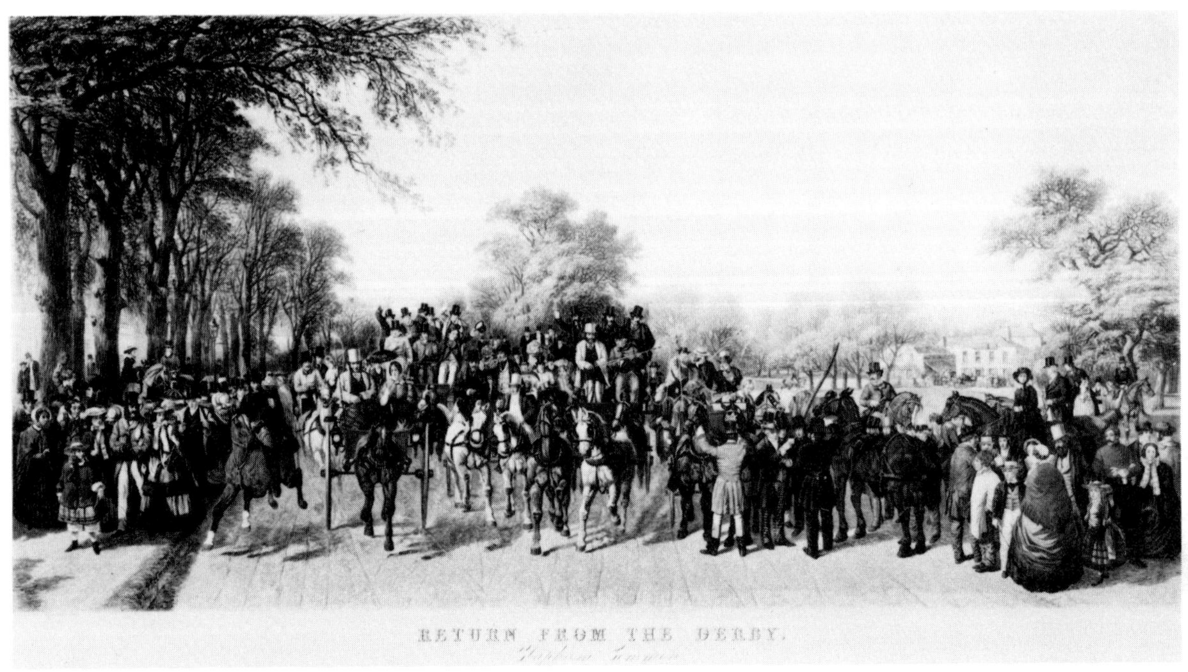

92 **Return from the Derby 1862.** 20¾ × 39¾ ins.
Engraved by J. Harris. *List No 362*

15. Given by the Administration of the Royal Studs. Two miles and a half heat. Won at three heats by HRH the Duke of Orleans' br. h. Roquencourt by Logic out of Contrition, five years old, 9st 1 lb (Charles Edwards), beating Lord H. Seymour's br. h.

THE RUNNING – THE FINISH. Particulars in French and English upon each print. Oakstick by Royal Oak out of Maria, six years old, 9st 4lb (Boyce), Baron de Rothschild's br. h. Vendredi, six years old by Cain out of Naiad, 9st 4lb (Flatman), and M. de Saran's br. h. Quine by Pottery out of Galatee, five years old, 9st 1lb (Moss).
This race, between four of the finest horses bred in France, was the fastest yet run by French horses. Notwithstanding a very stiff hill, the two and a half miles were run at the first heat in 4 minutes 47 seconds, at the second heat in 4 minutes 42 seconds and the third in 4 minutes 43 seconds. Roquencourt waited the first heat, which was won by Vendredi, Quine, being second; won the second heat cleverly by two lengths, Oakstick second, and won the third heat by a neck after a good race with Oakstick. The print is dedicated to the Duke of Orleans. Colours of the Riders: HRH the Duke of Orleans (Blue velvet cap with gold tassel, red silk jacket, silver buttons), Lord H. Seymour (Orange satin jacket, black velvet cap), Baron de Rothschild (Light yellow cap and blue silk jacket), M. de Saran (Black velvet cap, purple body, dark blue sleeves).

329 **Chantilly Derby**. A pair. 27 × 17 ins. Engraved by C. Hunt. (By G. B. Campion and J. F. Herring.) London, 31 December 1841: published by J. Moore at his wholesale looking-glass and picture-framing manufactory, 1 and 2 Corner of West Street, Upper St Martin's Lane, by special appointment printseller to HRH the Duke of Orleans; at Paris, Goupil & Co, Boulevard Montmartre, No 15.
PREPARING TO START – THEY ARE OFF (Publication line dated November 1, 1841.) Particulars in French and English upon each print. Seven thousand francs for three-year-old colts and fillies. Six hundred francs entrance, h. ft (?) Colts 8st 9lb and fillies 8st 6lb. Once and a distance round. Three hundred subscribers; eighteen paid forfeit; ten started. HRH The Duke of Orleans' Tragedy, by Altercetar out of Sweetlips (Edwards); Lord Henry Seymour's Poetess, by Royal Oak out of Ada Boyer and Florence; M. A. Lupin's Fiammetta, by Acteon or Camel out of Wings; M. Aumont's Beeswing, by Syntax out of Destiny; M. Lupin's Faustus, by Emilius out of Fleur-de-Lis; M. Depare's Peter, by Hercules out of Elvira, and Prince Paul, by Felix out of Amiable. The print is dedicated to the Duke of Orleans.
Colours of the riders: HRH the Duke of Orleans (Blue cap, scarlet jacket), Lord H. Seymour (Black cap, orange jacket), M. Aumont (Black cap, rose jacket), M. Lupin (Scarlet cap, scarlet and black jacket striped).

1842

330 **Lady Hampton**. 25½ × 18 ins. Engraved by C. Hunt. London: published 21 June 1842, by J. & C. Fuller, Repository of Arts, Rathbone Place, Oxford Street, W. This extraordinary Bay mare has performed two matches in harness, completing 15, 16, and 17 miles within the hour, for a wager of £150, which she completed seven seconds within the given time. The parties thinking she could not repeat it a second time, made a further bet of £150 a side, which was performed in 1 minute 8 seconds under the hour. Such a performance was never done in harness by any other animal. She was driven by Alexander Burke. This plate was republished by Mr G. Calverley, Warwick House, Shepherd's Bush.

331 **Beeswing**. 20 × 15 ins. Engraved by C. Hunt. The property of the late Mr W. Orde of Nynnykirk, near Morpeth, was got by Dr Syntax out of an Ardrossan mare. London: A. H. & C. Baily, Sporting Library, 83 Cornhill, 19 November 1842. As a two-year-old she started in 1835 three times and won twice. In 1836 five times and won twice. In 1837 eight times and won seven times. In 1838 nine times and won seven times. In 1839 twelve times and won eleven times. In 1840 twelve times and won ten times. In 1841 ten times and won eight times. In 1842 five times and won four times, making in the whole, sixty-four starts and winning fifty-one races, comprising seventeen stakes, nine King's and Queen's Plates, and twenty-five cups.

332 **Beeswing**. 13 × 9 ins. A smaller plate executed from a painting of 1842 by Mr H. Griffith's chromographic process, representing the mare standing in a tinted landscape with jockey up.

1844

333 **Running Rein**. Woodcut. Sketched expressly by Mr J. F. Herring, and published in Bell's *Life in London*, Sunday 26 May 1844. Placed first in the Derby, 1844; afterwards disqualified on the ground of fraud, being a four-year-old. The plate of Orlando, declared the winner, who came in second, is described under Winners of the Derby.

1845

334 **The Race for the Emperor's Cup**. 27½ × 17¾ ins. Engraved by J. Harris. Value 500 sovereigns. Ascot, 12 June 1845. The annual gift of His Imperial Majesty the Emperor of Russia. Showing the Emperor (G. Whitehouse) beating Faugh-a-Ballagh (H. Bell) and Alice Hawthorn (James Robinson). London: published 17 September 1845, by Messrs Fores, 41 Piccadilly; Paris Goupil & Vibert, depose.
A writer in *Bell's Life* of Sunday, September 21, 1845, in criticising this print, said: 'Messrs Fores, the printsellers in Piccadilly, have perpetuated the memory of this important race at Goodwood (– an error, it was at Ascot) in which Lord Albermarle's Emperor beat Faugh-a-Ballagh and Alice Hawthorn, by a magnificent engraving from a painting by J. F. Herring senr, engraved by Harris, in which the portraits of all the animals at the moment of the termination of the struggle, are beautifully and faithfully sketched in Mr Herring's best style. The grand stand, with Her Majesty and Prince Albert at the windows, are in the background, and the whole work is got up in a style of excellence worthy of the event, and in all respects creditable to the artist, publisher and engraver.' *(See Plate 91.)*

*c.*1845

335 **Alice Hawthorn**. 20 × 15 ins. Engraved by C. Hunt, coloured by C. Simpson. The property of Mr Plummer, was got by Mulcy Moloch out of Rebecca by Lottery. Six years old. Published by C. & E. Baily, Royal Exchange Buildings, Cornhill. No date.

1846

336 **The Race for the Great St Leger**. 19¾ × 6½ ins. Sir Tatton Sykes winning, Iago second. Probably a supplement to a paper edited by 'Vates'.

337 **Slane** (interior). 19¾ × 14¾ ins. Engraved by J. Harris. The property of Colonel Peel (picture dated 1846). Published by Messrs Baily, Cornhill.

*c.*1846

338 **Sweetmeat**. 20¼ × 14¾ ins. Engraved by C. Hunt, coloured by C. Simpson. The property of Mr A. W. Hill. Published by Messrs Baily, Royal Exchange, Cornhill. (See also the engraving by E. Hacker.)

339 **Gladiator** (interior). 20 × 15¾ ins. Engraved by J. R. Mackrell, coloured by C. Simpson. JFH described as 'Animal-painter to HRH the Duchess of Kent'. Picture dated 1846. The property of Colonel the Hon. G. Anson; was got by Partisan out of Pauline. Published by Baily Bros, Royal Exchange Buildings, Cornhill; Paris: Gambart et Junin, depose. No date.

1847

340 **Waiting for the Ferry-Boat**. 34½ × 22¼ ins. Engraved in mezzotint by W. Giller. From the original picture in the collection of Charles Theobald Maud Esq. Published 2 August 1847, by Messrs H. Graves & Co, 6 Pall Mall.

*c.*1847

341 **Rest and Labour**. A pair. Both 25¾ × 19¾ ins. Engraved by W. T. Davey. London: published 2 August 1847, by Ackermann & Co, 96 Strand.

342 **Hero**. 20½ × 15½ ins. Engraved by C. Hunt. The property of Mr John Day. Winner of the Doncaster Cup in 1846, the Emperor's Plate at Ascot, and the Goodwood Cup in 1847, the Goodwood Cup in 1848, and the Ebor Handicap in 1849. Published by Baily Bros, Royal Exchange Buildings, Cornhill.

1848

343 **The Frugal Meal**. 30 × 21½ ins. Engraved by John Burnet, FRS. London: published 1 February 1848, by H. Graves & Co, 6 Pall Mall.

344 **The Straw-Yard**. 25½ × 19¾ ins. Engraved by W. T. Davey from the original picture in the possession of the publishers. London: published 16 March 1848, by Messrs Fores at their sporting and fine art print repository and manufactory, 41 Piccadilly, Corner of Sackville Street.

345 **Feeding the Horse**. 30¾ × 24¼ ins. Engraved by T. L. Atkinson, from the original picture in the possession of John Mather Esq, of Liverpool, to whom this plate is dedicated by Messrs Henry Graves & Co. London: published 1 May 1848, by Henry Graves & Co, publishers in ordinary to Her Majesty and HRH Prince Albert, 6 Pall Mall; R. G. Grundy, Liverpool; and Goupil & Co, Paris depose.
Also, a smaller plate, engraved by C. Tomkins (13 × 17 ins) was published by Messrs Dickenson & Co, and declared at the Printsellers Association, June 21, 1872.

346 **Inheritress**. 24 × 18¼ ins. Engraved by J. Harris. By the Saddler out of Executrix, the property of James Meiklam Esq, to whom the plate is dedicated. London: published 1 August 1848, by E. Gambart & Co, 25 Berners Street, Oxford Street, W.
Inheritress at two years old won once, at four years old won four times, at five years old fourteen times, at six years old seven times, at seven years old nine times, and at eight years old, in 1848, several times previous to the publication of this print, and is still in training.

347 **The Farmer's Friends**. Large Oval. Three horses looking out of a stable door, with three pigs in the foreground and a pigeon. Litho by D. Fabronius. London. Published by Messrs Lloyd Bros, 22 Ludgate Hill, 1848.

348 **Tranquil Enjoyment** (three horses feeding with two pigeons). 11½ × 11½ ins. Engraved by R. G. Watkins from a picture in possession of Mr George Rossi, Norwich. Published London 1 December 1848 by Lloyd Bros, 22 Ludgate Hill.

c. 1848

349 **The Cab-Horses**. St James's and St Giles. – A pair. Both 20 × 14¾ ins. Engraved by J. Harris. London: published by Baily Bros, 3 Royal Exchange Buildings, Cornhill. No date.

350 **Scanty Meal**. 22¼ × 17½ ins. Engraved by E. Hacker. (Further particulars missing.) The same plate illustrates vol xii of the *Art Journal* for 1850, 'In the Vernon Gallery'. Of this picture the same journal says: 'The Scanty Meal' is one version of a story that the artist has before told in several different ways. A group of three horses' heads variously engaged has long been a favourite theme with him; yet, although we recognise the same animals, their occupations are so diversified as to dispel the idea that he has copied himself. The attitude assumed by the horses feeding is exceedingly well rendered in each of the heads. There is the dreamy listlessness about them that shows their relish, for the dry fodder is not equal to its abundance, or, in other words, that they are making a 'frugal meal' in a land of plenty. The beautiful pigeons introduced into the picture make an agreeable variety in the scene, and afford the artist an opportunity of giving to his work some brillliant bits of colour.'

351 **Alarm**. 20¼ × 15¼ ins. Engraved by J. Harris. The property of Charles Greville, Esq. Published by Baily Bros, Royal Exchange Buildings, Cornhill. No date. A small plate engraved by E. Hacker illustrates the *Sporting Magazine* for April 1848.

1849

352 **Society of Friends** (two horses' heads and pigeons). 23½ ins circular. Engraved by T. L. Atkinson. Published 1 January 1849, by H. Graves & Co, printsellers in ordinary to Her Majesty and HRH Prince Albert, 6 Pall Mall.

353 **Pharaoh's Horses**. Large circular. Engraved in line and mezzotint by Charles Wentworth Wass. Published 8 February 1849 by James Gilbert, Sheffield.

354 **Farmer's Daughter** (girl feeding horse from a sieve). Upright 24 × 17¾ ins. Engraved by W. H. Simmons. London: published 27 June 1849, by E. Gambart & Co, 25 Berners Street, Oxford Street, W.

1850

355 **The Baron's Charger**. 24¾ × 19½ ins.

Engraved by Robert Graves ARA. The print is dedicated to the Hon. Arthur Kinnard. London, published 4 June, 1850, by Henry Graves & Co, Printsellers in ordinary to Her Majesty and Prince Albert, 6 Pall Mall.

1851

357 **The Great Match, between Flying Dutchman and Voltigeur** at York on the 13th May, 1851, for 1,000 Sovs a side. 27½ × 17½ ins. Engraved by J. Harris. Published 31 July 1851, by Messrs Fores, 41 Piccadilly. The Earl of Eglinton's Flying Dutchman, five years, 8st 8½lb, ridden by C. Marlow, beating the Earl of Zetland's Voltigeur, four years, 8st, ridden by N. Flatman. Distance two miles.

358 **Fox-Hunting Scenes**. The Death. 30½ × 17½ ins. Engraved by J. Harris. London: published 21 November, 1851, by Henry Graves & Co, printsellers in ordinary to Her Majesty and HRH Prince Albert, 6 Pall Mall; Goupil & Co, Paris, Berlin and New York; B. Brooke, Doncaster; James Wyman, Oxford.

1857

359 **An English Farm-Yard** (companion to 'English Homestead'). 34 × 22½ ins. Engraved by G. Paterson. London: published January 1857, by Lloyd Bros & Co, 22 Ludgate Hill. Entered according to Act of Congress by Williams, Stevens, Williams & Co, in the Clerk's Office of the District for the Southern District of New York. Printed by T. Brooker.

1859

360 **Farm-Yard**. 34¼ × 22½ ins. Engraved by G. Paterson. London: published 1 November 1859 by Goupil & Co, 17 Southampton Street, Strand; Paris: 19, Boulevard Montmartre.

1861

361 **Kentish Farm-Yard**. 36 × 24 ins. Engraved in mezzo and stipple by W. Giller. Published by Messrs B. Brooks & Sons, 171 Strand. Declared at the Printsellers' Association 28 March 1861.

1862

362 **Return from the Derby** (the scene – Clapham Common opposite the Wheatsheaf Inn). 39¾ × 20¾ ins. Engraved by J. Harris. Exhibiting Mr Herring's marvellous powers of foreshortening in the most delightful manner. London: published 1 May 1862, by Henry Graves & Co, printsellers to the Queen, 6 Pall Mall. *(See Plate 92.)*

363 **A Straw-Yard**. 36 × 26 ins. Engraved by W. Giller. Published by Messrs Brooks & Son, 171 Strand. Declared at the Printsellers' Association 7 July 1862.

1867

364 **Market Morning** (Posthumous publication). 34 × 22½ ins. Engraved by Alfred Lucas. London, Goupil & Co; Paris, Goupil & Co; New York, M. Knoedler. Printed by R. Holdgate. Entered according to Act of Congress in the year 1867 by M. Knoedler in the Clerk's Office of the District Court of the United States for the Southern District of New York.

365 **The Smithy** (Posthumous publication). 34 × 22½ ins. Engraved by Alfred Lucas.

1886

366 **Old England** (Posthumous publication). 29¼ × 23 ins. Engraved by J. B. Pratt. London: published 1 May 1886, by Messrs H. Graves & Co, publishers to Her Majesty the Queen, and HRH the Prince and Princess of Wales, 6 Pall Mall. Declared at the Printsellers' Association 1 May 1886.

ENGRAVED WORKS OF J. F. HERRING

22 Derby Winners

Herring painted every winner – bar three – of the Derby Stakes at Epsom from the year 1827 to 1851, twenty-three in all. All except one were engraved by various hands, and a complete set was published by the firm of S. & J. Fuller at their Sporting Gallery, Rathbone Place, London, W, up to the year 1841.

In 1842, Attila's year, an uncompleted sketch of the horse was noted, but it was never engraved owing to the fact that Attila was exported to Germany, but died on the way. However, two finished paintings of the horse taken in stables, were offered for sale at Christie, Manson & Wood in May, 1893. In 1843, publication was taken over by A. H. & C. Baily, 83 Cornhill, London, and by Gambart et Junin in Paris, until 1846. The winners of the years 1847 Cossack, 1848 Surplice and 1850 Voltigeur are missing.

Messrs Fores, 41 Piccadilly, published the last two plates, of Flying Dutchman in 1849, and the 1851 winner, Teddington, in August of that year, in their series of Celebrated Winners. The Teddington print includes the owner, Sir Joseph Hawley holding the horse, and the jockey, J. Marson. It was engraved by J. Harris.

C. Hunt engraved thirteen plates on his own, three others that he engraved were coloured by C. Simpson, and one was done with Smart (1834).

J. Harris engraved two (1849 and 1851), and Pyrrhus the First was engraved by J. R. Mackrell and coloured by C. Simpson (1846).

Up to 1835 the plates were published jointly by Herring himself and Fuller's, initially from Herring's abode in Doncaster, and then from Six-Mile-Bottom, Newmarket. In 1836, when Herring was living in London, publication was undertaken solely by Fuller's. The financial arrangement about the proceeds is not known, although it looks as though Herring retained an interest up to that time – apart from his fee as painter.

In the absence of further particulars, the details and dimensions given follow the list as given in Mr Muir's invaluable inventory, with more information where warranted.

It is noteworthy that in that period, only one horse won both the Derby and the St Leger, namely Flying Dutchman, so in that year only one plate was issued.

After Herring's death, the firm of G. P. McQueen published a set of his Foxhunting prints, and then took up the task of publishing a series of Derby winners, from offices in Tottenham Court Road. Many of these were from paintings by Harrington Bird, ARCA, with engravers such as Eug. Till and C. R. Stock, and included the Triple Crown winner, Common in 1891. These, while being efficiently executed, lack the Herring touch. This is also notably missing from the small engravings of winners such as Favonius, owned by Baron de Rothschild, drawn and engraved by Hunt & Son.

367 **Mameluke** (1827) Doncaster. Engraved by R. G. Reeve. 17 × 12½ ins. Eighty-nine subscribers; twenty-three starters. Late the property of the Right Hon. The Earl of Jersey, to whom the plate is dedicated by the publishers J. F. Herring and S. & J. Fuller. London: published 18 September 1827, by S. & J. Fuller at their Sporting Gallery, 34 Rathbone Place, and at J. F. Herring's, Doncaster. (See also Annals of Sporting, March, 1828.)
(Author's note: This magnificent horse was by Partisan out of Miss Sophia, bred by Mr Elwes who sold him to Lord Jersey, who sold him to Mr John Gulley, Member of Parliament for Doncaster, for whom he would have won the St Leger and a great deal of money instead of being narrowly beaten by Matilda, had the starter not been bribed to spoil his chance. He went on to win other races as a four- and five-year-old, finally being retired to stud at Stockwell in Surrey by his then owner, Mr John Theobold. He was later exported to the US. Also painted by Ben Marshall and James Ward RA. He was trained by James 'Tiny' Edwards and ridden by John Robinson.)

368 **Cadland** (1828) Doncaster. Engraved by R. G. Reeve. 17½ × 12¾ ins. Eighty-six subscribers; fifteen starters. The property of His Grace the Duke of Rutland, to whom the plate is dedicated by his obliged servants, J. F. Herring and S. & J. Fuller. London: published 15 July 1828 by S. & J. Fuller, at their Sporting Gallery, 34 Rathbone Place, and at J. F. Herring's, Doncaster.
(Author's note: Ridden by John Robinson. In 1830, Cadland was beaten into third place at the Newmarket Houghton meeting by Albert and Oppidian.)

369 **Frederick** (1829) Doncaster. Engraved by R. G. Reeve. 17½ × 12¾ ins. Eighty-nine subscribers; seventeen starters. The property of Mr Gratwicke, to whom the plate is dedicated by the publishers, J. F. Herring and S. & J. Fuller. London: published 14 September 1829 by S. & J. Fuller at their Sporting Gallery, 34 Rathbone Place.

370 **Priam** (1830) Doncaster. Engraved by R. G. Reeve. 17 × 12¾ ins. Eighty-six subscribers; twenty-three starters. The Property of Mr William Chifney, to whom the plate is dedicated. London: published September 1830 by S. & J. Fuller at their Sporting Gallery, Rathbone Place, and at J. F. Herring's at Doncaster.
(Author's note: Priam, a beautiful bay, was trained by the famous William 'Bill' Chifney at Newmarket. He won the race on 27 May, and was sold to King George IV who died on June 26. This event marked the decline of the Chifneys and of Newmarket for many years.) *(See Plate 93.)*

371 **Spaniel** (1831) Doncaster. Engraved by C. Hunt. 17 × 12½ ins. One hundred and five subscribers; twenty-three starters. The property of the Right Hon. Lord Lowther, to whom the plate is dedicated by his Lordship's obedient servants, J. F. Herring and S. & J. Fuller. London: published 15 August 1831 by S. & J. Fuller at their Sporting Gallery, 34 Rathbone Place, W. See under *New Sporting Magazine*, and Wildrake's 'Cracks of the Day' and p. 3 of Tattersall's Picture Gallery of Race horses. (Also painted by John Fernely.)

372 **St Giles** (1832) Newmarket. Engraved by C. Hunt. 16 × 12½ ins. One hundred subscribers and one; twenty-two starters. The property of Mr Robert Ridsdale, to whom the print is dedicated. Published August 1832 by S. & J. Fuller and J. F. Herring, Six Mile Bottom, near Newmarket.
(See also *New Sporting Magazine*, *Wildrake and Tattersall's Gallery*.)

373 **Dangerous** (1833) Newmarket. Engraved by C. Hunt. 16½ × 12½ ins. One hundred and twenty-four subscribers; twenty-five starters. The property of Mr Sadler, to whom the plate is dedicated by the publishers, J. F. Herring and S. & J. Fuller. London: published 25 August 1833 by S. & J. Fuller at their Sporting Gallery, 34 Rathbone Place, and by J. F. Herring, Six Mile Bottom, near Newmarket.
(See also *New Sporting Magazine* Sept. 1833, *Wildrake and Tattersall's Gallery*.)

374 **Plenipotentiary** 1834 Newmarket. Engraved by Smart & Hunt. 16¾ × 12½ ins. One hundred and twenty-four subscribers; twenty-five starters. The property of S. Bateson, Esq to whom the plate is dedicated. London: published 12 August 1934 by S. & J. Fuller at their Sporting Gallery, 34 Rathbone Place, and at J. F. Herring's, Newmarket.
(See also *New Sporting Magazine* vol. vii, *Wildrake and Tattersall's Gallery*. Also quote in *Bell's Life* appendix).

375 **Mundig** (1835). Engraved by C. Hunt. 16½ × 12½ ins. One hundred and thirty subscribers; fourteen starters. The property of J. Bowes, Esq to whom the plate is dedicated by the publishers, J. F. Herring and S. & J. Fuller. London: published in 1835 by S. & J. Fuller at their Sporting Gallery, 34 Rathbone Place.
(See also *Bell's Life*, Sunday, 14 June 1835, and Mr Herring's letter to the Editor, p. 47).

376 **Bay Middleton** (1836). Engraved by C. Hunt. 16½ × 12½ ins. One hundred and twenty-eight subscribers; twenty starters. The property of the Right Hon. the Earl of Jersey, to whom the plate is dedicated by the publishers, J. F. Herring and S. & J. Fuller. London: published 1 July 1836 by S. & J. Fuller at their Sporting Gallery, 34 Rathbone Place, W.
(Author's note: Bay Middleton was a rich bay horse, not a sherry-bay, as he was described. As a two-year-old he ran as 'brother to Nell Gwynne', and as such won the Derby. After winning that race, he was named by the Earl of Jersey, after a

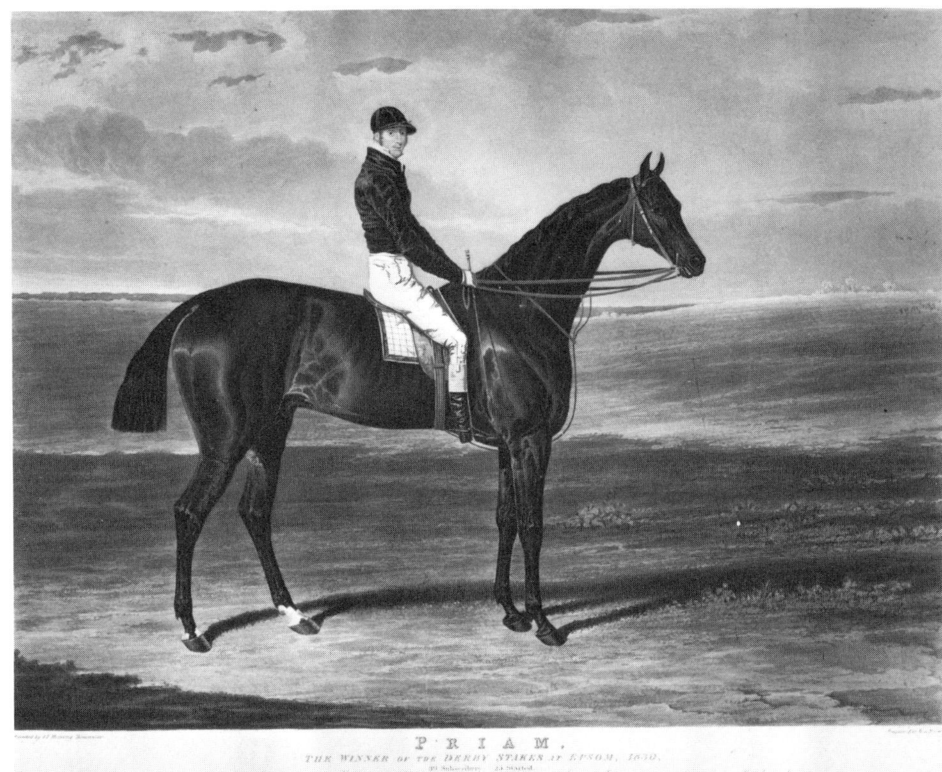

93 **Priam** winner of 1830 Derby Stakes.
Engraved by R. G. Reeve. *List No 370*

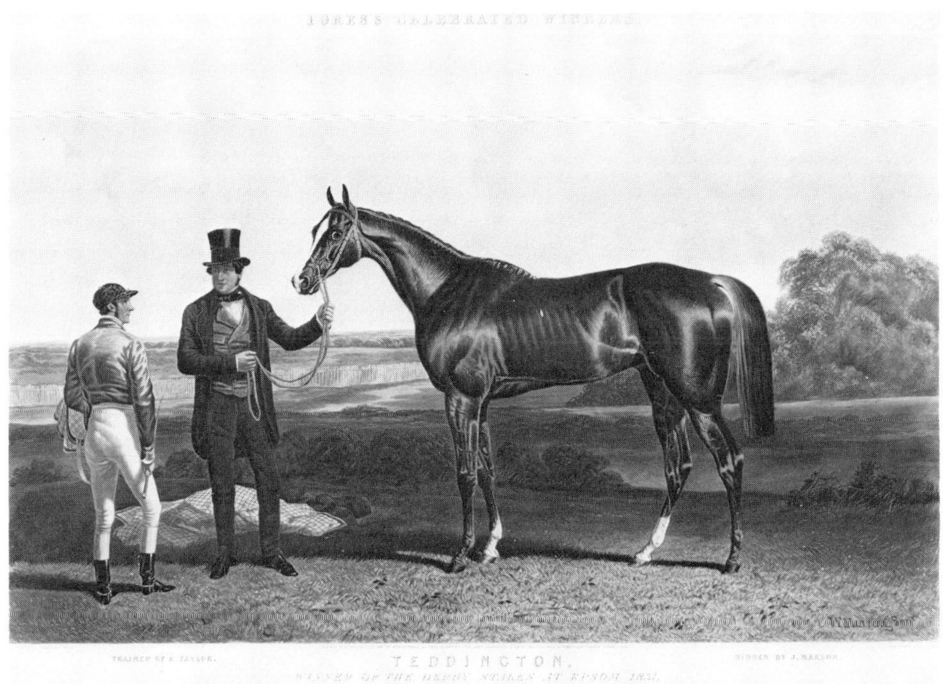

94 **Teddington** winner of 1851 Derby Stakes.
Engraved by J. Harris. *List No 389*

former winner, Middleton, belonging to him, Bay Middleton. James Robinson, his jockey, received 200 gns as his riding fee. This was heartily disapproved of by the bluff old autocrat, Admiral Rous, on the grounds, not of parsimony but as tending to corrupt the sport.
The Druid in 'Scott and Sebright', relating his visit to the artist's home at Meopham Park, Tonbridge, some years later, said: 'We came across the original sketch of Bay Middleton just as it was left about a quarter of a century ago. It occupied only one hour ten minutes, but it looks like the work of a day. No horse impressed Mr Herring more firmly than this son of 'Sultan' with the belief that he had the heart and the muscular energy to do what he liked with his fields. 'George Villiers', too, stood by the easel watching every stroke as it was dashed in, and never had painter a higher stimulus to bring all his manhood to his hand'.)
(See also *New Sporting Magazine* vol. xl, *Wildrake and Tattersall's Gallery*, p. 122, also *Sporting Magazine* July 1836.)

377 **Phosphorus** (1837). Engraved by C. Hunt. 16½ × 12½ ins. One hundred and thirty-six subscribers; seventeen starters. The property of the Right Hon. Lord Berners to whom the plate is dedicated. London, published July 1837 by S. & J. Fuller, Rathbone Place, W.
(See *Sporting Magazine* July 1837. Also *Bell's Life* appendix.)

378 **Amato** (1838). Engraved by C. Hunt. 16¾ × 12½ ins. One hundred and thirty-four subscribers; twenty-three starters. The property of Sir G. Heathcote, to whom the plate is dedicated. London: published July 1838 by S. & J. Fuller, at their Sporting Gallery, 34 Rathbone Place.
(See *Bell's Life* appendix.)

379 **Bloomsbury** (1839). Engraved by C. Hunt. 16¾ × 12½ ins. One hundred and forty-three subscribers; twenty-one starters. The property of Mr W. Ridsdale, to whom the plate is dedicated. London: published June 1939 by S. & J. Fuller, at their Sporting Gallery, 34 Rathbone Place, W.
(See *Bell's Life* appendix; *Bell's Life* in London, 19 May 1839.)

380 **Little Wonder** (1840). Engraved by C. Hunt. 16½ × 12¼ ins. One hundred and forty-four subscribers; seventeen starters. London: published in 1840 by S. & J. Fuller at their Sporting Gallery, 34 Rathbone Place. The property of Mr D. Robertson, to whom the plate is dedicated.
(This horse was purchased for sixty-five guineas. See also *Bell's Life*, Sunday, 7 June 1840.)

381 **Coronation** (1841). Engraved by C. Hunt. 16½ × 12½ ins. One hundred and fifty-four subscribers; twenty-nine starters. The property of Mr Rawlinson, to whom the plate is dedicated. London: published July 1841 by Messrs S. & J. Fuller at their Sporting Gallery, Rathbone Place, W.
(See also *Sporting Review* July 1841.)

382 **Attila** (1842). Not engraved, although the artist did take a sketch of him, and painted two pictures of him in stable, one signed J. F. Herring, 1842; both were offered for sale at Christie's in 1893.

383 **Cotherstone** (1843). Engraved by C. Hunt, coloured by C. Simpson. 20¼ × 15 ins. One hundred and sixty subscribers; twenty-three starters. The property of John Bowes Esq, MP. London: published by A. H. & C. Baily, 83 Cornhill and 18 Change Alley; Paris: Gambart et Junin.
(See *Bell's Life* in London, Sunday, 4 June 1843.)

384 **Orlando** (1844). Engraved by C. Hunt, coloured by C. Simpson. 20½ × 14¾ ins. One hundred and fifty-four subscribers; twenty-nine starters. The property of Colonel Peel. London: published by A. H. & C. Baily, Cornhill.
(See *Sporting Review* August 1844, *Sportsman* and *New Sporting Magazine* August 1844, and *Farmers Magazine* September 1844 and *Tattersall's Gallery* p. 290.)
(Author's note: Orlando, with Nat Flatman up, passed the post three parts of a length behind Running Rein, but was awarded the race on his supporters – aided by Lord George Bentinck – claiming that it was a fraud, and Running Rein was actually four years old. A similar accusation the year before, i.e. that the horse was a year older than claimed, had failed from the evidence of a stud groom who swore otherwise. On this occasion, the plaintiffs were thwarted by the disappearance of the owner, Goodman Levi and also of the horse itself, but, even so, Orlando was named the winner.)

385 **Merry Monarch** (1845). Engraved by C.

Hunt, coloured by C. Simpson. 19¾ × 14¾ ins. One hundred and forty subscribers; thirty-one starters. The property of W. G. K. Gratwicke Esq, to whom the plate is dedicated. Published by Messrs Baily, Cornhill.
(See also, *Bell's Life* Sunday, 1 June 1845; *Sportsman* July 1845, *New Sporting Magazine* July 1845, *Farmers Magazine* August 1845, and *Tattersall's Gallery* p. 308).

386 **Pyrrhus the First** (1846). Engraved by J. R. Mackrell, coloured by C. Simpson. 19¾ × 14¾ ins. One hundred and ninety-three subscribers; twenty-seven starters. The property of Mr John Gully. London: published by Messrs Baily Bros, Royal Exchange Buildings, Cornhill.
(See also, *Bell's Life* appendix; *Sporting Magazine* and *New Sporting Magazine* July 1846, and *Tattersall's Gallery* p. 323).

1847. Cossack. No known engraving.

387 **Surplice** (1848). Engraved by Henry Alken junr.

388 **Flying Dutchman** (1849). Engraved by J. Harris. 27 × 17½ ins. Also won Great St Leger at Doncaster in 1849, and all his engagements as a two-year-old. Beaten by Voltigeur in 1950 Doncaster Cup. Bred in 1846. In 1850 won the Emperor of Russia's Cup at Ascot, the sweepstakes of 300 sovs each at Goodwood, 1851, and the great match at York for 1,000 sovereigns a side, beating Voltigeur by a length, proving himself the champion of the turf. Ridden by C. Marlow. Published August 2 1849 [sic] by Messrs Fores, 41 Piccadilly.

1850. Voltigeur. No known engraving.

389 **Teddington** 1851. The property of Sir Joseph H. Hawley Bart. Bred in 1848. Got by Orlando (winner of the Derby 1844) out of Miss Twickenham. Trained by A. Taylor. Ridden by J. Marson. Engraved by J. Harris. *(See Plate 94.)*

11 Oaks Winners

Herring had eleven of his paintings of winners of the fillies' classic published as engravings; one by J. R. Scott, four by C. Hunt, alone, two by C. Hunt, coloured by C. Simpson, two by G. & C. Hunt and one of Mendicant, the last in the series, by J. R. Mackrell, coloured by C. Simpson.

Engravings for the years 1834, 1842 and 1845 are missing. It is on record that he made a sketch of Cyprian, the winner in the year 1836, preparatory to publication by Messrs Fuller, but owing to the engraving from F. C. Turner's picture (the usually accepted representation) being so quickly executed by Mr John Moore, it was probably decided to withdraw, leaving the field clear for Moore to continue publishing the Oaks winners, while Fuller covered the Derby and the St Leger.

Herring would have been in the position by then of being able to work for whichever firm could offer the best deal, while remaining faithful to Fuller with regard to the Derby pictures. It would obviously be of great interest if anyone was able to lay their hands on copies of engravings of the missing years.

390 **Vespa** (1833). Probably engraved by C. Hunt. Owned by Sir Mark Wood, Bt. Ninety-seven subscribers; nineteen starters.
(See also *New Sporting Magazine* January 1834, *Wildrake and Tattersall's Gallery* p. 67).

391 **Queen of Trumps** (1835). Engraved by C. Hunt. Owned by The Hon. E. M. Mostyn. Ninety-eight subscribers; ten starters.
(See St Leger list.)

392 **Cyprian**, bay filly by Partisan out of Frailty. Won the Oaks 1836 and Northumberland Plate. Engraving by J. Englehart in Taunton's *Celebrated Racehorses*.
(See also *Sporting Magazine* July 1836, *New Sporting Magazine* vol. xl, *Wildrake and Tattersall's Gallery* p. 128.)

393 **Miss Letty** (1837). Engraved by G. & C. Hunt., 16½ × 12½ ins. Ninety-two subscribers, thirteen starters. The property of the Hon. T. O. Powlett, to whom the plate is dedicated. Published July 1837 by J. Moore, Corner of West Street, Upper St Martin's Lane.
(See also *Sporting Magazine* July 1837.)

394 **Industry** (1838). Engraved by C. & G. Hunt. 16¾ × 12¾ ins. Ninety-eight subscribers; fifteen starters. The property of the Right Hon. the Earl of

Chesterfield, to whom the plate is dedicated. London: published July 1838 by John Moore, Corner of West Street, Upper St Martin's Lane.

395 **Deception** (1839). Engraved by C. Hunt. 16½ × 12½ ins. Ninety-six subscribers; thirteen starters. The property of Fulwar Craven, Esq, to whom the plate is dedicated. London: published June 1839 by John Moore at his wholesale glass and picture-frame manufactory, Corner of West Street, Upper St Martin's Lane.

396 **Crucifix** (1840). Engraved by C. Hunt. 17 × 12½ ins. One hundred and three subscribers; fifteen starters. The property of Lord George Bentinck, to whom the plate is dedicated. Published by J. Moore, 18 July 1840, at the Corner of West Street, Upper St Martin's Lane.
(See also *Sporting Review* August, 1840.)

397 **Ghuznee** (1841). Engraved by C. Hunt. 17½ × 12½ ins. One hundred and eighteen subscribers; twenty-two starters. The property of the Marquis of Westminster, to whom the plate is dedicated. London: published 1 July 1841 by John Moore at the Corner of West Street, Upper St Martin's Lane, printseller to HRH the Duke of Orleans.
(See also *Sporting Review* August 1841.) *(See Plate 95.)*

398 **Poison** (1843). Engraved by C. Hunt, coloured by C. Simpson. 20¼ × 15 ins. The property of George Samuel Ford, Esq. Ninety-one subscribers; twenty-three starters. London: A. H. & C. E. Baily, 83 Cornhill and 18 Change Alley; Paris: Gambart et Junin, depose.

399 **Princess** (1844). Engraved by C. Hunt, coloured by C. Simpson. 20¼ × 15 ins. One hundred and seventeen subscribers; twenty-five starters. The property of Colonel the Hon. G. Anson. London: A. E. & C. E. Baily, Cornhill. No date.
(See also *Sporting Review* July 1844, *Sportsman* and *New Sporting Magazine* same date, and *Farmers Magazine* November 1844 and *Tattersall's Gallery* p. 294).

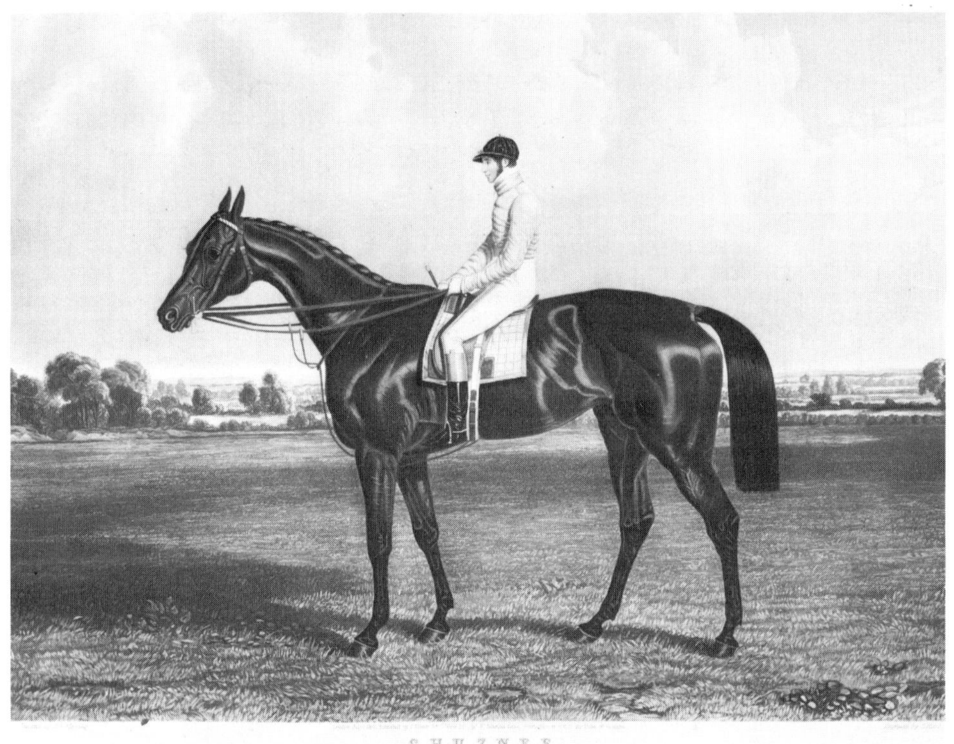

95 **Ghuznee** winner of 1841 Oaks Stakes. 17½ × 12½ ins. Engraved by C. Hunt. *List No 397*

400 **Mendicant** (1846). Engraved by J. R. Mackrell, coloured by C. Simpson. 20 × 15 ins. One hundred and forty subscribers; twenty-four starters. The property of Mr John Gully. Published by Baily Bros, Royal Exchange Buildings, Cornhill. (See also *Sporting Magazine* September 1846 and *New Sporting Magazine* same month, and *Tattersall's Gallery* p. 326.)

31 Great St Leger Winners

'St Legers' were also run at Newmarket and York, and other venues, but it is the race run at Doncaster which became known as the 'Great St Leger', the last Classic of the year.

From the year 1815, when Herring first entered the lists as a professional sporting artist, he painted every winner of this race up to and including the year 1849 – 34 in all – excepting those in the years 1841,[1] 1842 and 1848, and thirty-one were engraved. The last, Flying Dutchman, he had already had engraved as winner of the Derby. This extraordinary achievement is remarkable as much for the stamina showed by the artist in its accomplishment, as in the generally high standard of work.

In most cases, the winning owner granted Herring exclusive rights to paint the animal before anyone else, and the speed and accuracy with which he carried out the commissions, so soon after the race, were universally acknowledged, as were the likenesses he caught of the jockeys where included in the composition.

The fact that he lived in Doncaster (until 1830) and was well known and liked by many of the leading sporting gentry in the district, no doubt was a great help to him, but even when he left for the South, he still kept on with his annual assignment.

He was well served by Mr Thos. Sutherland who engraved the first eleven pictures, and thereafter C. Hunt (nine), R. G. Reeve (5), R. W. Smart and C. Hunt (1), C. Hunt with C. Simpson, the colourist (3), and J. Mackrell and C. Simpson, carried out the engravings.

The Publishers were the 'Doncaster Gazette' Messrs Sheardown, for the first twelve years, but their plates were taken over by S. & J. Fuller, who continued to publish the series thereafter on their own, until 1839, when the task was assumed by the Baily Bros, for one year. Then Fuller published one more, and then there is the gap of 1841 and 1842, before Baily Bros once again take over. It might be assumed from this that there was some dispute between the publishers themselves or Herring, that somehow allowed this unique series to be interrupted by other artists.

401 **Filho da Puta** (1815) Doncaster. Engraved by Sutherland. 16½ × 12¼ ins. Fifty-six subscribers; fifteen starters. The property of Sir W. Maxwell, Bart, to whom the plate is dedicated by the Publishers, Messrs Sheardown & Son. This plate and those following until the year 1825, was issued with the publication line altered to Messrs S. & J. Fuller, bearing their address at 34 Rathbone Place. No date.
(See also *Annals of Sporting*, 1 May 1822, and *Sporting Review* May 1844 – E. Hacker – and *The Sportsman* and the *New Sporting Magazine* May 1844.)

402 **Duchess** (1816) Doncaster. Engraved by Sutherland. 16½ × 11 ins. Forty-six subscribers; thirteen starters. The property of Sir R. B. Graham, Bart, to whom the plate is dedicated.

403 **Ebor** (1817) Doncaster. Engraved by Sutherland. 16½ × 14 ins. Fifty-two subscribers; eighteen starters. The property of Mr H. Peirse, to whom the plate is dedicated. *(See Plate 96.)*

404 **Reveller** (1818) Doncaster. Engraved by Sutherland. 16½ × 12½ ins. Fifty-one subscribers; twenty-one starters. The property of Mr H. Peirse, to whom the plate is dedicated.

405 **Antonio** (1819) Doncaster. Engraved by Sutherland. 16½ × 12½ ins. Fifty subscribers; fourteen starters.

406 **St Patrick** (1820) Doncaster. Engraved by Sutherland. 16½ × 12½ ins. Seventy-two subscribers; twenty-seven starters. The property of Sir E. Smith, Bart, to whom the plate is dedicated.

407 **Jack Spigot** (1821) Doncaster. Engraved by Sutherland. 16½ × 12¼ ins. Thirty-nine subscribers; thirteen starters. The property of the Hon.

[1] 1841: Colour aquatint by C. Hunt from G. B. Spalding, S. & J. Fuller 1 November 1841 *'Satirist'*.

T. O. Powlett, to whom the plate is dedicated. It is believed that some prints published by Sheardown were circulated, but Messrs Fuller issued a subscriber's edition with the Minerva stamp. A later edition was also published by them uniform with the others from plates purchased from Sheardown. (See also *Annals of Sporting* April 1822.)

408 **Theodore** (1822) Doncaster. Engraved by Sutherland. 17 × 12 ins. Seventy-three subscribers; twenty-three starters. The property of the Hon. E. Petre, to whom the plate is dedicated. Published by Sheardown, and afterwards by Fuller with publication line altered to their address at Rathbone Place. (See also *Annals of Sporting* December 1822, J. Webb.)

409 **Barefoot** (1823) Doncaster. Engraved by Sutherland. 16¼ × 12¼ ins. Eighty-four subscribers; twelve starters. The property of Mr Richard Watt and Mr Gilbert Crompton, to whom the plate is dedicated. Published by Sheardown, and afterwards by Fuller with publication line altered to their address at Rathbone Place. Another issue was also made with publication line erased.

410 **Jerry** (1824) Doncaster. Engraved by Sutherland. 16½ × 12¾ ins. Seventy-seven subscribers; twenty-three starters. The property of R. O. Gascoigne Esq, to whom the plate is dedicated. Published by Sheardown, and afterwards by Fuller with the publication line altered to their address at Rathbone Place.
(See also *Annals of Sporting* December 1824, W. R. Smith, engraver, where it is stated that Mr Herring is issuing proposals to issue this print with Mr Crofts, the training groom, and B. Smith, the rider, together with several favourite horses . . . quite novel in design, and to follow same with prints of succeeding winners of the race.)

411 **Memnon** (1825) Doncaster. Engraved by Sutherland. 16½ × 12½ ins. Eighty-one subscribers; thirty starters. The property of Mr R. Watt, to whom the plate is dedicated. Published by Sheardown, and afterwards by Fuller with the publication line altered to their address at Rathbone Place.
(See also *Annals of Sporting* November 1825, W. Scott engraver. A further reference to this print in May 1826 mentions that the jockey, William Scott 'very like and well put upon the saddle' is featured in the composition which also includes a view of the grand stand and spectators.

412 **Tarrare** (1826) Doncaster. Engraved by R. G. Reeve. 17 × 13¼ ins. Ninety-five subscribers; twenty-seven starters. The property of the Right Hon. the Earl of Scarborough to whom the plate is dedicated. London: published November 1826 by S. & J. Fuller at their Sporting Gallery, 34 Rathbone Place, W. and at Messrs White's, Doncaster.

413 **Matilda** (1827) Doncaster. Engraved by R. G. Reeve. 16½ × 12¼ ins. Ninety subscribers; twenty-six starters. The property of the Hon. E. Petre, to whom the plate is dedicated. London: published in 1827 by Messrs S. & J. Fuller at their Sporting Gallery, Rathbone Place and at J. F. Herring's, Doncaster.
(See also a woodcut in *Bell's Life* in London, Sunday, 23 September 1827, taken by Herring with the permission of Hon. E. Petre. Also *Sporting Magazine* February 1829, R. Woodman engraver.)

414 **Colonel** (1828) Doncaster. Engraved by R. G. Reeve. 16 × 12 ins. Eighty subscribers; nineteen starters. The property of the Hon. E. Petre, to whom the plate is dedicated. London: published January 15, 1829, by S. & J. Fuller at their Sporting Gallery, 34 Rathbone Place, and at J. F. Herring's Doncaster.
(See also woodcut in *Bell's Life* Sunday, 21 September 1828, by Herring with permission from Hon. E. Petre. No particulars of the horse are given.)

415 **Rowton** (1829) Doncaster. Engraved by R. G. Reeve. 16½ × 12 ins. Ninety-seven subscribers; nineteen starters. The property of the Hon. E. Petre, to whom the plate is dedicated. London: published 21 December 1829, by S. & J. Fuller at their Sporting Gallery, 34 Rathbone Place, and at J. F. Herring's, Doncaster.
(See also woodcut in *Bell's Life*, Sunday, 20 September 1829, by Herring with the permission of the Hon. E. Petre).

416 **Birmingham** (1830) Doncaster. Engraved by R. G. Reeve. 16½ × 12 ins. Sixty-eight subscribers; twenty-eight starters. The property of Mr Beardsworth, to whom the plate is dedicated. London: published 21 March 1831, by S. & J. Fuller at their Sporting Gallery, Rathbone Place, and at J. F. Herring's, Doncaster.

96

Ebor. Winner of Great St Leger Stakes, 1817. 16½ × 14 ins. Engraved by Thomas Sutherland

List No 403

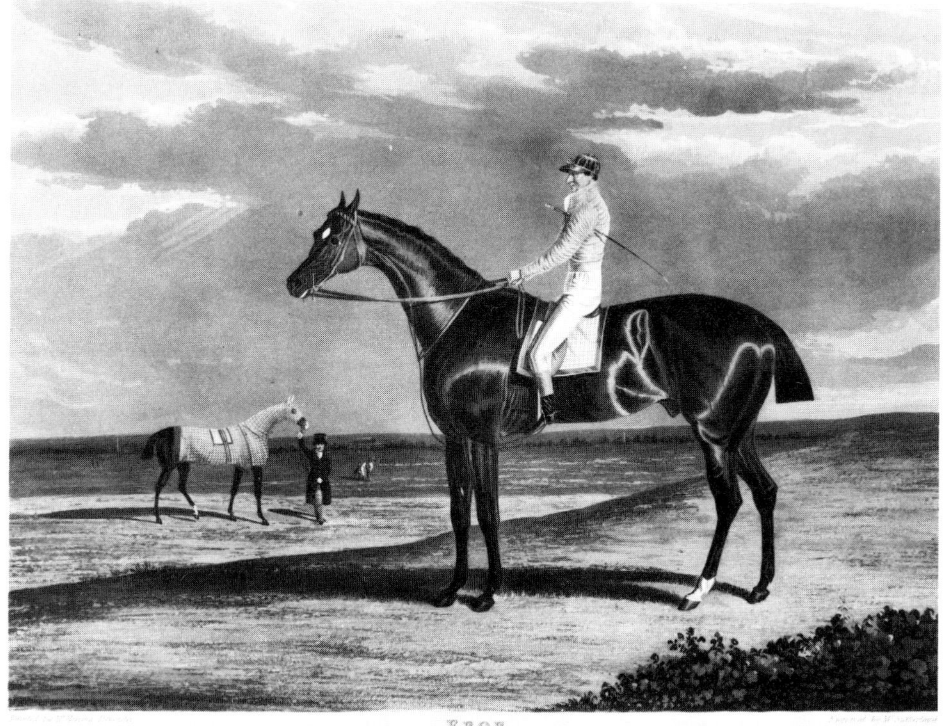

97

Don John, winner of Great St Leger Stakes 1838. 17 × 12½ ins. Engraved by C. Hunt

List No 424

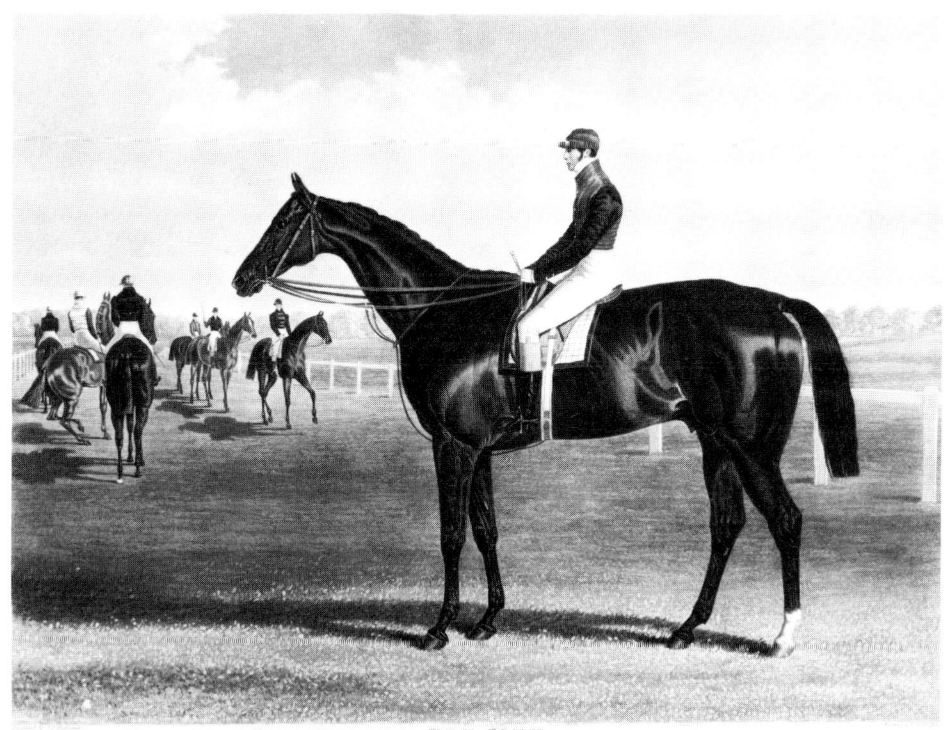

(See also woodcut in *Bell's Life*, Sunday, 26 September 1830, by Herring with Mr Beardsworth's permission).

417 **Chorister** (1831) Doncaster. Engraved by C. Hunt. 20 × 11¾ ins. Eighty-six subscribers; twenty-four starters. The property of the Most Noble the Marquis of Cleveland, to whom the plate is dedicated by J. F. Herring and S. & J. Fuller, London: published 14 February 1832, by S. & J. Fuller at their Sporting Gallery, 34 Rathbone Place, and J. F. Herring's, Doncaster.
(See also woodcut in *Bell's Life*, Sunday, 25 September 1835, with no description. Also *New Sporting Magazine*, December 1831, and Wildrake's *Cracks of the Day*, and *Tattersall's Pictorial Gallery of Race-horses*, p. 20.)

418 **Margrave** (1832) Six Mile Bottom, Newmarket. Engraved by C. Hunt. 16¾ × 12½ ins. Seventy-three subscribers; seventeen starters. The property of Mr John Gully, to whom the plate is dedicated. London: published 21 February 1833 by S. & J. Fuller at their Sporting Gallery, 34 Rathbone Place, and at J. F. Herring's, Six Mile Bottom, near Newmarket.
(See also woodcut in *Bell's Life*, Sunday, 23 September 1832, by Hering – 'the celebrated animal-painter. It was taken for us by permission of Mr Gully by Mr Herring, and gives a perfect idea of the "ugly features" of this lucky horse'. Also *New Sporting Magazine* June 1833 (J. R. Scott), *Wildrake and Tattersall's* p. 47.)

419 **Rockingham** (1833) Six Mile Bottom, Newmarket. Engraved by C. Hunt. 16½ × 12½ ins. Seventy-five subscribers; twenty starters. The property of Mr Richard Watt, to whom the plate is dedicated. London: published 2 December 1833 by S. & J. Fuller at their Sporting Gallery, 34 Rathbone Place, and at J. F. Herring's, Six Mile Bottom, near Newmarket.
(See also woodcut in *Bell's Life*, Sunday, 6 October 1833, by Herring, including portrait of Sam Darling, the jockey, whose likeness 'is admirably preserved'. Also *New Sporting Magazine* Vol. VII (J. R. Scott) and *Wildrake and Tattersall's* p. 70.)

420 **Touchstone** (1834). Engraved by R. W. Smart and C. Hunt. 16 × 12 ins. Seventy-one subscribers; eleven starters. The property of the Most Noble the Marquis of Westminster, to whom the plate is dedicated. London: published December 1834, by S. & J. Fuller at their Sporting Gallery, 34 Rathbone Place.
(See also woodcut in *Bell's Life* Sunday, 5 October 1834.* And *New Sporting Magazine* June 1835 (H. R. Cook), *Wildrake and Tattersall's* p. 97, *Sporting Magazine* August 1837 (T. S. Engleheart), *Sporting Review* and *Sportsman*, February 1844 and *Farmers Magazine* March 1844, E. Hacker.)

421 **Queen of Trumps** (1835). Engraved by C. Hunt. 16½ × 12 ins. The property of the Hon. E. M. L. Mostyn, to whom the plate is dedicated. London: published November 20, 1835, by S. & J. Fuller at their Sporting Gallery, 34 Rathbone Place.
(See also woodcut in *Bell's Life* Sunday, 20 September 1835, with a note: 'sketched at Doncaster where Mr Herring, had a sitting of both mare and Jockey with Mr Mostyn's consent'. And *New Sporting Magazine* December 1835 (R. Parr), *Wildrake and Tattersall's* p. 112, and *Sporting Magazine* December 1835 (J. R. Scott).

422 **Elis** (1836). Engraved by C. Hunt. 16½ × 12½ ins. Seventy-five subscribers; fourteen starters. The property of the Right Hon. the Earl of Lichfield, to whom the plate is dedicated by the publishers, J. F. Herring and S. & J. Fuller. London: published 1836, by S. & J. Fuller at their Sporting Gallery, 34 Rathbone Place.
(See also woodcut in *Bell's Life*, Sunday 25 September, 1836 by Herring, with a note to say that the assertion in a daily contemporary that Lord Lichfield is not the owner of Elis is without the slightest foundation. The news of his success reached Lord Lichfield in the theatre at Lichfield at nine o'clock the same evening, and was received by the audience with loud cheers'.
(See also *Sporting Magazine*, November 1836 (J. R. Scott), and *New Sporting Magazine* December 1836 (R. Parr) also in *Wildrake and Tattersall's* p. 130.)

423 **Mango** (1837). Engraved by C. Hunt. 16¾ × 12½ ins. Sixty subscribers; thirteen starters. Bred by Mr T. Thornhill in 1834, and is own brother to Preserve, Marmalade, Morella, Pickle and Perfume. The property of the Hon. C. C. Greville, to whom the plate is dedicated by the publishers, J. F. Herring and S. & J. Fuller. London: published November 1837, by S. & J. Fuller at their Sporting Gallery, 34 Rathbone Place, W.

(See also woodcut in *Bell's Life* Sunday 28 September 1837, by Herring to whom the owner gave exclusive permission as an addition to 'that popular work' The Great St Leger Winners.)

424 **Don John** (1838). Engraved by C. Hunt. 17 × 12½ ins. Sixty-six subscribers; seven starters. The property of the Right Hon. The Earl of Chesterfield, to whom the print is dedicated by the publishers, S. & J. Fuller. London: published November 1838, by S. & J. Fuller at their Sporting Gallery, 34 Rathbone Place.
(See also woodcut in *Bell's Life* by Herring, Sunday, 23 September, 1838; and *Sporting Review* February 1844 (J. R. Scott). *(See Plate 97.)*

425 **Charles XII** (interior) (1839). Engraved by C. Hunt, coloured by C. Simpson. 20 × 15¼ ins. One hundred and seven subscribers; fourteen starters. The property of Andrew Johnstone Esq, Helleath House. As a three-year-old, he started in 1839 three times and won. In 1840, six times and won once. In 1841, eleven times and won ten. In 1842, three times and won twice, making in all twenty-three starts; winning sixteen races, including the Doncaster, Great St Leger, and eight cups. Published by A. H. & C. E. Baily, Cornhill. No particulars available of Messrs Fuller's print.
(See also woodcut in *Bell's Life* by Herring, Sunday, 22 September 1839. And *New Sporting Magazine* Vol XVII (W. B. Scott), same in *Wildrake and Tattersall's* p. 200.)

426 **Lancelot** (1840). Engraved by C. Hunt. 16½ × 12½ ins. Rode by William Scott. One hundred and twelve subscribers; eleven starters. The property of the Most Noble the Marquis of Westminster,[1] to whom the plate is dedicated. London: published 1 November 1840 by S. & J. Fuller at their Sporting Gallery, 34 Rathbone Place.
(See also woodcut in *Bell's Life* by Herring, Sunday, 20 September 1840.[1])

427 **Satirist** (1841). Painting not engraved by Herring, but there is an aquatint by C. Hunt, from a painting by G. Spalding, 12¼ × 16½ ins.

428 **Blue Bonnet** (1842). Painting not engraved for Herring.

[1] Maroon, who ran second to Lancelot, also belonged to the Marquis of Westminster (bred by the Earl of Chesterfield).

429 **Nutwith** (1843). Engraved by C. Hunt, coloured by C. Simpson. 20¼ × 15 ins. One One hundred and twenty-seven subscribers; nine starters. The property of Mr S. Wrather. Published by A. H. & C. E. Baily, 83 Cornhill, and Gambart et Junin, depose.
(See also woodcut in *Bell's Life* by Herring, Sunday, 17 September 1843; *Sporting Review* November 1843 (E. Hacker) and ditto *Farmers Magazine* December 1843.)
His trainer, Robert Johnson, remarked his 'small hocks, rather curby in their appearance, and 'a noble Marquis (Exeter?) sent his agent to Middleham to see him when a two-year-old, and the latter gave it as his opinion that his hocks were not to be trusted to; or in all probability he would have gone south!

430 **Faugh-a-Ballagh** (1844). Engraved by C. Hunt, coloured by C. Simpson. 19¾ × 15¼ ins. One hundred and eight subscribers; nine starters. The property of Mr E. I. Irwin. He was purchased from his breeder, Mr Knox, by Mr Irwin, in 1842 with eight other horses for £2,000. Although beaten in the Champagne Stakes at Doncaster in 1843, his next win, the St Leger, was worth over £2,600, he also won the Grand Duke Michel Stakes and the Cesarewitch for the same year, so was a cheap purchase for Mr Irwin. Published by A. H. & C. E. Baily, Cornhill.
(See also woodcut in *Bell's Life*, Sunday, 22 September, 1844 – unsigned, but Herring responsible for the sketch; also *Sporting Review* November 1844 (E. Hacker), also in *Sportsman* and *New Sporting Magazine*, November 1844, *Farmers Magazine* February 1845 and *Tattersall's* p. 297.)

431 **The Baron** (interior) (1845). Engraved by J. R. Mackrell, coloured by C. Simpson. 19½ × 16 ins. One hundred and one subscribers; fifteen starters. The property of Mr George Watt (publication line missing).
(See also woodcut in *Bell's Life*, Sunday, 21 September 1845 by Herring – 'Animal painter to HRH the Duchess of Kent' (first time this appears); also *Sportsman* October, 1845 and ditto *New Sporting Magazine* November 1845 and *Tattersall's* p. 315.)

432 **Sir Tatton Sykes** (1846) looking to the right, with a portrait of Sir Tatton Sykes, Bart. Engraved by J. R. Mackrell, coloured by C. Simpson. 20 × 15 ins. Published by Baily Bros, 3 Royal Exchange

Buildings, Cornhill. (No details of number of runners.)

also

433 **Sir Tatton Sykes** – looking to the left. Engraved by C. Hunt. 20 × 15 ins. One hundred and fifty-one subscribers; twelve starters. The property of William Scott (jockey) (given by Sir Tatton), to whom the plate is dedicated by his obliged servant, John Moore. London: published by John Moore at the Corner of West Street, Upper St Martin's Lane. This latter plate was again issued, bearing the name and address of Mr George Newbold, 304 Strand.
(See also *Sporting Magazine* November 1846 (E. Hacker) and ditto *New Sporting Magazine* November 1846; and woodcut in *Illustrated London News*, 26 September 1846 with a description of the horse by Herring from the *Doncaster Gazette*.

434 **Van Tromp** (1847). Engraved by C. Hunt, coloured by C. Simpson. 20¼ × 15 ins. One hundred and forty-six subscribers; eight starters. The property of the Right Hon. Earl of Eglinton. London: Baily Bros, 3 Royal Exchange Buildings, Cornhill.

435 **Surplice** (1848). Not Engraved.

436 **Flying Dutchman** (1849). See Derby list.

19 Thoroughbred Stallions

Bell's Life, Sunday, 15 May 1836, says: The first number of Messrs Fuller's new work, *Portraits of Celebrated Thoroughbred Stallions*, is just out. It consists of an admirable likeness of Whisker from a painting of Mr Herring's, with his pedigree, performances, list of his stock, and their winnings. The style in which it is got up, and the small price at which it is published, cannot fail to ensure a large sale. It ought to be in the portfolio of everyone who professes to be a lover of the turf or of the fine arts!

(Some dates are missing.)

(All this set were published by S. & J. Fuller, 34 Rathbone Place, and engraved by C. Hunt.)

437 **Whisker**. 11¾ × 9½ ins. Bred by His Grace the Duke of Grafton. The plate is dedicated to His Grace the Duke of Cleveland. 1836.

438 **Blacklock**. 11¾ × 9½ ins. Bred by Mr Jirby, 1814. The print is dedicated to Mr Richard Watt. 1836.

439 **Catton**. 11¾ × 9½ ins. Bred by the Right Hon. the Earl of Scarborough [sic]. 1836.

440 **Camel**. 11¾ × 9½ ins. Bred by the Earl of Egremont, 1822. The print is dedicated to Mr Theobald. 1836.

441 **Partisan**. 11¾ × 9½ ins. Bred by the Duke of Grafton in 1811. To the Right Hon. Lord Lowther, to whom the plate is dedicated. 1836.

442 **Sultan**. 11¾ × 9¾ ins. Bred by Mr Crockford. 1836.

443 **Zinganee**. 11¾ × 9½ ins. Bred by the Marquis of Exeter, 1825. The plate is dedicated to the Right Hon. the Earl of Chesterfield. 1836.

444 **Velocipede**. 11¾ × 9½ ins. Bred and owned by W. Armitage Esq, to whom the plate is dedicated. 1836.

445 **Gohanna**. 11¾ × 9½ ins. Bred by Lord Egremont in 1790. Painted from the original in the collection of the Earl of Egremont. The plate is dedicated to the Hon. George Wyndham. 1838.

446 **Walton**. 11¾ × 9½ ins. Bred by Sir Hedworth Williamson, Bart in 1799. Got by Sir Peter out of Arethusa. To His Grace the Duke of Grafton to whom the plate is dedicated. 1838.

447 **Whalebone**. 11¾ × 9½ ins. Bred by the Duke of Grafton in 1807. A copy from the original painting in the collection of the Earl of Egremont.

The plate is dedicated to Colonel George Wyndham. 1838.

448 **Langar**. 12 × 9½ ins. Bred by Lord Lowther, 1817. The print is dedicated to the Hon. Lumley Savile. 1840.

449 **Glaucus**. 11¾ × 9½ ins. Bred by Lord Lowther in 1830. The print is dedicated to Messrs Tattersalls. 1840.

450 **Comus**. 11¾ × 9¾ ins. Bred by Sir John Shelley in 1809. The property of Christopher Wilson Esq.

451 **Venison**. 11¾ × 9¾ ins. Bred by Mr J. Day in 1833. 1840.

452 **Sheet Anchor**. Bred by Mr Golden in 1832. Now the property of Mr Thompson. 11¾ × 9½ ins.

453 **Defence**. 12¼ × 9¾ ins. Bred by Mr Sadler, 1824. 1843.

454 **Muley**. 11¾ × 9¾ ins. Bred by Sir Charles T. Bunbury, Bart in 1810.

455 **Actaeon**. 11¾ × 9¾ ins. Bred by Mr Newton in 1822. The property of his late Majesty King William IV.

From the Art Journal *p 192, 1856*

The Royal Pictures – The Queen's Horses

J. F. Herring, Painter. C. Cousen, Engraver. Size of the picture 35¼ × 27 ins.

A peculiar feature of our national character is a strong attachment to domestic animals, especially to horses and dogs. This feeling pervades, in a greater or less degree, every class, from the nobleman or country gentleman, who possesses his stud of racers, or of hunters, or his pack of deep-baying hounds, to the poor mountain shepherd whose collie keeps solitary watch with him day by day on the hills, or the wandering gipsy, whose donkey carries on his back the whole household wealth of the family, and asks no other shelter from the night-dews of heaven than the canopy of the thick-leaved oak, under which his master's tent has been pitched till the rising of the new day's sun. This national feeling has had its effect on our school of art, by calling into existence a few painters who have made it almost a special business to become portrait-painters of animals because there are few owners of a favourite horse or dog, who are not desirous of seeing him represented on the canvass of the artist; hence have arisen Landseer, J. Ward, A. Cooper, Ansdell, Herring, Barraud, and others.

Mr Herring is among that class of artists who, by the strength of their own genius alone, have raised themselves from comparative obscurity into fame and distinction; and in his case this result has been realised without any of those early indications of talent which 'cast their shadows before'. It is, we believe, about forty years back that he left the metropolis for Yorkshire, without any especial object in view; but a fondness for animals in general, and for horses in particular, and a strong desire to 'handle a team' of the latter, induced him to occupy the driving-box of a stagecoach; an ambition which, at that period when the glories of the turnpike-road were at their zenith, was exhibited by not a few of our aristocracy and wealthy commoners.

How it was he imbibed a taste for painting we do not know, but it is certain that he filled up his spare hours at this time by making portraits of the favourite horses which came under his guiding rein; and that he painted them and drove them with equal skill, his constant association with the animals making him a perfect master of their forms, habits, and character. His position on the box – it was the famous York 'Highflyer', we believe, which he drove – and his success in the department of art he practised, introduced Mr Herring to the notice of many individuals noted on the turf and in the chase, by whom he was frequently engaged to paint portraits of their horses.

This artist very rarely exhibits at the Royal Academy: he was one of the earliest supporters of the Society of British Artists, in whose gallery and in that of the British Institution his works may annually be seen. The picture here engraved was a commission from the Duchess of Kent, to be presented to her Majesty on her birthday. Her Royal Highness was so pleased with it, that she appointed Mr Herring her animal painter. The Queen also testified her approbation of the work, by commanding the artist to paint a portrait of a favourite black horse, the picture being a present from Her Majesty to Prince Albert on his birthday.

Of the two horses which appear in the engraving, the

darker is a beautiful chesnut, named Hammon; he was bred in the stud of the King of Prussia at Trakehn, and was presented to her Majesty by the King in 1844. Though the animal is now nearly twenty-two years old, we are assured by the Queen's riding-master, M. Meyer, that he is as fresh as a 'four-year-old'. The grey horse is called Tajar; he was bought by M. Meyer in 1844 of Count Hatzfeld, having been reared at Twenark in Mecklenberg, by Count Hahn; his age is about a year beyond that of Hammon; but, like the latter, he is as fresh as ever. Both horses are of pure Arab sires. Tajar is still used by her Majesty when she takes horse exercise in the riding-school. They are represented as standing at one of the private entrances to Windsor Castle. The picture is in the collection at Osborne.

From the Art Journal *p 172, 1865*

Selected Pictures

From the collection of Alderman Copeland, M.P., Stoke-upon-Trent

Mazeppa, J. F. Herring, Painter; John Cousen, Engraver

Byron's poem of 'Mazeppa' – less well known, perhaps, than most of his other writings – has furnished Mr Herring with an excellent subject for the display of his skill in drawing that noble animal the horse; and we have no artist more competent to do it full justice. Even animal painters have their speciality, though each may be able to portray well other creatures than that in which he particularly excels, or, in other words, one tribe takes precedence of the rest.

Thus, Sir Edwin Landseer has established his claim to the dog, Mr T. S. Cooper to sheep and cows, Mr Abraham Cooper and Mr Herring to the horse, as did the late James Ward, RA while Morland was 'great' in pigs and donkeys. Each of these artists seems to have made the character of the several animals his especial study.

There is something more in this picture than a series of portraits such as might be selected from the stud of a monarch or a nobleman. Here is a vast herd of wild horses, that seem to have swept down into the valley from the adjacent mountains; such a herd as travellers tell us is sometimes seen on the prairies of America, where the animal is known as the Mustang, and congregates in numbers so immense as scarcely to fear the attack of any enemy but man. These herds are always under the leadership of one of the herd, who is able, by some extraordinary means, to convey his orders simultaneously to the whole body. There is not one of the horses in Mr Herring's picture but calls to mind the magnificent description of the warhorse found in the Book of Job, than which nothing of its kind more poetical in idea, grander in language, and more truthful in delineation of character, was ever written.

'Hast thou given the horse strength? hast thou clothed his neck with thunder? Canst thou make him afraid as a grasshopper? the glory of his nostrils is terrible. He paweth in the valley, and rejoiceth in his strength; he goeth to meet the armed men. He mocketh at fear and is not affrighted; neither turneth he back from the sword. The quiver rattleth against him, the glittering spear and the shield. He swalloweth the ground with fierceness and rage; neither believeth he that it is the sound of the trumpet, Ha, ha; and he smelleth the battle afar off, the thunder of the captains and the shouting.'

The prevailing idea in the thoughts of this herd is surprise, or curiosity, rather than fear, at the strange sight presented to them; fear would have caused them to rush away; but they look on with manes and heads erect, yet with an air of uncertainty as to whether it would be wise to flee or stay. The horses in the foreground are drawn with much spirit and animation, while the attitude of the animal whereupon Mazeppa is bound is most natural. Weary with his flight, his eyes bereft of their fire, his nostrils sending forth a stream of hot breath, he has stumbled, and in another instant will roll over and crush his rider to death.

This is undoubtedly the artist's most poetical and original composition, qualities as evident in the treatment of the landscape as in that of the herd of horses.

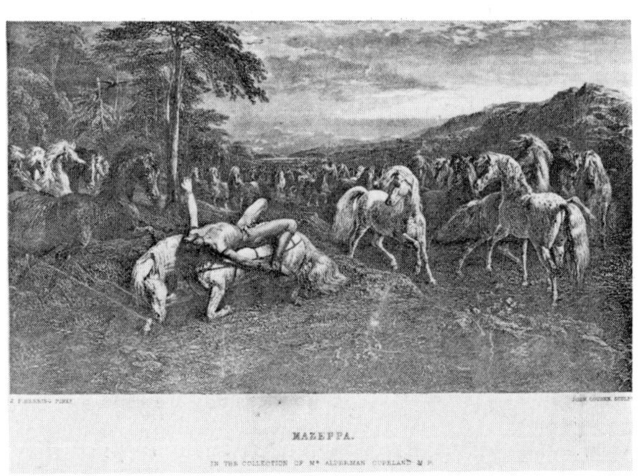
MAZEPPA.

Engraved Sets under separate titles

456 **Sketches on the Road**. 30 × 22 ins each.
1. Coach-Horses.
2. Post-Horses.
These two engraved by C. Hunt, London, Baily Bros, Royal Exchange Buildings, Cornhill. No date. These plates were afterwards issued with the following publication line: London, published 1863 by A. J. Isaacs, 56 Bishopsgate Street Within, E.C.
3. Royal Mail-Coach (Glasgow coach). Engraved by T. W. Huffam. London, Baily Bros, Royal Exchange Buildings, Cornhill. No date. This plate was issued later with the publication line erased.

457 **Stable Scenes**, 26½ × 17½ ins each. A smaller set, 12 × 7½ ins was also published by Fores.
1. The Mail Change. Engraved by J. Harris, from a picture in the possession of Sir W. W. Wynn, Bart. Published 2 August 1844. *(See Plate 98.)*
2. The Hunting Stud. Published 10 February 1846, Paris: Goupil & Vibert, déposé à la direction. *(See Plate 99.)*
3. The Team. Published 19 May 1846, Paris: Goupil & Vibert, déposé à la direction.
4. Thoroughbreds – a stable interior showing four horses preparing for a race, three jockeys mounted in colours. Published 17 March 1846 by Messrs Fores, 41 Piccadilly; Paris: Goupil & Vibert, déposé à la direction. *(See Plate 100.)*

458 **Fox-Hunting**. 30 × 22 ins each.
1. The Meet. Engraved by T. W. Huffam.
2. The Find. Engraved by T. W. Huffam.
3. Full Cry. Engraved by J. Mackrell.
4. The Death. Engraved by J. Mackrell.
London: published 1 November 1846 by Messrs Baily Bros, No 3 Royal Exchange Buildings, Cornhill.

459 **The Seasons**. 27½ × 17¾ ins each.
Spring, Summer, Autumn, Winter.
Inscribed: Animal Painter to HRH the Duchess of Kent. Engraved J. Harris. Each print is inscribed 'To Charles Cammell Esq, Wadsley House, Sheffield', from the original pictures in his collection. London: published 10 March 1847 by Messrs Henry Graves & Co, printsellers to the Queen; Paris: Goupil, Vibert & Co, déposé. *(See Plates 101, 102, 103, 104.)*

460 **National Sports**. A series of ten plates. Each 41¼ × 20¾ ins.
1. The Start for the Derby (for 1844 – Running Rein's year), with horse's names, colours and jockeys (the 'Dirty Derby'). Engraved by C. Hunt. Published May 1845, by Messrs Fores, 41 Piccadilly. The picture is accompanied with a key from which the name of every horse and jockey is distinctly ascertained. Leander, green, white sleeves, Bell; Ugly Buck, black, orange cap, J. Day junr; Orlando, purple, orange cap, Flatman; Running Rein, all white, S. Mann; Bay Momus, all white, F. Butler; Campanero, crimson, grey cap, Perrin; Ionian, all orange, G. Edwards; Ratan, white, red cap, S. Rogers; Akbar, crimson, grey cap, Robinson; Phalaris, black, white sleeves and cap, R. Sly; British Tar, green and white stripe, white cap, M. Jones; T'Auld Squire, all black, J. Holmes; Beaumont, crimson and white stripe (hoop), white cap, Calloway; Ashtead Pet, brown, yellow sleeves, black cap, W. Boyce; Needful, drab, green sleeves and cap, W. Cotton; Telemachus, lilac, black cap, Marson; Loadstone, red and white stripe, white cap, Darling senr; King of the Gipsies, lilac, drab sleeves, white cap, Marlow; Elemi, white, scarlet sleeves, white cap, S. Chiffney; Votri, black, white cap, W. Day; Lancet, yellow, black cap, Templeman; Delightful Colt, white, blue sleeves, red cap, Whitehouse; Croton Oil, blue, white cap, W. Howlett; Beaufront, light blue, black cap, J. Howlett; Mount Charles, white, Bumby; Dick Thornton, pea-green, Darling junr; Cockamaroo, yellow, gorge-de-pigeon sleeves and cap, Simpson; Amulet Colt, white, red sleeves and cap, Heseltine. *Bell's Life*: 'The spirit and reality infused into the picture surpasses anything of the sort ever witnessed. The position of every horse is accurately delineated, while the likenesses are not less true . . . the engraving by Charles Hunt is in his most masterly style.'

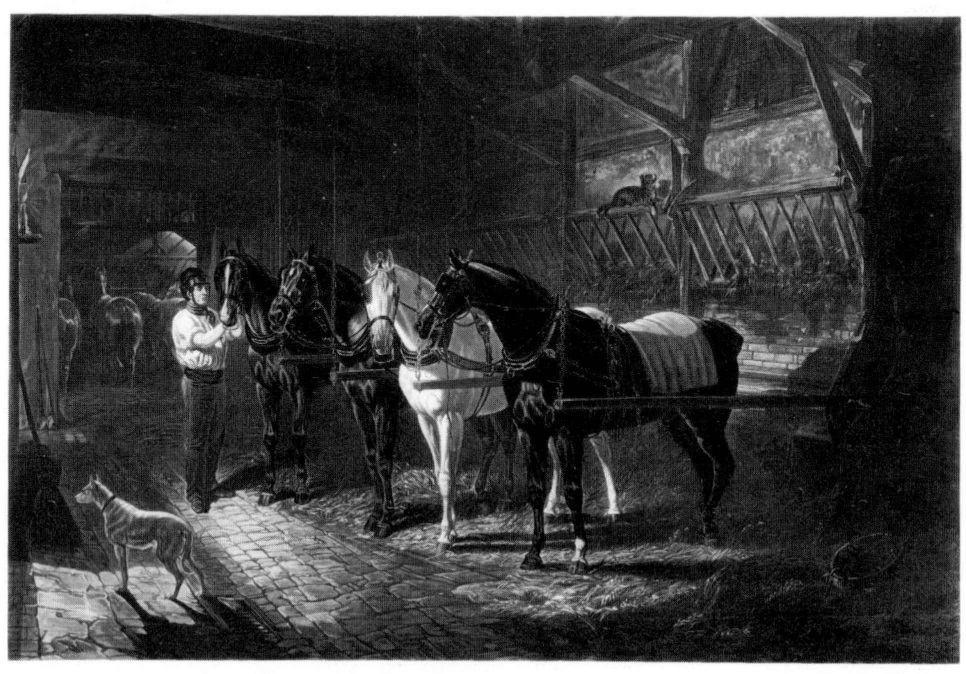

98 **The Mail Change** from Fores's Stable Scenes, 1844. 26½ × 17½ ins.
Engraved by J. Harris. *List No 457*

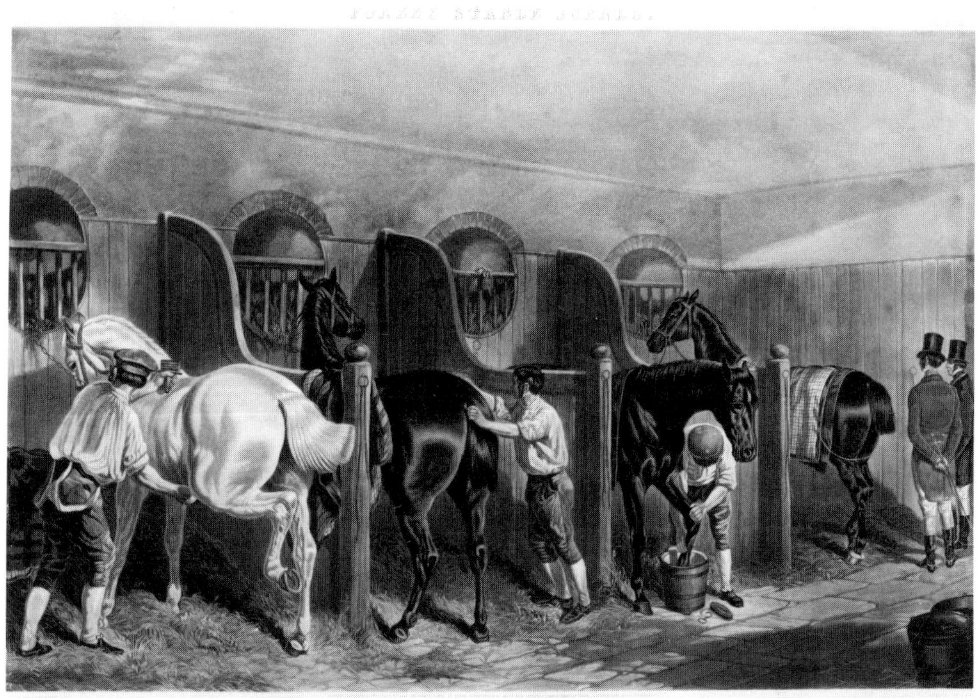

99 **The Hunting Stud** from Fores's Stable Scenes, 1844. 26½ × 17½ ins.
Engraved by J. Harris. *List No 457*

2. STEEPLECHASE CRACKS. Engraved by J. Harris. London: published 25 October 1847 by Messrs Fores, 41 Piccadilly, W.
Picture accompanied by a key: Salute, violet, white sleeves, violet and white cap, Captain Powell; Discount, black, orange cap, T. Oliver; Switcher, light blue, drab stripe, black cap, Lord Strathmore; Cigar, white blue stripe, black cap, Captain Broadley; Peter Simple, scarlet, light blue cap, P. P. Rolt Esq; Brunette, crimson, black cap, A. M. M'Donough; Pioneer, purple, orange cap, Captain Peel; Culverthorpe, scarlet, white cap, Rowland; Tramp, black, white sleeves and cap, J. Bradley; Marengo; blue, black cap, P. Barker; Lottery, blue, black cap, James Mason.

FOX-HUNTING: four prints engraved by J. Harris.
3. The Meet.
"... Delightful scene,
When all around is gay, men, horses, dogs,
And on each smiling countenance appears
Fresh blooming health and universal joy.
... Then to the copse
Thick with entangled grass or prickly furze,
With silence lead the many coloured hounds
In all their beauty's pride" – *Somerville*

4. The Find.
"Hark! on the drag I hear
Their doubtful notes precluding cry
More nobly full and swell'd with every mouth.
Hark! what loud shouts
Re-echo through the groves – he breaks away,
Shrill horns proclaim his flight, each struggling hound
Strains o'er the lawn to reach the distant pack.
'Tis triumph all and joy." – *Somerville*

5. The Run.
"... The riders bend
O'er their arched necks, with steady hands by turns
Indulge in speed or moderate their rage.
Happy the man who with unrivalled speed
Can pass his fellows and with pleasure view
The struggling pack." – *Somerville*

6. The Kill.
"The pack inquisitive with clamour loud
Drag out their trembling prize, and on his blood
With greedy transport feast.
... A chosen few
Alone the sport enjoy, nor droop beneath
Their pleasing toils." – *Somerville*

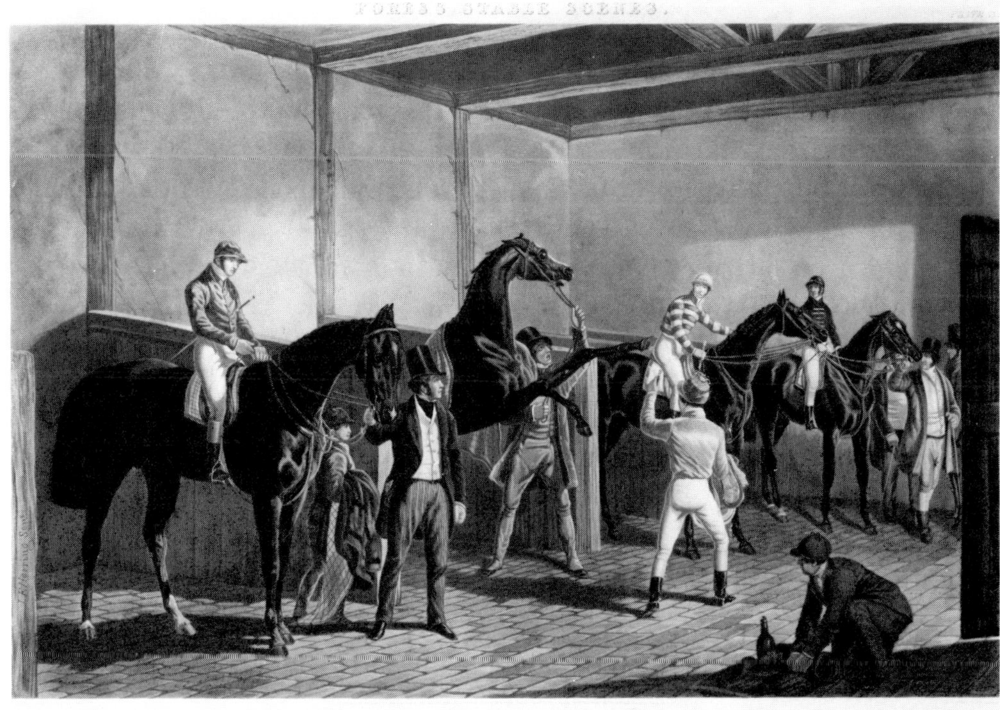

100 **Thoroughbreds** from Fores's Stable Scenes, 1844. 26½ × 17½ ins.
Engraved by J. Harris. *List No 457*

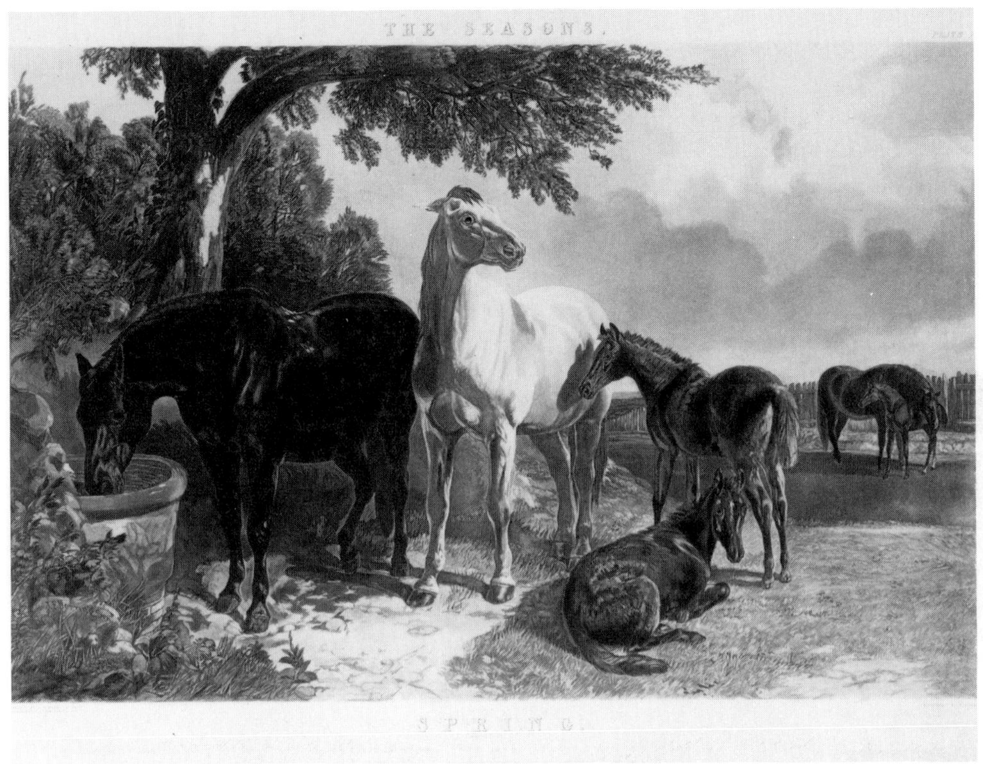

101 **Spring** (from the Seasons). Set of four, each 27½ × 17¾ ins.
Engraved by J. Harris. *List No 459*

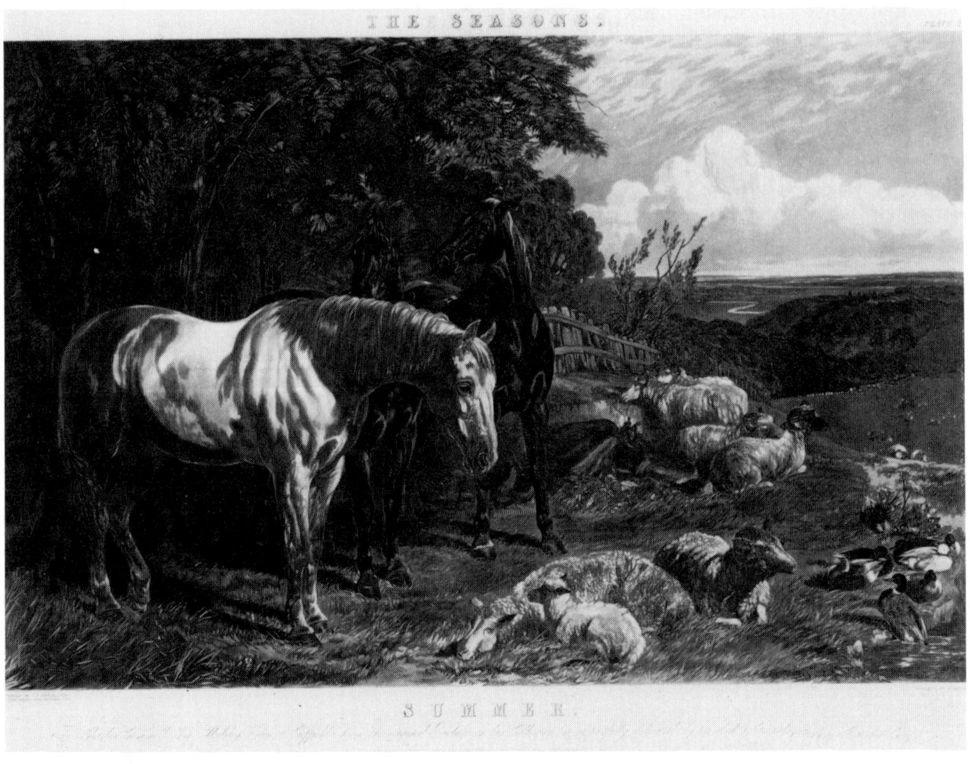

102 **Summer**
Engraved by J. Harris. *List No 459*

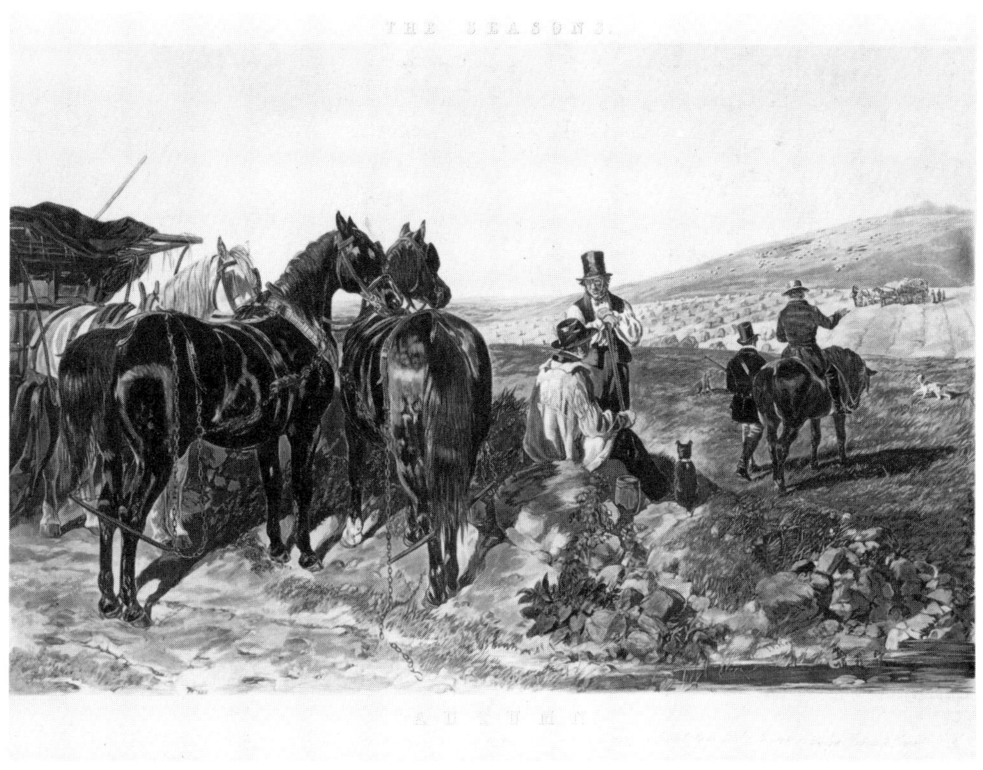

103 **Autumn**
Engraved by J. Harris. *List No 459*

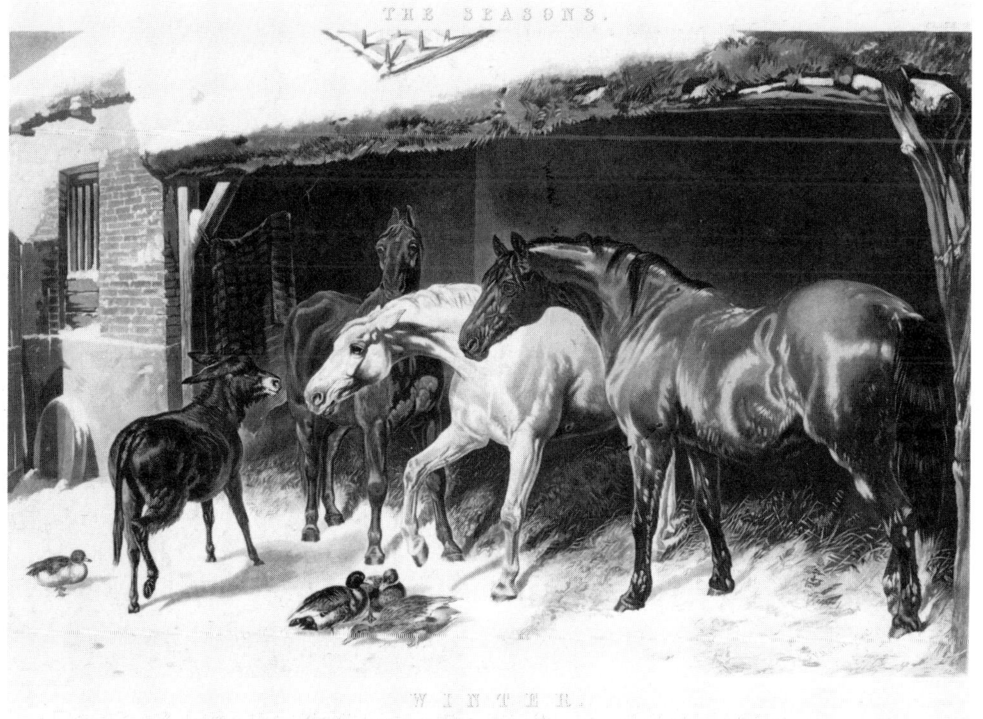

104 **Winter**
Engraved by J. Harris. *List No 459*

London: published 12 April 1852 by Messrs Fores, at their Sporting Repository, 41, Piccadilly, W. *(See Plates 111, 112, 113, 114.)*

RACING – Four prints engraved by J. Harris and William Summers.
7. Saddling.
8. False Start.
9. The Run In.
10. Returning to Weigh.
Representing Mr Martin Starling as clerk of the course, leading the way for returning to weigh of the following 'cracks' after a supposed race: Flying Dutchman, in the colours of the Earl of Eglinton, led by Fobert; West Australian, in the colours of Mr Bowes, led by John Scott; Teddington, in the colours of Sir Joseph Hawley, Bart, led by A.-Taylor; Stockwell, in the colours of the Marquis of Exeter, with the famous 'Aske spots' in the distance (Voltigeur?), and horses in the colours of Mr Nichol and Mr 'Dangerous' Sadler, etc. Published by Messrs Fores & Co, 41 Piccadilly, 1 September 1856, and entered according to Act of Congress in the year of 1856, by Williams, Stevens, Williams & Co, in the Clerk's Office of the District Court of the Southern District of New York.
A small set of the four plates of 'Racing' was also published, size – 24½ × 13¼ ins.

461 **The Horse** – illustrated with twelve plates from the original pictures by J. F. Herring, in a wrapper. Engraved by the most celebrated artists. Published by Lloyd Bros, Gracechurch Street, and to be had of all printsellers in town and country alike. No date.

LIST OF SUBJECTS
The Baron's Charger. Engraved by H. Davis.
The Cavalry Charger. Engraved by W. Holl.
The Hunter. Engraved by J. Knight.
The Racehorse. Engraved by H. Davis.
The Postman's Horse. Engraved by J. Patterson.
The Scotch Cart Horse. Engraved by J. Patterson.
The Dray Horse. Engraved by G. Davey.
The Brougham Horse. Engraved by W. Holl.
The Lady's Palfrey. Engraved by D. G. Thompson.
The Park Hack. Engraved by J. Knight.
The Farmer's Hack. Engraved by D. G. Thompson.
The Shooting Pony. Engraved by G. Davey.

India artist's proofs	£12.12.0
India before letters	£ 8. 8.0
Prints	£ 4. 4.0

462 **Farm Series**. Four prints each 27¾ × 18 ins. Engraved by J. Harris.
Morning, Noon, Evening, Night.
London: published 15 March 1849 by E. Gambart & Co, 25 Berners Street, Oxford Street; Paris: Goupil, Vibert & Co, déposé. A smaller set, size 10¾ × 7½ ins was published by Messrs E. Gambart & Co, 25 Berners Street, Oxford Street. No date. *(See Plates 105, 106.)*

463 **Portraits of Celebrated Stallions and Mares**, whose performances and produce are well known on the turf. 27½ × 17¾ ins each.
[1. Sir Hercules and Beeswing painted by Laporte.]
2. Touchstone and Emma.
3. Pantaloon and Languish.
4. Bay Middleton and Barbelle (sire and dam of the Flying Dutchman).
5. Camel and Banter.
6. Muley Moloch and Rebecca.
7. Lanercost and Crucifix.
Published by Messrs Fores, 41, Piccadilly. *(See Plates 107, 108, 109, 110.)*

464 **Fox-Hunting** (published posthumously). 30¾ × 17½ ins. Engraved by J. Harris.
The Meet, Full Cry, Breaking Cover, The Death.
London: published 7 August 1874 by Mr G. P. McQueen, 37 Great Marlborough Street, Regent Street, W.

465 **Farm-Yard Sketches**. Horses etc. Six plates 10¾ × 7¾ ins each.
London: published by Messrs G. Rowney & Co, Oxford Street, London, W. No date.

466 **Studies in Two Crayons**. 20 × 13½ ins each, heads of
Horses Eating.
Horses Drinking.
London: published by Messrs G. Rowney & Co, 64 Oxford Street, London, W. No date.

467 **The Poultry Yard**. 25½ × 19¾ ins. Engraved by F. Taylor.

468 **The Traveller's Rest**. 29 × 24 ins. Engraved by C. E. Wagstaff.
Ovals, 28 × 26¾ ins. The Friendly Meal, Temperance Meeting, Agricultural Members. Engraved by A. Lucas. Published by Solomon Marks,

Continued on page 170

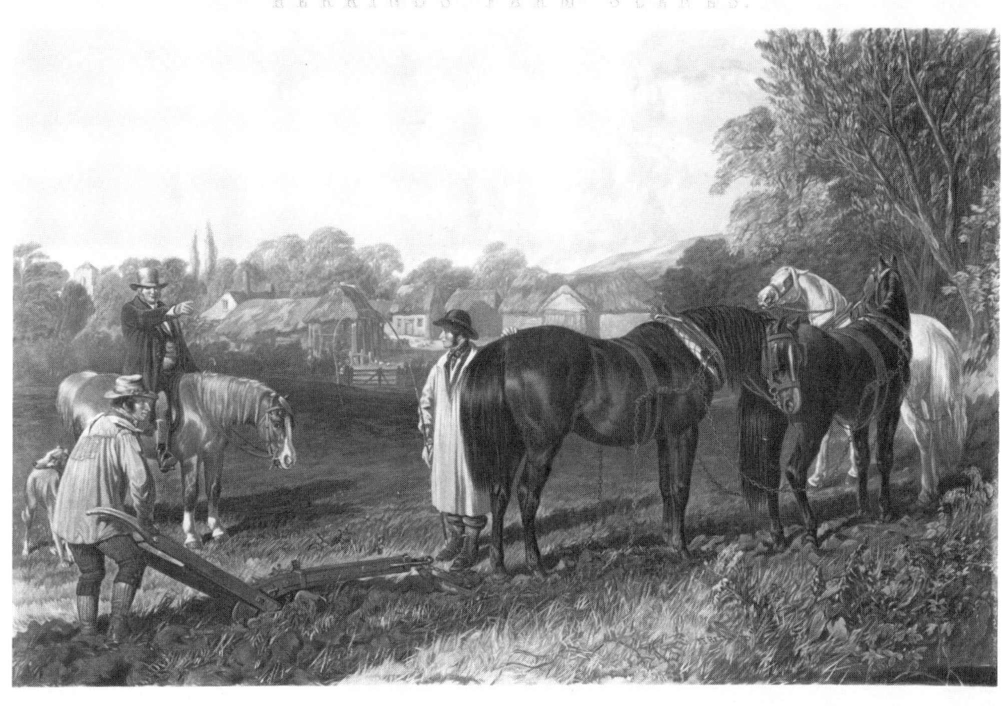

105 **Morning** (from Herring's Farm Scenes) 1849. Set of four, each 27¾ × 18 ins.
Engraved by J. Harris. *List No 462*

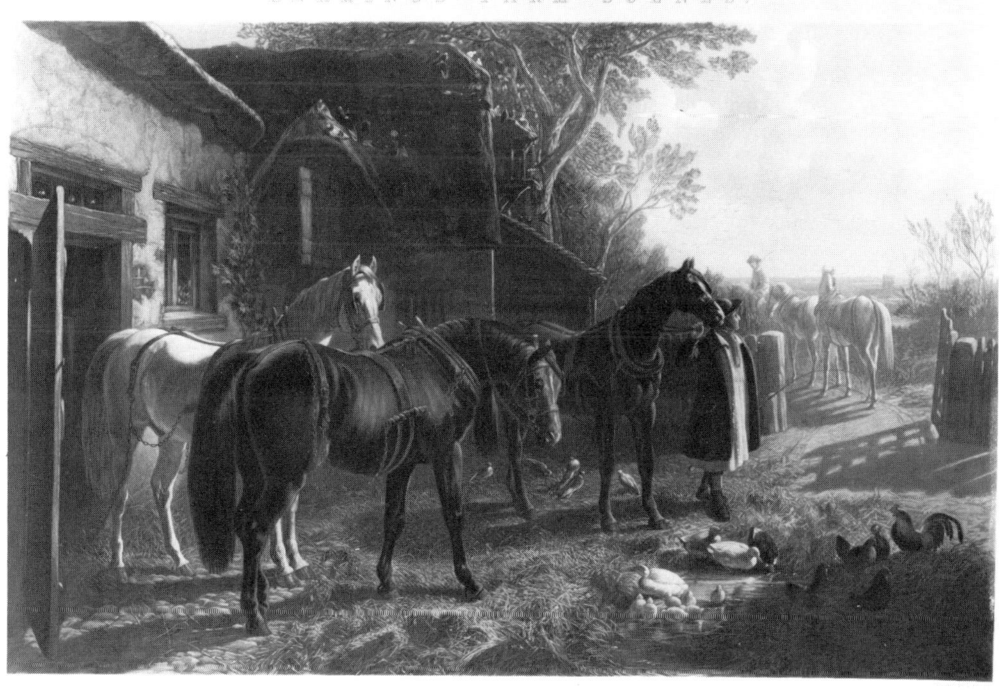

106 **Noon**
Engraved by J. Harris. *List No 462*

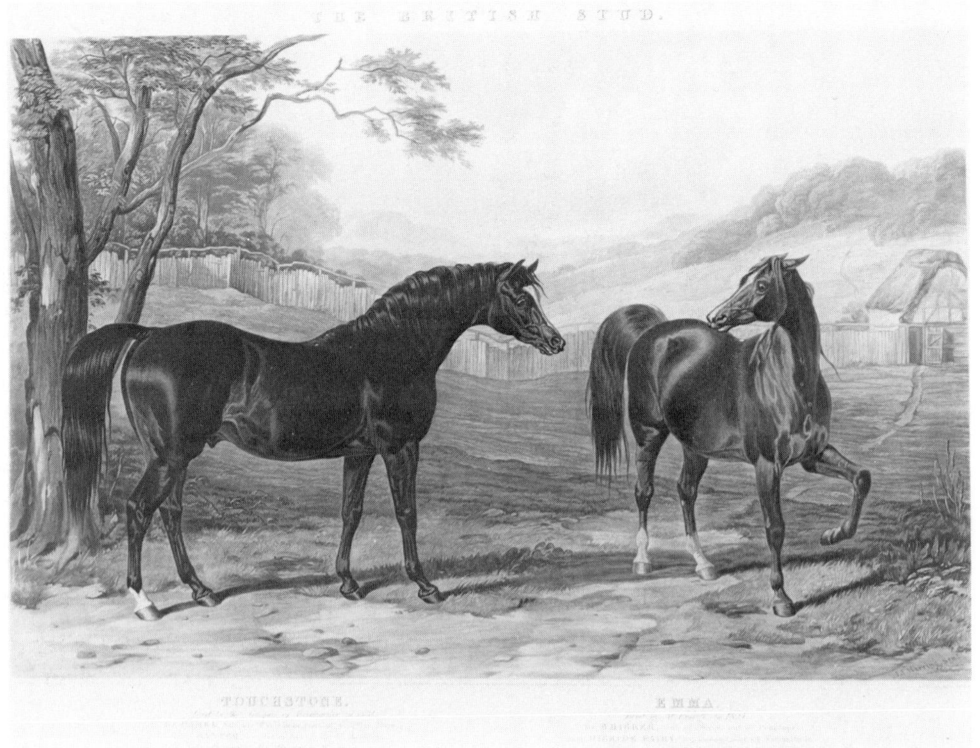

107 **Touchstone and Emma** from The British Stud 1845. Set of seven, each 27½ × 17¾ ins. Engraved by J. Harris. *List No 463*

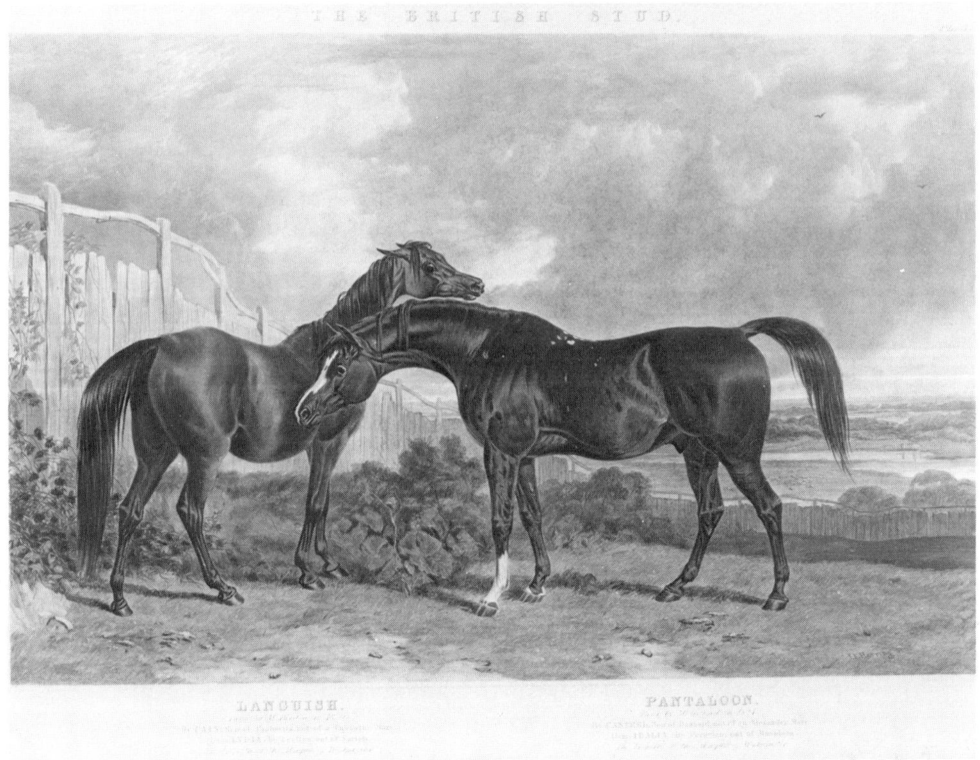

108 **Languish and Pantaloon** from the British Stud. Engraved by J. Harris. *List No 463*

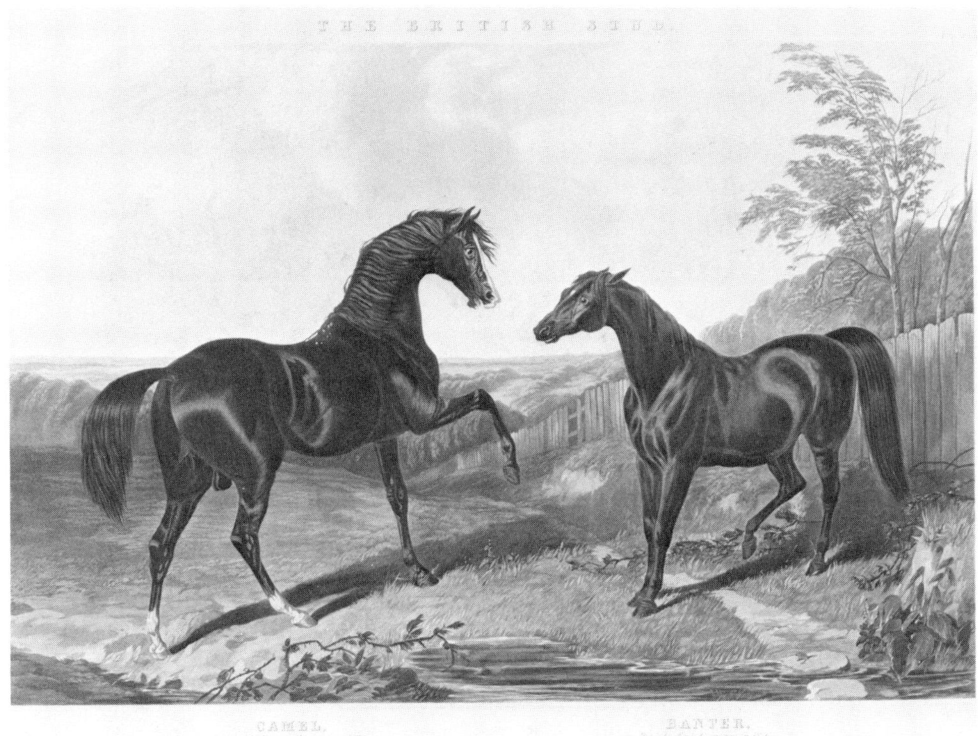

109 **Camel and Banter** from the British Stud.
Engraved by J. Harris. *List No 463*

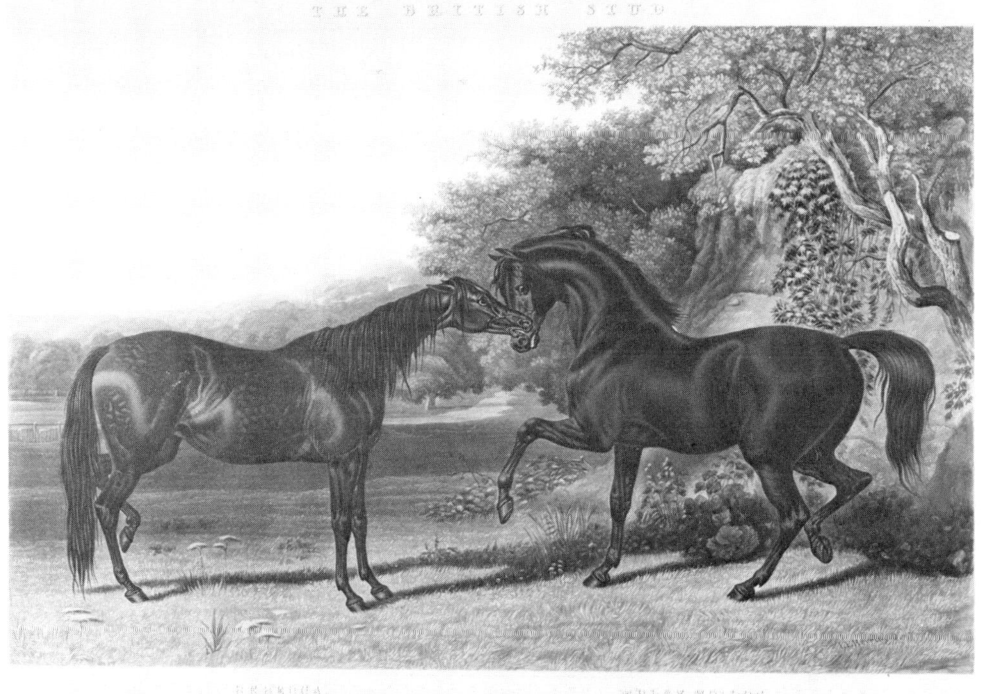

110 **Rebecca and Muley Moloch** from the British Stud.
Engraved by C. Hunt. *List No 463*

Foxhunter
from National Sports
Four prints engraved
by J. Harris. Each
41¼ × 20¾ ins.

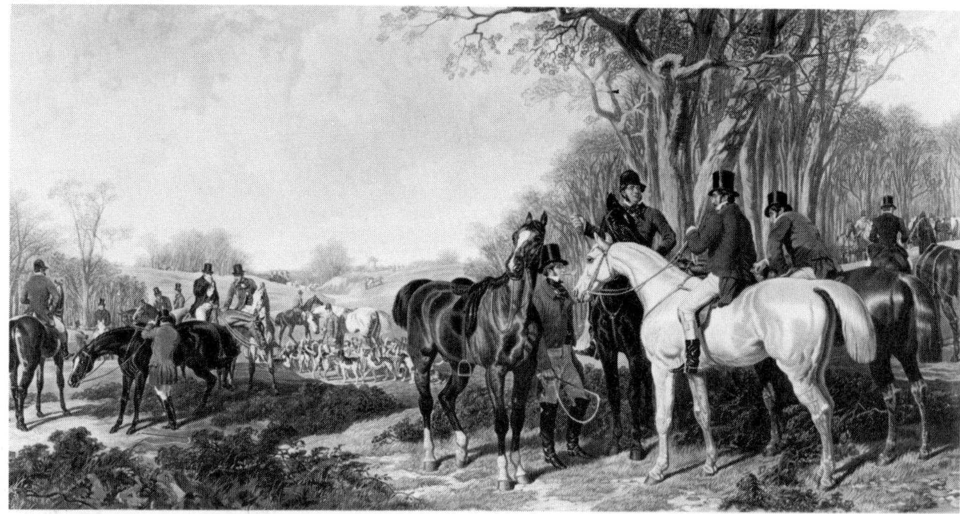
111 **The Meet.** *List No 460*

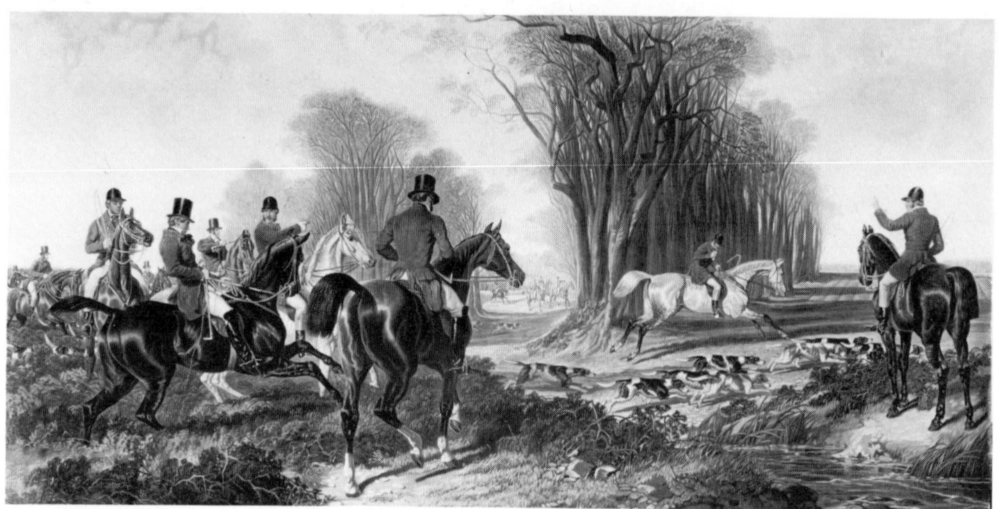
112 **The Find.** *List No 460*

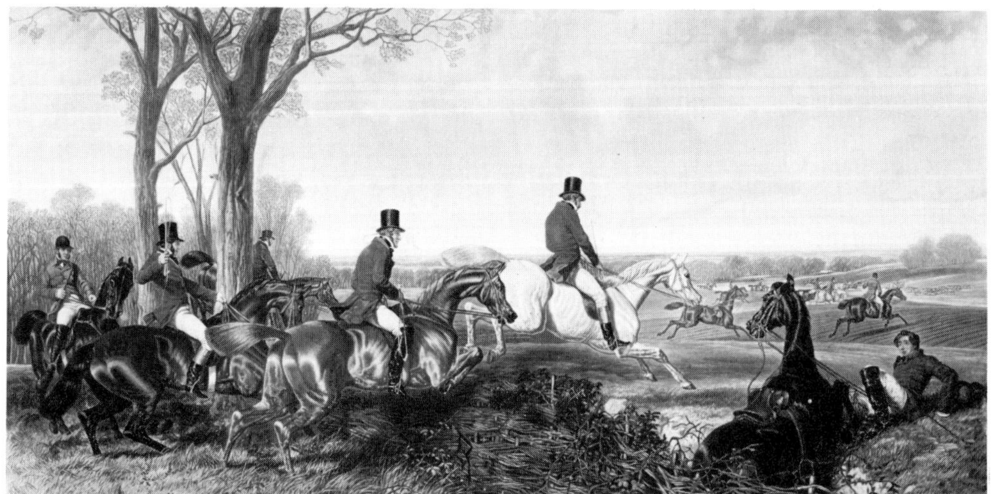
113 **The Run.** *List No 460*

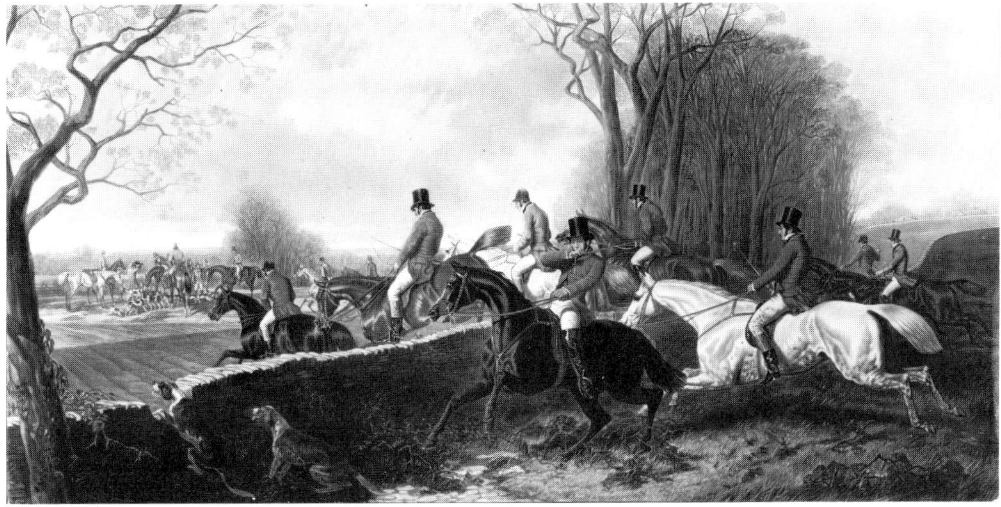

114 **The Kill.** *List No 460*

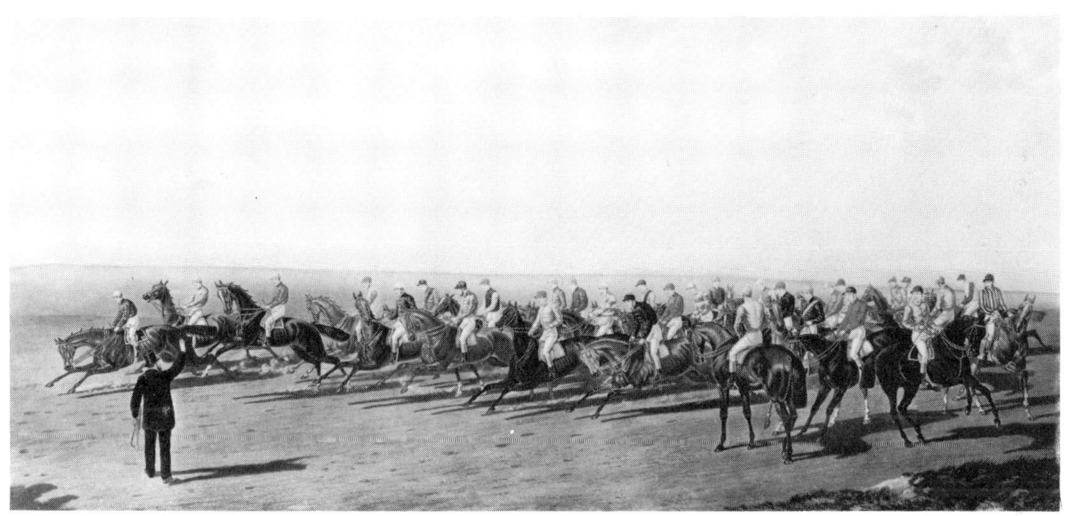

115 **Flat Racing** – The Start by Ben Herring Junr

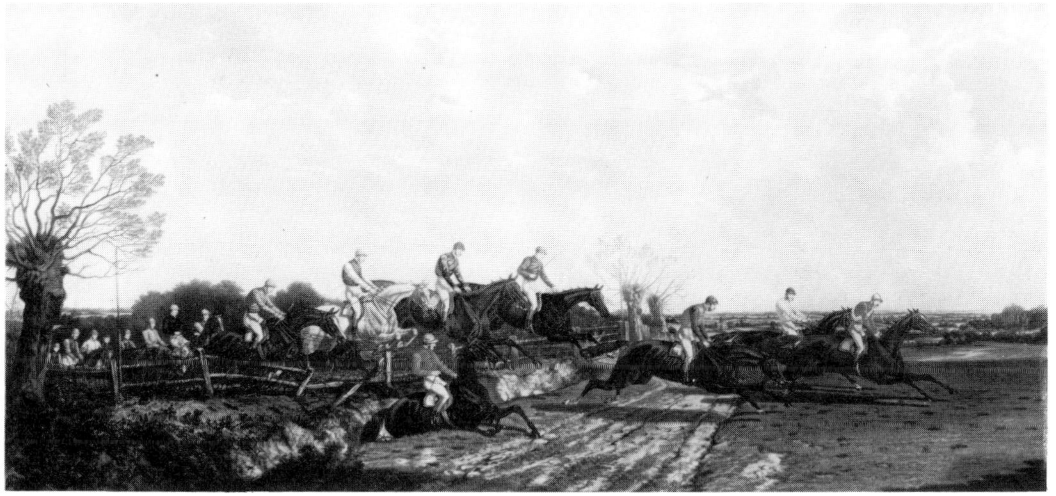

116 **Steeplechasing** by Ben Herring Junr

Fleet Street about 1856. These plates were re-issued by Thomas Rose of 70 Hampstead Road, NW.

469 **The Rev. J. M. Bellew**. SEL. 27 × 21½ ins. Engraved by Mr Edwards.

470 **An Interior**. Published by E. Atchley, Library of Arts, 106 Great Russell Street, Bedford Square.

471 **Gossip**. Published by E. Atchley, Library of Arts, 106 Great Russell Street, Bedford Square.

472 **Waiting for Master**. 34½ × 22 ins. Engraved by H. G. W. Watkins.
Published by Messrs H. Graves & Co, declared at the Printsellers' Association, 2 August 1847.

473 **Three Members of the Temperance Society**. Inscribed: Animal Painter to HRH the Duchess of Kent. Engraved by Thomas Landseer (Edwin Landseer's elder brother). Dedicated by permission to HRH the Duchess of Kent.
London: published 1 February 1847 by S. & J. Fuller, 34 Rathbone Place; Paris: Goupil & Vibert, 15 Boulevard Montmartre, déposé.

Lithographs

Farm-Yard Series. Lithographed by J. West Giles. Circular, about 16 ins in diameter.
1. Donkey and Horse; 2. Pony, Horse and Pigs; 3. Ducks; 4. Dogs; 5. Cows and calf in stable; 6. ? (Published 1 January 1949.) 7. Horses; 8. Oxen; 9. Sheep; 10. Pigs, peacock and fowls; (Published 1 February 1850.) 15½ × 15¾ ins (arch tops). 11. Rabbits; 12. Goats. (Published March and May 1852.)
London: published by E. Gambart & Co, 25, Berners Street, Oxford Street, W.

Stable Scenes. 15 × 15 ins (oval tops) by J. W. Giles.
No 1. Horse and pony with fowls.
No 2. Farmer's horse harnessed at the manger, with ducks etc.
London: published 2 December 1850 by E. Gambart & Co, 25 Berners Street, Oxford Street, W.

Stable Scenes. 25 × 19½ ins by J. West Giles.
No 1. Carriage Horses.
No 2. Roadsters.
London: published 22 July 1852 by E. Gambart & Co, 25 Berners Street, Oxford Street, Day & Son, Lithographers to the Queen.
Entered according to Act of Congress in the year 1852 by Knoedler in the Clerk's Office of the District Court for the Southern District of New York.

Farmyard Scenes. 4 × 3¾ ins. Coloured. In sheets.

No 1

Plate 1. Horses.
Plate 2. Bull and cow.
Plate 3. Horses in a straw-yard.
Plate 4. Horse and donkey with ducks.
Plate 5. Cow and calf (interior).
Plate 6. Bull and cows.

No 2

Plate 1. Dogs (interior).
Plate 2. Goat and kids.
Plate 3. Rabbits feeding.
Plate 5: Sheep and lambs.
Plate 6. Pigs, fowls and peacock.
London: published 30 March 1853 by E. Gambart & Co, 25 Berners Street, Oxford Street; Goupil & Co, Paris and New York.

Straw-yard, Summer (horses, pigs, ducks etc.). 25½ × 19¾ ins. J. West Giles, lithographer.
London: published 14 June 1850 by Messrs E. Gambart & Co, 25 Berners Street, Oxford Street, W.; Goupil, Vibert & Co, New York. M. & N. Hanhart, lithographic printers.

Sporting Sketches. Approx 10¾ × 7½ ins each. Chromo-lithographs.
Before (the race). Vincent Brooks. 1 December 1853.

After (the race). Vincent Brooks. 1 December 1853.
Present Times. Vincent Brooks. 1 December 1853.
Times Gone. Vincent Brooks. 1 December 1853.
The Welter. Day & Son. 10 January 1854.
Follow. Day & Son. 10 January 1854.
The Wrong Sort. Vincent Brooks. 10 January 1854.
A Smash (Steeplechase scene). Day & Son. 10 January 1854.
The Right Sort. Day & Son. 10 January 1854.
And No Mistake. Day & Son. 1 March 1854.
Hunters Going to Cover. Day & Son. 1 March 1854.
Going to the Meet. Vincent Brooks. 1 March 1854.
The Rise. Day & Son. 10 May 1854.
The Fall. Day & Son. 10 May 1854.
Too Fast to Last. Day & Son. 10 May 1854.
Taking a Little Drop (or bank). Day & Son. 10 May 1854.
Crossing the Line. Day & Son. 10 May 1854.
The Fix. Day & Son. 1 November 1856.

London: published on the above dates by Lloyd Bros & Co, Ludgate Hill, and 96 Gracechurch Street.

Fox-Hunting. 34 × 22¾ ins. Large lithographs by J. West Giles.
The Meet, The Start, The Run, The Death.
Printed by M. & N. Hanhart. London: published 15 March 1854 by E. Gambart & Co, 25 Berners Street, Oxford Street; Goupil & Co, Paris and New York.

A smaller set, size 20 × 14 ins, of the above were engraved by J. Harris and W. Summers. London: published 7 January 1857 by E. Gambart & Co, 25 Berners Street, Oxford Street, W.

A second issue of these plates has been published bearing the name of F. Herbault, 166 Strand. No date.

A Glimpse of an English Homestead. 34 × 22½ ins. G. Paterson (picture dated 1852).
London: published 13 October 1854 by Messrs Lloyd Bros & Co, 22 Ludgate Hill.
Entered according to Act of Congress by Williams, Stevens, Williams & Co, in the Clerk's Office of the District Court for the Southern District of New York.

A scene in the Highlands. 33¼ × 20½ ins. J. West Giles, litho.
London: Published 1 November 1854, by E. Gambart & Co, 25 Berners Street, Oxford Street, W; Goupil & Co, Paris and Berlin. Printed by M. & N. Hanhart.

A scene in the Lowlands. 33½ × 20¼ ins. J. West Giles litho.
London: published 1 February 1855 by E. Gambart & Co, 25 Berners Street, Oxford Street, W; Goupil & Co, Paris and Berlin. M. & N. Hanhart, lithographic printers.

Mountain Ponies (Scotch hills). 25 × 17½ ins. Picture dated 1854. Lithographed by Day & Son, Lithographers to the Queen.
London: published by Messrs Lloyd Bros & Co, 22 Ludgate Hill, August 1, 1855 and Messrs Williams, Stevens, Williams & Co, 153 Broadway, New York.

A Highland Home. 34 × 22¾ ins. Lithographed by Day & Son, Lithographers to the Queen.
London: published 24 January 1856, by Henry Graves & Co, printsellers and publishers to Her Majesty the Queen and HRH Prince Albert, 6 Pall Mall, East.
Entered according to the Act of Congress by Williams, Stevens, Williams & Co in the Clerk's Office of the District Court for the Southern District of New York.

Agricultural Series. Lithographs by Vincent Brooks.

No 1. Haymaking. 34¼ × 19¾ ins.
London: published 13 March 1856 by Messrs Henry Graves & Co, printsellers and publishers to Her Majesty the Queen and HRH Prince Albert, 6 Pall Mall, East.

No 2. Hop-Picking. 34 × 19¾ ins.
The publication line is the same excepting the date, as this plate was not published till February 2, 1857.
The Druid in *Scott and Sebright* says: 'In the other (referring to Mr Herring's Hop-Picking picture) the artist in a straw-hat with a black ribbon and mahogany tops plays 'Farmer Oldfield' and does not look, as he gazes complacently at the fast-filling bins, as if the iron of Gladstone was piercing his soul so acutely. The jaunty ribbons and tunics, with the green avenues which they are so ruthlessly rifling, and the farmer's daughter with her bonnet

carelessly tossed back, is taking the tally as the widow brings up her bin to be measured.' (The reference to Gladstone presumably implies that his Free Trade policy and taxation did not appeal to farmers – he would be against beer-making anyway. *Author*)

No 3. Ploughing. 34 × 18½ ins. The publication line is the same as Plate No 1, but was not published till 6 July 1857.
Each plate bears the following: 'Entered according to Act of Congress by Williams, Steven, Williams & Co in the Clerk's Office of the District Court for the Southern District of New York.'

Farmyard Series. Lithographed by J. West Giles.
No 1. Donkey and Horse (Round, 16 ins diam.). Published 1 January 1849.
No 2. Pony, Horse and Pigs (15½ × 15¾ ins). Published 1 January 1849.
No. 3. Ducks (15½ × 15¾ ins). Published 1 January 1849.
No 4. Dogs (Round, 16 ins diam.). Published (?).
No 5. Cows and calf in stable (Round, 16 ins diam.). Published (?)
No. 6. Title missing (Round, 16 ins diam.). Published (?)
No 7. Horses (Round, 16 ins diam.). 1 February 1850
No 8. Oxen (Round, 16 ins diam.). Published (?)
No 9. Sheep (Round, 16 ins diam.). Published (?)
No 10. Pigs, peacock and fowls (Round, 16 ins diam.). Published (?)
No 11. Rabbits (15½ × 15¾ ins – arch tops). Published 1 March 1852.
No 12. Goats (15½ × 15¾ ins – arch tops). Published 1 May 1852.
London: published by E. Gambart & Co, 25 Berners Street, Oxford Street, W.

COLOURED AUTOTYPES

The York Stage (20 × 12 ins). Facsimile of the original picture. Published by Messrs Dickenson & Foster, 114 New Bond Street, London, W.

The Mail-Coach (17 × 12 ins – upright). 'On the road – full pace', facsimile of the original picture in the collection of Sir W. W. Wynn, Bart. Published by Messrs Dickenson & Foster, 114 New Bond Street, London, W.

Engravings which appeared in various journals

Published in the *Sporting Magazine*

The fractured leg of Spartan. J. F. H. delt. Published February 1819.

Sultan. A celebrated hunter. Engraved by J. Scott. Published October 1820.

Mulatto. Engraved by J. Webb. Published August 1828.

Fair Helen. Engraved by J. R. Scott. Published February 1831.

A favourite cob – Stiff Dick, the property of the late Lieut-General Sir John Heron Maxwell, Bart. Engraved by H. R. Cook. Published September 1831.

Dover – son of Patron. Engraved by J. R. Scott. Published June 1836.

Pantomime. Engraved by J. R. Scott. Published December 1836.

October Shooting. Engraved by T. S. Engleheart. Published January 1837.

Camarine. Engraved by H. Beckwith. Published February 1837.

Lucetta. Engraved by J. R. Scott. Published April 1837.

A moor scene. Engraved by J. H. Engleheart. Published August 1837.

Hornsea. Engraved by J. H. Engleheart. Published September 1837.

Gazelle. An Arabian. Engraved by J. H. Engleheart. Published November 1842.

Sweetmeat. The property of A. W. Hill Esq. Engraved by E. Hacker. Published February 1846.

Even Betting. Two horses clearing a stone wall at the same moment. Engraved by E. Hacker. Published October 1846.

The Brush Bespoke. Hunting scene. Engraved by E. Hacker. Published December 1846.

'The Times' Change. Coaching scene. Engraved by E. Hacker. Published January 1847.

The fate of the favourite. A broken down racehorse at agricultural work. Engraved by E. Hacker. Published March 1847.

The Switcher. The property of the 8th Earl of Strathmore, winner of the Worcester and Newport Pagnell Steeplechases, 1846. Engraved by E. Hacker. Published 1847 (originally April 1847).

A bit of blood. Engraved by E. Hacker. Published June 1847.

Used-up. Thoroughbred in harness with broken knees. Engraved by E. Hacker. Published September 1847.

A case for the kennels. A dead horse in a knacker's cart. Engraved by E. Hacker. Published December 1847.

The Steeplechase. Set of six plates engraved by E. Hacker.

Plate 1. What about the Grey? Published February 1848.
Plate 2. Now they're Off. Published May 1848.
Plate 3. Well over the First Flight. Published September 1848.
Plate 4. The Grey Beats Anything. Published December 1848.
Plate 5. Nobody Names the Winner. Published February 1849.
Plate 6. And the Grey Wins. Published April 1849.

The Passions of the Horse. Set of six plates engraved by E. Hacker. Published on the corresponding dates in the *Sporting Magazine*.

Plate 1. Affection (mare and foal). Published March 1853.

Plate 2. Rage (thoroughbred kicking). Published September 1853.
Plate 3. Emulation. Published March 1854.
Plate 4. Fear. Published September 1854.
Plate 5. Joy. Published May 1855.
Plate 6. Agony (fall at a fence). Published October 1855.

Four plates on various subjects issued between 1855 and 1859 engraved by E. Hacker.

Not Exactly (hunter refusing a water jump). Published March 1855.
Done Handsome (clearing a fence). Published February 1856.
Has been Ridden with Hounds (after a fashion). Published March 1857.
The Warren Hill (rough terriers, My Hat, and the bag of rabbits of a day's sport). Published March 1859.

Published in the *Annals of Sporting*

Magistrate. Engraved by Mr Thomas Sutherland. Published June 1823.

Blacklock. With jockey mounted. See also under 'Thoroughbred Stallions'. Engraved by Mr Sutherland. Published August 1823.

Wanton, **Theodore**, and **May Day**. Represents the race for the Gold Tureen, run for at the Leeds Commencement Meeting in 1824, resulting as follows: Mr Ferguson's Wanton (J. Jackson) 1, Hon. E. Petre's Theodore (Wm. Scott) 2, Lord Kelbourne's May Day (J. Garbutt) 3. Engraved by J. R. Smith. Published April 1825.

Fly. A celebrated greyhound, the property of Mr Littlewood of Arnthorpe near Doncaster. Engraved by J. R. Scott. Published June 1825.

Figaro. (The property of A. Farquharson, Esq, who purchased the horse at the sale of the Hon. T. O. Powlett for £2,000. This gentleman had previously purchased him from the Duke of York. He was sold at Tattersall's in February 1827 to Mr George Payne for 1300 guineas.) Engraved by Scott. Published August 1825.

Whisker. (See also under 'Thoroughbred stallions'.) Engraved by J. R. Scott junr. Published January 1826.

Wild Horses Fighting. Engraved by W. Scott. Published March 1826.

Lottery. (Of this portrait a writer in the same publication says, 'We have ourselves seen him often, and we were in the judge's chair when, by the exertions of horse and rider, he just won the gold cup against Longwaist (the others being beat a long way) at Doncaster, and we therefore can confidently speak of the faithfulness of the picture Mr Herring has produced, to which the engraving does justice.) Engraved by Scott. Published April 1826.

Mandane. Engraved by P. Roberts. Published August 1826.

Bedlamite. Engraved by Scott. Published February 1827.

Fleur-de-Lis. Engraved by J. Westley. Published August 1827.

Sam. A celebrated pointer. Engraved by Thomas Landseer. Published November 1827.

Marmeluke. Derby winner 1827. Published in issue March 1828, small plate engraved by J Westley.

Published in the *New Sporting Magazine*

Saddler (frontispiece to Vol V 1832). Engraved by J. R. Scott.

Throwing off. Hunting Scene. Illustrates Vol VI 1833. Engraved by J. Engleheart, junr.

Beiram. The same plate illustrates Wildrake's 'Cracks of the Day'; also page 41 of Tattersall's *Pictorial Gallery of Racehorses*. Engraved by J. Webb. Published April 1832.

Euclid (frontispiece) – with portraits of Mr Petit, his trainer, and Pat Conolly, his jockey. This horse ran a dead heat with Charles XII for the Doncaster St Leger in 1839, and lost the deciding heat by a head. The same plate illustrates Wildrake's 'Cracks of the Day'; also page 201 of Tattersall's *Pictorial Gallery of Racehorses*. See also *passim*. Engraved by W. B. Scott. Published January 1840.

In for a sharp thing across the grass. Hunting scene, or, 'A Day with the Willowford Hounds'). Engraved by E. Hacker. Published April 1845.

Emma (dam of Mundig). The property of Mr Bowes. Engraved by E. Hacker. Published April 1845. (Also in *Sportsman*, illustrating page 223, January to June 1845.)

Hetmann Platoff. Engraved by J. Scott. Published February 1845. After in *Farmer's Magazine*, April 1845.

Aristides. Engraved by E. Hacker. Published June 1845.

High-Mettled Racer. Set of 12 plates engraved by E. Hacker.

No 1 The Foal. Published January 1846.
No 2 Breaking. Published March 1846.
No 3 The Sweat. Published April 1846.
No 4 The Start. Published May 1846.
No 5 The Race. Published June 1846.
No 6 The Steeplechase. Published October 1846.
No 7 The Chase. Published December 1846.
No 8 The Road. Published January 1847.
No 9 The Farm. Published March 1847.
No 10 The Shop. Published June 1847.
No 11 The Street. Published September 1847.
No 12 The Fate. Published December 1847.

Three Plates for *Sporting Review*

The magazine for March 1842 remarks: 'We are indebted to the politeness of Sir B. Smith for the original (The Find) after which this engraving is made. The painting is remarkable for the truth and accuracy that distinguishes all Mr Herring's pictures. It affords us much pleasure to announce that through the courtesy of Sir B. Smith (whose gallery is enriched with several of the finest productions of Mr Herring's pencil), we shall be able to embellish this work with some of the best efforts of that distinguished artist'.

The Find (Hunting scene). From the original in Sir Benjamin Smith's collection. Engraved by H. B. Hall. Published February 1842.

The Finish (Hunting scene). From the original in Sir Benjamin Smith's collection. Engraved by H. B. Hall. Published March 1842.

The Watering-place (horses drinking). From the original in Sir Benjamin Smith's collection. Engraved by H. B. Hall. Published April 1842.

Published in *Sportsman*

Gibside Fairy (the property of John Bowes Esq). Engraved by E. Hacker. Published April 1844.

Mare and Foal (Levity the property of J. C. Cockerill Esq, and her foal, Queen Elizabeth, now the property of Lord Dorchester.) Engraved by E. Hacker. Published April 1844.

Published in *Art Union Prize Annual* – 1847–1848

The Farmer's Pet. London: R. A. Sprigg, Library of Arts, 106 Great Russell Street, Bedford Square. This picture was exhibited at the British Institution in 1847, and the Art Journal in its notice says, 'A grey pony in excellent condition, which has received ample justice at the hands of the Painter'.

An Interior. Published by E. Atchley, Library of Arts, 106 Great Russell Street, Bedford Square.

Gossip. Published by E. Atchley, Library of Arts, 106 Great Russell Street, Bedford Square.

Published in *Art Journal*

Hammon and Tajar, The Queen's Horses. C. Cousen, sculpt. Published June 1856. In the Royal Collection. This picture was a commission from the Duchess of Kent to be presented to Her Majesty on her birthday. Her Royal Highness was so pleased with it that she appointed Mr Herring her animal painter. The Queen testified her approbation of the work by commanding the artist to paint a portrait of a favourite hack horse, the picture being a present from HM to Prince Albert on his birthday. Published June 1856.

The Cavalier. J. C. Armytage, sculpt. Painted by J. F. Herring, Bright & Baxter. From the picture in the collection of Frederick Chapple Esq, Liverpool. Published March 1866. London: Virtue & Co.

Mazeppa. John Cousen, sculpt. In the collection of Mr Alderman Copeland MP. Published June 1865. London: J. S. Virtue. *(See page 158.)*

The Trooper. C. Cousen, sculpt. From the collection of Frederick Chapple Esq, Huyton Hall, Liverpool. Painted by J. F. Herring, Bright & Baxter. Published April 1866. London: Virtue & Co.

The Mothers. A series of nine plates (1854–1855).

No 1. Hack Mare and Foal. Engraved by J. Harris. Published 19 May 1854.

No 2. Cart Mare and Foal. Engraved by J. Harris and C. Quentery. Published in 1854.

No 3. Duck and Ducklings. Published 19 May 1854.

No 4. Hen and Chick(en)s. Engraved by J. Harris. Published 19 May 1854.

No 5. Sow and Pig(let)s. Engraved by J. Harris and W. Summers. Published 18 January 1855.

No 6. Thoroughbred Mare and Foal. Engraved by J. Harris and C. Quentery. Published in 1855.

No 7. Draught Mare and Foal. Engraved by J. Harris and C. Quentery. Published 8 November 1855.

No. 8. Cow and calf. Engraved by J. Harris and C. Quentery. Published 8 November 1855.

No 9. Hunting Mare and Foal. Published by Messrs Fores, 41 Piccadilly.